SELLING THE RACE

HISTORICAL STUDIES OF URBAN AMERICA

Edited by Timothy J. Gilfoyle, James R. Grossman, and Becky M. Nicolaides

ALSO IN THE SERIES

Parish Boundaries: The Catholic Encounter with Race in the Twentieth-Century Urban North
BY JOHN T. McGREEVY

Modern Housing for America: Policy Struggles in the New Deal Era
BY GAIL RADFORD

Smoldering City: Chicagoans and the Great Fire, 1871–1874
BY KAREN SAWISLAK

Making the Second Ghetto: Race and Housing in Chicago, 1940–1960
BY ARNOLD R. HIRSCH

Faces along the Bar: Lore and Order in the Workingman's Saloon, 1870–1920
BY MADELON POWERS

Streets, Railroads, and the Great Strike of 1877
BY DAVID O. STOWELL

The Creative Destruction of Manhattan, 1900–1940
BY MAX PAGE

Brownsville, Brooklyn: Blacks, Jews, and the Changing Face of the Ghetto
BY WENDELL PRITCHETT

My Blue Heaven: Life and Politics in the Working-Class Suburbs of Los Angeles, 1920–1965
BY BECKY M. NICOLAIDES

In the Shadow of Slavery: African Americans in New York City, 1626–1863
BY LESLIE M. HARRIS

Building the South Side: Urban Space and Civic Culture in Chicago, 1890–1919
BY ROBIN F. BACHIN

Places of Their Own: African American Suburbanization in the Twentieth Century
BY ANDREW WIESE

Downtown America: A History of the Place and the People Who Made It
BY ALISON ISENBERG

Block by Block: Neighborhoods and Public Policy on Chicago's West Side
BY AMANDA I. SELIGMAN

The Elusive Ideal: Equal Educational Opportunity and the Federal Role in Boston's Public Schools, 1950–1985
BY ADAM R. NELSON

Chicagoland: Suburbs of the Railroad Age
BY ANN DURKIN KEATING

City of American Dreams: A History of Home Ownership and Housing Reform in Chicago, 1871–1919
BY MARGARET GARB

Millennium Park: Creating a Chicago Landmark
BY TIMOTHY J. GILFOYLE

The New Suburban History
EDITED BY KEVIN M. KRUSE AND THOMAS J. SUGRUE

SELLING THE RACE

CULTURE, COMMUNITY, AND BLACK CHICAGO, 1940–1955

ADAM GREEN

THE UNIVERSITY OF CHICAGO PRESS
CHICAGO AND LONDON

ADAM GREEN is associate professor of history and of social and cultural analysis at New York University.

The University of Chicago Press, Chicago 60637
The University of Chicago Press, Ltd., London

Printed in the United States of America

16 15 14 13 12 11 10 09 08 07 1 2 3 4 5

ISBN-10: 0-226-30641-0 (cloth)
ISBN-13: 978-0-226-30641-4 (cloth)

Library of Congress Cataloging-in-Publication Data
Green, Adam, 1963–
Selling the race : culture, community, and Black Chicago, 1940–1955 / Adam Green.
p. cm.
Includes bibliographical references and index.
ISBN 0-226-30641-0 (cloth : alk. paper) 1. African Americans—Illinois—Chicago—Intellectual life—20th century. 2. African Americans—Race identity—Illinois—Chicago. 3. African Americans—Illinois—Chicago—Social life and customs—20th century. 4. African American arts—Illinois—Chicago—History—20th century. 5. Cultural awareness—Illinois—Chicago—History—20th century. 6. City and town life—Illinois—Chicago—History—20th century. 7. Community life—Illinois—Chicago—History—20th century. 8. Chicago (Ill.)—Intellectual life—20th century. 9. Chicago (Ill.)—Social life and customs—20th century. 10. Chicago (Ill.)—Race relations—History—20th century. I. Title.
F548.9.N4G72 2007
305.896'073077311—dc22

2006021626

♾ The paper used in this publication meets the minimum requirements of the American National Standard for Information Sciences—Permanence of Paper for Printed Library Materials, ANSI Z39.48-1992.

CONTENTS

ILLUSTRATIONS

ACKNOWLEDGMENTS

This book conjoins diverse sources of support and sustenance, all of which encouraged my own growth, intellectually and personally, as this book took shape. Though I, like other University of Chicago undergraduates of my day and since, found scarce encouragement to delve into the wider world of the South Side while studying there, I had the good fortune my senior year to meet James Grossman, who had just been hired as an assistant professor and agreed to advise my honors project. Jim and I maintained contact as I completed graduate school, as he published his own landmark study of Black Chicago migration during and after World War I, and as I first attempted to follow his historical thread through subsequent decades. As my engagement in Black Chicago deepened the further I ranged from the South Side, Jim offered a reliable beacon back to that "same old place." His final reading of this manuscript, not surprisingly to those that know him, was among the most thorough, challenging, and affirming in its engagement. Though many colleagues, friends, and loved ones have anticipated my completion of this work, he may well have waited the longest—I hope that it proves worthy of his interest through the years.

Doctoral work at Yale University, an institution I entered intending to research antebellum African-American thought, was also integral to this book's development. Jean Christophe-Agnew, Alan Trachtenberg, David Brion Davis, David Montgomery, and Michael Denning offered ever richer glosses on the possibilities of cultural history. Indeed it was Michael's seminar on the Depression-era United States that first brought me to the sociology of Cayton and Drake and the poetry of Gwendolyn Brooks, the first glimpse of the rich archive I have happily rummaged through up to the present. My love of teaching—and respect for its symbiotic enhancement of scholarship—began through assisting David Davis and Melvin Ely in their exemplary lecture classes. Hazel Carby radically broadened my imagination of what African-American studies might encompass, exemplified its grounding in an ethic of service and political engagement, and convinced me and so many others that our work could and would matter. Deborah Thomas, then a graduate dean, facilitated most of my funding, and hired me to head the campus Minority Summer Research Exchange Program for two years. I cannot possibly acknowledge all the fellow students—graduate and undergraduate—who influenced me there. Hilari Allred, Emily Barnard, Herman Beavers, Lisa Daugaard, Ari Fitzgerald, Mark Harding, Tom Kluboek, Adrian Lunn, Joanne Mariner, Carlo Rotella, Sandhya Shukla, Sally Singer, Stephanie Smallwood, Heidi Tinsman, and Harald Weilnbock were indispensable colleagues, and even better friends. Leaders and fellow members of the Graduate Employee Student Organization, along with Locals 34 and 35 at Yale, generated a different and richer notion of what intellectual work might mean.

Funding support for my research and writing came from the Dorothy Danforth Compton Fellowship program, the Minority Scholar-in-Residence Program at Occidental College, the Center for Black Studies at the University of California at Santa Barbara, and generous provisions of faculty leave time at both Northwestern University and New York University. A year's sabbatical at the Center for African American Studies at the University of California at Los Angeles facilitated the project's development from thesis to book. Colleagues and friends at these campuses—Monique Taylor and Raul Villa (Occidental College); Ken Alder, Wallace Best, Henry Binford, Martha Biondi, L. Stanley Davis, the late Leon Forrest, Erik Gellman, Christopher Manning, Aldon Morris, Alex Owen, Charles Payne, Sandra Richards, David Schoenbrun, Mike Sherry, Liz Whittaker, Easter Young, Esther Young, Ji-Yeon Yuh (Northwestern University); and Thomas Bender, Arlene Davila, Lisa Duggan, Linda Gordon, Phil Harper, Martha Hodes, Molly Nolan, Jeffrey Sammons, and Danny Walkowitz (NYU)—were more important to this book's completion than they may know. Ken Alder, Martha Biondi, Steven Hahn, Michael Hanchard, Nancy MacLean, Charles Payne, and Mike Sherry all read some or all of this manuscript in its early form, while Walter Johnson, Phil Harper, and Arlene Davila read later versions: each provided acute observations, criticisms, and encouragement. The graduate students of the American Studies Program at New York University, raised the level of my own thinking routinely through their acute insights, ambitions, and engagements, while the hundreds of undergraduates I have met through teaching at Yale, Occidental, UCSB, Northwestern, and NYU have been a constant source of inspiration.

Over the years I have delivered portions of this book to the Ethnic Studies Department at University of California at San Diego, the Institute for American Cultures and the American Studies Conference on Urban Culture, the DISCORD Conference on Popular Music at the University of California at Los Angeles, the Social History Workshop at the Newberry Library (Chicago), the St. Clair Drake Center for African and African-American Studies at Roosevelt University (Chicago), the UIC–DuSable Museum Conference on African American Designers (Chicago), the Institute for Research in African-American Studies at Columbia University, and panels at the Organization of American Historians, the American Historical Association, the Association for the Study of African-American Life and History, and the American Studies Association. I thank the organizers of these sessions, and those attending and participating as well. Friends and colleagues met through these sessions have helped me sharpen my approach and thinking, in particular Houston Baker Jr., Victor Margolin, Robert Pruter, Christopher Reed, Sonnet Retman, Rita Roberts, Tricia Rose, Valerie Smith, Alys Weinbaum, and Penny Von Eschen.

Full grasp of this project eluded me until I expanded research related to it during a year's leave in 1999–2000. Work with the Claude Barnett Papers was ably assisted by my research assistant Elizabeth Mullen, and supported in inimitable fashion by the archival staff of the Chicago Historical Society, in particular the late Archie Motley, who took every opportunity to encourage my efforts—I, like others, miss him dearly. If Jim Grossman is this book's original parent, Michael Flug of the Vivian G. Harsh Collection at the Woodson Branch of the Chicago Public Library has been its insistent midwife. I cannot begin to say how much Michael's wise counsel and his grasp of this project's potential inspired me to work to improve it. He, the rest of the Woodson staff, and fellow board members of the Harsh Society are among my "ideal readers" for this work. Not least among Michael's many assists to this project was putting me in touch with most of those whom I interviewed for the book. While a good deal of this material made its way into the final manuscript, just as much had to be left out. Nonetheless, I was invariably immersed in the feel and lore of the postwar South Side, thanks to the generously shared stories of Lerone Bennett Jr., Timuel Black, Esther Burns, Dr. Margaret Burroughs, Chester Commodore, Charles Davis, Clarice Durham, Truman Gibson Jr., Sue Ish, Vernon Jarrett, Bennett Johnson, Larry Kenan, Etta Moten, Herbert Nipson, Doris Saunders, Charles Walton, LeRoy Winbush, and Susan Cayton Woodson. While finishing this book in New York, I received sad word that Vernon Jarrett, a landmark figure in black journalism, social activism, and letters, and Charles Walton, an indispensable font of wisdom on local music, who opened his home many times to me, had both passed away—their wise words alone could have filled this book, no doubt to more profound effect. That both of them, like Archie Motley and Leon Forrest, will not have the opportunity read this book, that I might benefit from their responses, is no small source of pain for me.

At a late stage of this project I received invaluable assistance from famed photographer Wayne Miller. First meeting on a panel in Chicago in honor of his Guggenheim-sponsored visual archive of black life in Chicago during the 1940s, Wayne kept in touch, encouraged my efforts, and welcomed me to his home in Orinda, California, where he and his wife Joan walked me through thousands of contact prints, and talked me through their rich life together in Chicago. A large portion of the photographs reproduced in this book are his—I believe that they convey the depth and texture of black life and outlook in Chicago in a uniquely evocative manner. Other images were made available through the Chicago Historical Society and the Harsh Collection at the Woodson branch of the Chicago Public Library. I am indebted to the entire Harsh staff, especially Cynthia Fife-Townsell, who hunted down and digitally scanned a number of singular images to make sure this work would benefit from the Harsh's ever-growing holdings. Linda Evans and Rob Medina at the Chicago Historical Society effected an eleventh-hour save in helping locate several key photographs related to Claude Barnett's life and career.

Doug Mitchell at the University of Chicago Press signed this project up for publication, and offered encouragement even after he ceased to be its editor. Robert Devens, who inherited it from Doug, was a model of creativity, patience, and enthusiasm over the several years it took for this book to find its two covers. Elizabeth Branch Dyson expertly steered me through a thicket of rights and permissions questions, while manuscript editor Mara Naselli greatly enhanced the books stylistic quality. I am also indebted to the two sets of anonymous readers who read versions of the manuscript and offered many helpful suggestions, and also to Jim Grossman, Kathy Conzen, and Timothy Gilfoyle, coeditors of the Historical Studies of Urban America series.

Though all those mentioned were crucial to this book's completion, there are several individuals in particular who deserve special recognition. Martha Biondi has been a constant comrade in arms, heart, and mind since we met at Northwestern. Her balance of cutting-edge scholarship with a grassroots dedication to justice offers a model for my own work, in the broadest sense: I am grateful to count her a friend. Though I knew Steven Hahn and Stephanie McCurry only briefly as our paths intersected in Evanston, their friendship and solidarity have proven crucial since our coinciding relocations. Michael Hanchard has been the brother I never had: only now am I truly coming to appreciate the insights on thought and life traded over dinners, hang outs, and deep raps. *Muito obrigado,* my brother. Matt Hale, Mark Maxwell, and Laurie Tractman, in different ways, were central to this project, even though they stand at thankful remove from the arcane world of academe. Without them, my frequent L.A. escapes would not have been possible, and, more importantly, I would suffer the lack of three unique friendships. Neither Nico Israel nor I could have predicted while in graduate school that our respective perambulations would run the same L.A./Chicago/New York triangulated groove: that happy coincidence has provided ample occasion for advice, support, and spirit-lifting laughter, even when there was scarce cause for good humor. Robin Kelley and Andrew Ross's encouragement that I consider applying for a position in American Studies at NYU enabled the completion and, I hope, enhancement of this book—I cannot say enough about their faith and trust in me, as well as that of my many coconspirators there in my new home. Walter Johnson saw me through my NYU hire up to tenure, always with singular humor and generosity of mind and spirit. Nikhil Singh brought joy and wisdom to me for well over a decade, as my deepest interlocutor and dear, dear friend. Here's to helping remake a world through thought, as we always hoped, in close friendship for so long.

Those who know me well know that I inevitably return, in the end, to family. Herewith I vow to bring the first copy of this book to my grandmother LaNora Markell, who asked "when will it be done" so many times, yet never once without providing her own reassuring answer, "when it's ready." My blended family of Bergs in northern New Jersey and New York—in particular my grandmother Ruth—offered like encouragement through weddings, seders, and bar mitzvahs. My father Ernest Green, stepmother Phyllis, and sister MacKenzie kept me thankfully focused on the big picture, in work and in life generally. Dad, now we can finally enlist all your big shots in the Windy City for promotional assistance. My stepfather Carl Berg and mother Judith Green-Berg have given all—morale boosts, proofreadings, provisions from their bountiful upstate garden, countless diversions large and small, and above all love. My sister Jessica has interwoven her singular intelligence and critical consciousness with mine throughout shared lives, I hope she can see herself in my efforts here. Whatever comes from the publication of this book, I look forward to sharing it with them.

Which goes as well for my other family. While at Northwestern, I entered a friendship, and ultimately a love, with Tessie Liu. In the face of all manner of disruption and asymmetry, she has welcomed me into her life, and that of her daughter, An-Lin. Ani has been a constant source of joy and inspiration throughout our years together, and the fact that she reads more than most academics I know has surely kept me on task. If young and old can indeed enjoy meaningful friendship, then surely we enjoy one of the closest. I could say so much about Tessie, yet the fullest acknowledgment I can make of her here is that she, more than anyone, reminded me to find the person in the book—which in turn made it possible for me to find this book in my person. For that, and so much else, I dedicate it to her.

SELLING THE RACE

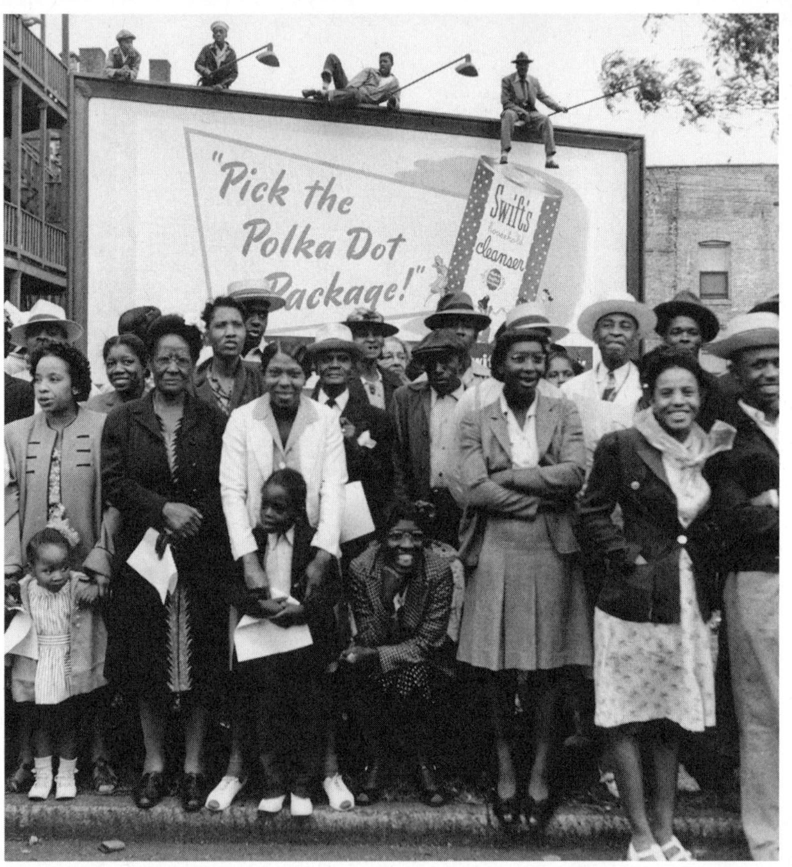
"Pick the Polka Dot Package!"
Swift's
Cleanser

IN SEARCH OF AFRICAN-AMERICAN MODERNITY

AN INTRODUCTION

There in that self-conscious city, we caught
whispers of the meanings that life could have.
RICHARD WRIGHT

This book argues that African Americans in Chicago, during and after World War II, engendered unique senses of group life and imagination, restructuring ideas of racial identity and politics that remain influential today. In so doing, it confronts and reworks the standard view that black life in the Windy City has constituted an ongoing test of fitness for modern life. Confessing a debt to social research in his day and since, Richard Wright called Chicago "the known city," implying that black life there was a transparent social condition, needing only documentation and realist explication in order to be understood. Yet as the late novelist and educator Leon Forrest (who, like Wright, was among Black Chicago's most acute observers) consistently maintained, the deeper meaning of this community, if often presumed, remained to be fully told. The most studied black urban enclave in the country then, still retains its secrets, promising revelation for those willing to chase after them. Among these veiled qualities is the degree to which, following migration, blacks' imaginative powers—what might be called their cultural ini-

Facing page: 1. Spectators at the Bud Billiken Parade, an annual ritual for South Siders from 1929 to the present. Photograph by Wayne F. Miller. Courtesy of Wayne F. Miller.

tiative—reworked core conditions and institutions of urban life, even as they themselves were transformed by experiences encountered in Chicago.[1]

Remapping the coordinates of this study—Black Chicago, black migration, race, and the twentieth-century city—requires casting aside definitions of African-American history as either teleological or tragic. Though both joy and pain appear prominently in the following pages, I have become fascinated with how contingent and unpredictable the encounter of African Americans with the Windy City has been. Ever attuned to the uncertainty, perversity, and profound improvisation of local black life, Leon Forrest's observations are once again helpful. Declining "to think of [their] ethos as symmetrically consummated," African Americans in Chicago were, in his estimation "a people in process, even in metamorphosis." I have found frequent occasion to return to this statement, for it offers a counterpoint to the positivism—what Paul Gilroy trenchantly called the "sociologism"—informing most studies of Chicago over the past half century, a time when the city has constituted the preeminent laboratory of urban racial conditions in the United States. My interest in local black culture—culture at once quotidian and commercial, institutional as well as vernacular—drew on this alternate vision of black life in Chicago as vital and unresolved process, rather than as dreams deferred or betrayed. As well, I found encouragement in its invitation to see the city as a site of creativity, rather than constraint: a space of imagination as much one of brute fact. The anthropologist Clifford Geertz defines culture as "stories we tell ourselves about ourselves." Reworking reflexivity into innovation, this analytic approach fits well with the history of black cultural initiative in the United States and other parts of the Americas. It has proven difficult, though, to find such emphasis on generative action in accounts of contemporary black life in cities, where expansive imagination is often counted a luxury, or distraction from the harsh realities of proscription. Consequently, urban blacks have generally been seen as history's victims, rather than its makers. This has exacted a steep cost from our overall knowledge and perspective, for it obscures African Americans' central role in fashioning the world all of us live in today.[2]

Accounts of African-American life transformed and transforming through the twentieth century more often than not make some gesture toward what is called modernity. Migration, proletarianization, Pan-Africanism, orthodox and vernacular forms of radicalism, even the ironic presumption of racial emancipation announce the modern turn in black existence, in all its complexity and contradiction. I, too, argue that events and processes taking place in Black Chicago between 1940 and 1955 constitute a noteworthy episode in black engagement with the challenges of the modern condition. Indeed, I seek to prove that this history marks a defining turn toward circumstances we equate with modernization, modernism, and modernity generally. Making this claim, of course, requires definition of modernity's meaning and relation to black folk, in Chicago and beyond. At base, modernity as a premise rests on the idea—frightening to some, inspiring to others—that common conditions determine life for humankind everywhere at once: secular universals succeeding the prior authority of faith and spiritual mission. Recent scholarship has called these presumptions of human totality to question, interrogating modernity, as it were, at its roots by emphasizing the core ethnocentricism of its philosophic progenitors. Increasingly these accounts maintain that blacks tracked their own course toward subjectivity and self-consciousness—one signaled not by irony or ennui, but instead sterner stuff of existential privation and terror. Like many others, I have learned much from this work, and retain great affinity for it. Yet even as black modernism established its own terms of inquiry, much remains to be learned from the more conventional tenets of the modern, even when these fail, in part or outright, to account for human life and action beyond the European continent.[3]

Like others before me, I see no reason to forego the well-worn caveat that modernism and modernity are categories that defy easy summation. Whether seen as fifty years of aesthetic innovation, or as five centuries of epochal transformation in thought, production, and power, that which is defined as modern marks all corners of life and sensibility, in a variety of ways. World finance, futurism, primitivism, Freudian psychology, the annihilation of space and time, the old imperialism and the new empire, the cosmopolitan intellectual and immigration control, planetary naturalisms and the machine age: each and more count as progeny of the modern age, indicating at once its overwhelming scope and its intrinsic sense of antinomy.[4] Each of these items, of course, can be related to specific conditions of black life, giving lie, for example, to Hegel's dismissal of Africans and their descendants as "people without history." Who, after all, registers and ascertains the fractal and contingent state of modern existence better than black folk? Two social structures loom large in relation to U.S. blacks' modernity in the United States, factoring with special significance in this study: the city and the nation as community.

While modernity's advent can be traced through multiple contexts, it is clear that the city offers one of its central fields of play. Here human beings' reworked identities as market consumers, as nomadic workers, as motile, atomized selves are most in evidence. As with war, exchange, and statecraft, the dichotomous faces of the modern are revealed in the city. The merry amblings of Baudelaire's *flaneur* and the steely technocracy of

Corbusier's Radiant City announce the intertwining of freedom and control at modernity's core. The great stations of modernist experiment—Vienna, Paris, New York, Los Angeles, St. Petersburg, Hong Kong, Accra, and so on—have more often than not been cities. Globalized production, consumption, and investment, administration of planetary flows of people, seemingly universal mediascapes, all derive from the communities of scale cities offer. It is impossible, of course, to say whether modernism follows urbanism, or the other way around: though cities have constituted exemplary structures of community in premodern and even classical periods of social history, the intense symbiosis between the modern and the urban conveys how mutually constitutive one is of the other within our current imagination. In a century when human life indisputably *changed,* one persistent universal has been the deepening orientation of social life toward urban rather than agrarian conditions. To speak of a modern turn in individual and collective life, then, is more often than not to speak of encounter, negotiation, and response to the city. This helps explain the unique sense of imagination, the mental kinesis, marking the modern: the labyrinthine mystery and protean energy of urban existence are by now familiar points in accounts of its fashioning. Modernism and modern life, Raymond Williams observed, first and foremost involved experiment in form—not just for elite creators, but for all inhabitants of the age, up to our own time. Such experiments in form were best pursued within the atmosphere of change, stimulus, and shifting obligation and filiation in cities, even given the potential for them to end in frustration or disaster.[5]

None of this is surprising to those familiar with African-American life in the twentieth century. Histories of migration and expatriation, analyses of jazz and improvisational arts generally, and discussions of cultural fluorescence hinge on the turns of black people toward one or another city, signaling their own historic exchange of life conditions of agrarian confinement for something else—not necessarily better, but certainly different. For most scholars, it is the Harlem Renaissance that remains the modern moment *par excellence* for black people in the United States, if not the African diaspora generally—so much so that previous attempts to account for cultural innovation in Black Chicago have often transplanted the Renaissance template there, down to matching lists of awards cycles, patronage structures, and parlor festivities. This sense of historical derivation helps explain why, despite the efforts of Robert Bone, Margaret Walker, Bill Mullen, and others, arguments that Chicago provides a landmark seat of black creativity have yet to take root in recent African-American cultural history. Harold Cruse's well-known maxim that "as Harlem goes, so goes the rest of black America," remains the operative logic for most of those dedicated to studying this history. But this is one explanation, and not necessarily the most critical one. Black Chicago, indeed, already enjoys a prominent place in discussions of modern black life—just not one privileging creativity, imagination, experiment in form, or expansive consciousness among its people.[6]

If Alain Locke, flush with the ferment of the Jazz Age, optimistically read African-American urbanization from the vantage point of 1925 as a forward march of progress, the "hurdle" of "several generations of experience at a leap," Chicago's story to date has traced a different vector from the urban turn in black life. Withering segregation in homes and schools, political clientage, and persistent restriction within the industrial economy, followed by the devastating consequences of deindustrialization from the mid 1960s into the 1980s, together signaled a perfect storm of racial proscription, memorializing Black Chicago's story as one of slippage, stagnation, and declension. One need only recall how the rules of social relation among successive generations of Chicago-school sociologists—from Robert Park's racial cycle and Ernest Burgess's ecological zones to E. Franklin Frazier's pathologized family and William Julius Wilson's jobless ghetto—grew ever more foreboding to see how the group motive assigned to black urban existence has shifted, from development to stark survival. By 1960, James Baldwin would define the local black community as "a million in captivity": a striking rejection of Locke and other utopians' hopes for blacks' alignment with urban life. In one sense, this simply (if brutally) suggested the savage pun of modernity's dark side: the disintegrative flip side of its coin of invention and renewal. Yet this scholarship, with a few exceptions, invariably carries with it a still more devastating speculation: were blacks capable of functional existence in the city—and, by extension, within the modern world?

Let us return once more to Richard Wright, surely an observer who maintained special interest in local black life's relation to the modern world. Though Wright was among the most trenchant critics of personal and structural racism in the midcentury North, it is striking even today to observe the probationary character he attributed to blacks' strivings in Chicago. "Perhaps never in history has a more utterly unprepared folk wanted to go to the city," Wright wrote in 1941: their naïveté, he further concluded, constituted an innocent yet tragic ignorance leaving blacks blind to how, in the city, "life would begin to exact of us a heavy toll in death." Looking at the migrant masses fashioning new homes in cities at the time, Wright saw frays and tears in their existential fabric at all turns, foretelling a deeper unraveling to come. Marginalized from occupational advance and mobility, interdicted by custom and, quite frequently, force from white neighborhoods, exploited by "gangster-politicians," urban blacks suffered what seemed an irreversible diminishment. Though melding of "a thousand rivulets of blood . . . into a common stream of human unity" marked the promise of the modern American city, blacks could not similarly gain entry, thus failing to gain "the sensitive features of modern men." Intrinsic traits, as much as structural racism, were to blame for this state of affairs: "the unbearable closeness of association," "the [blighted] personalities of our children," even "the outdoor boisterousness of the plantation" worked to funnel black lives "toward ruin and death on the city pavements." If Chicago was the known city, its meaning and codes here seemed beyond the capacities of African Americans: Wright's fear, recurrent in fiction and commentary alike, was that the city's lessons might prove "facts too big for us." It is not hard to project these thoughts forward toward pejoratives like "culture of pathology" or "ghetto underclass" denoting black life in Chicago and other cities today—terms, given their policy effects, that make clear the stakes involved in how we represent blacks' encounter with and negotiation of the modern city historically.[7]

Because modern urban black life has been presented as a tale of regress, rather than one of experiment and expansion, Chicago in particular has served as test challenge that twentieth-century African Americans were obliged to meet. Could they master the time-clock of the routinized workday? Could they retain familial coherence? Were they capable of educational achievement? Could they improve their surrounding environment? Did (and do) cities benefit, or suffer, from their presence? While many might wish to believe these questions, widespread at the time Richard Wright was writing, no longer hold currency, few of us could convincingly argue this to be the case. My book applies a different line of vision to urban, and by extension, modern black life. Chicago in the aftermath of mass black migration, to quote one of its classic histories, was a "land of hope"—but that vision and aspiration extended beyond basic material access, or even everyday ideas of personal freedom. It involved establishment of what Arna Bontemps, addressing another juncture in racial history, called an alternate "angle of vision": one proposing new perspectives on relations with institutions and conventions of society, as well new ideas of self and community. The special significance of media institutions in my account underscore how this angle of vision helped constitute a novel—and enduring—black modern posture. Raymond Williams described the contemporary metropolis as a transmitting city—a nodal site for projecting new forms of meaning outward. Revisiting Chicago as a site of integrating black life well beyond its limits not only reworks definition of cultural institutions among African Americans. It compels us to acknowledge that blacks did more than survive the twentieth-century city: they initiated and appropriated its core conventions, thereby revising their terms of engagement with American society.[8]

One of the most significant of these revisions concerns the premise of national fellowship and feeling among African Americans. As with modernity, nationalism enjoys a distinct meaning within black thought and imagination. Yet, even as black nationalism has served as nomenclature for centuries-old dynamics of self-determination and diasporic amalgamation, it is worth remembering that *nation,* like *city,* is a term of modern vintage. The elements we think of as distinguishing the nation as an architecture of society—passports, civil law, vertically integrated and regulated economies, censuses, powers of war and treaty, the popular press—are important modernisms in their own right, emerging in force during the twentieth century. To be sure, such specifics have been superfluous to most accounts of black national feeling, especially in the United States. More aspiration than actualization, black nationalism lent evocative meaning to autonomy, self-determination, even freedom itself—that which has proven so difficult to call by other names since the purported end of race bondage throughout the West in the nineteenth century. There is a timeless quality to black nationalism as a concept, reinforcing the sense of perpetual struggle recommending it to so many versions of race insurgency and resistance. Nonetheless, "nation," like "modern" or "city," is the result of historical origin and variation: a signifier not only of black continuity, but also change. The specific conventions of national consciousness are no more inherent among African Americans than any other human group. The emergence of this elaborate mindset thus requires not only the desire to determine one's own affairs, but the peculiar conventions of thought and relation that characterize it as a complex and resonant idea of community.[9]

These conventions emerge with special force in Black Chicago during the 1940s and 1950s, constituting one of the more manifest occasions when black people in the United States broadly—across region and generation, gender and class—came to think of themselves as national, existentially more so than politically. This does not mean that Garveyism, Africanity, the Black Popular Front, class consciousness, the women's club movement, or migration as a group politics were not themselves important precedents of expansive identification and action. Rather, developments in postwar Chicago led to finer lineaments of association among blacks: engagement with horizontal public fields such as markets or law, affinity for the unique sense of simultaneity engendered by media cultures, gravitation toward more abstract and even anonymous structures of social feeling, alongside more traditional environments of family or church. These tendencies, unlike traditional constructions of black feeling like race interest or diasporic affinity, were neither timeless nor wholly vernacular—they signified specific achievements and dilemmas of black people in the twentieth century, and, as parallel tracks present within African-American and U.S. society alike, they embodied the carry-over of double consciousness from the turn of that century to our own time.[10]

What was transmitted from Black Chicago to the United States and the world during this time was an evolving premise of national black feeling. That feeling served simultaneously to authorize a racially distinct sense of direction and also an enhanced identification with the United States as a national community. This may strike some readers as a cop-out. Works examining racial nationalism often present that process as epiphany: the occasion when the mass base stands up and asserts their distinct and inalienable interests. As will become clear over the course of this book, I see the emergence of national feeling among African Americans in more equivocal terms, mainly due to its encouragement of race distinction and civil identification at once. But this seems to me the more honest view of the past half century of history, as well as the more promising way to think through the contortions of black thought today, not to mention the still deeper tangles of how blacks are seen in this country.

My intent to relate Black Chicago's history to these and other broad patterns of historical change is evident in the peculiar wording of the book's subtitle. For decades, scholars have addressed the particulars of African-American life *in* Chicago, in order to signal their deferral to community study as a methodology. Horace Cayton and St. Clair Drake's description of the South Side as a "city within a city" (a shorthand performing its own fascinating project of rendering urban segregation almost consensual) was but the first study to treat black life in Chicago as discreet existence, often to compelling narrative effect. Consider, for instance, this famous passage from their book *Black Metropolis:*

> Stand in the center of the Black Belt—at Chicago's 47th Street and South Parkway. Around you swirls a continuous eddy of faces—black, brown, olive, yellow and white. Soon you will realize that this is not "just another neighborhood" of Midwest Metropolis. Glance at the newsstand on the corner. You will see the Chicago dailies . . . But you will also find a number of weeklies headlining the activities of Negroes—Chicago's *Defender, Bee, News Ledger,* and *Metropolitan News,* the Pittsburgh *Courier,* and a number of others. In the nearby drugstore colored clerks are bustling about (they are seldom seen in other neighborhoods). In most of the other stores, too, there are colored salespeople, although a

> white proprietor or manager looms in the offing. In the offices around you, colored doctors, dentists, and lawyers go about their duties. And a brown-skinned policeman saunters along swinging his club and glaring sternly at the urchins who dodge in and out among the shoppers.

The virtual tour of African-American urban life at street level, first introduced by W. E. B. Du Bois in his famed study *The Philadelphia Negro*, was already by 1945 a convention of sociology and ethnography, and remains so today. Here the sense of vibrant human community and space, the array of sturdy public institutions—a free press, a variegated professional and merchant class, an alert officer of the law—evoke a captivating sense of functionality in the central black district of Bronzeville. An extended walk in any direction from this crossroads would have brought other key institutions of local black life into view—the Wabash YMCA west on 39th Street and the Provident Hospital east along 51st Street, Supreme Liberty Life Insurance up South Park at 35th, and the offices of the *Defender* and the Associated Negro Press just west along 35th, and a progression of churches and spiritual homes, from Olivet Baptist Church at 31st and South Park, to Metropolitan Community Church ten blocks south, to the small but growing Second Temple of the Nation of Islam further south and west on 63rd and Cottage Grove. Further ambits through and around Bronzeville, then, would have confirmed Drake and Cayton's deeper message: that this "city within a city" functioned well, on its own terms, and of its own accord: "On a spring or summer day this spot, '47th and South Park,' is the urban equivalent of a village square. In fact, Black Metropolis has a saying, 'If you're trying to find a certain Negro in Chicago, stand on the corner of 47th and South Park long enough and you're bound to see him.'"[11]

The barometers of urban wellness that indicated a high quality of life within Bronzeville—institutions, interaction, exchange—have to date been the main counterpoint to a dystopian portrayal of urban black life. Among the twenty or so long time residents I spoke with in researching this book, these proved a reliable touchstone: once upon a time, Bronzeville was an effective, exciting, and wholly self-sufficient community—it could and did exist *within itself*. Yet while attention to Bronzeville's robust and partisan localism offers a compelling defense of the quality of its social and human life, it is also important to project beyond the limits of neighborhood and village square—to see Bronzeville, and Black Chicago, as a point from which black people could imagine race, nation, and world anew. "Culture" and "community" were categories that took on meaning through the symbiotic interrelation of Black Chicago with wider worlds. They were not terms that could be understood as subsumed or contained within its local boundaries. This explains my choice to depart from the community-study convention that largely informs research on African Americans in Chicago, important though that convention is. Surely I will miss some of those secrets hinted at from the start in so doing. Yet I feel, in the end, such a choice helpfully reorients investigation of twentieth-century black urbanization, from "how well did African Americans adjust to the modern city," to "how did African Americans transform the modern city upon arriving there?"

Several key turns in recent scholarship are engaged by this book, though my intent in doing so is more to borrow techniques and perspectives, than to endorse one or another as the proper approach to postwar black experience. Growing attention to African-American class distinctions and antagonisms as an engine of historical formation have been central to accounts of black urban life since the high point of social historical method a generation ago, and received an important boost from the work of Kevin Gaines, Joy James, and others emphasizing the constraints of uplift ideology among black elites. My representation of Black Chicago after 1940 notes these points of class tension, yet ultimately emphasizes the hybrid affinities of class feeling among African Americans, more than their clear differentiation along lines of material condition and social position. Uplift and clientage, ultimately, are two ideas undergoing some significant interrogation in this place and time, and I present them in more contingent form than has been the case to date in recent work.

This revision seems all the more necessary when one considers wage and occupational indicators showing the 1940s and 1950s as a period of gains, not only for an emergent black middle class, but also for African Americans generally, nationwide and particularly in Chicago. While the national median income for urban blacks increased between 1940 and 1950 from $700 to $1,263, and went up again to $2,911 by 1960, in Chicago median income for black male workers rose to $2,361 in 1950 and to $4,104 in 1960: for women, the figure was $1,234 in 1950 and 2,393 in 1960. Black median income in 1950s Chicago—$1,919—was higher than all other cities except for Detroit, the leader in wage levels because of the auto manufacturers. Black unemployment between 1948 and 1955 remained under 6 percent for half of the eight years, reaching as low as 4.5 percent in 1953. Specific occupations showed dramatic increase in the number of African Americans, in particular for men. Black male clerical and sales workers nationwide rose from 58,000 in 1940, to 145,000 in 1950, and to 261,000 in 1960. The number of black men working as craftsmen, foremen, and operatives—the high-end jobs in manufacturing and industry—grew from 497,000 in 1940 to 1,346,000 in 1960: over 30 percent of the black male workforce. National conditions were less positive for black women, with close to 1,000,000 employed as domestics, resulting in a depressed median income of $764 in 1950. In Chicago, however, black women saw employment in domestic work drop precipitously, from 38 percent of the local black female labor pool in 1940 to 20 percent in 1950, and only 13 percent in 1960, rates far lower than the 17.5 percent of black women who worked as clerical workers by that time. A range of local employers, from the Ford Motor plant to the black-owned Supreme Liberty Life Insurance sustained the upward push in income and occupational status. At Ford by 1960, blacks held 37 percent or nearly 2,000 jobs, 17 percent of which were salaried, as opposed to hourly, positions. Supreme Liberty Life Insurance employed 2,000 black workers mainly in white collar and clerical positions. These developments, in turn, indicated very different collective material conditions for African Americans in Chicago than might be presumed from accounts of inexorable community declension there.[12]

Accounts concentrating on African-American history during and after World War II have increasingly emphasized the bifurcating impact of the Cold War on intraracial black relations and agenda. This work has been most important in defining African-American thought and action as constitutive of, rather than incidental to, the emergence of the U.S. state as the main global actor, while also offering a critical interpretation of the civil rights movement as partnership with as much as challenge to that state's domestic authority. Instructive and thought-provoking as this work has been, my approach will be to emphasize the complexities of black loyalty and civil affiliation, especially given the contradictory pursuit of both public belonging and racial distinction inherent in their nationalizing turn. The growing field of diaspora scholarship has introduced a different revisionist category of political imaginary to recent black life. I suppose that my approach has more equivocal relation to this work, though by saying so I do not mean in any way to question the significance or utility of this burgeoning field. Rather, I think it remains important to consider African-American culture, expansive racial imagination, and even black nationalism in relation to the U.S. nation-state specifically. Even as African diaspora studies offers its own compelling formulations of visionary, alternative black perspective, I believe we have yet to exhaust the complex terms with which U.S. blacks wrestled with existence in their adoptive environment—a land both strange and strangely familiar at once.[13]

Probably the most significant recent innovation in scholarship related to African Americans is the move to reorient recent U.S. history by placing black people at its center and positing resistance as their perpetual form of social agency. There is no question that this turn has not only changed the practice of black history, but changed it for the better, for the simple reason that this has meant that black people are today presented as progenitors of their own history as never before. In this sense, I am working from the suggestion of countless scholars today who emphasize this paradigm, insofar as I seek to tell the story of how blacks in Chicago, simply put, acted in a manner profoundly influencing the conditions of their present and future, as well as the conditions of others in the nation generally. Nonetheless, by focusing on the motive of creation as much as the will to struggle, I stress a different notion of proactivity of African-American history. Here the debate more than a generation ago between E. P. Thompson and Raymond Williams over whether culture was best described as a "total way of struggle" or a "total way of life" proves relevant still. Though protest and insurgency feature prominently in the lives of African Americans in Chicago between 1940 and 1955, and would emerge more prominently soon after, it did not exhaust their collective and public ambitions. The project of fashioning institutional, entrepreneurial, market-driven, and national forms of black culture from the pivot point of Chicago is a story of creative and strategic alignment as much as resistance. This, once again, strikes me as an approach that better evokes the complex equivocation of African Americans as both blacks and Americans today. Perhaps, in reckoning with their (and our) ambiguity, we might better suggest acknowledge African Americans' ongoing sense of divided aims, and become more precise in itemizing the benefits and costs of their alignment, however ambivalently, with this country.[14]

Chapter 1 of *Selling the Race* recounts the 1940 American Negro Exposition, the most ambitious black national exposition to that point, and an event meant to commemorate the emancipation of slaves seventy-five years earlier. Convening Black Chicago's leading lights of public and media culture, in particular Claude Barnett, the Associated Negro Press founder who proved the event's driving force, the exposition gave first evidence of the community's awareness of its pivotal place in national black life. Cognizant of the arts accomplishments emanating from Harlem in the 1920s and 1930s, Chicago's Negro Exposition proved an episode of still more expansive intentions, drawing black exhibitors and contributors from all areas of the country, mounting the most comprehensive retrospective of black visual arts at the time, and constituting a landmark in cooperative programming with the government. Yet despite its impressive list of contributors and sponsors, the American Negro Exposition proved anything but a landmark success, as evidenced by its near-anonymity in the historical record. In part, this was due to a series of farcical developments within the organizing and management of the festival: labor troubles, problems in securing sought-after attractions, and disappointing attendance all combined to leave the event with a less than lustrous legacy. But also at play were deeper contradictions implicit in the event's very mission. Contradictory loyalties to race and state, an awkward grasp of the centrality of popular and commercial arts to black imagination and interest, and in particular the challenge of fashioning an enduring legacy of black freedom from the discreet event of emancipation: these and other difficulties rendered the project, in many ways, untenable from inception. As a crucial and summary celebration of race history and experience, the exposition was a crucial locus of collective memory in its time, due to its failures as well as its achievements. And, like all memory sites, it was as much a projection of future as retrospective of past, providing an illuminating example of how its organizers envisioned their later lives as creators and citizens. For these reasons, this analysis begins with the exposition, a rehearsal of many of the initiatives undertaken in the decade and a half that followed.

Popular music, the subject of chapter 2, carries this inquiry into the most celebrated field of local culture. Chicago has long enjoyed a central place in narratives of popular black music, as evidenced by the extensive bibliographies in blues, gospel, jump blues, soul, and other styles touched on here. Too, Chicago has been seen as a special exemplar of twentieth-century black music's syncretic character. For many, the blues' melding of Black Belt folkways with the rhythms of industry, or gospel's syncopation of the hymnal embodies for many the melding of city and country resulting from black migration. Though these qualities are given consideration here, more attention is paid to popular music as the basis of a robust local commercial and cultural infrastructure: the original black culture industry in the city and, perhaps in the country as well. Chicago's seedbed relation to postwar popular music is well known: Chicago blues, to name one genre, was parent to both American and British styles of rock and roll, while a list of postwar artists emerging from the Windy City over time—Sam Cooke, Muddy Waters, Mahalia Jackson, Nat King Cole, Dinah Washington, Joe Williams, Curtis Mayfield, Jerry Butler, Chaka Khan, and Earth, Wind, and Fire—makes clear the city's preeminent role, together with Detroit and Memphis, in moving black music toward an especially soulful identity. But this was no spontaneous or inevitable force of racial nature. Various structures of production and dissemination refined these forms as new sounds, creating the conditions for the synthesis of sacred and secular styles constituting what is perhaps black folk's most universally acclaimed modernism. Crucial in this process were black appeal disc jockeys like Jack Cooper and Al Benson, who innovated potent systems of delivery and promotion for the new sound. Chapter 2, then, addresses commercial infrastructure as the basis for the city's unique musical forms, showing how the market played a catalyzing, rather than diluting or compromising role in these arts' developments during and after World War II.

Chapter 3 takes up the story of the Associated Negro Press, the preeminent black news wire service nationally, and its founder, Claude Barnett. Patrician elder within local media and commercial culture, Barnett grasped before anyone Chicago's emerging nodal role in national black life, as demonstrated by his efforts related to the American Negro Exposition in 1940. His work within the press after that time, along with several supplemental projects—in particular the fascinating *Negro America* newsreel project beginning in 1952—sought to translate that ferment into viable media initiatives, partly for his enrichment but as well out of a sense that these efforts would generate a more empowered black public consciousness in a period of pronounced challenge and change. Yet Barnett—among the more personally sympathetic figures within the book—ultimately proved his own worst enemy. Indulgence of subordinates and partners compromised the ANP's effectiveness in several crucial locales, notably Los Angeles. A still greater problem was Barnett's allegiance to the credo of clientage, learned during his undergraduate years at Tuskegee Institute and honed over a career of racial custodianship. The adverse effects of this orientation became pronounced during the cold war, as Barnett sought with ever diminishing success to hold course between state demands of loyalty and the widespread insurgent spirit animating black life following World War II. Examination of the ANP, then, extends recent examinations of African Americans' complex relation to the cold war, but with a twist. Hamstrung by ties to an archaic code of race relations, Barnett illuminates the cost of clientage on the eve of that code's impending collapse. His was the old ambassadorial style advocated by Locke at the dawn of the Harlem Renaissance, but perfected a generation earlier by Barnett's mentor, Booker T. Washington.

Barnett's problems seem all the more striking when compared to the fortunes of his local competitor and successor (in many senses), magazine publisher John Johnson. Johnson's personal success has generally been seen as adequate summation of the significance of his business initiative, Johnson Publishing Company. Too, the ambition of Johnson, unabashedly celebrated in his own writings and remarks, has often been presumed sufficient explanation of his magazines' notorious mystification of black life with entertainer profiles, unfettered consumerism, and rags to riches stories—a "world of make believe" providing fodder for critiques of the emergent black middle class' lack of racial solidarity and responsibility. My examination of Johnson Publishing and in particular its flagship magazine, *Ebony* in chapter 4 revises these accounts in a range of ways. I present *Ebony* as the shared accomplishment of an eclectically diverse and talented staff: one whose varied experiences and social orientation equipped it to represent postwar black life in uniquely ambitious ways. Rooted in Black Chicago institutions and topics, *Ebony* nonetheless ranged well beyond the local interest, remapping black life on national and international scales, and exemplifying the social imagination driving new notions of community related to race and nation. While its advocacy of African-American market consciousness and consumer identity is well known, *Ebony* highlighted other modern affiliations among blacks—attention to law, celebrity, improvised family and domestic arrangements, and a surprising array of cultural diasporic affinities all indicated the magazine's modernizing orientation toward black life and thought. In the end, *Ebony* presented itself as champion not of assimilation or race apostasy, but instead of classic liberalism as a dominant structure of modern black life. This development, which alongside racial resistance and diasporic identification remains the governing mode of social and political feeling among African Americans today, makes clear *Ebony*'s impact as a cultural enterprise, and offers the most compelling proof of Black Chicago's pivotal place in redefining black life and thought nationwide.

The implications of this redefinition are made clear in chapter 5, which addresses the outcry against Chicago boy Emmett Till's lynching in 1955. Like the American Negro Exposition, the protests and insurgencies emerging in the wake of Till's death encouraged reflections at once retrospective and forward-looking. The saga of where black people had been and where they were going found new and eloquent voice in 1955: now the impetus was not the praise song of postemancipation progress, but rather the lament of racial terror. Till, of course, was not the first black—or black youth—murdered in the South. Indeed, several blacks lost their lives under similar circumstance in Mississippi that year—a wave of reactionary terrorism that cast the coming civil rights battle not as a benign campaign for American hearts and minds, but as a bloody struggle for that society's soul. What distinguished the Till case from these atrocities, and from past episodes of racial terror, was its universal circulation among African Americans, through the resolve of Till's mother Mamie Bradley and other organizers, and through publication of an open-casket photo of Till's brutalized body in *Jet* magazine, sister journal to *Ebony* begun in late 1951. Recognized as the initiating insurgent action of the civil rights movement, response to Till's lynching realizes a different epiphany in my account: that of manifesting the simultaneity sought by Black Chicago impresarios and entrepreneurs since 1940. Juxtaposing coverage and comment on the Till episode to conditions of racial violence both in Chicago and in Mississippi, my treatment of this profound historical juncture agrees with the consensus regarding its significance, but attributes that significance to the nationalizing of cultural meaning emanating from Chicago since 1940, as much as the tradition of protest against racial terror.

This last chapter explicitly returns, as well, to the book's main mission—to place black Chicagoans at the center of the postwar historical narrative, not only that specifically related to African Americans, but also the history of the country as a whole. Viewing the Emmett Till controversy as a social spectacle and memory project generated in part by way of race media—making it a *production* as much as a spontaneous episode of protest—reminds us of the innovation and sophistication characterizing cultural production in Black Chicago over these years. Though conventional histories credit broadcast television's coverage of the brutality of Birmingham in 1963 with placing civil rights struggles before a national audience for the first time, it is clear that this had happened among African Americans and all those who took their media seriously nearly a decade before. While photorealist style has undergone criticism since its heyday during the Depression as a distorting mirror of social and political conditions, the activating effect of the Till photos as artifactual record of black pain and outrage mark them the deepest accomplishment of racial documentary style. And though analysts then and since have protested the corrosive impact of market alignment on black social structure and politics, *Jet*'s half-million circulation distinguished response to the Till lynching from countless episodes of racist atrocity preceding it. Each of these circumstances demonstrates the active relation of African Americans to the historical patterns and developments they encountered. Each as well indicates the complex, even contradictory character of African-American culture and politics.

This, finally, constituted the true legacy of black folks' modernity. Initiative at the personal level and development at the group level led not to epiphany or deliverance, but rather contradictory meaning and outcomes. Nowhere was this more apparent than in the ways that national integration of black cultural experience and exchange encouraged both a sense of racial distinction and also a sense, however tenuous or unsatisfying, of civil connection. That these developments originated in Chicago, among the most racially segregated and brutish communities in the twentieth-century

United States, is its own indication of how modern life rests often on sobering irony. The problems inherent in this situation have proven resistant to any simple or transparent correctives—I do not presume to add to that long list. Instead, I want to present African Americans as modernity's agents, rather than its casualties. Such an orientation, it seems to me, is the best way to reimagine terms of discussion that might one day lead to equitable coexistence, in Chicago and beyond.

AMERICAN NEGRO
EXPOSITION
1865
1940
CHICAGO COLISEUM
JULY 4 TO SEPT. 2
AMERICAN NEGRO EXPOSITION HEADQUARTERS, 3632 SOUTH PARKWAY, CHICAGO

IMAGINING THE FUTURE

CHAPTER ONE

And yet, being a problem is a strange experience.
W. E. B. DU BOIS

Throughout the first half of the twentieth century—especially during the 1910s and 1920s—Chicago was the nation's focal point for African-American congregation. Lodges and fraternal groups such as the Elks and Odd Fellows, small but growing professional associations, expansive religious assemblies like the National Baptist Convention—all routinely came to Chicago for annual meetings and special events. Waves of itinerant artists and intellectuals, proselytizers of spirit and wallet, worldly train porters and mouth-agape masses broke upon the city's concrete shores, channeling an extraordinary human confluence. Terminus more than crossroads, Chicago's illustration of the modern saga of Black mass migration derives significantly from this precedent of destination. Personal journeys, along with the collective restlessness of a sojourning people, were promised an end in the Windy City, hopefully for better, though all too often for worse.

The first chapter of this book considers one noteworthy attempt to harness Black Chicago's role of convention: the American Negro Exposition in 1940, commemorating the

Facing page: 2. Official poster for the American Negro Exposition, 1940. Artwork by Robert Pious. Courtesy of the Claude Barnett Collection/Chicago Historical Society (ICHi-39058).

seventy-fifth anniversary of the end of the Civil War and Blacks' official emancipation from slavery. Held at the 18th Street Armory on the near South Side, the exposition sought to inventory the progress made by African Americans since slavery, and therefore buttress claims to full civil status and belonging. That this event—meant to constitute the first Black-organized World's Fair—has been essentially forgotten today indicates that it failed to realize these aims. Yet in its failure lies a revealing story of the logistics and politics of cultural programming in Black Chicago, on the eve of its emergence as a national center of cultural enterprise. In the end, the challenge embodied in the 1940 exposition was not only to represent Chicago as destination for the race, but also as a site of renovation for group imagination and discourse. Falling short of these goals, paradoxically, set the stage for later projects and institutions among African Americans in the Windy City that would better suggest how blacks' legion travels might culminate not only in a common experience of arrival, but also a new and modern sense of collective being, waiting to be broadcast across nation and even world.

With 1940 approaching, Claude Barnett, founder of the Associated Negro Press in Chicago, was not a happy man. "What on earth is the hold-up in the matter of the Afra-American Emancipation Exposition?" he demanded in a letter to James Washington, the local businessman who had first proposed commemorating the seventy-fifth anniversary of slavery's end in the United States. "We have gone along with your program supporting it and seeking to aid you, but I confess we are beginning to be a bit dubious," Barnett warned, noting that only months remained before the scheduled Fourth of July opening. Though an event commission had been organized, it was unclear to what extent—or whether—it had deliberated. A $75,000 grant from the Illinois legislature remained untouched, casting doubt upon claims of both progress and a plan. Barnett now grew anxious, fearing discredit to more than just Washington: "You are on trial in this matter and so is the whole race . . . I suggest that you fight through whatever the barriers are and get some action. Get us some news so that we can keep praising instead of picking flaws." There was no response from Washington, but if there had been one, it failed to allay Barnett's concerns. By February 1940, Washington had been demoted to a figurehead role on the reconstituted board, with Barnett and his associates in Chicago now lining up contacts and funds for the gala, renamed the American Negro Exposition.[1]

The change in leadership promised an event grander than what James Washington initially had in mind. As the *Chicago Defender* put it, the event would be "the first real Negro World's Fair."[2] Named as executive director was attorney Truman Gibson Jr., who while at University of Chicago had helped research Professor Harold Gosnell's groundbreaking book *Negro Politicians,* introducing the young law student to the movers and shakers of Windy City politics.[3] His father, Truman Gibson Sr., headed Supreme Liberty Life Insurance Company along South Parkway, which meant the exposition was backed by the largest black-owned business in the country. Local notables joined the drive: among those named to governing boards were cosmetics magnate Anthony Overton, attorney and future municipal judge Wendell Green, labor leader Willard Townsend, community leader Irene McCoy Gaines, and city councilman Earl Dickerson. Earlier that year, Dickerson had helped argue the *Lee v. Hansberry* case before the Supreme Court, beginning the process of nullifying restrictive covenants, a first step in enlisting the federal courts against institutionalized bulwarks of segregation nationally.[4]

Others went to work producing materials and promoting the event. Arna Bontemps, head of the Negro Division of the Illinois Writers Program (under the Works Project Administration) and Harlem Renaissance alumnus, was tapped to coordinate exhibit planning and construction. Together with Erik Lindgren, another WPA supervisor, Bontemps drew from a pool of IWP talent: Horace Cayton, Joseph Evans, Margaret Taylor Goss, Charles Dawson, and Katherine Dunham all worked researching themes and designing exhibits.[5] As head of the Associated Negro Press, Barnett was well positioned to plan publicity, a task he delegated to his editor Frank Marshall Davis, known both for journalism and poetry in the urban realist style.[6] Other local journalists, notably Lucius Harper, columnist and former editor for the *Defender,* joined the effort to excite popular interest in the exposition.

Given its scope, the drive shortly taxed the resources of local blacks: support was needed from beyond the boundaries of race community. Prominent Chicago whites, for whom politics of color had been a point of tension since the horrific Race Riot of 1919, assisted at several junctures. The $75,000 legislative grant signaled the state government's interest: seeking to insure proper use of the appropriation, Governor Henry Horner tapped Robert Bishop to represent the state on the exposition board.[7] Aware that sponsorship might translate into votes, city politicians from alderman and school board members up to Mayor Edward Kelly lined up behind the project. Financial help came from the Rosenwald Fund, the local philanthropic organization administered by well-known negrophile Edwin Embree. Known for its stake in school construction throughout the black South, spread of the YMCA system in black urban enclaves, and increasing fellowship support of black artists and scholars during the Depression, the Rosenwald Fund underwrote education and health exhibits at the exposition, to a total of $15,000.[8]

Help from more distant sources proved decisive in putting the exposition on track. Though blacks were emerging as a political constituency of note—especially in urban centers like Chicago—federal leaders remained averse to acknowledging blacks' special needs. Inattention to racial equity had proven an Achilles' heel for the early New Deal, due to the distorted leverage white southern congressmen and appointees enjoyed during the Roosevelt era, as well as doctrinaire administration liberals who perversely frowned upon race conscious policy as smacking of favoritism. Thus, Claude Barnett could have been forgiven dim hopes while traveling in late February to Washington, D.C., in search of support. A meeting with agriculture secretary Henry Wallace—personally progressive, yet to date grievously neglectful of black sharecroppers and farmers—surprisingly saw Barnett's expectations not only met but exceeded. Wallace committed all branches of agriculture to exhibit in Chicago at a cost of $40,000; suggested contacts in other departments and agencies, including Labor, Commerce, Social Security, and the alphabet agencies of the New Deal; and laid the groundwork for a matching federal grant of $75,000 to exposition organizers.[9]

A flurry of contacts built on this beachhead, including several directed toward black advisors embedded within various government departments in Washington: Mary McLeod Bethune and Robert Weaver at the most visible levels of the Black Cabinet, as well as lesser figures like William Trent and Emmer Lancaster, advisors on Negro Affairs at the Federal Works Agency and the Department of Commerce respectively.[10] Through their efforts, multiple branches of the government signed onto the exposition, helping insure that as a program, it would be national in scope. It now constituted the most ambitious cultural partnership between blacks and the federal government to date: an experiment with relations of race and state that in the best moments since emancipation had been characterized by patronizing clientage and in the worst by withering contempt.

Thus, the exposition effort gained momentum through the spring of 1940, offering promise not only of an intriguing curiosity, but a watershed in public perception of blacks as a group. Communication with Jackson Davis of the Southern Education Board, Gunnar Myrdal's guide across the South during his early research on U.S. race relations, resulted in a $25,000 grant to the American Film Center for a film on southern black education—the most elaborate documentary on black life to date.[11] Letters to Grove Edwards at the Civil Aeronautics Authority and Willa Brown, the well-known pilot whose Coffey School in Chicago was an epicenter for the flight training craze captivating black America at the time, led to plans for a black aviation exhibit.[12] E. Simms Campbell, alumnus of Englewood High School and now a featured artist at *Esquire* magazine, agreed to show a selection of his acclaimed cartoons.[13] Albion Holsey of Tuskegee Institute and the National Negro Business League solicited black businesses across the country to rent booths, while Dorothy Porter, supervisor of the Moorland Collection at Howard University, proposed an exhibit of books by prominent black authors.[14]

Anchoring the developing effort was Barnett. Nominally coordinator of government and arts exhibits, Barnett was the driving force in most aspects of the exposition project. His own start had come during the Golden Freedom Jubilee held in Chicago twenty-five years earlier, when as a young Tuskegee graduate he established a mail-order portrait service of "prominent Negroes through history and in contemporary life." Now, having parlayed his experiment into a global wire service counting nearly one hundred black newspapers as subscribers, Barnett was among the best connected African Americans in the country, making him the logical point person to oversee programming.[15] Woodbridge E. Morris, director of the Birth Control Federation of America, enthusiastically replied to Barnett's invitation, promising cooperation "to the fullest extent possible." If Barnett held doubts concerning endorsement of contraception in the heavily Catholic city of Chicago, his subsequent letter reiterating interest gave no indication.[16] Barnett showed nimble feet again in the matter of the federal appropriations bill, whose main sponsor was Arthur Mitchell, the vainglorious black congressman from Chicago. Reassuring the prickly Mitchell that plans were proceeding smoothly, he kept the bill on a slow but steady path to passage in mid-May.[17] Barnett wrote officials in the Virgin Islands, Liberia, and Haiti inviting exhibits representing their countries and territories, and sent letters to African missions in nine different colonies, asking for documentation of "life and progress in Africa," with emphasis on indigenous newspapers and magazines.[18] Closer to home, Barnett pressed William Nickerson Jr., founder of Golden State Mutual Life Insurance Company, to continue efforts to revive the exhibit from Los Angeles, despite Nickerson's fears that the project might prove "a complete flop."[19]

Securing another community's involvement posed a thornier challenge. All efforts at depicting black life in 1940, of course, had eventually to reckon with the outsized place of New York City and, in particular, Harlem. Barnett acknowledged as much in his deferential letter of invitation to Mayor La Guardia requesting a representative exhibit ("Harlem ranks as the greatest Negro city in the world," he wrote).[20] Most leading lights of

African-American culture and intellect viewed Harlem as their spiritual home, and though the reputation of the Renaissance nearly a decade after its puzzling end was not what it would become, there was still a catchy ring to the notion that black life in Gotham sounded the key for race existence throughout the country, if not the world. Chicago blacks, by contrast, rarely found their own lives spoken of in such terms, despite the political clout, extensive business enterprise, and advanced social organization of Bronzeville. In late spring organizers took stock of their more promising attractions: Augusta Savage's sculptures, previewed to an enthusiastic audience in early May; Aaron Douglas's panels inspired by James Weldon Johnson's *God's Trombones,* set to show in the Temple of Religion; Langston Hughes's and Richard Wright's appearances, scheduled for key dates during the exposition.[21] It would have been hard to resist the conclusion that, whatever its location, the exposition would further burnish New York and Harlem's claim as race capital.

Yet that the exposition was set for Chicago and not New York marked a crucial, if not immediately apparent, shift in the balance of cultural power in black America. Assessment of the Harlem Renaissance—in its own time and since—has noted its inability to generate native structures of production, distribution, and support to sustain its artistic progeny.[22] When white patrons, wavering by the late 1920s, took flight with the Depression, ingénues like Bontemps, Langston Hughes, and Zora Neale Hurston soon found themselves cast to the winds. Chicago, to be sure, had its own conventions of white philanthropy and cross-racial validation. But these arrangements were not as self-important as they had been in Jazz Age New York, nor did they supersede the dense web of black commercial, civic, and media institutions offering a nascent base for creative work and group imagination locally. Indeed, an alternate reading of the relationship between New York and Chicago, in light of the exposition effort, might emphasize the gravitational pull of Chicago on blacks across the country, including Harlem, as the 1940s began. Figures like Bontemps and Hughes were in many ways Renaissance refugees, drawn by chance or design to Chicago to connect with a broad black public audience that, despite all efforts, had thus far eluded them.

Nowhere was this new calculus more evident than in plans for the arts exhibit, rapidly becoming the centerpiece for the exposition. Visual arts was a latecomer among the imaginative genres for blacks: despite talents like Douglas, Savage, and Richmond Barthe, painters, printmakers, and sculptors rarely received the acclaim—or funding—that drama, music, and literature had in the high days of the Harlem Renaissance. Ironically, the Depression had seen improved prospects for black visual artists—due, to be sure, not to improved market conditions, but rather the emergence of new lines of support, none more important than the Harmon Foundation in New York. Since 1928, Harmon had subsidized black achievement in the arts: by the Depression years, their traveling show (reaching fifty cities and 150,000 people in 1931) signaled that black artists were being sponsored and promoted to an unprecedented degree.[23]

Once Claude Barnett opened communication with Mary Beattie Brady, the prim, efficient director at Harmon, through an exchange of letters exploring an art show for the exposition, he accessed the foundation's weighty reputation, further validating the event's credentials.[24] Yet this undertaking would test Harmon's capabilities, along with those of Barnett and other organizers. The proposed exhibit would be twice the size of any prior showing of African-American art. Certainly there were risks, as Brady reminded Barnett in discussing the intricacies of selecting, transporting and storing works. But there were as well the benefits of staging a blockbuster show to authorize black painters and sculptors, as race writers had been a decade earlier. Too, there were the possibilities of strengthening links between black artists based in the East, the South, and the remaining parts of the country—including Chicago, where established figures like Archibald Motley Jr., William Edouard Scott, and Charles Dawson anchored a cohort of rising talents. As planning progressed through the spring, both Barnett and Brady realized that Chicago's freedom fete offered a unique opportunity to place black visual arts on the nation's cultural map.

Others noted this potential with interest: virtually without exception, Barnett's invitations to artists and impresarios met with hearty assents. Calls for poster designs drew nearly a hundred entries, with Harlem-based Robert Pious winning the $100 prize: his panel of two dark brown figures with raised arms bearing sundered chain links, and other artifacts of black freedom, provided the logo for the exposition (fig. 2).[25]

Writing from the dean's chair at Fisk, Charles Johnson, former editor of *Opportunity,* agreed to serve on the arts committee, counseling invitations to several young artists, among them Selma Burke, Jacob Lawrence, and Roy De Carava.[26] Joining Johnson on the committee was a still more august patriarch, Alain Locke. Brought in at the early stages of planning, Locke proved a key advisor and booster, contacting artists, tending to the partnership between Brady and Barnett, and lending his singular prestige to the exposition.[27] With June approaching, Barnett, Brady, and the others involved in organizing the arts exhibit had commitments from black artists across the country to submit over 300 works for public viewing in a hall to be named for the Henry Ossawa Tanner, the African-American master who had passed away in Paris three years earlier.

Thus, even if many artists were New York–based, was it not more significant that only in Chicago had it proved possible to propose a show convening their works, as well as those from other points? With the Tanner Gallery validating the exposition as a whole, other New York–based contributors scrambled to join the party. L. D. Reddick, curator of the Schomburg Library collection, submitted a proposal for a 164-item sample of the library's book and archival holdings, on topics ranging from Paul Lawrence Dunbar and *Uncle Tom's Cabin* to early newspapers, politics, and war.[28] Julius Adams, publisher of the *Amsterdam News,* wrote Frank Marshall Davis requesting "an intimate story" portraying black life in Chicago and emphasizing the "I Will" spirit of the city, in order to recommend the event to readers.[29] Barnett promised further shipment of official posters to New York representatives to supplement the initial run of 20,000 already used up advertising the gala in Chicago.[30] Whatever feelings of geographic rivalry, Harlem, like the rest of black America, had little apparent choice but to plan its summer in Chicago. Brady's request that New York artworks have their own room drew no objection from Barnett and other organizers, sufficiently flush with their prospects to brush aside all gestures of regional gamesmanship.[31]

With Harlem safely in orbit, the lure to participants elsewhere grew stronger. William Smith, head of Karamu House theater group in Cleveland, and Andy Razaf, songwriter and collaborator with Fats Waller, offered their services to the exposition.[32] The International Sweethearts of Rhythm, the all-women's swing band out of Pine Bluff, Arkansas, that was just beginning to break into the national circuit, went one better, sending Rae Lee Jones to preview their act. An impressed Barnett applauded Jones as a "capable saleswoman" who "threw herself into her exposition," before tabling their bid, explaining that event stages were already booked up with better-known bands.[33] Organizations ranging from the NAACP to Mabel Staupers's National Association of Colored Graduate Nurses drew together exhibits, joining a bevy of black fraternities and sororities, church groups, and civic organizations from communities across the country.[34] Emory Ross, director of the Africa Bureau in New York, cataloged 200 photos shot throughout the continent for display.[35] Margaret Walker submitted a poem of thirty-three stanzas titled "Epic for the Jubilee Year of Negro Freedom" for the juried competition. With its panorama of forced labor ("we have gone into the too hot sun"), genius ignored if not desecrated ("Do not forget, America, how we made your songs; do not forget,

America, how we bore your thongs"), and radical lessons of African-American existence ("I say I will make you hear me, America. I will make you know the meaning of my working and my living and my dying on your shores"), Walker's epic sounded the transforming potential of the upcoming commemoration:

What is yours, America, is mine
and what is mine, America, is yours.
Have I not made you what you are?
Have you not made me what I am?
Have I not joined hands, too, with you?
Did I not rise without gold
and without your love?
Did I not span the distance
of the jubilee years
with the liquid swiftness
of a shooting meteor?[36]

Walker's reading of the integral character of blacks' presence in America, anticipating the later literary syncretism of Ralph Ellison and Albert Murray, failed to sway the jury of Davis, Hughes, and Bontemps, who awarded the precise "Dark Symphony" by Texan Melvin Tolson first prize.[37]

As July approached, all indications were that the exposition, at death's door a half year earlier, would prove a gala without precedent in black cultural history. To be sure, the inevitable fires arose. A local citizens' group protested the exclusion of "ordinary Chicagoans" from planning tasks, resulting in a testy meeting of community members and organizers brokered by *Defender* publisher John Sengestacke.[38] Anticipating that the demoted James Washington might encourage further grumbling, organizers shuttled him off to tour black colleges and universities "for the purposes of explaining the merit of the Negro Exposition" throughout all of May and June.[39] Squabbles over a national press exhibit were initiated by the Murphy family, iconoclastic publishers of the *Afro-American* newspapers in Baltimore.[40] A minor scandal erupted as local Catholics and politicians moved to block the Birth Control Federation's exhibit, leaving Barnett to consult black ministers on alternate sites while commiserating with a vexed B. Kenneth Rose, federation vice president.[41]

Yet these concerns did not dim the optimism of organizers in the final days of preparation. Reporting back to Senator James Slattery (IL), who had teamed with Arthur Mitchell in sponsoring the federal appropriation, Barnett relayed how a "tremendously impressed" congressional monitor "expressed himself as amazed at the scope of the program," noting that he was "happy he had been chosen to work with the Exposition."[42] Upon receiving an exhibit grant for the National Council of Negro Women, Mary McLeod Bethune sent plans to come to Chicago, along with her "congratulations upon the success of your splendid efforts."[43] Roy Wilkens, editor of the *Crisis* magazine of the NAACP, confirmed the association's participation, noting that "personally, I believe that this exposition offers us an opportunity to reach many thousands of people, and that the results from a publicity and propaganda standpoint . . . will more than repay the cost of a trip to Chicago."[44] There was even talk of President Roosevelt opening the exposition by wire from his Hyde Park home in New York.[45] All seemed in place for an historic show, one that would affirm race progress since emancipation, and the central role of black folk in the work and culture of the nation.

Once President Roosevelt opened the American Negro Exposition with the press of a button on July 4, his telegram was read to the crowd gathered at the Chicago Coliseum:

> It gives me great pleasure to send cordial greetings to you and through you to all who are participating in the opening of the American Negro Exposition in Chicago . . . The steady progress of our Negro citizens during the three quarters of a century that has elapsed since their emancipation emphasizes what can be accomplished by free men in a free country. Moreover, their achievements in art, letters, science, and public service during a brief seventy-five years of freedom should give all Americans renewed determination to marshal all of our strength to maintain and defend and perpetuate our priceless heritage of free institutions . . . In extending my greetings may I express confident hope that a race that has achieved so much in so few years may go forward to ever nobler things in the generations ahead.[46]

Roosevelt's proclamation came a little less than a year before his ban of war production discrimination, meant to head off A. Philip Randolph and the March on Washington movement. His statement was an appreciable if patronizing gesture, coming from an administration still inactive in the face of mounting discrimination and terror against blacks. Yet the content of Roosevelt's address, in the end, proved incidental: exhibits crowding the hall spoke more eloquently to blacks' accomplishment and potential than any words of a president.

Upon paying forty cents (or the ticket book rate of a quarter), visitors entered the coliseum: multistoried and larger than a football field, the hall comfortably accommodated the ninety-two different installations.[47] At its center was a replica of Lincoln's tomb, located downstate in the capital of Springfield.[48] Though race scholars from George Washington Williams to W. E. B. Du Bois had questioned the Great Emancipator's commitment to black freedom past the occasion of slavery's end, visitors saw no cause to temper their tributes, making the tomb among the lead attractions of the summer.[49] Beyond the information desk, where guidance and schedules could be obtained, exhibits lined up to the left and right. Those intrigued by the exposition's partnership with the federal government could peruse nine different booths, organized by the Federal Works Agency (FWA), the National Youth Administration (NYA), Social Security, the Civilian Conservation Corps, the Civil Aeronautics Agency, Public Health, Departments of Labor and Agriculture, and the Post Office, which displayed a full run of stamps, including one commemorating Booker T. Washington released in April—the first ever dedicated to an African American.[50] While Agriculture, with its $40,000 installation, and Labor, whose Mechanical Man's tape-recorded message "contrasted the Negro worker of today with the colored worker of years ago" provided the most elaborate displays, departments with proven commitments to black constituents, such as NYA or FWA, appealed equally to visitors. Onlookers seeking local exhibits were not disappointed. Booths dealt with leading South Side institutions, such as Supreme Life or Provident Hospital, while more thematic displays—like the sports hall sponsored by boxing champ and local hero Joe Louis, or the Temple of Religion employing a thousand-person choir drawn from neighborhood churches—spotlighted home talent.[51] Chicago's entry contrasted a replica of the cabin of Jean Baptiste Pont Du Sable, mulatto trader and Chicago's first nonnative settler in the late eighteenth century, with a scale model of the Ida B. Wells Homes, the $9 million public housing development scheduled to open on the South Side that fall, as testament to blacks' long and pioneering residence in the area.[52]

Of course, Barnett had secured space for the Associated Negro Press, but he was hard-pressed to lure observers away from the national press exhibit, dominated by a striking mural executed by Charles White, one of the rising stars of local arts.[53] Numerous exhibits filled out categories beyond local and federal. In addition to booths for black colleges, civic and self-help associations, church groups, and secret societies, there were areas for public education, the Negro soldier, and "Negro inventions." Towns and cities from Peoria, Illinois to Buffalo, New York to Los Angeles, California had booths, as did groups like the National Baptist Sunday School Board and the Hobby Lobby.[54] Encouraged to offer a comprehensive exhibit,

Liberia responded curiously with a miniature model of a rubber plant supplied by the Firestone Company, the dominant industrial presence in the republic, and power behind the country's oligarchic administration.[55] Haiti fell short of even this disappointing entry: despite Barnett's ceaseless inquiries, no exhibit came from the black nation that had initiated the epic arc of New World emancipation.[56] Dorothy Porter's Literature booth hosted signings and lectures, including ones by Langston Hughes and Richard Wright who were back in Chicago to research *Twelve Million Black Voices,*

the landmark photo-essay of black migrant life to be published in 1941. Onlookers remarked that Wright seemed fully at ease with his newfound celebrity following publication of his bestseller *Native Son*.[57] The Temple of Religion incorporated materials from ten different denominations, and held interfaith services on Sundays, while the Chicago Archdiocese and the Bahai Temple presented their own exhibits.[58] The Birth Control Federation, in the end, proved no match for local Catholic muscle, and was left to protest its barring to Barnett and the *New York Times*.[59]

Some observers, no doubt, would have only glanced at the booths on their way to staged attractions. The North Hall of the coliseum was used to screen films in daytime, including the Film Center's education documentary, titled *One Tenth of a Nation*. But it was at night that the exposition presented its most compelling entertainments. Initially, a double bill of live shows had been planned: a revue of blacks' achievements on stage titled *Cavalcade of the Negro Theater,* to be written by Hughes and Bontemps, and *Chimes of Normandy,* a "jazzed-up version" of the Gilbert and Sullivan operetta to be performed by the Federal Theater Project (FTP). This was not the first time that Victorian theater had swung: the FTP's *Hot Mikado* had been premiered in New York and Chicago a year earlier, to capacity crowds and glowing reviews.[60] *Chimes* sought to repeat this success, bringing in Sammy Dyer, choreographer at the South Side's Club DeLisa, to produce the show. After a slow start, the show became one of the great attractions at the exposition, compelling organizers to scrap *Cavalcade*. Upstairs in the South Hall was Tropical Gardens, which alternated nightly between Horace Henderson's dance orchestra and the revue *Tropics after Dark,* a collaboration joining Hughes, Bontemps, songwriters Margaret Bond and Zilmer Henderson, and local singers, dancers and comedians in a rendition of "the exotic and mysterious nights in Haiti and other Caribbean isles." It is unclear what Katherine Dunham made of such hyperbole, but her company performed, as did Ethel Waters, who reduced her $4,750 weekly appearance fee by two thirds to take part in the exposition.[61]

The Tanner Gallery, below the gardens, offered its own attractions. Besides Locke, Brady, and other Eastern *cognoscenti,* the gallery committee

Exhibition
of
THE ART
OF THE
AMERICAN
NEGRO
(1851 to 1940)
ASSEMBLED BY THE
American Negro
Exposition
ON VIEW
JULY 4 TO
SEPTEMBER 2
1940
TANNER
ART GALLERIES
AMERICAN
NEGRO
EXPOSITION
CHICAGO, ILLINOIS
PRICE TWENTY-FIVE CENTS
First Award in Black and White
"There Were No Crops This Year"
by Charles White, Illinois.

3. Cover of the program for the Exhibition of the Art of the American Negro, American Negro Exposition, 1940. Courtesy of the Harsh Research Collection/ Chicago Public Library.

had included Wendell Dabney from Cincinnati, Hale Woodruff from Atlanta, and Charles Johnson, insuring regionally diverse presentation. Selection juries reflected broad expertise: James Herring, art chair at Howard, and Daniel Catton Rich, director of Chicago's Art Institute, joined Richmond Barthe, Charles Dawson, and Archibald Motley Jr. as well as Federal

Arts Project head Holger Cahill and Peter Pollack, whose Chicago gallery had recently broken the downtown color bar on black artists. The end result, according to Locke, was "the most comprehensive and representative collection of the Negro's art . . . ever . . . presented to public view": 316 pictures, sculptures, carvings, and ceramics, representing 115 artists from around the country. Eleven paintings from Henry Ossawa Turner, including his acclaimed *The Three Marys* (on loan from the Art Institute) joined works of Malvin Gray Johnson, Albert Alexander Smith, and others in the memorial section of the gallery.[62] In the contemporary section, Jacob Lawrence's forty-one watercolors depicting Toussaint L'Ouverture vied for attention with ten equally vivid panels from cartoonist E. Simms Campbell. Works from familiar names—William Johnson, Palmer Hayden, Horace Pippen—shared space with those beginning to garner notice. Lois Mailou Jones submitted three works, including *Artist's Kitchen,* shown previously at the Grand Salon in Paris in 1938, along with Frederic Flemister, whose oil painting *Man with the Brush* received first prize. Barthe, Woodruff, Selma Burke, and the other sculptors proved a special draw. Elizabeth Catlett's *Negro Mother and Child,* bested better known rivals for first prize in the category, while the irrepressible Augusta Savage returned in July for a tea in her honor, causing Albion Holsey to complain to Barnett about reduced attendance at the nearby agricultural exhibits.[63]

In the end, the Harmon Foundation was granted its own room, but the distinction would have made little impression on onlookers. While the thirty-seven New York contributors made up the largest contingent in the collection, Illinois, with thirty-one artists, was not far behind. Along with established figures like Archibald Motley and the late William Harper, the Chicago group included a cadre of young black artists poised to establish Chicago as a center for visual arts. Charles White's offerings, including *Fellow Workers Won't You March with Us* and his prize-winning black and white *There Were No Crops This Year,* exemplified the radical spirit within the group. Bernard Goss and Eldzier Cortor depicted abusive local housing conditions in oils, while Margaret Taylor Goss took time from her docent's position to offer two watercolors, *Mama Takes in Washing* and *Social Worker.* Local painters Henry Avery, Charles Sebree, Charles Davis, and sculptors Marion Perkins and David Ross submitted compelling works, as did Leroy Winbush, young designer of stage sets at the Regal Theater.[64] Upon visiting the collection, Holger Cahill gave his blessings to Barnett, predicting that "the Negro Exposition will point out the fact that the Negro has a splendid creative contribution to make to American art."[65] Endorsing the Chicago group's realist vision, Alain Locke pointed out how the Tanner collection demonstrated that "today's beauty must not be pretty with sentiment but solid and dignified with truth." For him, as for others, the collection had fulfilled its core mission to "put Negro art on the map . . . and carry its inspiring message to the heart of every visitor to this Exposition."[66]

As compelling as the Tanner Gallery was, it did not exhaust visitors' aesthetic attention. Informed during spring of plans for a circuit of historical portraits and murals above the coliseum floor, James Herring conceded that, while not to his own tastes, the balcony series might prove "a worthwhile compliment to the more serious art."[67] When finished, however, the pieces registered more significantly than Herring had imagined. Including twenty portraits ranging from Sojourner Truth to Paul Robeson, and fifteen murals depicting an eclectic array of themes, from Ku Klux Klan night riders disrupting a Reconstruction-era classroom to the Fisk Jubilee Singers appearing before the Queen of England, the Court of Honor was visible to onlookers throughout the hall. Below the panels, alongside the facsimile of Lincoln's tomb, were eighteen dioramas conceived by local craftsman and designer Charles Dawson, depicting more outlandish scenes, from the building of the Sphinx and the discovery of iron in West Africa to the exploits of Isaac Murphy, first black jockey to run in the Kentucky Derby.[68]

These dioramas vied for attention with others at the Social Science booth, where sociologist E. Franklin Frazier "worked out a very timely theme on the Negro family."[69] Five installations depicted the fortunes of the African-American family over time—the House of the Master, demonstrating embattled conditions of marriage and childcare under slavery; the House of the Mother, detailing the matriarchal family structure of most blacks upon emancipation; the House of the Father, equating stable households with male-defined rights of land ownership and economic independence; the City of Destruction; and the City of Rebirth. Observers related the City of Destruction to declining home environments of freedmen in Southern cities after the Civil War, while the City of Rebirth was seen as illustrative of "wholesome surroundings" of domestic stability derived from improved labor conditions after the Great Migration.[70] Over time, these readings would turn in less optimistic directions. Frazier's book *The Negro Family in the United States* (1939) would prove a landmark in urban sociology, and an intellectual touchstone for cycles of interventionist and regressive public policy in decades to follow.[71] Though organizers could not know it at the time, it would be Frazier's thought that offered the most enduring legacy of the exposition, one undergirding devastating conclusions about blacks' place in—and fitness for—modern national life.

But such sobering outcomes were obscured, for the moment, by the kaleidoscope of experience, achievement and imagination on display. Attending on the eve of his vice-presidential nomination at the Democratic Convention a few blocks away, Secretary Wallace endorsed the effort as "100 percent Exposition instead of 50 percent Exposition and 50 percent hokum as is the general custom."[72] Lucius Harper sounded a similar note, but with emphasis on implications for blacks specifically: "As I walked through the labyrinth of Negro achievement as depicted at the American Negro Exposition prior to its opening, I marveled at the work that had been done in such a short space of time—just about four months of actual work. It is undoubtedly the greatest cultural exhibition that the black man has presented to the American public. There is nothing in it that smacks of a 'mammy-made' carnival that has heretofore characterized similar efforts on our part in presenting the Negro in culture, art, and education." To Harper, the exposition was a bargain for its black attendees, since for the price of admission, "a Negro couldn't purchase as much pride and glory in himself . . . anywhere else in the world."[73] Yet even as the kudos rolled in, the seams in the grand effort began to show.

Though Wallace and Harper applauded the exposition's refrain from sensationalism, organizers themselves regretted the absence of mass culture's irresistible thrills. While homespun programs like International or Pan African, Asiatic, European, and North and South Americas Day, brainchild of Afrocentric orator and programmer Fidipe Hammurabi, extended the exposition's geographic scope,[74] tapping the energies of popular entertainment was vital to the enterprise's popularity as it had been in previous expositions, notably the 1893 World's Fair in Chicago.[75] Difficulties in representing blacks' contributions to music illustrated the dilemma. Initially, Frank Marshall Davis wrote John Hammond, famed impresario at Columbia Records, requesting the company's participation in a multilabel exhibit, and promising a restaging of the Spirituals to Swing concerts Hammond had organized the previous two years in New York.[76] By June, though, no progress had been made, and Barnett advised Truman Gibson to settle for a display from the National Association of Negro Musicians—an organization focused on classical and recital artists—to represent the rich scope of black music.[77] The complications generating the music exhibit were matched by problems concerning programming. Writing Duke Ellington soon after the opening, Truman Gibson relayed that his scheduled performance might be canceled due to strained finances, though he still held out hope that "some good luck will enable us to have [your] band."[78]

Similar problems arose concerning film. Historically black actors had been consigned to demeaning role play mere steps from minstrelsy; yet recent years had seen breakthroughs. Barnett, whose wife, the acclaimed singer Etta Moton, appeared in Warner Brothers musicals in the 1930s, was tireless in his efforts to interest major studios to the exposition, writing MGM, United Artists, Walter Wanger Productions, and the Motion Picture Producers and Distributors of America.[79] By June, efforts focused on David Selznick, maverick producer of *Gone with the Wind,* which had its premiere the previous January. Provoking near universal protest by blacks at first, the film inspired grudgingly favorable comment as the year progressed, particularly given its unprecedented number of speaking roles for blacks in a major studio film.[80] The most prominent of these, Hattie McDaniel's "Mammy" character, had garnered the first Academy Award for a black performer: a hint, however compromised, of the prominence young black stars like Lena Horne and Dorothy Dandridge would enjoy in coming years.[81] Sensing an opportunity, Barnett pressed Selznick to have McDaniel appear for a week sometime during the summer.[82] Displaying surprising sensitivity, Selznick directed an assistant to coordinate McDaniel's appearance, reassuring Barnett that his request would "receive the most sympathetic consideration."[83] Shortly after the exposition's opening, welcome news of McDaniel's availability beginning July 20 arrived.[84] By July 18, though, Daniel O'Shea, Selznick's representative in the McDaniel negotiations, informed Barnett that the actress would be forced to cancel due to illness.[85] With McDaniel's cancellation, hopes of tapping the growing if still-dim allure of black Hollywood faded, indicating the still-shallow stake film studios had in black talent in 1940, as much as it did the low influence of Barnett and the rest of the black press in the world of feature film at that time.

Special difficulties surrounded attendance, a problem for expositions generally, including New York's own World Fair, in its second year by 1940. In letters to sponsors, Barnett offered rosy prognoses based on a simple if misguided formula. Given that the 1915 Golden Jubilee had attracted 250,000 people, despite lasting only two weeks and drawing most of its audience from a local black enclave of 50,000, projections of 2,000,000 visitors in 1940, based on a local community of nearly 300,000 African Americans and an entire summer to build interest and appeal, seemed within reach.[86] Yet sparse crowds from the start lowered revenue projections.[87] Within the first week, 141 employees had been laid off. Responding to Elizabeth Simon's letter inquiring about work, Barnett noted regretfully that "the Exposition is engaged in reducing employees rather than adding them." Arthur McLendon, a law student at Northwestern among the first to be let go, wrote Barnett that if he did not regain his post at the exposition, "he would surely starve."[88] Nor did financial woes end with the reduction of staff. Informing Hale Woodruff that his design for Tanner prize medals had been accepted, Barnett warned that poor finances might prevent his promised commission. Confronted with similar warnings, book exhibit organizer Dorothy Porter chose to cut losses by accepting reduced payment. Given the "severe slashing" the event's budget was subject to, Barnett termed her decision "a wise one."[89]

Other financial issues proved more resistant to negotiation. As early as late April, Barnett had alerted Truman Gibson to "the subject of unions and possible friction with them."[90] Barnett, whose undergraduate years at Tuskegee included a stint as Booker T. Washington's personal assistant, was far from neutral on matters of organized labor. Unfailingly pro-management in posture and association, Barnett in 1929 had entered into secret partnership with the Pullman Company to discredit the Brotherhood of Sleeping Car Porters during its initial organizing drive.[91] Such attitudes were reflected in the roster of participants chosen for the exposition. Along with Firestone's diorama glossing deplorable conditions of labor for Liberian rubber workers, exhibits from Chrysler and Pepsi-Cola joined in celebrating the company line. By contrast, no countervailing representation of the nearly half million black trade unionists nationally was to be found.[92] Indeed, the exhibit best evoking worker insurgency, however inadvertently, came from the United Taxicab Owners' Association, locked in a bitter strike with black drivers through June and July.[93]

At the same time, the exposition was no typical shop floor. Volunteers such as Margaret Goss and Katherine Dunham had been hired casually and worked flexible hours, technically constituting unfair competition to unionized craftsmen, performers, and technicians making up the event's natural labor pool. Negotiating with unionized projectionists to show motion pictures in the North Hall resulted in unanticipated expenses, forcing use of short documentary subjects rather than more elaborate offerings, including those from the major studios.[94] Disputes over layout, construction, and instillation work proved even more difficult to address. Carpenters working with black-owned firm Rousseau and Douglass were pushed on by J. Levert "Illy" Kelley, the colorful leader of Local 444 of the Waiter, Bartenders and Cooks Union (AFL), to stage a slow-down through June so as to extract overtime payment.[95] The result, as Barnett lamented to all who would listen, was a $50,000 overrun for installation costs, an unanticipated loss from which organizers never recovered.[96] Similar problems arose with Local 206 of the American Federation of Musicians, which protested use of nonunion players throughout the summer, and eventually boycotted the exposition when it discovered that amateur youth players had been used during Catholic Day festivities.[97]

The double hit of poor attendance and labor strife left the exposition in dire straits, forcing deferral of its many obligations. Langston Hughes and Arna Bontemps wrote Barnett demanding their promised payment for the shelved *Cavalcade of the Negro Theater,* and complaining that "conversations with [Truman] Gibson have been hurried, interrupted, vague and unsatisfactory regarding . . . compensation for our time and labor."[98] Responding to Thomas Young, editor of the Norfolk *Journal and Guide,* Barnett apologized for not paying for exposition advertisements, citing a lag on the part of the state government in making good on its $75,000 appropriation.[99] Delayed reimbursement to Fred Patterson, president of Tuskegee Institute and a long-time associate of Barnett's, brought an anxious letter lamenting the "most distressing news" and fearing that the growing fiscal impasse would "be another black eye for Negroes in general."[100] Robert Bishop, the governor's watchdog on the board, wrote in August that proposals for a Tanner Gallery catalog were "entirely out of the question . . . in view of the Exposition's present financial condition."[101] Barnett, unwilling to relinquish the chance to highlight the event's greatest attraction, directed that his organizer's stipend, totaling $500, be applied to production of the catalog, "as well as certain little bills owed the Art Institute and other similar organizations."[102]

As the summer progressed, organizers cast about for solutions, with little success. Frank Marshall Davis proposed that publicity funds be reserved for promoting *Chimes of Normandy* through the *Chicago Tribune* and other dailies.[103] Complimentary passes were sent to Jules Herbuveaux of the National Broadcasting Company's Chicago affiliate, as well as to representatives of other local broadcasting concerns. Though Herbuveaux promised to send staff to "give the show the once over," there was no evidence of their visit, nor of any positive effect on attendance.[104] Putting aside displeasure over their late checks, Arna Bontemps and Langston Hughes wrote up *Cavalcade of the American Negro,* an overview of blacks' recent history and achievements, as the official publication of the exposition, with Barnett arranging for 50,000 hardcover and paperback copies to be printed.[105]

It was a more unlikely campaign, though, that reversed the fortunes of the exposition, if only momentarily. On August 10, Gibson announced that daily prizes would be awarded at random to attendees. Making up for the absence of consumer exhibits at the event (Pepsi and Chrysler proved the sole representatives of national goods manufacture), local retailers donated Philco and Zenith radios, General Electric washing machines, Hammond clocks, Columbia records, bags of groceries, and packs of Coca-Cola, among other products.[106] Contributors of door prizes were identified by

David Kellum, city editor of the *Defender*, with local merchants assured of the promotional advantages of having "several substantial gifts on display [to be] awarded [to] the lucky number holder."[107] Following Gibson's announcement, thousands of circulars were distributed in the Chicago area advertising the giveaway.[108] By the end of August $10,000 worth of prizes had been distributed, boosting daily attendance figures.[109] Observers noted that "it became customary for visitors to linger" until the closing hour "in the hope of receiving an award."[110] As of 1940, mainstream manufacturers generally refused to market to blacks in any concerted and respectful fashion. The exposition giveaway, then, constituted a brief interruption in the marginality of black consumers as it boosted the event's finances. In time, more dramatic and lasting departures of this sort would issue from Chicago, reshaping conceptions of black life across the country.

While crowds picked up as Labor Day approached, the boost could not reverse earlier financial woes. Though radios and groceries attracted new attendees, no other strategy proved successful. In late July, Robert Bishop had encouraged partnership with the August 25th Spiritual Song Fest, a benefit for the Red Cross chaired by Marva Louis, wife of the boxing champ, and slated for Soldier Field.[111] Several weeks later, Barnett found himself still mired in unsuccessful negotiations with the famed Southernaires concerning an appearance at the exposition's own Song Fest.[112] Attempts to run *Chimes of Normandy* past the closing of the exposition also failed: William Trent broke news of the proposal's rejection by Federal Writers' Project (FWP) superiors opposed to commercializing federal cultural initiatives.[113] By the event's end, only the Miss Bronze America Beauty Contest, involving twenty-five contestants nominated by black newspapers across the country, and Duke Ellington's performance at the closing ball generated any appreciable interest among the exposition's closing attractions.[114]

The late flurry of unrequited efforts did not bode well for the exposition's legend, and, hard on its close, a chorus of criticism emerged. Predictably, the Baltimore *Afro-American* published critiques as early as July, which Frank Marshall Davis dismissed publicly as the equivalent of "browsing about garbage pails."[115] By winter, Davis's protestations proved less effective against more sustained negative commentary from the NAACP's *Crisis*.[116] Informed of a $96 deficit from the book exhibit, Barnett was left with the unenviable task of settling accounts with sales supervisor Horace Cayton. An acrimonious series of letters and meetings followed, with Cayton fingering his assistant Carl Loneia for the discrepancy ("there is, I can assure you, 'a gentleman of color in the wood'"). Barnett responded that Loneia and others had cleared themselves through kept

4. Horace Cayton and St. Clair Drake, late 1940s. Photographed by Wayne F. Miller. Courtesy of Wayne F. Miller.

receipts. Cayton, unable in the end to exonerate himself, expressed hope that Barnett "would understand his situation so that I can continue to enjoy your friendship which I regard most highly." Horace Cayton's fuller legacy, of course, would be secured by his 1945 publication, together with St. Clair Drake, of the masterwork *Black Metropolis:* still for many the definitive chronicle of midcentury Black Chicago. As to the young sociologist's deficits with the exposition, no further record remains concerning their resolution.[117]

Other shortfalls proved embarrassing to lead organizers themselves. Frederic Flemister, prizewinner in the oil painting contest, informed organizers that his check had bounced, as did Emory Ross, coordinator of the Africa Bureau's photography exhibit.[118] Word came in October that James Gentry, organizer of the beauty pageant, had arranged for an attorney's lien to be placed on the exposition's assets to force payment of his outstanding reimbursement.[119] Attorney Irvin Mollison threatened similar actions on behalf of Langston Hughes and Arna Bontemps: neither had received promised payments for the *Cavalcade* booklet.[120] By December 1942, Mary Beattie Brady, unpaid for her efforts, would alert Barnett of inquiries from yet another lawyer, Chicago-based J. Thomas Moore, promising uncompensated contributors aggressive representation and eventual settlement. Though Barnett advised Brady not to retain Moore because he wanted her "to get all of your money," Brady found neither reassurance nor compensation ultimately, recalling the exposition over the years as "a very painful experience."[121]

No doubt Brady's discomfort was matched by that of organizers, as complaints and controversies related to the exposition persisted. Requests that the Illinois legislature make an additional appropriation to retire the event's deficits made no headway. According to observers, many legislators tied the event's woes to its own "bad management for which the state could not make itself responsible." Truman Gibson's point that the World's Fair in New York, saddled with a deficit $15,000 larger than the exposition, had nonetheless been bailed out had no impact.[122] Soon after, $18,000 remaining from the state's grant was frozen by the legislature, essentially dooming hopes of retiring outstanding debts.[123] For Barnett, consumed now with stalling creditors—many of them associates and friends—the neverending frustration took its own toll, as his plea to Brady that she recognize "how keenly I feel about the whole matter" made clear.[124]

In a final, farcical coda, Barnett wrote Brady again in 1944—not with news of success in securing funds, but instead with news that the governor's office had released floor dioramas impounded after the close of the event.[125] Relocated to Tuskegee and "in sad need of repair," the exhibits were handed over to commercial artist Charles Dawson, himself relocated to the Alabama campus from Chicago, where he had spent most of his legendary career. Dawson successfully completed the job in September 1945: yet less than a year later, Albion Hosley wrote Barnett asking information on the design and execution of the dioramas, to challenge Dawson's original claim to them. Barnett ruefully responded that Dawson had in fact been lead designer for the project, joining with Horace Cayton to "work out some of the historical backgrounds and research on the proposed dioramas."[126] With this last controversy settled, the books on the American Negro Exposition closed figuratively and literally, and the once-anticipated gala endured its final fall, from disrepute into oblivion.

As the exposition dropped from memory, its celebration of black freedom past and future found discredit as well. Hopes of establishing Bronzeville as a seat of black creativity and enterprise were in the end replaced by identification of Chicago as the urban site of want and suffering. Frazier's vision of cities of destruction proved more credible to those interested in Black Chicago's story, with apocryphal tales of unlivable housing, cyclical poverty, and preadolescent murder dominating later research and reportage. Given waves of deindustrialization, disinvestment, middle-class flight, and neighborhood blight that eroded the spirit of Chicago's blacks in the decades after 1940, it is hard to imagine how it might have turned out otherwise. A well-attended, successful exposition would have had difficulty holding subsequent generations' attention, in the face of such devastating conditions. What then can be learned from this event, that proved so disappointing and, by all accounts, so forgettable?

Perhaps through the unrealized promises of the exposition, one may discern rehearsal for more sustained imaginative enterprises within Black Chicago in years to come. As premonition of the broad infrastructure that emerged after 1940, the American Negro Exposition anticipated much local cultural history to follow: crises along with achievements, questions as well as answers. Some of its individual and institutional constituents reemerged in later years. Some faded from view, together with memories of the grand commemoration itself. But its broader ambition—that blacks rework the story of their race's presence within the modern nation—proved more resilient than did its reputation.

Against the announced intent of organizers, the exposition manifested the ephemeral character of integration as an ethos in 1940s Chicago, and the United States generally. To be sure, there were individuals whose sense of project focused more closely on values of racial inclusion in the event's aftermath. Claude Barnett and Truman Gibson, for example, would both subsequently enlist their services within the wartime state. Barnett became a special aide to the secretary of agriculture, and Gibson, more significantly, an attaché of the War Department, where his investigations of military discrimination and racial abuse proved foundational to the postwar campaign to desegregate the Armed Forces, the most significant race reform initiative prior to the 1954 *Brown* decision. More ceremonial figures, such as Willard Townsend or Earl Dickerson, assumed important federal posts as well—in Townsend and Dickerson's cases, seats on the Fair Employment Practices Commission, watchdog for the 1941 executive order banning war industry discrimination. Nor were blacks alone steered toward such amalgamative ends. Henry Wallace, the event's most enthusiastic white sponsor, saw his stake in racial reform deepen precipitously after

1940, speaking out as vice president against racial injustice, and mounting his 1948 presidential run: the most racially progressive national campaign by a white politician prior to the civil rights era. Outcomes like these seemed to validate Barnett's early prediction that the exposition would point to way toward "further integration [of blacks] into the fabric of American life."[127]

In its fuller dimensions, however, the exposition's endorsement of interracial fellowship proved less consequential. Black attendance, to be sure, was disappointing, but the number of white visitors, besides those directly connected to the event, was virtually nonexistent. Given such low interest among the general public, the exposition's ability to "establish the extent to which [blacks have] been integrated into American life" was hampered from the start.[128] For every white leader like Wallace, interested in more level engagement with black constituents, there were others, like secretary of the navy Charles Edison, who proved indifferent, even when their role in replicating patterns of discrimination was called out.[129] Various event outcomes, such as Liberia's implicit celebration of multinational clientage over national independence, or the legislature's freeze of disbursements, or even the momentary advantage of white owners in propaganda wars surrounding the taxi strike, together demonstrated paternalism's persistence as a structure of racial feeling in 1940.

Of course, paternalism was not the only architecture of racial action and outlook operative at this time. Fiercely oriented toward self-determination from its start, Black Chicago exemplified racial initiative by the middle of the twentieth century. Its residents had engineered restoration of black Congressional presence in Washington and leveraged substantive partnerships within party politics, even as they grafted Garveyist remnants into separatist institutions like the Nation of Islam, not yet through its first decade by 1940. They sustained business enterprises in fields ranging from insurance to cosmetics, even as they constituted the largest cadre of African Americans in the Communist Party, helping remake that organization as an antiracist vanguard along the way. Though never free of reference to surrounding white society, Black Chicago was an environment where reversal of standing lines of racial authority seemed plausible: in which group existence could be envisaged in self-defined form. In this light, Margaret Walker's poetic reading of blacks' collective progress "without gold . . . and . . . love" recalled the widely shared view of racial history articulated in the stand-alone language of autonomy rather than cooperation. To be sure, some of this collective pride was compensatory, meant to salve wounds opened by segregation, discrimination, and emphatic assault. Still, the paradoxical premise of black community in Chicago—that in spite of proscription it constituted a viable "city within city," as St. Clair Drake and Horace Cayton later put it—meant that appeals to racial independence found fallow ground there.

This proud—and familiar—black worldview was apparent in the exposition, hidden though it was by testimonials to amalgamated national culture or solicitations of white patrons. At times, the partisan claims were relatively innocuous, as when Barnett lobbied Erik Lindgren for exhibit dioramas to be fashioned by blacks rather than whites, or when Pepsi Cola consented to staff its booth with an African-American spokesman, or when local and black-owned Young Drug Company was awarded the concessions contract for the event.[130] In other cases, they were well-articulated, and far-reaching in significance. Though the dystopic urban vision of E. Franklin Frazier proved the primary intellectual legacy to emerge from the exposition, its most meaningful institutional survivor was the South Side Community Arts Center, still today the oldest community arts center in the country. Dedicated in 1941 after an intense fundraising campaign boosted by the Tanner Gallery's success, the Arts Center proved an anchor of local cultural life. Twenty-eight thousand visited in its first year alone, viewing exhibits and attending classes on subjects ranging from interior decorating to Gordon Parks's photography classes. And while the center affirmed an empathically universalist conception of art—naming as its first director Peter Pollack and including among its early shows an overview of the French political cartoonist Honore Daumier—it drew primarily on the local cohort of black artists, and the deep aesthetic sensibility of South Side Chicago to inform that vision. Among its many regular offerings, the two most prominent were the annual Collector's Show, where South Side residents were invited to lend personal pieces; and the legendary Artists' and Models' Balls, the society event among local blacks in the 1940s—young and old, respectable as well as less reputable. That visual arts could suggest a center for collective black imagination and society—the hope, it should be remembered, of Barnett, Locke and other organizers of the Tanner Gallery—confirmed the exposition's engagement with more autonomous visions of African-American life.[131]

Yet this and other achievements did not yet speak to the most pronounced formulation of racial autonomy. Committed to a patriotic framing of African-American life and equating effective black freedom with active civic role, the exposition's engagement with less derivative ideas of nationalism was limited, to say the least. Programs like Hammurrabi's Pan African Day, itself universalist as much as separatist, were exceptional among exhibits that, though affirming independent qualities of race arts and enterprise, did not dispute whether such elements could—indeed, could only—emerge within a context of liberal American democracy. When apparent, the exposition's consideration of the idea of black national community was driven by pragmatic concerns, rather than ideology. Looking to promote the event among blacks across the country, exposition organizers designated special days for states delegations—twenty-one were scheduled by July, including all southern states save Texas and Arkansas, as well as most industrialized states offering destination to African-American migrants from World War I on. Alongside commitment to a diverse Tanner Gallery, or entreaties to the hesitant California contingent, the States' Days initiative demonstrated organizers' interest in defining the exposition as national in scope and therefore in appeal.

That the exposition failed to sustain an audience suggests important lessons about the finer mechanics of group imagination among African Americans. Over time, accounts of nationalist spirit among African Americans have become so common as to make it seem an obvious and natural feature of black worldview. But nationalism is neither organic or primordial: it is instead, along with race, the rubric of group identity most salient to specifically modern conceptions of human society. As such, it is historically symptomatic rather than omnipresent—it should tell us about individuals' and constituencies' engagement with the contradictions *of* their times, as much as register their shared resolve to persevere *over* time. Recent theoretical work stresses this perspective, tracing nationalism's parallel relationship to key features of modernity: capitalism's rise in mercantile, industrial, and market form; secularized conceptions of human action and purpose; the proposal of individuated political authority, or liberty; the advent of institutional media as precept of human relations and as technology for ever more expansive and ambitious ideas of a public.[132] When those interested in nationalism's manifestation among African Americans treat it as enduring tradition, they miss the chance to glean its resonance with conditions of the moment, and how patterns and ideas of group identity can serve to assess those specific circumstances.

Though the exposition demonstrated at multiple points blacks' interest in nationalist and nationalized orientation as strategy, in order to secure decent treatment, to sustain comprehensive enterprise—and for its organizers, to conduct a credible commemoration—the event's failings make clear the limited capacity to realize this approach in 1940. Paraphrasing Benedict Anderson, African Americans broadly speaking were not yet a national people, because they still lacked capacity to think of themselves in nationalized terms. Projects in decades and centuries past—from the Garvey movement and the Great Migration to the melding of various African ethnicities into a shared New World diaspora following the Middle Passage—had established blacks' commitment to a broad and self-determined sense of self and group. Yet none of these revised collective imagination to the point where the necessary fictions of national identity—that dispersed individuals shared mores and goals to the point where they felt they had more in common with one another than not, or that they viewed one another in simultaneous and interchangeable relation and routine correspondence—could take hold among most African Americans. Though the exposition's organizers yearned to harness such sensibilities through defining their attractions in national scope, poor attendance indicated that they could not be called on, because they were not yet adequately developed.

In short time this would change. African Americans throughout the country would be moved to see themselves in such simultaneous terms by purveyors of music, radio, and journalism: individuals already disproportionately concentrated in Chicago. Spheres of intellect, amusement, social comment, and protest central to black life would take profound new shape as a result of this process. While dreams of asserting Black Chicago as the new Negro capital in 1940 proved premature, by 1955 Chicago would reveal itself as pivotal to the project of reimagining blacks as a national people in thought and deed, and therefore as a thoroughly modern community. Yet, it is important to remember that African Americans' nationalization would not constitute a simple teleology, an irrefutable story of empowerment. All the dubious inheritances of modern identity—bombastic self-reference, mediated conception of social will, equation of commodity with human feeling, suppression of human variety—would prove outcomes of blacks' formation as a modern, nationalized group, shaping their shared cultural, social, and political identifications for better and for worse.

Most importantly, confusion between a nationalism of autonomous ideals and rituals, and a nationality derived from an extant, dynamic American state, marked the exposition indelibly. The event's patriotic trappings, from its July Fourth opening to its determinate arrangements of federal sponsorship, registered endorsement of what Walter Johnson has called "the metanarrative of racial liberalism": the notion that public freedom and civil acculturation were the twin cornerstones of black amelioration, and that emancipation represented an inexorably progressive narrative substituting the American citizen for the African slave.[133] That ideological alignment with the U.S. nation could coincide with recognition—and even denunciation—of the racist practices of its state exemplified the contortion in exposition attempts to display African America in nationalized terms, as well as the deeper contradiction of the dissident yet patriotic black public style that would reshape American politics and society for the next half century. It would be wrong to point to this circuit of affiliations as the root of the exposition's particular failures, since virtually all of its organizers and contributors, and doubtless many of its attendees, wrestled with similarly complex senses of allegiance. But slippage between notions of racial nationalism and the obligations of American nationality marked the confusion in the exposition's representation of the meaning of "black freedom," a confusion that endured for subsequent artists, managers and entrepreneurs engaging the meaning of national black community from the pivot point of Chicago.

One way to better appreciate the unsettled meanings of blacks' identification as a national group is to examine to the exposition's most striking omission: engagement with the history and memory of slavery. The year 1940, after all, was not just the jubilee of Emancipation, but also an early crest of efforts to revise slavery's legacy according to black slaves' own terms of experience. W. E. B. Du Bois's 1935 landmark history, *Black Reconstruction,* had recast slave life in terms of labor insurgency and solidarity, providing a comprehensive precedent for asserting black historical agency. Scattered yet noteworthy articles by literary and historical scholars through the preceding decade had called for refutation of the Plantation School of Southern History, by means of closer attention to the records and testimonies of slaves rather than masters. In an even more direct rejoinder to the Plantation School, researchers at Fisk and Southern Universities in 1929 conducted 500 interviews with African Americans born as slaves. In 1934, L. D. Reddick, a Kentucky State University professor before his hiring at the Schomburg Center, secured funding to interview another 250 ex-slaves in Kentucky and Indiana. Between 1936 and 1938 the Federal Writers' Project took up the cause, collecting what ultimately amounted to 2000 interviews gathered from across the South. The priority FWP director Henry Alsberg gave to collecting the testimonies, the work of its national folklore editor B. A. Botkin and Sterling Brown in promoting awareness of the growing archive, and the involvement of Reddick in both slave interviews and the exposition all indicate that their existence were well known by 1940.[134]

It is striking then, that no systematic account of slavery was offered at the exposition. Visitors encountered only a few dioramas, murals of Sojourner Truth and Frederick Douglass, a corner devoted to *Uncle Tom's Cabin* at the Schomburg booth and a few titles displayed at the book exhibit, and isolated renditions such as Lawrence's paintings or lines from Walker's poem. Given this understated treatment, organizers' interest in exploiting the public celebrity of *Gone with the Wind,* or their unrequited efforts to secure exhibits of the emancipatory legacies of Haiti or Liberia betrays a deeper disconnect with a black slave past. There was little chance it could have been otherwise, given the failure to embrace a more activated and self-defined set of antebellum memories. No invitations were issued to academic or FWP researchers to recount the growth of the archives of slave testimony. No appearances were made by surviving elders to help put emancipation in proper perspective by recounting their own lived experience of bondage.[135] As late as 1937, Reddick had lamented in an article that "there is not yet a picture of the institution [of slavery] as seen through the eyes of the bondsman himself." And though steady if not yet authoritative academic and folkloric interest attended the emergence of the slave testimony archive, the exposition's choice to forgo serious appreciation of it signaled the rule rather than the exception. The broad public response to the project of remembering slavery from the slave's point of view, in 1940 and for many years to come, was to ignore it. Even with the publication of Botkin's anthology of slave interviews, *Lay My Burden Down* (1945), most representations of slavery in the United States derived from planters' materials when they rested on an archival basis at all, until the 1970s. The other great repository of slave experience, the fugitive slave narratives, fell back into disuse after a resurgence during the 1920s and the onset of the Negro Renaissance. Arna Bontemps would later lament that on the eve of the *Brown* decision in 1954, only one title (most probably Frederick Douglass's *Narrative*) out of the several hundreds he recognized as constituting the slave narrative genre remained in print.[136]

All imagined communities—national, racial, and otherwise—revise, embellish, and invent history to suit desired ends: this is after all crucial to their authority as structures of collective existence and will. That those involved in the exposition did so by overlooking the narrative of slavery undergoing dynamic and progressive revision by 1940 says much about which elements of the black past did—or did not—serve preferred visions of racial present and future at that moment. Given the bourgeois profile of the exposition's organizers, one might summarily characterize their lack of interest in the archive of slave memory as class elitism: anxiety about associating with the race community's less elevated members. Surely this was at least in part true. But there were other problems that concerned integrating memories of slavery and freedom for African Americans in 1940. What if considering that central aspect of the black past led to recognition of all the ways that Emancipation had ushered a state of being that was in fact, less than free? What if pride in the resilience and resourcefulness of those first to gain freedom led to questions about the value of progress and modernity, about the validity of celebration of blacks as a people of the future rather than the past? What if consideration of the growing record of still living freed people made clear, as George Rawick would later put it, "the important continuity between slavery and freedom?"[137] Seen in this light, the fundamentally subjunctive character of the exposition as memory project becomes clear. Consideration of African Americans' collective legacy would serve the cause of a validating memory of the future more so that it would answer to the responsibilities of remembering a viable memory of the past.

To think in modern terms about black community and black life involved repression of past memories that might contradict that idealized image. The ties of the exposition—and, more broadly, the ties of the "homogenous comradeship" implicit in nationalized notions of community—to black commercial enterprise illustrated this better perhaps than any other condition. What did it mean to promote and sponsor—to sell—a vindicated spectacle of race, in the face of a history in which race's sale constituted the defining condition of a people's history? That the exposition as a collective project chose to evade this question constitutes its most significant and instructive failure. That its direct descendants—the impresarios and artists who would assert Chicago's primacy as the center of African-American popular arts in the next decade and a half—wrestled with this question in similarly awkward fashion calls for us to closely inspect their actions and motives. That this question remains a vexing challenge in our purportedly integrated age makes careful reading of these memories and this history all the more necessary.

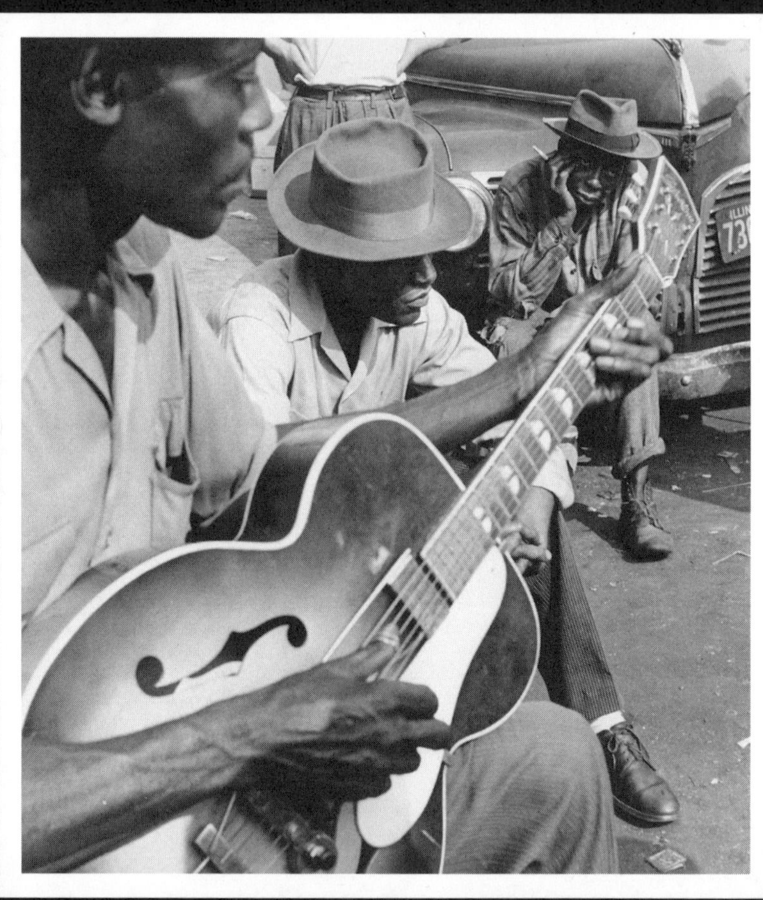
ILLIN
73

MAKING THE MUSIC

CHAPTER TWO

> They do not know that our songs are our
> banner of hope flung desperately up in the face
> of a world that has pushed us to the wall.
>
> RICHARD WRIGHT

Few dispute that Black Chicago has remained a capital city of popular music for more than a century. It represents the birthplace of the modern forms of jazz, blues, gospel, and soul. Foundational conventions of style such as Louis Armstrong's attack note, the melisma of gospel pioneers like Mahalia Jackson and soul stars like Chaka Kahn, or the stop-time rhythm of the blues combo, all originated in its clubs, churches, and bars. The city's internationally recognized festival culture advertises not only an ongoing abundance of home-grown talent, but also the degree to which local music heritage constitutes a veritable civic institution. The ease with which Black Chicagoans refer to their music as mirror of self evokes its frequent association with essential identity, suggesting that true black music, alone among the creative and expressive genres, endures regardless of historical change or circumstance.

Which makes the history of the commercial transformation of multiple genres of black popular music in Chicago all the more striking. Far from being exempt from forces of

Facing page: 5. Big Bill Broonzy playing at the Maxwell Street Market. Photographed by Wayne F. Miller. Courtesy of Wayne F. Miller.

change, key forms and artists prove sensitive barometers for their times. In this chapter, the story of black popular music in the 1940s and 1950s is presented not as a familiar series of discreet genre narratives, but rather as a more holistic account of shared structural change and increasingly capitalized conditions of performance and production. Focusing on a group of exemplary figures—Mahalia Jackson, Louis Jordan, Muddy Waters, Willie Dixon, and black-appeal disk jockey Al Benson—modern black music's roots are traced back to motives of commercial appeal, as much as the inspiration of personal genius or presumed points of cultural origin. In their stories, as well as many others, rests a compelling argument that the impact of the market on black music's integrity was neither adverse nor diluting—indeed, in many cases it constituted an indispensable spur to innovation and development.

When asked in 1955 to account for the successes of Black Chicago's music, guitarist Bill Broonzy remarked that it was "just born in us to sing and play the blues." Naturalizing genius in this way remains the signature of most accounts of African-American music in the Windy City. Black music, by most lights, signifies the staying power of blackness itself: LeRoi Jones once described it as "the one vector out of African culture impossible to eradicate." Given Chicago's historic representation as the site of change and even destabilization for its black inhabitants old and new, such promises of enduring nature held special attractions. Little wonder then that accounts of Black Chicago so often present musical culture and community as synonyms for one another, reminding us of Jones's further variation on Bill Broonzy's theme: "the song and the people is the same."[1]

Without question there is appeal within the notion of black music's staying power: its capacity, as Stuart Hall put it, to ground black people's sense of place through shifts in their existence. Yet if African-American music connotes sameness (even "changing sameness," to quote Jones still again), what is its own relation to these same shifts, especially in the past century: urbanization, industrialization, commodification, transnationalization, more explicit politicization?[2] How might we address black music as a charged field of statement and counterstatement, negotiation, reinvention—even contradiction—rather than as enduring mirror of collective will and goal? Such inquiries require addressing black music in context, rather than invoking it as cause. In the case of Chicago, black music provides crucial opportunities to consider how notions of race community in the broadest sense register change for black folk, as much as establish the resilience of their identities.

In this chapter that story of change is taken up to demonstrate how the

1940s and 1950s were pivotal years in black music's equivocal yet unmistakable transition from art to industry, both within Chicago and, more indirectly, within the country as a whole. Several key performers—Mahalia Jackson, Louis Jordan, Muddy Waters, and Willie Dixon—are closely examined in terms of their Chicago roots and careers. Their composite identities as both artists and cultural entrepreneurs are featured to underscore how opposition of cultural integrity and commercial orientation oversimplifies the motivations of the midcentury black musician.

Through these individual studies, the linked stories of some of Chicago's most celebrated genres of popular music—gospel, jump blues, urban blues, rhythm and blues, and soul—emerge, suggesting the unified conditions of development for forms of music generally presented as discreet categories by their more committed devotees. The ways in which the turn toward market-related goals and institutions remade black music and black life after World War II is also illustrated in the case of local black-appeal radio and its popularization beginning in the 1940s. The radio disc-jockey format was a crucial marriage of market and cultural values in the world of modern black music. Here transformation in Black Chicago radio and broadcasting style, while resonant with changes elsewhere, proved rather site specific, underscoring the idiosyncrasies and particularities of black music as a cultural field. Yet despite such qualifications on unity, the institutions and practices of Black Chicago music proved harbingers for shifts in black music and ultimately broader cultural sensibilities nationwide, indicating how the local turn of black life toward market orientations precipitated change well beyond its specific boundaries.

To discuss the market turn within Black Chicago's music, one must refer to broad changes within the music industry at the time. During the 1940s and 1950s, while African-American music transformed at levels of institution and genre, American popular music as a whole worked through its own period of flux. The two stories are not merely coincidental: one should see this period of cultural change as an opening for black artists and their supporters, a chance to realize greater authority over musical conception and production.

Throughout this century, American popular music has been a system at war with itself, caught between great material promise and equal potential for self-destruction. Following the 1909 Copyright Act, dispute over composition and performance revenues in particular created conflict. At first, song publishers possessed the upper hand—song sheets were the standard commodity form for the music business prior to the Depression, and publishers and songwriters were the best organized group within the industry, as evidenced by the influence of the American Society of Composers, Authors, and Publishers (ASCAP), founded in 1914. Musicians were organized within the American Federation of Musicians (AFM), but their position was less secure. Before World War II, neither group paid much attention to the interests of black artists and audiences: the AFM kept to a Jim Crow membership policy, and the ASCAP was notorious for its condescension toward black talent.[3]

During the 1920s, new forces challenged the positions of both musicians and writers in the industry. Recording companies—which developed rapidly after the 1909 Copyright Act—sold $126 million worth of records in 1926, of which $5 to $10 million were from purchases by black customers. The parallel emergence of radio (less than a decade separated the first professional broadcast in 1920 from the emergence of corporate media such as NBC and CBS) created a sudden boom market for home equipment, tuned increasingly to music programming. Both the ASCAP and the AFM turned away from battling one another, focusing instead on these new sources of revenue. Publishers pursued royalties on records through the 1920s, and (with the help of a series of court rulings) compelled the radio industry in 1932 to agree to profit sharing with the ASCAP.[4] The musicians' union, led by aggressive chapters like Chicago's Local 10, also secured payments from the new industries. By the eve of the Depression, though, it was clear that radio and recording would redefine popular music, transforming the roles of all who worked within it.

It is important to discuss black music in light of these changes, given our understanding of the Jazz Age as one of black creative fluorescence, and of greater influence upon American culture broadly.[5] The impact of the improvisational method of Jelly Roll Morton, Louis Armstrong, and other pioneer jazz performers is often cited as evidence of the enhanced role of black artists. But shifts in production, as well as technique, also hinted at an alternate calculus of power. The sheer reach of radio and record technologies promised greater public access to popular music; for blacks this raised hopes of an end run around the discriminatory control of traditional arms of the industry—the ASCAP, AFM, and Theater Owners Booking Agency.[6] Artists like blueswoman Bessie Smith benefited from this leveling effect, defiantly achieving commercial success despite being thought too unsophisticated by the music establishment. A similar challenge to standards occurred after 1925 when J. Mayo "Ink" Williams, a black agent for Paramount Records, recorded guitarist Blind Lemon Jefferson. The success of Jefferson's releases, along with those of Delta pioneers Charley Patton and Son House, revealed the existence of a market for rural blues in both

Northern and Southern areas stirred by the Great Migration. With such successes, the emergent race record trade promised increased cultural authority for African-Americans, in particular popular capacity to demand material truer to vernacular taste, and thus communal experience.[7]

Despite the prominence of race records, however, the leverage enjoyed by black musicians and audiences on the industry at this time was not great. Major record companies, though attuned to demands of black public taste, still controlled recording, promotion, and of course revenues—musicians recalled standard compensation for studio work as a $15 or $20 fee and a bottle of liquor. The bottom line on Bessie Smith's Columbia Records career indicates the tenuous position of black artists during this time. Although her records sold between six and ten million copies from 1923 to 1933, Smith's income for these years was less than $30,000, at best a half penny per record.[8] Few black artists could have enjoyed fair compensation given professional conditions at the time—almost none could claim publishing rights due to the virtual color bar within the ASCAP. Even those shepherded by black agents and company insiders complained of betrayal.[9] Attempts by blacks to own record companies, such as the launch of Black Swan Records in 1921, faltered soon after inception. The situation within radio was similarly poor—although black on-air performance was common late in the 1920s, no African-Americans worked as programmers prior to Jack Cooper's 1929 debut in Chicago.

The vulnerable position of African-Americans within the music business was made starkly clear during the Depression. The race records market shrunk to $60,000 by 1932, with average sales for a release at only 400, down from 10,000 in the mid-1920s. Companies annulled their commitment to black audiences, when they did not collapse outright. Paramount, whose 1920 release of Mamie Smith's "Crazy Blues" began the race records era, failed in 1931.[10] Artists who had been major stars earlier, such as Smith or jazz cornetist Joe "King" Oliver, saw their careers evaporate along with the record market. Those who weathered the period with some success were either self-managed (like Ma Rainey), insulated by traditional structures of power (like ASCAP member Duke Ellington), or reliant upon underworld promoters in New York, Chicago, and Kansas City.[11] Few black musicians, though, lived these years as flush ones, and black audiences suffered from decreased access to recorded as well as live performances. The effects of the Depression made it clear that black music—like other forms of racial cultural expression[12]—would remain subordinate to structures of mainstream production so long as it lacked its own institutional base.

The popular music industry also contracted during this period, but its recovery was quick and robust. Record companies were devastated by the Depression: sales dropped from $126 million in 1926 to $6 million in 1932. By 1939, though, the figure had rebounded to $44 million, increasing to $140 million by 1942.[13] Radio, along with movies, the most resilient cultural system during the 1930s,[14] began to regularly broadcast records on shows such as *Make Believe Ballroom,* conceived by Los Angeles announcer Al Jarvis in 1933 and made famous later by Martin Block in New York. Commitment to the new disc-jockey format made explicit radio's stake in the record companies, a gesture soon returned in kind. In 1942, Capitol Records became the first studio to provide free releases to radio for "promotional purposes."[15] The alliance was concretized in 1940 with the creation of Broadcast Music Incorporated (BMI), a music publishing organization created by broadcasters to challenge ASCAP authority over royalty and publishing rules. Emphasizing genres and artists ignored by its highbrow predecessor, BMI quickly secured a strong market share, allowing radio and record companies to exert greater leverage upon the ASCAP and the musicians' union. Ironically, though, BMI's emergence helped prevent full consolidation of power by the record companies: the inclusive spirit of the new association fueled the growth of independent radio and recording companies during the 1940s, keeping the music business decentralized for several decades more.

While these developments undercut traditional interests, the old guard did not retire quietly: the 1940s were particularly volatile years for popular music. Because of BMI's challenge, and also the shift from song sheets to records within the industry, the ASCAP's influence was markedly curtailed. That left the musicians' union, led after 1940 by former Chicago local leader James C. Petrillo, to take the lead in the struggle over revenue control. Format changes from live music to records within broadcast radio inspired union fears of being shut out of the revenue loop, since existing contracts dealt only with on-air performance. Heightening these concerns was the growing popularity of jukeboxes: the number of automatic records players nationally increased from 25,000 in 1934 to 500,000 in 1940, as bars and restaurants sought to provide customers access to music without paying performance fees. The jukebox was a perfect fit for the recording industry—jukebox orders made up an estimated 60 percent of record sales in 1938—and its use accelerated the reorientation of popular music around record production and distribution.[16] Faced with the prospect of live musicians becoming supplemental to the industry, the AFM responded dramatically: in 1942, Petrillo declared a recording ban by union members—a music strike—that halted work for almost two years before contracts were rewritten. Initially, the action seemed a success. New royalties allowed the

AFM to establish a $4 million fund for unemployed musicians, and improved contracts with all the major labels led union historian Robert Leiter to describe the poststrike music industry as a "closed shop."[17] Subsequent events, though, proved these were fragile gains—in 1948 the AFM went on strike again, concerned that the existing agreement had not sufficiently reigned in the record industry.

With this history in mind, one could question Theodor Adorno and Max Horkheimer's 1944 characterization of American popular music as party to an administered culture industry; a system "uniform as a whole and in every part."[18] The developments of centrifugal effect of independent radio and recording, growth of diverse management structures, persistent struggles over revenue, and even open labor strife all challenge claims of a coherent production process. As Richard Middleton has argued, the very concept of culture industry may be credible as an ideal aspired to by management, but actual culture manufacture is more a system of "continuous co-production" in which lines of authority are obscure, particularly at moments of crisis.[19] Evident in Middleton's thesis is an application of Antonio Gramsci's theory of hegemony as it relates to cultural work—notably the idea of authority as neither permanent nor stable, but instead contingent, historically specific, and prone to restructure.[20]

The value of Middleton's (and Gramsci's) insight becomes clear when one notes present cultural studies' deferral to Adorno and Horkheimer's argument from the start. By defining oppositional cultural practice as discursive intervention or assertion of identity, scholars concede more functional levels of production—levels of management—to established authority. In other words, activities of commerce and trade are understood, inverting Gramsci's language, to be terrain beyond contestation.[21] Examining the instability of managerial authority, by contrast, allows an understanding of cultural production—along with practice—as a site of challenge and struggle.

In the case of African-American music after 1940 the need for such theoretical reworking is especially clear. Each of the structural developments discussed above—the switch to records as benchmark product, the popularization of the jukebox, the formation of BMI and the legitimation of marginal song catalogs, and the rise of independent radio and recording—all spurred development of black music during and after World War II. As was the case during the 1920s, new music and artists resonated with communal tastes, encouraging growth of innovative cultural forms. After 1940, though, not only was the music business decentralized to a point where black artists and audiences could leverage institutions of cultural authority—increasingly African-Americans exercised that authority, at fundamental levels of production and dissemination. Intervention took place at structural and interior positions, as well as more familiar sites of performance. The need to map these developments brings us to Chicago, which, more than any other community, exemplified this shift.

Control of Bronzeville's music scene, as any local historian or older resident can confirm, has long been a vexed matter. Ever since stories of local impresario Robert Motts haunting his former property, the famed Pekin Theater, upon its purchase by white investors after his death in 1911, questions of music performance and production have resonated with anxieties over communal subordination. Like residents of Harlem who fretted over the influence of segregated venues such as the Cotton Club or Connie's Inn, or those in Kansas City who questioned Boss Pendergast's motives for "protecting" local Depression-era talent, Chicago blacks balanced celebration of race musicians with unease over their obligation to patrons. Consolidating the production of Black Chicago music after 1940 had important roots, then, in the frustrations of earlier artists and audiences.

The first years of the Regal and Savoy Theaters summarize the tensions present through the Depression. Opened in 1928 by Baliban and Katz Management, white owners of the Savoy in Harlem, the theaters are remembered mostly, as jazz historian William Howland Kenny put it, for having been "the most elegant and expensive entertainment complex ever built in black Chicago."[22] As Dempsey Travis points out, though, the theaters played a part in undermining Bronzeville's first commercial center. Seeking distinction from competing venues such as the Pekin, Plantation Cafe, or Lincoln Gardens—all located on State Street between 27th and 35th—Baliban and Katz chose 47th and South Park as the site for the theaters. This, in spite of warnings from business leaders Jesse Binga and Robert Abbott of the threat the proposal posed to the core district of the Black Belt, which ran along State Street and was anchored by the Binga Bank, the *Defender* offices, and Supreme Liberty Life Insurance, as well as the older entertainment houses.[23] The growth of the Savoy and Regal helped fulfill these predictions—Binga's holdings failed early in the Depression, and several competitor theaters also collapsed. What seemed to Cayton and Drake a vital self-governing locus of community life, then, is open to a different reading in light of actual institutional history.

Subsequent developments at the Regal heralded still another arrangement of cultural authority, however. In 1939, Baliban and Katz named Ken Blewett as manager of the theater, the first black to reach that level in the chain's history. Blewett, a Kentucky migrant, had worked up the theater's job ladder in classic fashion, beginning as an usher in 1929 and advancing to assistant manager in 1935 before his final promotion.[24] From 1939 until 1959, when Blewett left the Regal, the theater provided the best bookings of black artists in town, and grew from local prominence to become a national tour stop.[25] Blewett's success as a promoter accorded him an important place within Chicago music history—the Regal was a key site for Black Chicago's musical development. For now, it is important to think of Blewett's ascension—a development unthinkable a decade before—as a prediction of the later authority wielded by blacks over the local music scene.

Beyond the Regal, popular music had been controlled by still more suspect patrons than Baliban and Katz. Along with New York and Kansas City, Chicago was a center for criminal syndicates, involved not only in bootlegging and racketeering but also entertainment.[26] By the mid-1920s, the organization headed by Al Capone ran most of the South Side's bars and nightclubs. Tales of the notorious boss's courtesies toward black Chicagoans have become the stuff of folklore. Bandleader Earl Hines recalled Capone's regular $100 tips when his requests were performed. Vibraphone pioneer Lionel Hampton, whose uncle Richard Morgan was a well-placed bootlegger, remembered his mother receiving weekly courtesy calls from the syndicate leader.[27] At the same time, though, Capone ruthlessly controlled performance on the South Side. Several major spaces had organization ties: the Club DeLisa on 55th and State was opened in 1933 by bootleggers Mike, Louie, and Jim DeLisa; while Dave's Club further east on 55th Street was run by Sam "Golf Bag" Hunt, overseer of South Side gambling operations and trusted hit man.[28] Capone's organization constituted another level of control over the fortunes of black musicians, one of often irresistible influence. Duke Ellington narrowly escaped extortion and threats of harm by gangsters during one visit to Chicago, while Hines was forced to perform exclusively at the Grand Terrace, owned by Capone associate Ed Fox, from 1928 until 1941.[29]

But as was the case at the Regal, management of South Side nightclubs was changing hands on the eve of World War II. After Capone's arrest and imprisonment in 1931 and the legalization of alcohol sale in 1933, gangster control of local entertainment began to erode. Dave's Club passed to another owner in 1937, and then in 1940 to black investor Charlie Glenn and boxing champion Joe Louis, who together renamed it the Rhumboogie Club. Other black entrepreneurs began locating in overflow areas created by renewed migration in the 1940s. Joe's DeLuxe Nightclub, at 63rd and South Park, and the El Grotto, in the Pershing Hotel at 64th and Cottage Grove were among the new venues.[30] Although the DeLisa remained the

6. Interior of the Club DeLisa, 1939. Courtesy of the Harsh Research Collection/ Chicago Public Library.

property of the namesake brothers, it mirrored the management structure at the Regal; retired black stage performers Earl Partello and Sammy Dyer served as floor managers at the club. Throughout the war and postwar years, the DeLisa was famous for the floor shows Partello and Dyer presented: dance revues using elaborate Afro-Caribbean stagings anchored by the house band of drummer Red Saunders, a mainstay at the DeLisa from 1937 to his promotion to head of the Regal's house band in 1954.[31] Also working to overturn white control of race music was the all-black AFM Local 206, headed after 1937 by Harry Gray, who gained a reputation for facing down threats from club owners seeking to exploit black musicians.[32] To be sure, this shift in control of Bronzeville's music should not be viewed simply as communal empowerment. Impresarios like Blewett and Dyer were businessmen as much as "race men," with complicated relations with the general African-American population.

Special tensions grew from issues of class: as recent scholarship on black migration makes clear, power wielded by black occupational and social elites could result in uneven returns for poorer members of the race community.[33] Such was at times the case at Bronzeville's nightclubs: criteria such as admission fees, familiarity with employees or performers, and celebrity worked to filter customers, codifying the distinction between haves and have-nots within Black Chicago. Emphasis on social standing was stated policy at many spots. Black-owned clubs such as Joe DeLuxe's, the El Grotto, and Square's Boulevard Lounge held weekly "celebrity nights" where entertainers were provided tables to host friends and admirers, while enhancing the club's own prestige.[34] These moves, consolidating what Ben Sidran called a "black star system," reinforced other mappings of local power. The *Defender* often reported sightings of community leaders such as its own publisher John Sengestacke or sociologist Horace Cayton jitterbugging at various spots.[35] At times, club selectivity had a more pejorative side. Singer Joe Williams, among the most acclaimed of postwar black male vocalists, recalled being turned down by both Rhumboogie co-owner Charlie Glenn and DeLuxe head Joe Hughes in the early 1940s because his dark skin did not conform to the "pretty boy" image of light-skinned balladeers such as Billy Eckstine and Herb Jeffries.[36] Given such discrimination against performers, it is not surprising that prejudice shaped audiences as well—the DeLisa and Joe's Deluxe, while rejecting full Jim Crow codes common in other cities, routinely seated white customers at choice tables closest to the dance floor.

Yet it would be inadequate to treat black nightlife in post-Depression Chicago solely as a study in intraracial or class prejudice. Despite social airs—as well as internalized racism—working-class and more "marginal" constituencies in the black community were familiar with the best-known nightclubs and claimed them as a part of their own personal geographies. Blues great Willie Dixon, a spot laborer and hobo before his arrival in Chicago, recalled frequent visits to the DeLisa and Rhumboogie clubs during his early years in the Black Belt.[37] Dempsey Travis remembers blues singers Chippie Hill and Clarence "Gatemouth" Moore headlining at the DeLisa stage, in addition to the more respectable jazz acts. The Savoy ballroom had programs directed at diverse audiences, from performances by the Count Basie, Ellington, and Chick Webb bands, to Tuesday amateur boxing matches, to roller-skating programs for youths several nights a week.[38] Joe's DeLuxe served an even broader audience in the late 1940s, devoting portions of each year's January schedule over to a revue of female impersonators.[39] Following the example of Ken Blewett, aspiring talents held entry-level jobs at the clubs, waiting for important breaks. Dinah Washington, working as a nightclub washroom attendant, signed her first singing contract with the Lionel Hampton band in 1943 after an impromptu performance at the Regal arranged by Blewett. Joe Williams, employed as a doorman at the Regal at the time, also signed with Hampton during the same set of dates.[40] While it is an exaggeration to describe black-owned or run clubs during the 1940s as egalitarian spaces, it is clear that class and status lines were permeable, particularly for customers who could agree with the conventions of society and celebrity promoted there.

As cultural context, the nightclub is often represented as antithesis of black spirituality: conflict between sacred and secular spheres is a common device in discussions of modern black experience. It is striking, then, that in post-Depression Black Chicago, church music melded faith, performance, and commercial ambition into a fertile cultural system, analogous to the emerging local club circuit. As Michael Harris's study of Thomas Dorsey shows, the genre of gospel blues rapidly evolved in Chicago during the 1930s.[41] Local establishment in 1933 of the National Convention of Gospel Choruses and Choirs inspired church singers nationwide to switch to the solo-based style of Dorsey and other young composers. By 1937 the National Baptist Convention—the foremost black spiritual institution—featured gospel blues at its conventions. During the 1940s the movement accelerated, with the Soul Stirrers Quartet and soloists Rosetta Tharpe and Clara Ward exemplifying the now-definitive style of sacred music. Gospel's growing popularity derived from recording as well as church performance—labels such as Savoy (Newark) and Specialty (Los Angeles) worked to supply the music to growing audiences.[42]

The career of Mahalia Jackson—most celebrated of gospel artists—highlights the changes within the world of black sacred music at this time. Leaving New Orleans for Chicago in 1928, Jackson involved herself in church music upon arrival; through the 1930s, she soloed at the Greater Salem and Pilgrim Baptist Churches. At Pilgrim, which under the leadership of Reverend Junius Austin was one of the most powerful area houses of worship, Jackson was trained by Dorsey, director of the church choir. Despite these references, Jackson's early reception was mixed; she was thrown out of more than one church by ministers offended by her vital, often sensual style, and told by one voice teacher that her technique was "no credit to the Negro race." A 1937 Decca recording session supervised by Ink Williams went nowhere; Williams canceled her contract after a few months. Devoted to singing, but resigned at the time to its precariousness as a livelihood, Jackson followed a more common occupational path for black women in Chicago—starting as a domestic in 1928, she took work as a produce packer and then as a maid at a North Side hotel in 1933.[43]

Despite these hardships, Jackson soon established a reputation as a singer. During the Depression and war Jackson traveled the black church circuit on the South Side and in nearby Indianapolis and Detroit, often accompanied by Dorsey. Her appeal as a soloist as well as the popularity of

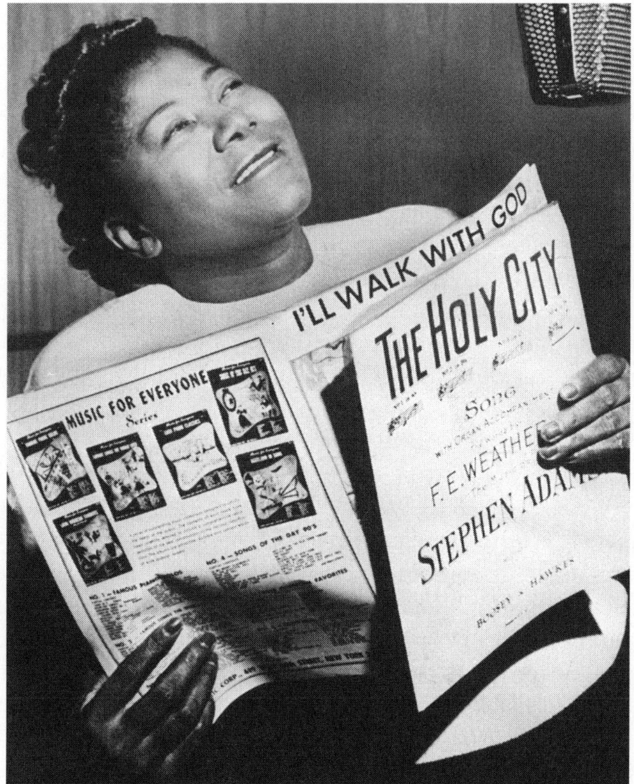

7. Mahalia Jackson. Courtesy of Corbis Photos.

other groups and artists renewed hopes of success as a singer. In 1946, she agreed to record at Apollo Records, a New York independent label. Initial sessions, like those earlier with Decca, were lukewarm, and Apollo head Bess Berman also considered letting Jackson go. By 1948, however, Jackson's appeal was confirmed: her version of "Move on Up a Little Higher" surpassed figures for all prior black gospel releases. Much of her market was concentrated in Chicago: during the first month of the record's release, 50,000 copies were sold to Bronzeville fans.[44] "Move on Up," which sold two million copies in the end, was the first of many hits for Jackson—"Even Me" later in 1948 and "Over the Hill" in 1950 were also million sellers—and the start of a singular career. Soon after her initial success, Dr. D. V. Jemison, president of the National Baptist Convention, named her official soloist for the organization. In 1950, Jackson became the first gospel singer—and the first black artist since Duke Ellington and his band—to perform at Carnegie Hall.[45] Projections by CBS consultants in 1953 of Jackson's national radio audience approached three million people.[46] With a Columbia Records contract in 1954 and an increasingly wide-reaching tour itinerary, Jackson had achieved a rare level of crossover appeal—combining an expanding white audience with near-universal support among blacks—generally reserved for jazz greats such as Ellington, Ella Fitzgerald, or Louis Armstrong.

Given the expanse of Jackson's career, it is possible to overlook the local roots of her music and life. Anthony Heilbut has suggested that the populist character of Jackson's music did not agree with sophisticated Bronzeville congregations, but community support for her records and performances argue otherwise. Indeed, the local appeal of her songs (which recall spiritual practice from her New Orleans childhood) indicates how much an exemplar of migration experience Jackson was, and underscores the complexity of cultural tastes in Black Chicago. In addition, her place in Bronzeville was augmented by her involvement in the community as a businesswoman. Through the 1940s Jackson supported herself through various enterprises, opening up a beauty parlor in 1939, and adding a flower store a decade later. In 1943 she became a landlord, purchasing a building for tenant rental. Even with her music, Jackson demonstrated commercial acumen: upon the release of "Move on Up," she served as her own distributor, picking up boxes of records for delivery to stores, beauty parlors, and barber shops on the South Side.[47]

Along with her business activities, Jackson's ties to the Second Ward Democratic organization, led by William Dawson, also helped to establish her sense of place in Bronzeville. Dawson had utilized Jackson in campaigns since 1932, when he was still a Republican. As Jackson's reputation grew, Dawson, also ascending from municipal to national prominence, relied on her increasingly. During the 1948 election, Jackson performed at rallies for the roster of party candidates: Dawson, Governor Adlai Stevenson, Senator Paul Douglas, and President Harry Truman. Truman, whose famed victory over Thomas Dewey hinged in part on a landslide South Side vote, later invited Jackson for a personal White House tour in recognition of her work. In 1955 Jackson, again at Dawson's request, stumped for the mayoral candidacy of Richard Daley, combining public concerts with clergy canvassing at her home. Jackson's ties to Daley would prove controversial, as tensions over local housing and school segregation grew acute in later decades.[48]

In their account of African-American religion, C. Eric Lincoln and Lawrence Mamiya argue that urbanization resulted in partial, as opposed to full, differentiation of black sacred and secular spheres, maintaining the union of social practice and communal spiritualism that had characterized Afro-Christianity since slavery.[49] Clearly, Mahalia Jackson raised this notion of partial differentiation to the level of high irony: a near-sanctified artist who declined countless invitations to front jazz bands on principle, yet was slyly recalled by one gospel accompanist as "our original belly dancer."[50] Dorsey acknowledged this contradiction when, after one performance in 1940, he referred to her as "Empress of the gospel singers," identifying Jackson by the stage name of her earliest idol, Bessie Smith.[51] Within post-Depression Black Chicago where Jackson lived and sang, the boundary between spiritual and temporal was becoming more pliable—here less a site of moral conflict than one of cultural dynamism and exchange. Refusing to perform in secular surroundings, Jackson proved more adventuresome in her use of musical styles. As Charles Wolfe points out, the appeal of "Move on Up" derived in part from the repetitive chord scheme, or vamp, supplied by pianist James Lee and organist James Francis, which provided Jackson a harmonic platform upon which to improvise, in the same way that blues singers such as Smith and Ma Rainey had improvised earlier.[52] Later songs such as "Said He Would" and "In the Upper Room" (1952) found Jackson singing over small choirs and quartets using vocal techniques derived from do-wop groups such as the Orioles and the Ravens.[53] Others extended Jackson's example of marrying sacred and secular cultural practice. Dinah Washington began her career as a pianist for Sallie Martin in 1940 before shifting to rhythm and blues later in the decade. Washington's conversion was but the first of several such detours locally—soul crooners Lou Rawls and Johnnie Taylor began their careers with area gospel quartets, while Sam Cooke sang at Highway Baptist Church before joining the Soul Stirrers in 1950, and later achieving pop stardom in 1957.[54]

Mahalia Jackson's career also raises questions about the dependence of "authentic" black culture upon a working-class context. Dorsey's equation of Jackson with Bessie Smith—each unquestioned exemplars of vernacular style—hints at the tendency to foreground an artist's grasp of the durative[55] conditions faced collectively by black people under histories of slavery and uneven development. This equation of cultural legitimacy to stories of scarcity—part of what Jerry Watts calls the "blues ontology"[56]—codes racial representation through social class: the perspectives of the working-class are validated because of their proximity to the material harshness of black life, while those of the more privileged are suspect due to their misrepresentation of plausible options under racist constraint. In this sense fellow singer Robert Anderson's comment that Mahalia Jackson's singing "took the people back to slavery times" has particular significance.[57] Her music bore witness to her personal trials in childhood and early adult life, and also invoked the long and hard memories of African-American experience. As Lawrence Levine points out, components of Jackson's art—her vital and kinetic style, her storefront spiritualism—resonated not only with the tastes of a black mass audience, but also with a deeper common sense regarding social and material possibilities for African-Americans.[58] This, of course, is one more fascinating aspect of the combination of gospel and blues fashioned by Jackson. Not only shared style but also status as credible collective memory marked her linkage of the genres.[59]

Given this context, what are we to make of Jackson's identity as entrepreneur? How was it that her music could "take the people back to slavery times" even as her own work—on and off stage—followed a different trajectory, one linked to the modern emergence of the black middle class? What Jackson's case suggests is that after migration and urbanization, the inverse relation between cultural legitimacy and class identity among black people was becoming less tenable. For Jackson and other women artists, there was of course a practical explanation for this turn: subject to double exploitation by the white world and also black male associates, black women performers needed to establish control over their material fortunes to insure viability. Here Jackson was a paragon of self-management, cultivating a tough negotiating style to secure good terms and prompt payment from promoters and ministers alike, and insuring against theft by holding tour receipts at her home in Chicago. But Jackson's entrepreneurship functioned as a gendered survival skill, while also exemplifying a broader tendency: linkage of communal cultural authority with personal economic ambition.

Another celebrated local musician, bandleader Louis Jordan, followed similar strategies. Often described as the prototypical black pop musician,[60] Jordan, like Jackson, was based in the Chicago area during the years of his greatest popularity, 1941 to 1950. After leaving Chick Webb's band in 1938, Jordan soon established himself as head of the Tympany Five, a dance group combining a spare horn section (three to five pieces) with standard rhythm elements (bass, drums, piano, and guitar). This streamlined band was of course the sign of things to come for jazz and dance music: in 1940, though, it was an anomaly for music fans awash in the swing craze. After modest success, Jordan's band was invited in 1941 to play the Capitol Lounge in downtown Chicago, which was under the management of Berle Adams.[61] From this point on, the careers of Jordan and the group took off. Louis Jordan and the Tympany Five recorded five million-selling songs during the 1940s, and created one of the highest profiles in the business.

8. Louis Jordan. Photographed by Wayne F. Miller. Courtesy of Wayne F. Miller.

Jordan's appeal rested on an array of talents: well-trained in both blues and big band technique, his group combined double entendre narrative (often drawing on folk imagery) with music and lyrics, role play, dance, and costume evoking the urban hipster. The group enjoyed popularity across the color line: Jordan would later boast, "I made just as much money off of white people as I did off colored."[62] Like Jackson, Jordan was at his best playing in a range of venues before diverse audiences. By 1947, his group had broken gate records at Chicago's Savoy and Regal theaters, was a favorite at New York's Apollo, and played the Trocadero and Billy Berg's in Los Angeles, choice stops on the Hollywood club circuit.[63]

Writing about African-American music during and after the Depression, Ben Sidran states that these years marked the emergence of a "black underground" sound, with new genres—Kansas City jazz, jump blues, bebop—constituting a significant counterculture.[64] Key to this argument is the establishment of a race-specific set of musical codes—what Sidran calls the "singular idiom"—conveying the specificity of cultural practice and, by extension, social politics for black people. This thesis has been most prevalent in case of bebop jazz: Eric Lott's definition of the genre as "making disciplined imagination alive and answerable to the social change of its time"[65] is one of many to emphasize this music's fundamentally oppositional nature. But the work of Louis Jordan and other jump blues artists has also been discussed in this manner. Several writers, notably George Lipsitz and Nelson George, have traced allegories of transgression in the lyrics of songs such as "Ain't Nobody Here but Us Chickens" and "Saturday Night Fish Fry," arguing that these and other Jordan pieces were available as political texts within black communities.[66] Indeed, Jordan's aesthetic had subcultural resonance beyond lyrics: use of hipster dress and argot, song themes ranging from sexual politics to wartime scarcity, and a commitment to interface with the audience support Jordan's claim that while other musicians played for themselves, "I still wanted to play for the people."[67] This populist credo, coupled with the style politics[68] in which his performances were rooted, identifies Jordan as a vernacular artist, one hinting a more transgressive purpose than was the case with Mahalia Jackson.

Yet Jordan's cultural identity was more complex still than the cryptic subversive previous accounts describe. Avoiding late nights following performances and using invasive policies to similarly control bandmembers, Jordan offstage was a study in contrast to the bawdy hep cat seen in performance. His attention to order resulted in one of the more exacting regimens among musical groups of the day: band members recall Jordan holding marathon practices, with tours used to drill the musicians even more. Helping to establish the group's urbane image were rules governing appearance and demeanor—saxophonist Eddie Johnson recalled always packing a spare pair of shoes after being fined for wearing soiled ones to a South Carolina concert in 1945.[69] Of course, adherence to rules and routine were not an anomaly within professional black music: in Jordan's case these qualities simply emphasize that discipline was just as important as imagination in fashioning Jordan's appeal.

More striking here is the recording process for the group. After arriving in Chicago, Jordan established a complex promotional plan, and an open-door policy on collaborators. This resulted in a broad songbook, drawing from national, transnational, and diasporic sources: "Open the Door, Richard" (1945), was an interpretation of a slapstick act performed by local comedian and Regal Theater regular Dusty Fletcher, while "Run Joe"

(1947) and "Push-Ka-Pee-She-Pie" (1949) were conceived by Trinidadian backup singer Peggy Thomas and Jordan's own physician Walter Merrick, a native of the Caribbean island of St. Vincent.[70] Jordan regularly sought artistic advice from Dan Burley, former *Defender* writer and well-known urban folklorist.[71] White songwriters were also instrumental to Jordan's success. Several of Jordan's best-known songs—"Five Guys Named Moe" (1942), "Is You Is or Is You Ain't (Ma Baby)?" (1943), "Buzz Me" (1945), and "Beware" (1946)—were written by whites, whom Jordan often met on tour.[72] During this period, performances in all-white towns or clubs were quite common. Some of these dates were crucial to the band's development—Jordan described a 1942 run at a bar in Cedar Rapids, Iowa, where the band first performed novelty tunes, as "a great turning point in my career."[73]

Viewing the multiple sources for Jordan's work, one can question Sidran's conclusion that black music "went underground" during and after the Depression. This assessment becomes less tenable when one examines actual creative and production processes of the time. Just as it is difficult to discuss bebop greats like Charlie Parker and Thelonious Monk without addressing their excursions through Hollywood and Broadway ballads (not to mention classical music), so too it is impossible to make sense of Louis Jordan without addressing the heterogeneous nature of his art. Indeed, given conditions of industrial leveling discussed earlier, rejection of the mainstream in order to formulate a "singular idiom" seems too simplistic an assessment of what black musicians at this time thought their interests to be: definitions of "the people" they sought to play for, and with, were fluid and expansive.[74] That the reputation of Jordan and the Tympany Five as oppositional figures persists suggests that the resilience of the black vernacular derives as much from powers of interpretation and commentary as from the capacity to conserve tradition. Here one is reminded of the work of literary scholars Houston Baker and Henry Louis Gates. Following the work of Alain Locke, Zora Neale Hurston, and Ralph Ellison, Gates and Baker define the vernacular as a field of (and in) transit: not a site of cultural preservation but "a matrix . . . a point of ceaseless input and output," undergirded by the critical strategies of blues and signifying.[75]

In Jordan's case something further is being proposed: that we discuss the vernacular not only in terms of interpretation, but also production. The premeditation of Jordan's oeuvre—from routine drilling of the band to weathering the AFM strike by recording under the government's "V" label for sales to the armed forces—emphasize how his own theory of the vernacular tied communal culture to commercial interest.[76] Jordan's planned development of himself and his band—his professionalism—

raises again the contradiction seen with Mahalia Jackson: within post-Depression Black Chicago, vernacular cultural work came from artists tied to the emergent entrepreneurial class. How these conditions led to a dynamic nexus between race, class, and culture in Bronzeville become clearer through discussion of its best known genre of music.

Few musical traditions so readily evoke Chicago as urban blues. Inspiration for global music genres marking transformation of social mores, Chicago's brand of blues music enjoys a storied place in national and global popular traditions. However, this venerable artistic legacy obscures how the growth of local blues was rooted in processes of work, production, and supply, as well as the genre's aesthetic genius.

By the eve of the war, an early blues infrastructure was forming in Chicago. The ubiquitous "Ink" Williams remained active, recording artists for Decca and later Mercury Records. His main competitor was Lester Melrose, a white agent who followed Williams at Paramount in the 1920s, and represented the Columbia, Okeh, and Bluebird labels during the lean Depression years. Melrose was already familiar with local talent—he had recorded Bill Broonzy's early work, as well as "It's Tight Like That," the 1928 hit for Tampa Red (Hudson Whittaker) and Georgia Tom.[77] With the founding of Bluebird in 1934 and renewal of the race record market, Melrose signed an array of artists to contract. Broonzy and Tampa Red were joined by Memphis Slim, Sonny Boy Williamson, instrumentalists such as pianists Josh Altheimer and Maceo Merriweather, and latter-day blueswomen Memphis Minnie and Lil Green. All these musicians were migrants to Chicago. The convergence of talent gave Bluebird an insurmountable advantage in the resurgent race record business: Melrose claimed control of 90 percent of the national blues market by the mid-1940s. It also marked the centralization of the blues industry in Chicago—a previously itinerant system serving dispersed regional tastes.[78]

One reason for the success of the Bluebird artists was how their work melded blues techniques and urban experience into compelling art. Often described as the first "city" blues, the Bluebird sound—like that of Louis Jordan or Mahalia Jackson—articulated social experiences connected to migration within black communities. Along with perennial themes of movement, personal longing, and suspicion, early Chicago blues artists focused on specific features of the new cityscape: two of the biggest hits from the group—Memphis Minnie's "Me and My Chauffeur" (1941) and Sonny Boy Williamson's "Elevator Woman" (1945)—mixed erotic subtext with reference to technologies set in the urban context.[79] Lil Green's hit song

"Romance the Dark" was a decidedly modern ballad, combining instrumentation and lyrics evoking images of tenement love.[80] Important also was use of the electric guitar: Broonzy and Memphis Minnie were amplifying their instruments by wartime, inspiring other Chicago-based musicians to employ the new technology.[81]

A closer look at the process through which Bluebird artists made their music reveals that the emergence of the new sound was no coincidence. Part of the motivation for the label's musicians—most of whom enjoyed enviable reputations elsewhere—to relocate to Chicago was Melrose's use of long-term contracts. Previously only proven attractions could command such terms: but at Bluebird even backing musicians were given extended deals. To be sure, not all artists were happy with Melrose's terms, but there were fewer questions about his ethics than was the case for other agents, white or black. The benefits of consistency at Bluebird went beyond matters of compensation, though. By reliably contracting with diverse musicians, Melrose encouraged establishment of a common sound connected to the Bluebird label, influencing the work of each musician and leading to coordination—what Mike Rowe refers to as rationalization[82]—of their collective talent. In a sense, then, the more urban sound of the Bluebird musicians and early Chicago blues derived from the music's conception within a consistent, replicable process. The significance of this becomes clear when one notes that the very idea of a distinct sound connected to a label, a routinely noted trait of postwar popular music, was rare before 1940 given irregular retention of musicians.[83]

Assembling the Bluebird artists in this manner also nourished the growth of blues institutions rooted in Black Chicago. Informal sites were transformed into work or professional spaces, where training took place, contacts were made, and money changed hands. Both Willie Dixon and Muddy Waters recalled Tampa Red's home at 35th and State as the point of entry to the Chicago blues community, as well as unofficial waiting room for the Bluebird operation.[84] The visibility gained from recording made blues musicians an attractive draw at local clubs. In many cases this led to extended gigs, or sometimes even commitment of weekly slots for musicians to showcase talent on their own terms. Memphis Minnie's famed "Blue Monday" party at Ruby Lee Gatewood's Tavern on Lake Street along the West Side was one example of this arrangement. Extending the premise of cross-fertilization within the Bluebird studio, musicians sat in on each other's live dates. At the Blue Monday parties, both Bill Broonzy and Memphis Slim were regular guests, while Sonny Boy Williamson, Tampa Red, and Maceo Merriweather took turns headlining at the Flame Club.[85] The success of the Bluebird artists inspired local black impresarios to enter the growing music market. Rhumboogie owner Charley Glenn started a record company named after his nightclub in 1945, while Hy-Tone, another South Side label, was founded by the owners of the Melody Lane Record Shop on 55th Street near Indiana. George Leaner, who worked at the Groove Record Store on 47th Street near the Regal and Savoy, was hired in 1946 by Melrose as an assistant. In 1950, together with his brother Ernest, he founded United Record Distributors, later one of the major popular music suppliers in the Midwest.[86] Through the 1940s and afterward, musicians and producers revised the meaning of blues in Chicago—not only through focus on the urban context, but also a more professional understanding of black music, which encouraged artists to view their cultural work in more material terms.

It is often argued that the main innovation of blues music was foregrounding individual genius within the black cultural context. This turn toward autonomy—what critic Albert Murray calls the heroism of the blues[87]—has led Lawrence Levine among others to argue that the emergence of blues music early this century was a crucial moment of modernization in black life: the birth of personalized cultural practice that in turn reinforced notions of self-determination generally for African-Americans.[88] It is in large part a fixation on this spirit of "heroic" autonomy within blues artists and black performers generally that makes many writers and fans suspicious of the connection between music and commerce. Yet among the Bluebird artists this ethos of individual genius evolved into a strategy of collective production, rooted in a commercial context and capable of articulating shared understanding and codifying social practice. To be sure, the central role played by Melrose tempers any claim that black artists themselves fully controlled music production in 1940s Chicago. Nevertheless, these artists altered communal cultural practice by coordinating activity and resources within a decidedly commercial agenda—a kind of modernization within black cultural practice as significant as any previously.

One indication of how life was changing for blues musicians was the shifting fortunes of Local 208, the black chapter of the musicians' union. We have already noted the role that Local 208 and its leader Harry Gray played in redirecting music management away from gangster syndicates. Greater opportunity in the resurgent music industry, the doubling of membership for the union nationally during the 1940s,[89] and the general increase in musician activism connected to the musicians' strikes, gives reason to think that Local 208 would have grown markedly. Indeed, many popular local performers of this period—Louis Jordan, Memphis Minnie, Muddy Waters, and Willie Dixon, among others—did become members. However, union records indicate a contradictory pattern: after increasing from 428 members in 1940 to 550 members in 1948, membership decreased to 223 in 1955.[90] Involvement in the AFM was sufficiently erratic that guitarist Jimmy Rodgers, later Waters's sideman, recalled "scabbing"—performing without union approval—as common practice among postwar artists.[91]

How can declining involvement in Local 208 be explained, given simultaneous expansion of the industry, union, and community of African-American musicians in Chicago? The key issue was how systematization changed ideas of work and professionalism for those musicians. Early in the century, popular music circulated through performance and music publishing. Black musicians—who before the emergence of BMI could rarely claim publishing revenues—had to organize their professional identity around sites of stage and nightclub. As we have seen, performance remained critical to the careers of post-Depression Chicago musicians. The relationship between live and recorded work, however, was changing dramatically. Where before recorded music supplemented stage work, musicians during the 1940s inverted the formula. Now hit records established careers, and live performance augmented reputations made in the studio. These changes mirrored broader developments in the industry. While live dates for American musicians dropped from 99,000 in 1930 to 59,000 in 1954, the number of record companies—approaching zero during the Depression—grew to between 1,500 and 2,000 by the late 1950s, generating sales of $213 million in 1954 and $603 million in 1959.[92] Under such conditions, the utility of the union was less apparent to black musicians: Willie Dixon no doubt acted on commonly held feelings when he changed residences in 1956 to distance himself from the AFM and consolidate a career increasingly based in the studio.[93] The fortunes of black popular musicians—and their understandings of cultural work and collective interest—were now tied to emergent independent recording companies working in blues, dance, and gospel genres: Specialty in Los Angeles, Peacock in Houston, King in Cincinnati, Atlantic in New York.

Of these, the first major success was Chess Records, begun in 1947 on the South Side of Chicago. Successor to Bluebird and epitome of the studio blues sound, Chess's place in local music history is both central and controversial. Polish immigrants Leonard and Phil Chess—like the DeLisas, members of the Capone syndicate—were owners of the 708 and Macamba clubs, popular spots near 39th and Drexel that featured headline artists such as Billy Eckstine, Ella Fitzgerald, and Lionel Hampton, as well as local blues stars like Memphis Minnie. As blues audiences grew larger, the Chess brothers began recording professionally in order to tap the enormous public interest in the music. In 1947, they started the Aristocrat label, renaming the company Chess in 1950. Early successes were infrequent, but the label nonetheless established a notoriety of sorts: the label's first hit, Andrew Tibbs's 1947 release "Bilbo is Dead," was banned in Mississippi because of its unkind reference to the recently deceased segregationist Senator Theodore Bilbo. Leonard Chess showed personal initiative with the company's product, packing records into his automobile and dropping bundles at record sellers, convenience stores, and, like Mahalia Jackson, barber and beauty shops throughout the South Side.[94]

Chess might have remained an intriguing but minor player in the business were it not for the emergence of Muddy Waters as the label's headline artist in 1948. Waters, a migrant from the area near Clarksdale, Mississippi, was drawn to dreams of celebrity by records heard off local jukeboxes and phonographs on the nearby Stovall plantation, where Waters lived and worked into young adulthood. Stories of Waters's talent before coming to Chicago in 1943 are common knowledge by now, as are the trials he underwent early in his career. Despite a South Side reputation that, according to Willie Dixon, preceded his arrival by several years, Waters did not impress in the studio. Lester Melrose canned his sessions for Bluebird in 1946 and Leonard Chess almost let Waters go after lax response to several sides in 1947. Like Mahalia Jackson, Waters first worked outside professional music: first in a paper warehouse, then as a deliveryman, while keeping up a string of house party dates.[95]

Waters's first hit, "I Can't Be Satisfied" (1948), came close to suffering the same fate as his earlier work: Leonard Chess's dismissive response upon first hearing the song was; "What's he singing? I can't understand what he's singing!" With an energetic but spare (vocals, guitar, and bass) sound, the song made it onto tape only through the intervention of a company assistant. Chess, still skeptical, sent out a limited pressing. By the next day, the shipment had sold out. Waters recalled being denied an extra copy at a local record store, despite protesting to the owner that it was his own record. "I Can't Be Satisfied" turned out to be the first of many hits for Waters at Chess. Titles such as "Train Fare Home Blues," "Rollin and Tumbling," and "Rolling Stone" led up to Waters's best year in 1951, when release of "Louisiana Blues," "Long Distance Call," and "Honey Bee" ushered in what Mike Rowe called "the very springtime of Chicago blues."[96]

As the descendent of a blues tradition connecting Delta legends such as Charley Patton, Son House, and Robert Johnson, Waters is often characterized as part of a rural cultural continuum. Yet it is clear—from use of amplification and attention to migration themes—that he was a city artist as much as one with Delta roots. Crucial here is how Waters, like others, acknowledged his ties to the local music infrastructure. Note Waters's account of his life following release of "I Can't be Satisfied" in March of 1948:

> I had a hot blues out, man. I'd be driving my truck, and whenever I'd see a neon beer sign, I'd stop, go in, look at the jukebox, and see is my record on there. I might buy me a beer and play the record and then leave. Don't tell nobody nothing. Before long, every blues joint there was, that record was on the jukebox. And if you come in and sat there for a little while, if any one was in there, they gonna punch it. Pretty soon I'd hear it walking along the street. I'd hear it driving down the street. About June or July that record was getting *really* hot. I would be driving home from playing, two or three o'clock in the morning, and I had a convertible, with the top back 'cause it was warm. I could hear people all upstairs playing that record. It would be rolling up there, man. I heard it all over. One time, I heard it coming from way upstairs somewhere, and it scared me. I thought I had died.[97]

Within this passage one can see the influence cultural commerce—specifically independent recording and the jukebox—had on Waters's own sense of musicianship. What is most striking is how Waters based his artistic identity more on recording success than on visibility as a performer—hence his clandestine pleasure in following the song through the taverns and tenements of Bronzeville. As he drew together a regular band—Ernest Crawford on bass, Jimmy Rodgers on second guitar and, after 1950, Little Walter on harmonica—Waters's work came to revolve around what lyrics and sounds could be recorded to greatest effect. Regular collaboration after 1954 with Willie Dixon deepened Waters's commitment to the studio, as Dixon provided material that enhanced the group's commercial success.[98]

Waters's string of hit records (fifteen *Billboard* chart entries between 1950 and 1958) anchored a range of artists and styles at Chess during the 1950s. Other celebrated performers—stalwarts Memphis Minnie and Memphis Slim, vocalist Willie Mabon, guitarist Lowell Fulsom, harmonica player Little Walter, and Howlin' Wolf—became label regulars. The unparalleled blues catalog Chess put out facilitated the company's entry into other genres of music. Jackie Brentson's "Rocket 88" (1951), thought to be the first identifiable rock and roll release, was produced and distributed by Chess after being recorded in Memphis by Sam Phillips. Leonard Chess would later pass up Phillips' invitation to sign another prodigy, the young Elvis Presley, in 1954. Other pioneers bridging the gap between blues and early rock—Bo Diddley and Chuck Berry in particular—were Chess artists. The label even made inroads into the sacred market. Chess recorded the popular sermons of the Reverend C. L. Franklin of Detroit, father of

9. Muddy Waters tuning up in the lavatory, with fellow blues headliner Otis Spann. Courtesy of Corbis Photos.

future queen of soul Aretha Franklin. One wonders if the label might have avoided its demise in 1971 if it had pulled off an earlier signing coup involving James Brown, who at the last minute broke a verbal commitment and signed with King Records in 1956.[99]

It was blues songs and artists, though, that were the basis for Chess's success. Innovations defining postwar blues, and later rock and soul music—the use of harmonica or extra guitars as a second lead, "stop time" rhythm, and all-out commitment to amplification—grew out of the label's studio near 52nd Street and Cottage Grove Avenue. Even more so than Waters, the artist responsible for these developments was songwriter, bassist, and arranger Willie Dixon. Dixon, also a Delta migrant, enjoyed a diverse career through World War II—he worked as a laborer and deliveryman, professional boxer, gospel singer, and bassist for the Big Three Trio, a combo based in Chicago. He was also well known locally as a blues player and writer, playing on Memphis Slim's hit release "Rockin' the House" (1947) and other recordings, and selling copies of his version of "Signifyin' Monkey" at the Maxwell Street Market, a favorite outdoor venue for local black musicians. By 1951, Dixon was working for Chess both as musician and office assistant. He would become the logistical pivot for the company, shepherding Muddy Waters and other contracted artists, recruiting and developing new talent such as Berry and Diddley, and managing studio sessions with Leonard Chess.[100]

It would be an error to describe Dixon's tenure with Chess as an easy partnership. Dixon was always suspicious of Leonard Chess and even left the label from 1956 to 1959 because of contract issues. Nevertheless, it is clear that his influence on the company was germinal, similar to that of Ken Blewett at the Regal. All the key players at Chess—the Chess brothers, engineer Malcolm Chisholm, as well as various artists—remember Dixon as the stabilizing constant around the studio, particularly during recording sessions. The fact that his musicianship was surpassed in reputation by his technical and management acumen shows how Chicago blues music was defined as much by matters of production as qualities of genre. Although it was not until after 1960 that Dixon's influence reached its apex—inspiring Mike Rowe to call him the "second Melrose"[101]—one could see the central role he played even in earlier years.

Dixon's work at Chess exemplified also the entrepreneurial ethos of those working in postwar Chicago music: Mahalia Jackson, Louis Jordan, Charley Glenn, and Muddy Waters. Dixon devoted himself to honing and disseminating blues as a genre, always with an eye toward increasing the music's potential audience. As in the case of Louis Jordan, Dixon's sense of project raises questions about treating post-Depression black popular music as an insular or underground system. From regular Big Three gigs in remote ranching territories (he recalled especially memorable successes in Cheyenne, Wyoming, when performing there in the late 1940s) to a 1958 tour of Israel with Memphis Slim that inspired the famed European blues festivals of the 1960s, Dixon served as ambassador for Chicago blues, midwifing its emergence as exemplary popular music.[102]

One mark of Dixon's influence was his role in establishing the bluesman style of Waters and other Chess stars. Emblematic of what Charles Keil called "the expressive male role" in black social life, the bluesman as type can be seen as one of a series of archetypal representations of masculinity within black popular culture, extending into the present.[103] Paul Gilroy has argued that focus on heterosexual conflict has been central to blues' appeal, given the ritual role gender antagonism plays in projecting deeper senses of loss tied to the memory of slavery for Afro-diasporic communities.[104] Within this framework, the stock elements of the bluesman persona—sexual frankness, romantic transience, celebration of the socially unobligated male—have impact beyond entertainment, engaged as they were with vital traditions of historical meaning. While many commentators—Gilroy especially—have criticized the misogyny embedded within this structure of thought, all agree that black music's obsession with the male subject represents a deeply rooted, almost inherent, aspect of popular African-American culture. Perhaps this is why the over-the-top masculinity of such Chess classics as Waters's "Hootchie Cootchie Man" and "I'm Ready," or the inimitable "Back Door Man" by Howlin' Wolf, has been celebrated by fans of Chicago blues as requisite to the genre, and by extension, black culture generally.

The fact that each of these songs was written by Willie Dixon calls into question the inherent nature of this element of blues performance in Chicago. Looking closely at Waters's work before he began his association with Dixon in 1954, one finds nuanced treatments of heterosexual interaction in such songs as "Standing Around Crying" or "Honey Bee," where male agency was often contingent upon (if not subordinate to) the will of a female partner. To be sure, some Waters's songs prior to 1954 (notably "Louisiana Blues") do approach the machismo of later works; but before collaborating with Dixon, Waters's treatment of gender appears contradictory, as opposed to unambiguously celebratory of male autonomy and power. Thus what is taken as a "natural" declaration of male identity—particularly for black popular audiences—derived as much from specific production decisions by Dixon and Chess Records as it did from long-standing mores held by artist and audience. Given the attention directed—then and now—at such renditions of black masculinity, focus on figures such as Dixon allows a more contingent sense of how these beliefs are historically formed.

Behind the connection of blues and masculinity is another role often credited to black music: its function as critique of capital. Here the politics of culture reach beyond matters of style: most writers argue that the world of black music should be understood as a challenge to processes of formal work. Once again, Gilroy provides an eloquent formulation of the position. Discussing what he calls the "anti-productivism" of black music culture, Gilroy argues that collective practices tied to genres of blues, soul, and reggae have served to repudiate the labor process under capitalism. Emphasis on the world of leisure rather than that of work, pursuit of open-ended goals of romance and stimulation as opposed to known ends of piecework and the paycheck, celebration of the black (and usually male) body "as an instrument of pleasure rather than labor": all combine to invest black music with a critique of—if not outright resistance to—material exploitation of blacks in the West.[105] The key term here is *resistance:* within this framework, presumptions of black music's "inherent" political effect gain credibility, and focus on the effort to maintain its integrity—its authenticity—become more compelling, given black music's role in the struggle against racism and exploitation.

Yet the interrelation of blues music and processes of work in Chicago offers a different interpretive model. The example of Willie Dixon's career, like others mentioned in this chapter, indicates how structures of production and distribution were important not only to the personal interests of musicians, but also as credible models of black labor, for both musicians and their audiences. This is not to say that there was a full embrace of the business of popular music by Black Chicago artists and audiences. Institutions of authority were held in suspicion and often engaged critically, whether they were the syndicate of Al Capone, the musician's union, or the Chess brothers. But what becomes clear is that emerging black popular music genres provided not so much resistance to cultural capital as *alternative* versions of that same capital system. Musicians and entrepreneurs in post-Depression Black Chicago sought their own definitions of labor, just profit, and culture industry, rather than refusing the validity of music commerce *in toto*. Thus, greater acknowledgment of the black musician's status as worker as well as artist reinforced the growing understanding of black music not only as art or social ritual but also system of production. Here Willie Dixon provides an especially illuminating example. Aware through hard experience of the need for blues artists to retain composition rights, Dixon set up a booking agency that grew into a publishing company registered with BMI and serving Chicago blues' "second generation" of the mid- and late 1950s—J. B. Lenoir, Otis Rush, Buddy Guy, Koko Taylor. The name of the organization—Ghana Publishing Company—speaks volumes about Dixon's understanding of cultural production as site of both struggle over power, and also collective material interest.[106]

Postwar music entrepreneurship was pushed even further by the local rise of soul music. A marriage of blues and gospel, soul music was an apt progeny of Black Chicago's cultural scene; its development, though, could not have occurred without extension of existing commercial ambitions. In 1953, Vivian Carter and Jimmy Bracken, a black couple from nearby Gary, Indiana, started Vee-Jay Records in Chicago. One of the few black-owned independent labels in postwar period (Houston-based Peacock Records, owned by Don Robey, was the only other black label of note during this time[107]), Vee-Jay would produce and supply much of the nation's early soul music. The company's first hit in 1954, the Spaniels "Goodnight, Sweetheart, Goodnight," would be followed through the 1950s by a string of successful releases, most notably those of the Impressions, the legendary group led by Curtis Mayfield that grew out of the Cabrini Green Housing Project on the West Side in the late 1950s.[108] Carter and Bracken's operation represented the apex of local black control of popular recording: the company remained prominent until its sudden bankruptcy in 1966. It anchored a soul music system that by the early 1960s would eclipse the Chicago blues as the preferred local (and, to some extent, national) genre for black audiences, with new black-owned clubs such as the High Chapparal, Lonnie's Skyway Lounge and the Algiers Lounge serving as regular venues, along with the Regal Theater.[109]

By the mid-1950s, structures evolving from the work of postwar local musicians involved in recording were powerful testimony to the influence of black cultural entrepreneurship in Chicago. Lines of symbiosis extended through artists and producers, club owners and audiences, inspiring a sense of community feeling that lent credence to the decades-old idea that Bronzeville controlled its identity and direction. The legacy of Charley Glenn and Ken Blewett was carried on during the 1950s by Herman Roberts, who purchased an old taxi garage near 61st and Cottage Grove, reopening it in 1957 as the Roberts Show Lounge, a favorite venue for Dinah Washington and other stars that rivaled gate receipts for the Regal.[110] Willie Dixon's and Vivian Carter's achievements would be extended through the work of the preeminent black music entrepreneur, Quincy Jones, who relocated from Seattle to Chicago in 1955, supervised several Dinah Washington recording sessions at Mercury Records, and there ascended to the post of music director. He was the first African-American to hold such a position at a major label.[111] Yet these developments do not convey the full story of emerging black music commerce. For that we must turn to radio broadcasting, and the emergence of the black disk jockey.

Broadcast music and other forms of radio programming are such a familiar feature of contemporary entertainment that it is difficult to grasp the medium's transformative impact on American society, from its arrival in 1920 through the 1950s. Some of this amnesia is due to television, which during the postwar years replaced radio as the core of cultural media and in many ways, of the culture industry. Nonetheless radio transformed social habits in ways similar to how television has in our day—influencing leisure patterns, reshaping ideas of community, and deepening the relationship between industry and the public through advertising media. No segment of the population was more affected by early developments in radio than urban blacks, and no change within radio was more significant—for African Americans, the industry and American society broadly—than the rise of the black disc jockey in post-Depression Chicago.

The first black radio personality—ex-prize fighter and *Defender* columnist Jack L. Cooper—was a noted pioneer in the industry: many claim that he, not Al Jarvis, was the first to broadcast recorded music. Beginning his *All-Negro Radio Hour* in 1929 on WSBC, an independent station in Chicago, Cooper expanded his schedule to include talk and music shows, church simulcasts, and mobile news reporting, which totaled forty hours of programming on four stations by the time of the war. A late 1940s survey by a local retailer showed 90 percent of the African-American sample listened to Cooper's programs.[112] Cooper's career has been well documented by historian Mark Newman and needs no extensive discussion here.[113] However, it is important to note some aspects of Cooper's operation, as they set key precedents for the postwar expansion of black radio.

Although Cooper was known across the country, his programs were available only on the South Side. This arrangement, called "narrowcasting," resulted from the limited technology available to early black broadcasters; WSBC, for instance, had a signal of only 250 watts. While limited, Newman points out that for a still segregated South Side, narrowcasting had its benefits, since the discreet signal fit communal boundaries. Technical limitations encouraged programming focus, which supported and strengthened notions of cultural specificity. This was reflected in Cooper's work during the 1930s and early 1940s, when he was the only major local on-air presence. Although music shows followed strict formats whether swing or religious, other programs had broader appeal: Sunday sermon simulcasts, for example, came from nine different churches, along with choir performances during the week.[114] Talk programs also sought diverse Bronzeville audiences. Shows such as *Our Community Marches On* (hosted by a local social worker), *Situations Wanted* (where classifieds were read on air), and *Your Legal Rights* indicated Cooper's sense of public service. Two other shows, *Listen Chicago* and *Search for Missing Persons* were unique conduits for community concerns. While *Listen Chicago* served as a popular roundtable forum for various leaders from 1946 to 1952, it was *Search for Missing Persons* that best demonstrated Cooper's impact. Drawing from police records, the program gave names of lost residents, including migrants who had failed to make connections with family or friends. Begun in 1938, the show had reunited 20,000 persons into the late 1940s.[115]

In basic terms support for Cooper's programming indicates the interest black Chicagoans, like proud residents anywhere, had in their local affairs. But at a deeper level it shows how their notions of community transformed during and after the Depression. Attention to altered black sensibilities has long been central to discussion of the postmigration period. LeRoi Jones's belief that the act of migration represented "a reinterpretation by the Negro of his role in this country"[116] highlights its paradigmatic status as gateway from pre-modern to modern black life. Yet most accounts, echoing Jones, value this reinterpretation for its unprecedented register of communal agency. Few ask, as Alain Locke and others did at the time, how terms such as *community* or even *race* could and did change as the massive relocations ran their course.[117]

It is in relation to new notions of community, and thus race, that black-appeal radio played a crucial role in Chicago after 1940. Here we return to the work of Benedict Anderson, notably his discussion of social simultaneity: the fictive, modern sense of collectivity derived from the newspaper, novel, and other cultural forms that made more ambitious models of community, such as the nation, cognitively possible. This thesis is clearly relevant to interwar black history: scholars have noted how during migration race newspapers encouraged a more collective—and, through the melding of Northern and Southern regional experiences, more nationalized—sense of agenda in black communities.[118] Black-appeal radio extended these developments, since it embodied the idea of simultaneity literally. Black radio audiences, by virtue of the power of electronic media, were "in the same place at the same time" in ways that readers of even the largest newspapers could not match. In this light, Cooper's programs take on added significance: not just integrating the airwaves or spurring increase in black ownership of radios,[119] but also rehearsing more complex terms of postmigration community, be they specific racial audience, narrowcast territory, or "simultaneous public." Indicators of Cooper's popularity, such as the aforementioned retailer's poll, document a significant audience, one constituting a vital metaphor of social collectivity in Black Chicago.

That this sample was drawn from a customer database points to another innovation of Cooper's, and still another provocative notion of modern black community. While African Americans had of course bought and sold retail goods throughout history, their collective status within the world of mainstream commerce to date had been one of invisibility and alienation. Up to World War II it was customary for businesses, especially national businesses, not to advertise directly to blacks. This practice—the denial of what Roland Marchand called "consumer citizenship"[120]—was an especially bitter arrangement during the interwar years. With modernization in retail and advertising, legitimacy as a consumer helped constitute the core of popular ideas of social identity and belonging within the United States.[121] Indeed, the store boycotts that raged through black urban communities in the late 1920s and 1930s, often taken as signs of racial or labor militancy,[122] could also be characterized as "consumer dignity" campaigns, meant to assign positive meaning to black consumption within an indifferent, if not hostile, social context. One can think of the struggle to legitimate black consumption as a key—though understudied—point of entry for blacks into the emerging social order of the American Century, comparable to others emphasized in current historiography, such as the fight to abolish Jim-Crow labor organizing;[123] campaigns to consolidate constitutional rights;[124] or relation of domestic race politics to geopolitical currents of anticolonialism and nonalignment.[125] To be sure, the salience of consumer dignity as a social issue for African Americans individually depended on material circumstance. Yet, concern over black consumption transcended lines of class—in Chicago for example, leaders who sought (in varying ways) to render black consumers visible ranged from street orator and mystic Sufi Abdul Hamid to Associated Negro Press head Claude Barnett, indicating the breadth of feeling regarding these issues.

Within this climate, Cooper's work in radio was once again groundbreaking. The "timeshare" arrangement at WSBC, where broadcast slots were purchased for a flat fee, left location of sponsors and advertisers to the broadcaster. Here Cooper proved most adept, convincing local businesses in furniture, clothing, food, and other trades to solicit black customers through his radio programs.[126] Nor were Cooper's ties confined to white businesses. Black-owned Metropolitan Funeral System Association built him a studio in the early 1930s, in exchange for regular plugs.[127] Seeking to consolidate these gains, Cooper started what was probably the first official black advertising agency in 1937 to cultivate and retain clients: the Jack L. Cooper Advertising Company.[128] The arrangement represented another idea of black community through radio—not only that of cultural audience or virtual public, but also validated consumer market. Cooper would not secure national advertisers until the late 1940s, around when it became commonplace throughout black radio, as we will see shortly. But the interrelation of consumption and cultural communication within his work—the motto for Cooper Advertising Services was, "When We Get 'Em Told,

You've Got 'Em Sold"—show once again that in radio, like popular music, commercialism was becoming more central to black cultural identity and systems, and that these shifts heralded new and deeply modern understandings of race community in the United States.

It is these two notions of community—simultaneous black public, and viable race market—that define Cooper's and by extension radio's role in the transformation of Black Chicago. The appeal of black radio's marriage of cultural, public, and commercial identity meant that it not only anchored music infrastructures, but also engendered potent new senses of racial collectivity.[129] While Cooper made out handsomely—his annual pay from the shows and other ventures was nearly $200,000 by the late 1940s[130]—he soon found himself in competition with a new wave of black broadcasters that were more egalitarian and expansive, particularly around matters of taste and style. These newcomers secured Chicago's place as the center for black-appeal radio and, by extension, the emergent black popular music infrastructure.

Al Benson was the first and most influential of this second wave. Born Arthur B. Leaner in Mississippi in 1910, Benson, like others in this chapter, engaged diverse jobs and interests before his entertainment successes, holding staff positions with the Works Progress Administration and the Cook County Probation System, and also serving as a precinct captain for Alderman William Dawson.[131] Establishing himself as minister to a storefront congregation on 40th and State Streets sometime during the early 1940s, Benson was invited to do a fifteen-minute simulcast from his church by independent station WGES in 1945. He quickly secured more time slots and switched to a secular, blues-oriented play list, changing his name to Benson to protect his congregation from association with his worldly forays. His rise was more dramatic than Cooper's: by 1948, he broadcast ten hours *a day* on WGES and two other local radio stations, often seven days a week. He remained on the air until 1962, making nearly five million dollars for his decade and a half of radio work.[132]

There were several differences in the work of Cooper and Benson: Benson's use of blues versus Cooper's reliance on "respectable" music; Cooper's emphasis of public-affairs shows as compared to Benson's adherence to records, for example. The most remarked contrast between the two, though, was in on-air voice and personality. While Cooper projected the refined, striving black *sophisticate,* speaking with flawless precision, Benson affected an unstudied, deeply quotidian persona that quickly became a legendary exemplar of Bronzeville identity. Using folk colloquialisms and vernacular; gleefully dispensing with the burdens of proper grammar; struggling gamely with (and often playing off of) his chronic stutter,

10. Al Benson (second from right) with Jimmy Bracken (far left) and Vivian Carter (second from left). Courtesy of the Harsh Research Collection/Chicago Public Library.

Benson fashioned a style that seemed its own unique postmigration synthesis—a syncretism of northern being and southern memory that acclimated migrants far more effectively than the "socialization" projects of the Urban League or the *Defender* a generation before. For many, the difference between the two could be traced to the simple matter of class identity. Cooper, self-made and elitist, saw radio as an instrument of racial improvement, while Benson evidenced no such pretensions, thereby achieving greater public acceptance.[133] And yet such readings of race and class miss the two men's common material position: each epitomized entrepreneurial vision and success, as well as differing cultural and status commitments within Black Chicago. It is more accurate to think of Cooper and Benson, like others artists discussed earlier, as representing a range of class positions—in both their work and their lives—within the Bronzeville community.

Benson fast became a fundamental public figure in postwar Black Chicago—outside of Mahalia Jackson, one would be hard-pressed to find a more popular personality at the time. His fame made him the first choice of promoters and stage managers: many of Benson's nights were spent emceeing concerts, dances, and contests throughout Chicago.[134] Indeed, his popularity resulted in his election as "mayor of Bronzeville" in 1948 through a *Defender* administered poll.[135] Ever the businessman, Benson maintained his position by consolidating control over movement of his product. Working through the Leaner brothers of United Record Distributors (who were also his nephews), he parlayed his popularity into what amounted to first play rights on most black records produced during the

late 1940s and early 1950s. Although record companies (including Chess) chafed at this level of control, none could argue with Benson's capacity to insure a song or artist's popularity; by the early 1950s Chicago was known throughout the industry as the breakout market for black popular music largely because of his influence.[136] The balance of power between the recording industry and black disk jockeys like Benson is best illustrated through the case of payola. Although this practice of payment for record airplay, is seen as a blemish on the legacy of early broadcasters,[137] its growth after the war was indicative of the leverage enjoyed by disk jockeys on the rest of the music industry. As in so many other areas, Benson's circumstances epitomized broader conditions. In 1960, opening his books to stave off official investigation, Benson confirmed that he was receiving nearly a thousand dollars a month from nine different record labels and distributorships, including both Chess and Vee-Jay.[138] No doubt these figures were higher earlier in the decade when Benson's popularity was at its peak.[139]

With standing both in Bronzeville and the transforming music industry, Benson enjoyed an enviable position in relation to sponsors and advertisers. Like Cooper, Benson saw black radio as an instrument of commerce as well as community culture, and devoted time and energy to advertising. With an audience well beyond that of Cooper, though, Benson was able to break new ground: by the late 1940s his list of sponsors included not only local businesses, but national product lines such as Coca-Cola or Schlitz Beer.[140] Because of his appeal, Benson entered year-long contracts with sponsors up into the 1950s: a level of marketing commitment to black communities unheard of at that time.[141] Benson championed the products pitched on his show, on and of air. Black radio star Jack Gibson, who started out working for Benson, recalled his threatened boycotts of South Side bars that did not carry Schlitz or Canadian Ace beer.[142] But he also exercised initiative vis-à-vis advertisers. Given scripted commercials to read on air, Benson would invariably improvise his own versions of the slogans and jingles given to him; a signifying, of sorts, on retail commerce that enhanced his standing among Black Chicago listeners—and customers—all the more.[143] One is tempted, mixing vernacular and history, to see Benson as something of a trickster figure in relation to consumer capital—an image that, given the charged interrelation between race, popular music, and consumption in the last half-century, begs further study.

Tracing Benson's path through local radio, one sees the summit of an infrastructure of cultural production and distribution: a system involving blacks as managers as well as talent. The complexity of this formation becomes clear by noting those "obliged" to Benson for early boosts to their careers. Vivian Carter, cofounder of Vee-Jay Records, first became involved in popular music when she won an amateur disk-jockey contest organized by Benson in 1948.[144]

Both Muddy Waters and Mahalia Jackson, dubious prospects in the eyes of their respective recording companies, received crucial airplay of their earliest hit records from Benson on WGES, again in 1948. That Benson filled this role of cultural *padrone* in post-Depression Black Chicago says as much about the dynamic, variegated nature of black music commerce at the time, as it does about Benson's talent or personal dedication to the development of local popular music.[145] Indeed, the deepened interrelation of genres, performers, and institutions within local black music made possible by Cooper, Benson, and those that followed greatly encouraged replication of that music and those working with it. Black popular music would never again face the disastrous conditions of destitution and near-erasure it faced during the Depression.

Benson was but one of many who made a name in postwar Black Chicago radio. At WGES, Benson was joined by Sam Evans, a graduate of Northwestern University who shared Benson's commitment to promoting local blues on the air. Muddy Waters paid tribute to Evans's support of his music by titling one of his 1951 Chess singles "Evans Shuffle."[146] Competing with Benson and Evans for the local blues fans was Big Bill Hill, who began broadcasting during the 1950s on WOPA in Oak Park, near the emerging West Side black enclave.[147] Hill, like Benson, attracted other talented broadcasters to his station. One of these, McKie Fitzhugh, built on his reputation as Black Chicago's "most popular disk jockey for 1954" by opening the Disk Jockey Show Lounge, a famed jazz bar on 63rd and Cottage Grove Avenue.[148] The story of local jazz disk jockey Daddy-O-Daylie underscores the interrelation between black radio and other levels of the popular music system in an especially rich manner. Holmes Daylie, a bartender in the black-owned DuSable Lounge, was noted for his "rhyming service" when mixing and setting up drinks; and because the hotel upstairs (also black-owned) was a regular stop for touring musicians such as Louis Armstrong, Fats Waller, and Billie Holiday, Daylie became well known in the music community. After DuSable owner Charlie Cole leased the El

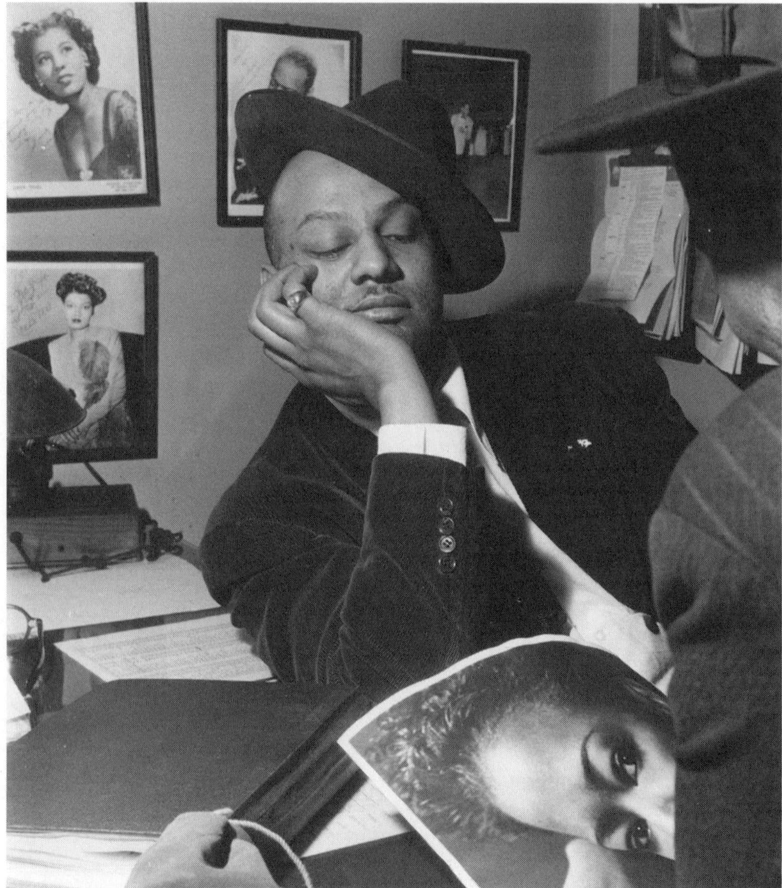

11. McKie Fitzhugh with client in office. Photographed by Wayne F. Miller. Courtesy of Wayne F. Miller.

Grotto Supper Club in 1944 and installed Daylie as bartender, he helped redirect Daylie's career, financing his study at broadcasting school later in the decade. Daylie went on to begin broadcasting at WAIT in 1948, and became one of the most respected (not to mention poetically adept) jazz broadcasters in the country.[149] Augmenting the public affairs work of Cooper were dramatic and news-commentary shows by Oscar Brown Jr., Art McCoo, and Richard Durham such as *Destination Freedom* and *Negro News Front*.[150]

With such dynamic growth in local black broadcasting, it is little wonder that Chicago was soon known as the capital of black radio. Between

1944 and 1956, the number of hours of local, black-appeal broadcasting went up from fifty-six to four hundred.[151] By 1960 six stations would carry shows targeting Bronzeville, with over 125 national businesses advertising on their programs.[152] Across the country, black radio expanded in similar fashion—the number of black disk jockeys nationally went from sixteen in 1946 to over five hundred in 1955.[153] Black Chicago radio continued to serve as fertile ground for imaginative ideas of racial community locally and nationally. After Chess Records began WVON in 1961, the first twenty-four-hour black-appeal station, it hired as broadcasters both Don Cornelius, later host and producer of the legendary syndicated TV dance program *Soul Train,* and Jesse Jackson, the indispensable "political entrepreneur" of the post–civil rights era.[154] Yet, as with most stories of resonant black vernacular culture, it is finally ironic how thoroughly these "authentic" forms became part of broader U.S. cultural practice. By the mid-1950s the on-air style of Al Benson, Daddy-O-Daylie, and others—along with their blues, jazz, and rhythm and blues playlists—were being used by white broadcasters all over the nation, fundamentally transforming the meaning of postwar music for both popular audiences and commercial producers.

In discussions of contemporary mergers of major media groups one often finds reference to the notion of verticality. This idea—where circulation of a product is assured through coordination of several lines or vehicles of dissemination so that a product is flooded through multiple markets simultaneously—has long been a buzzword of cultural corporate restructuring. It's a dismal feature of life in the late capital world, as any parent confronted with still another line of movie tie-in toys available at McDonald's or Burger King can attest. Yet the idea has intriguing historical parallels—in the utilization of Hollywood stars as representatives of various product lines in the 1940s and 1950s for example, or the appearance of musical artists signed to record labels in affiliated visual or sound media. Such arrangements of marketing and distribution point out how intertwined culture and commerce have been in this country throughout the past century.

With this in mind, one might call the variegated music infrastructure in post-Depression Chicago the first vertical phase of African-American cultural commerce. Clearly, other vibrant networks of black clubs and venues, and other compelling genres and groups of black artists, predated those discussed in this chapter, in Chicago and elsewhere. But no prior place or time enjoyed the diverse, interwoven modes of circulation—points of entry, as has been shown, often managed by blacks themselves—that

Bronzeville did after 1940. This should not be seen only as evidence of another cultural renaissance, like that in Harlem during the 1920s. Attuned to shifts and changes in the industry at the time, the local black music community underwent, to borrow Mike Rowe's term, a historically unique process of rationalization. Because of these developments, genres of music could more effectively borrow from one another—hence the interchanges between gospel, blues, and later soul that many see as the hallmark of black musical modernization. As well, individuals—both hidden working-class talents such as Dinah Washington or Daddy-O-Daylie, and migrant artists such as Muddy Waters or Quincy Jones—found themselves able to move into an efficient system of training and promotion, leading to unprecedented opportunities for both personal success and public fulfillment. Ultimately, all of these conditions deepened black popular music as a professional and commercial context, redefining meanings of work, art, and community along the way. One can see within Black Chicago music hints of a similarly sophisticated apparatus, one that forced a restructuring of those same corporate systems believed historically beyond the reach of African Americans.

With the development of the black music commerce in Chicago came a deeply altered vocabulary of race. At a most basic level, the rationalization of black music encouraged standardization of race culture across the United States, allowing African Americans to share a more simultaneous—a more national—sense of existence. Certainly this is shown in the salience of Chicago's musical genres themselves as signs of racial identity, from blues to gospel to soul. The evolution of these genres through a decidedly commercial process helped introduce still another idea of racial collectivity—that of the consumer market—which, at least at the time, promised legitimating, if less than liberatory, outcomes for postmigration blacks. The world of race popular music in Chicago was, now more explicitly and unapologetically, shaped by those who saw themselves as both artists and entrepreneurs. Rooted in these developments was perhaps the most far-reaching change within post-Depression black music, reworking presumptions of how and by whom common senses of racial identity were constructed.

In his celebrated work on the nature and history of African-American music, LeRoi Jones stated categorically, "such a thing as a middle-class blues singer is almost unheard of. It is, it seems to me, almost a contradiction in terms."[155] To what extent this statement, read over the broad sweep of twentieth-century black music from early vaudeville to modern bars and clubs, captures the long relationship of race, class, and culture remains open to debate. Looking at Black Chicago after 1940, though, one sees that while those working with the blues—or popular music as a whole—were generally not middle class in strict sociological terms, they pursued their crafts and modeled their careers along lines of entrepreneurship and commercial ambition. Indeed, one can see within Black Chicago some resolution of the contradiction put forth by Jones. Without such aspirant identifications, one could hardly imagine musicians in black Chicago reaching the level of artistic and professional development that has marked their fame for over half a century. As we move beyond local black music, these connections between cultural entrepreneurship and collective racial imagination—a symbiosis, in a sense, of black production and black vernacular—become more significant.

THE ENDS OF CLIENTAGE

CHAPTER THREE

The leader not of one race, but of two.
W. E. B. DU BOIS

Though the venerated Defender *newspaper is generally seen as the local exemplar of the black weekly press, the Associated Negro Press wire service offered better demonstration of Chicago's intrinsic relation of local race journalism to the national scene in the 1940s. Source of features, editorials, photos, and cartoons for scores of African-American papers across the country, the ANP was a unique measure of scope of the midcentury black press, and testament to the increasingly pivotal role of local journalism in transforming structures of African-American consciousness, in and beyond Chicago.*

This chapter considers the ANP during and after World War II, through its founder and leader Claude Barnett. Barnett, more so than any other figure in this study, represented a bridge between old and new sensibilities regarding black group life. An indefatigable racial emissary like his mentor, Booker T. Washington, Barnett nonetheless retained ties with major progressive and even radical voices among African Americans, including several on his staff. Devoted to old protocols of cross-racial sponsorship and underwriting, he nonetheless pushed to devise new modes of mass communi-

Facing page: 12. A young Claude Barnett. Courtesy of the Claude Barnett Collection/Chicago Historical Society (ICHi-16313).

cation geared toward still-exclusionary media like film and television. As with the American Negro Exposition that he had devoted himself to throughout 1940, Barnett saw most of his more ambitious initiatives at the Associated Negro Press bear less than full fruit. In particular, his embrace of the cultural and political mandates of the cold war proved something of a straightjacket for his several endeavors, and also for the sustained editorial independence of the ANP. More autonomous and institutionally viable forms of local press power would shortly succeed Barnett's and the ANP's pioneering efforts. Yet in many cases, these success stories repeated many of the innovative steps taken by the wire service, underscoring how it constituted a crucial template for the emergence of Chicago as African America's cultural capital during this time.

ANP founder Claude Barnett's story reads at first glance like a race-angled dime story: struggling young man calls on luck and pluck to find success if not, as would prove the case with later rivals, legendary wealth. The bootstrap ring of his story and of Associated Negro Press, suggests at once the comfort and confines of traditional black values. Through a century when African Americans overturned stereotypes of dependency and accommodation, Barnett's actions seemed to recall earlier days. He maintained a pioneer's stake in the party of Lincoln, even if his affinity for the intermittent race progressivism of the New Deal complicates assessments of him as a stalwart Republican.[1] Proud graduate of Tuskegee Institute, Barnett recalled his 1932 installation as school trustee—the first alumnus to be so honored—as his "signal achievement."[2] And using backroom skills to quell controversies and fast-track careers much as Booker T. Washington had earlier, Barnett proved arguably the school's most exemplary graduate of the twentieth century. Little wonder that Claude Barnett has proved awkward and even anachronistic for most scholars, a residual of the old life among blacks rather than an exemplar of the new.

Yet, despite (or more probably because of) his moderation, Barnett established a key role in the remaking of Black Chicago public culture as a national idiom through the 1940s and 1950s. Because of the nodal role his Associated Negro Press filled for black newspapers across the country, Barnett and his staff epitomized Chicago's growing function as transmitting metropolis. Most of this period's significant events and conditions converted to news copy through the press offices on South Parkway, while many more delicate developments drew Barnett's own discreet attentions. The singular scope of ANP—the most ambitious black press institution in the country before the advent of Johnson Publishing—assured its solicitation by a range of parties, including industrialists, labor activists, the State

Department, diplomatic offices, composers, writers, actors, conservative educators, left activists, inveterate nationalists, and unrepentant assimilators. Thus Barnett's ANP provides further important evidence of Chicago's role as pivot for black imagination (and imaginings about blacks) across the country. Yet mitigating its potent institutional effect were crippling material limitations. Barnett, according to Lawrence Hogan, routinely played the frustrated entrepreneur, searching for projects and partnerships that might put ANP on sound financial footing. This campaign to diversify, premonition of Johnson Publishing's blueprint a few years later, highlights the high stakes and uncertain prospects for black cultural enterprise during and after the war.[3]

Both in his old school brokerage between the races, and his desire to locate a more autonomous sense of base, Barnett offers revealing study in what Adolph Reed calls the "custodial approach" to black leadership and politics at a moment when its efficacy was coming under question.[4] Embedded within the clientage premise structuring race relations since Booker T. Washington, definition of the race leader as custodian was a familiar arrangement for Barnett, given his years at Tuskegee. More broadly, it posed a pressing question generally within Black Chicago. For all the rich institutional ferment marking local black life since the eve of the Great

13. Claude Barnett's induction as a trustee of Tuskegee Institute, 1932. Barnett is at the far right. Courtesy of the Claude Barnett Collection/Chicago Historical Society (ICHi-16316).

Migration, it remained, in a number of key ways, a formation beholden to white underwriting and oversight. Classic mechanisms of migrant socialization, from machine politics to industrial welfare, mandated that virtually all manifestations of cultural and social life among Chicago's blacks carry some determinate sense of obligation to the surrounding population of white folk. As we saw in the previous chapter, even in the dense cultural world of black music, the racial vector presumed to be impossible to eradicate in fact traced a dense web of interracial associations. There, the music's protean nature allowed an occasional upper hand to remain with African Americans, leveraging determinate exercise of both technologies and syntaxes of cultural meaning. Matters were more complex in the circles of public media and institutional power that Barnett interfaced with: the perpetual struggle was to somehow avoid "cross[ing] the line from accommodation to complicity."[5]

In the end, Barnett's success in respecting this line proved mixed: in part due to his own equivocation and the contradictions of the ANP; in part due to the strong press of historical factors, chief among which was the impact of the demands of the cold war on his work. The course of the ANP during this period charted the dilemmas implicit in attempts to generate both a viable institutional base for expansive black cultural work, more than they did its successes. Yet the often tortuous course of the enterprise and its leaders anticipated the initiatives and constituent elements of later and more consequential local black media. Barnett and ANP's story, then served as rehearsal for those entities that better demonstrated Chicago's centrality to black life in a modern, postmigration period, and its greater autonomy.

Born in Florida in 1890, Barnett was technically a migrant, but lived in Chicago for virtually all his life. His history is well documented in Lawrence Hogan's thorough biography and need not be recounted in detail here. Yet three early phases stand out for their reinforcement of a custodial approach to racial leadership and progress. Each of these moved Barnett toward benefactors and role models who were often white, offering useful explanation of his later tendency to mediate between racially separated worlds, and as well to sustain a vexed relationship with race-conscious positions throughout his later work at the press.

First, Barnett's faith in the powers of clientage hearkened past his Tuskegee days. Though moved by stories of free ancestors' flight north to avoid reenslavement, or of grandparents withstanding racial threats while living in downstate Illinois, Barnett's outlook was shaped by white beneficence more so than supremacist aggression. Hired in 1902 at "an impressionable age" as houseboy to Richard Sears, partner in the legendary mail order and department store, Barnett worked summers in the Chicago home store's grocery ("the only colored employee who was not a janitor"), received tickets to theaters and concerts (another exceptional perk, given the segregation codes of downtown entertainments at the time), and enjoyed the sponsorship of one of the nation's captains of retail industry. Such privileges often encouraged in other blacks an arrogant sense of distinction from the race group, as documented by Willard Gatewood, among others. Barnett, it seems, never permitted elite affiliations to degenerate into a complex of color aristocracy. What did emerge, though, was an unshakable faith in the tactical advantages of racial patronage. As Barnett struggled later in life with various collaborators—white and black—and pursued partnerships within and across racial lines, he invariably found his last, best advantage in the influence of sponsors from the white world. Tellingly, this left him incapable of envisioning black advance without the push of helping hands from beyond the color line. This would prove at once the basis for his near-unrivaled influence as a black power broker, and a stubborn ceiling on bids to achieve both personal and institutional autonomy in his later work with the press.

This comfort with patronage deepened, predictably, during Barnett's undergraduate years. No other black institution—educational, political, or otherwise—exemplified the racial clientage philosophy as did Tuskegee Institute. W. E. B. Du Bois's doubled-edged compliment of its founder, Booker T. Washington, as the leader of "not one race but of two" summarized the deft if unsustainable interracial dance Washington joined with numerous white benefactors.[6] Barnett, rapidly funneled to the school's inner sanctums, wrote rhapsodically of its leader's example, calling Washington's Sunday addressed to the student body "inspiring visits with genius" and using a post as student assistant to "[drink] in the magic of his strength, his vision, his matchless wisdom."[7] Barnett's impressions of life at Tuskegee were perhaps tested by severe challenges to Tuskegee's authority that emerged during his years there: Monroe Trotter's relentless and sensational critiques of its leader, Du Bois's more measured—and more devastating—analysis of Washington in *Souls of Black Folk,* and the emergence of the Niagara movement in 1905 that led to the founding of the NAACP. Yet Tuskegee stubbornly persevered through these trials, remaining relevant during—and long after—Barnett's enrollment. Washington's successors as university president, Robert Russa Moton and Fred Patterson, remained ex officio members of black and interracial leadership circles through the mid 1940s, and Tuskegee itself enjoyed an inordinate share of resources and attention from white America, especially the federal government. Surely Tuskegee's long if underestimated importance to an increasingly federally managed mode of U.S. race relations are among many lessons that Barnett took from his undergraduate years.

The third noteworthy aspect of Barnett's early experience redirects our attention from white largesse to the resources of black institutions, though this final element spoke more to the costs of interracial competition than the windfalls of racial solidarity. Alongside early ventures such as his Douglass Specialty mail-order portrait company and partnership (with Washington's former assistant Emmett Scott) in the Kashmir Cosmetics Company, Barnett worked with the *Chicago Defender,* promoting the paper's out-of-town customers and advertisers. With his affinity for influential company, it was natural that Barnett would gravitate to the most dynamic media concern of the day. The *Defender* and its founder Robert S. Abbott were acknowledged catalysts of the Great Migration, standard bearers of militancy during World War I, and audacious translators of Washingtonian accomodationism into a broad credo of autonomy, to the point where the paper seemed a synonym for the New Negro ideal emergent at this time. Traveling on doctor's orders in 1918 to remedy work-related exhaustion, Barnett characteristically recuperated by barnstorming the West on the *Defender*'s behalf. Talks with local agents made clear that blacks across the country found the paper "a sort of beacon of hope pointing the way to a new day."[8] When Barnett returned to Chicago with ideas for a national black news service, he sought partnership with the *Defender,* hoping to access its resources in exchange for rationalizing the paper's thousands of small town stringers into a comprehensive wire service for African Americans.[9] No doubt this would have secured the *Defender*'s flagship position in race journalism for decades to come. Nonetheless, despite enthusiastic endorsement from advisors, Abbott rejected Barnett's proposal out of hand, initiating a feud that continued until Abbott's death in 1940. In this case the lesson learned was one of intraracial rancor, rather than racial cooperation, leaving Barnett slow to endorse later offers of cooperation from other blacks.

The Associated Negro Press was founded in March of 1919, with a press announcement and an inaugural packet of stories sent out to eighty charter members. It weathered the *Defender*'s opposition, the ravages of the Depression, and other trials to reach a peak of 112 papers served nationally in 1945. Declining thereafter, it still counted 78 papers as members in 1952, with a combined circulation of two million subscribers. For initiation fees and graduated monthly payments, member papers received features, releases, opinion columns, and photographs totaling from twenty-five to forty pages, once or twice a week. Included were some of the most recognized features in black journalism. Hampton Institute economics professor Gordon Hancock coined the term "double duty dollar" in his column "Between the Lines," which the press began syndicating in 1940. William Pickens, field secretary of the NAACP from the mid-1930s until the early 1940s, also ran a regular column. When Frank Marshall Davis served as assistant editor of ANP from 1935 to 1948, he wrote or commissioned book, theater, and music reviews recognized by artists as exemplars of incisive comment. Louis Jordan spoke for many others when he thanked the press in 1949, claiming that he "owed much of [his] popularity" to reviewers like those at the press "who've kept my name before the public."[10]

Though the ANP's actual staff remained small—at no point did the personnel based in the Chicago office total more than eight—ANP generated a reliable and substantial service for its members. A reciprocity clause instituted shortly after the press's founding enabled releases to be gathered from member papers all across the country. To be sure, this was similar to how individual papers like the *Defender* established interregional coverage and audience simultaneously during the Great Migration. Still, ANP delivered a markedly better product: trained editors and staff writers, after all, could provide copy-ready releases more effectively than the legions of salesmen, small town ministers, and rail porters making up the *Defender*'s army of stringers, as well as those of the other black papers. Correspondents based across the United States and in other countries—including Haiti, India, France, England, Ethiopia, Liberia, South Africa, and colonized African territories—augmented this coverage through space-rate dispatches. As Brenda Gayle Plummer points out, the ANP's foreign dispatches were crucial to extending blacks' collective interest and stake in world affairs during the 1930s, a crucial precursor to demonstrations of black civic dissent during World War II.[11] Sports, entertainment, labor news, and vindicationist chronicling of black "firsts" helped round out the coverage, which was uniformly praised (even by rival black newspaper publishers throughout the 1930s and 1940s) as a unique resource in the world of black media and public information. Recalling how ANP "prided itself on mirroring black activities everywhere," Frank Marshall Davis declared that, in spite of various difficulties, he still marveled "at the comprehensiveness of our operation."[12]

Yet though gratifying, praise and accolades could not pay the bills. Throughout its long history, the ANP rarely broke even, running annual deficits at times approaching the thousands of dollars. Barnett observed ruefully that the press "produced so little revenue that every worker in the Chicago office held an extra job in order to make a living." The Depression and its effect on subscribers' capacity to pay fees increasingly obscured the humor in this arrangement.[13] Though the service was forced at times to play the heavy, as when Barnett invoked a sixty-day termination deadline on the account of L. C. Bates, *Arkansas Gazette* editor and husband of NAACP branch president activist Daisy Bates, rarely were such threats actually carried out.[14] The result was a well-respected yet cash-poor institution, with scant prospects to translate its reputation into material security. Attractive proposals for developing the services offerings generally went unrealized. Exemplary was W. E. B. Du Bois's offer to provide a serial "letter of interpretation" beginning in 1939—regretfully declined by Barnett due to the press's inability to offer the author a "fair sum" for his uniquely expert perspective.[15]

The hand-to-mouth conditions that the ANP generally labored under compelled Barnett to search incessantly for means of diversification or synergy. Though the wire service did yeoman's work in providing the vital nourishment of features, releases, and columns to black newspapers across the country during a period many remember as their apex of development, the institutional limits that plagued them similarly constrained the ANP. Increasingly, the service found it difficult to avoid shading coverage in order to accommodate and indulge the more powerful institutions, creating conditions of occasional journalistic compromise that not only reflected the old guard stance of its founder, but as well deeper dilemmas around the unstable balance between independent voice and material security that defined the black press into the 1940s.

The ANP's approach to the interests of black workers around the start of the 1940s gives some indication of the compromises of the time. There is little question that Barnett reproduced an outlook on labor politics inherited from Tuskegee days. Scholars agree that Barnett was among the most damaging opponents that black sleeping car porters faced in their struggle to gain and defend union recognition during the 1920s and 1930s. Barnett's own files reveal an almost uninterrupted campaign to stunt the efforts that eventually yielded the first black-organized national union of the twentieth century. This campaign included the founding of *Heebie Jeebies*, the Pullman company-funded journal that delivered promanagement positions directly to black porters, as well as frequent efforts on the part of Barnett to deliver intelligence, accomplishments, and weak points in the organizing drive to Pullman company executives.[16] Eager to effect alliances with powerful whites, Barnett strove to position his organization as witness to corporate fair play and reform, even when such accounts strained the truth. Barnett's contacts with local war industries during the early years of World War II demonstrate the point. Barnett was no stranger to companies like U.S. Steel, Inland, and other metalworks industries, having offered in 1936 to publish apologias on conditions for black workers at their plants, so as to parry organizing drives by the Steel Workers Organizing Committee (SWOC), working with the Congress of Industrial Organization (CIO).[17] With nationwide conversion and expansion of production to meet Allied war needs at the close of the decade, Barnett renewed these contacts. The National Association of Manufacturers, the main lobby for industrial firms, was forwarded offers to publish favorable stories on clients' hiring and promotion of African-American workers in the first years of wartime conversion.[18] Renewing his old ties with the Pullman Company, Barnett arranged in 1942 to have articles fed to the *Chicago Sun Times* celebrating the firm's employment of black labor as it shifted its production line over to the manufacture of warplanes.[19] Similar proposals went to U.S. Steel, who while demurring that focus on the general situation of black workers would distract attention from "activities to win the war," did reaffirm support of antidiscrimination and forward contacts for the company's oldest black employee, laborer Ward Fisher, employed thirty-seven years at the South Works plant near Gary.[20]

Of course, such accounts of job access and fair treatment clashed with the larger picture of wartime labor politics well known to African Americans at this time. The 1941 March on Washington movement, followed by black press and progressive leaders' monitoring of the Fair Employment Practices Commission (FEPC), meant that industrial resistance to hiring blacks was well known within the black public, as if years of discriminatory practice had not already made it clear. Figures from 1941 had documented deplorable conditions across the country, nowhere more than Chicago, where 71,000 African Americans—well over half the working-age population—remaining on relief despite the war-generated upturn in local manufacturing output.[21] More than a year after Roosevelt's ban of war industry discrimination, the picture remained mixed. Large aeronautical companies in Kansas City, Cincinnati, and California hired black workers in disappointing numbers despite the executive order, while Baltimore, with a population of 167,000 African Americans, maintained a cap on black hiring even though local manpower needs exceeded 35,000.[22] And for those black workers fortunate enough to gain entry to war production, prospects of equal compensation, much less promotion, were dim indeed. Ward Fisher's story, for whom thirty-seven years at U.S. Steel had won only shifts from one laborer's post to another, was the rule more than the exception for black war workers nationally. Given this deflating record, Barnett's willingness to launder heavy industry's record seems a troubling example of his affinity for old-style clientage, even as the ANP's own releases outlining hiring discrimination during the war argued the ultimate futility of this course.

Barnett was not alone in establishing editorial policy on these and other issues during the early 1940s. Frank Marshall Davis, well established as a progressive journalist and trenchant realist writer before assuming the editor's seat at ANP in 1935, was the latest in a line of strong editors with whom Barnett had collaborated. Davis's own leanings were as pronounced toward militant criticism as Barnett's were toward cooperation. He reported protests by black workers against discriminatory conditions, like the brief strike by 1500 black workers making armor plate at American Steel's East Chicago factories in July 1943. He notified Truman Gibson at the War Department in April 1942 that German-American stewards had made pro-Axis comments aboard the Santa Fe Railway line as they passed through areas in California, where thousands of Japanese Americans were interred as a threat to national security.[23] Clearly there were occasions when Davis's partisan spirit compelled Barnett to pull rank, as in 1948 when he reprimanded his editor for soliciting denunciations from other race leaders of red-baiting comments by Secretary of Labor Lewis Schwellenbach. Admonishing Davis not to allow his "own activities" to cause controversy, Barnett reiterated his own moderate doctrine, advising that the press "keep free and to the middle of the road."[24] Yet given Barnett's own conservatism, it is surprising that such clashes were not more frequent with Davis, or others in his organization of reporters, columnists, and stringers. Barnett's accommodation, then, proved able on occasion to accommodate diverse African-American opinion even as it catered to the paternalistic conceit of his white benefactors.

If Claude Barnett's precepts were branches of the Tuskegee root, his journalistic method was different—answerable to diverse black outlooks as well as to white elite demands for deference. Despite his stake in client/broker style of race politics, Barnett was fluent in the languages of black dissent, and well respected within its circles. Though early communications with Paul and Eslanda Robeson bordered on the presumptuous, with Barnett hectoring the performer to engage local Chicago clergy's condemnation of his "communistic views," by 1942 Barnett was encouraging Essie Robeson to refute skeptical remarks regarding racial grievances attributed to Pearl Buck.[25] In 1949, the ANP would circulate supportive reports of a benefit in Chicago before several thousand listeners, where Paul

Robeson dismissed controversy over his alleged remarks at the Paris Peace Conference that spring.[26] Thyra Edwards, promoter of Spanish Civil War relief and friend of Barnett, wrote thanking the press for their contributions to the loyalists' cause.[27] Alpha Phi Alpha leader Luther Peck invited Barnett in 1943 to hear New York councilmen Benjamin Davis—perhaps the most radical elected official, black or white, in the country—speak to a local Chicago audience. Though Barnett declined to attend, he called Davis principled, and predicted that the councilmen's "viewpoint should stir the thinking of some of the conservatives and tories with whom we abound."[28] Barnett himself had begun to call old allegiances into question as early as the eve of the 1940 election, observing to Albion Holsey that neither Democrats nor Republicans "seem to be doing the deuce of a lot for the brethren," and elaborating that while Roosevelt struck him as "only a politician," his respect for exposition ally and Vice President Henry Wallace provided sufficient incentive to refrain from opposing the sitting administration.[29]

Two exchanges indicate Barnett's ambidextrous sense of alignment, as well as his role as racial consigliere. In February 1941, Richard Wright wrote Barnett seeking ANP's help in arranging a three month assignment in Russia, China, and India. Asserting that since war's outbreak "the center of gravity of Western civilization has shifted from Europe to the Americas and Asia," Wright proposed to "get stories of how the brown, red and yellow people are faring . . . and how their attitudes are likely to influence the outcome of the war in Europe." Plans to write a ten-part series of dispatches circulating among member newspapers elicited "deep interest, even thrill" from Barnett in Chicago. Though scattered postings of African-American journalists, particularly J. A. Rogers's accounts of Italy's invasion of Ethiopia in 1936, had raised expectations as to the black press's global scope and capacity, never before had a figure of such renown set out after a story of such international portent. Wright's fame, evident the past summer at the exposition, had reached an apex with his January receipt of the NAACP's Spingarn Medal—the summit honor reserved for African Americans nationally—causing the writer to muse that, despite his radicalism, "the public is catching up to me."[30]

Yet the shared enthusiasm of Wright, Barnett, and the ANP could not close the deal in the end. With visas and publication agreements secured, the project hit a snag when Barnett wrote directly to Secretary of State Cordell Hull asking that Wright's passport request be expedited "on the same basis [as] other distinguished writers." The State Department responded by tabling the proposal: technically in protest against Soviet restriction of American journalists, yet also due to the insurgent potential of such color-conscious war coverage.[31] What would have been Wright's first trip overseas and to date the most ambitious foreign assignment undertaken within the black press, never came to fruition. Wright maintained contact with Barnett, requesting an ANP press card in 1948 for travels in both Europe and Africa, and offering to send reports on conditions for Africans and New World Blacks in his new home of Paris. Here, too, Barnett would be disappointed as well: follow-up letters to Wright asking to restart talks on a more developed relation with the service went unanswered. But just that Wright had sought out Barnett to generate, as Barnett put it, "a broad picture of what is happening to black people"—a project that later informed books such as *The Color Curtain*, *Black Power*, and *White Man, Listen!*—speaks to the ANP's utility to dissident as well as conservative expressions of black worldview.[32]

The second exchange of communications involved another noted writer: the irrepressible Zora Neale Hurston. Though averse to the ideological orbits favored by Wright, Hurston was no stranger to controversy. Consider her purported remarks on Southern race relations in 1943. Interviewed by New York *World-Telegram* staff writer Douglass Gilbert in February upon the release of her autobiography *Dust Tracks on the Road*, Hurston was quoted as calling conditions for blacks better in the South than the North. The statement, fodder for Hurston's most passionate detractors at the time and a vexing topic for Hurston scholars since, was a surprise to Hurston herself. Writing Barnett shortly after the story's run, Hurston denied having made any apology for Southern segregation, admitting only to terming it "frankly established." If anything, Hurston ventured, she sought to debunk optimistic claims as to blacks' situation in the North, revealed through personal experience to have its own problems. Terming the article "twisted and untrue," Hurston asserted dramatically she was "now a bitter person" in the wake of the controversy: "Since my god of tolerance has forsaken me, I am ready for anything to overthrow Anglo-Saxon supremacy, however desperate. I have become what I never wished to be, a good hater." Barnett's brief and sympathetic response promised to "do the sort of thing that we believe will be most helpful."[33]

As with Wright, no definitive resolution came of Barnett's ministry to Hurston's plight, certainly nothing that satisfied the aggrieved author, who descended into seclusion, and found herself cast as apologist for southern segregation several times later. Yet in both cases, the sense of access attending Hurston and Wright's communications say much about their regard for Barnett's empathy and potential intercession. Too, that such distinct registers of race politics—exemplifying global and local black perspectives of the day—found their way to Barnett's desk underscores, above all, his wide engagement of black opinion and life. Increasingly after the Depression, Barnett received similar requests for intervention. In 1939, Bill "Bonjangles" Robinson sought guidance on handling a feud with Will Rogers over racist remarks attributed to the "Cowboy Philosopher," while Hattie McDaniel enlisted the ANP to circulate an open letter defending her role in *Gone With the Wind* as a period tribute to black womanhood, resonant with "the common laborer, the washerwoman, and the cook" rather than "our social register people."[34] Pacifist organizer Bayard Rustin wrote in 1952 requesting letters of introduction for an extended trip to North and West Africa. His meetings while there with Nigeria's anticolonial leader Nnamdi Azikiwe were no doubt enabled in part by Barnett: Azikiwe was listed at this time as the ANP's correspondent in Lagos.[35] Barnett's work as counsel and facilitator recalled earlier interventions on behalf of the exposition, enhancing ANP's role as nexus for black public life across the country.

This integrating function corresponded to larger amalgamative trends in black life and imagination. African Americans during and after World War II often enacted nationalization tactically, in relation to strategies of collective advance.[36] Cooperation between the ANP and key blacks integrated in the formal machinery of the state demonstrate the significance of Barnett's own nationalizing vision. Though his work with the exposition suggested strengthened collaboration between government and African Americans, other indices—the lack of enforcement of victories for the FEPC or the frequency of stateside assaults on black troops, to name but two recurrent story lines for the ANP—cautioned that such hopes were premature. Especially disturbing was the persistence of employment discrimination within the federal system itself. According to Desmond King, the first half of the 1940s found blacks excluded from skilled, permanent staff positions in the civil work force, as they had been since the start of the Wilson administration in 1913. Advisory posts like those assumed by Barnett and Truman Gibson in 1942 were contingent: the impact of blacks on the federal job culture of the early 1940s therefore remained as minimal as in earlier years. Surveys conducted by the FEPC, whose jurisdiction included federal offices along with war industries, provided a dismal picture. In late 1942, although 22 percent of the Treasury Department's 32,000 employees were African American, only one was hired in a position classified as professional: the rest were either junior clerical or, more commonly, custodial or general labor. Overall, only 1.8 percent of the federal workers accounted for by the FEPC in 1942 were African Americans above junior or custodial job classes, with most of these temporary appointments slated to end once the war was over.[37]

Yet there were exceptions to these early conditions; ones which Barnett quickly identified and called on. Though the Commerce Department's record conformed to these deplorable norms in hiring, among its few black professional staff was Joseph Houchins, specialist on Negro statistics at the Census Bureau starting in the mid-1930s.[38] Houchins proved central in pushing the Census Bureau to research change in black population and social patterns, resulting in race conscious data and analysis never seen before. These releases proved invaluable to the ANP, which was in need of reliable statistics concerning black life given the flux of renewed mass migration to Chicago and the rest of country. Bulletins organized by Houchins detailed diversification of the national population, rates of black urbanization, and isolated characteristics of African Americans as a group. His studies included birth and death rates, improved literacy rates, decline in agricultural workers and increase in professionals and entrepreneurs, all intended to offer "a basis for evaluating the progress of the nation's largest racial minority."[39] Barnett and his staff pursued these connections actively, regularly requesting bulletins until Houchins's office was eliminated by the Commerce Department—a move protested for several months by ANP.[40]

Given the civil service bars affecting blacks through the 1940s, accounts such as those of Joseph Houchins must be kept in proper perspective. At the same time, the manner in which his work intersected the aspirations of Barnett and the ANP encourages closer consideration. Standard accounts of the modern quest for African-American citizenship trace a dramatic, agential historical arc: one where legal desegregation of public education, consolidation of franchise rights and, in later decades, election of a critical mass of black officials plot the unbroken ascent of blacks' civil standing. This validation is routinely read, as with other chapters of African-American history, as the expression of collective will more so than the result of structural shifts in perspective or condition. Yet common to all operative national and civil communities are arrangements of meaning conveying those communities in credible form. Among the most fundamental claims, for instance, governments rely upon to affirm legitimacy is their ability to account for population and resources comprehensively; to represent the sum total of a country's constituent parts, be they resources, currencies, or inhabitants. Censuses, then, constitute exemplary instruments of public order and authority, especially given their capacity, as Ted Porter notes, to rationalize the most unstable and obscure social contexts.[41] Censuses demonstrate particular effectiveness in containing claims related to race identification, for as Benedict Anderson observes, enumeration in both national and colonial contexts endorses racial classification, so long as all those counted declare "one—and only one—extremely clear place" in the administered order.[42] Seen in this light, census making becomes a crucial instrument of state will—a system of flexible surveillance and hegemony[43]—to the extent that one might question what benefit Houchins, Barnett, or the black press gained ultimately from viewing group life through its lens.

But there were other dimensions to the ANP's reliance upon federal enumeration, ones that demonstrated the census's susceptibility to appropriation, as well as the constraints of civil identification for African Americans. Traditionally, enumeration was an act imposed upon black folk, whether through plantation logs of slaves or turn-of-the-century insurance schedules of fatality rates, to justify denial of rights or services on a racial basis.[44] Government had proven no ally to African Americans in mitigating the adverse effects of these pejorative applications of numbers and statistics. Only the efforts of black educators such as Monroe Work at Tuskegee Institute or W. E. B. Du Bois at Atlanta University offered what might be termed appreciative enumeration of black life before the Depression. Thus when Barnett and the ANP drew on Houchins's efforts, they not only enriched black media coverage, but also helped concretize greater responsibility and interest on the part of the state in addressing African Americans in civil terms. The authority derived from census reports and bulletins also standardized reports of transforming black life that Barnett, the ANP and member newspapers proffered—especially those representing black community in integrated national terms. The same appeal to statistical law that routinized the most volatile political environments, then, could also consolidate, however momentarily, minority publics. This proved an important resource to the ANP—and would prove crucial again later to subsequent enterprises like Johnson Publishing.

Ultimately, appeal to the state's enumerative authority hastened the rise of new techniques of social management of blacks as a group, coordinated now from seats of federal power rather than the plantation ledger or the actuary's desk. As the twentieth century progressed, regimes of numbers served to mire black families within the welfare system, consign African Americans to underresourced housing and schools, and, most recently, fast-track black convicts through the criminal justice system. These outcomes are among the most compelling contemporary demonstrations of what Michel Foucault calls "governmentality," where social authority modernizes past the traditional form of sovereignty by redefining subjects en masse as "population," "labor force," "electorate"—and even "race"—eliminating the need to personify authority, and forcing constituents to abide their abstraction and, increasingly, their abjection.[45] The outcomes listed above resulting from the enhanced interchange between blacks and the state, impacting blacks in Chicago as dramatically as anywhere else in the country, surely exceeded the vision for Barnett and his staff as they consulted Joseph Houchins at the Census Bureau. For them, the prospect of better registering blacks' activity in civil life, and representing the amalgamation of black local life into an integral, nationalized whole would have seemed the only factors relevant to the new categories of information. Like so many other aspects of blacks' increased involvement in civil life through the latter half of the twentieth century, their enumeration ultimately proved a double-edged sword.

Federal offices such as the Census Bureau offered one impetus for complicating ideas of African-American community, and more ambitious definition of blacks' relation to national life generally. But Washington was not the only site inspiring broader understandings of black collective life and condition. Throughout the twentieth century media structures proved as important as civil institutions in codifying norms of collective identity and motive. Of these, film proved the most attractive as a topic of coverage for the ANP during and after the 1940s. Yet the difficulties experienced by the service in covering motion pictures say much about the structural contradictions and limitations of the ANP, and also about addressing the culture and industry of American film from a race angle.

Even by standards of the day, conditions for African Americans in film to the late years of the Depression were regressive. The widespread assumption that blacks were invisible within pre-1940s cinema is somewhat misleading. Blacks appeared in the scores if not hundreds in B-features such as *Trader Horn* and *Tarzan*, animated volatile Depression-era urban backdrops as hustlers and sporting types, and above all epitomized the servant/confidant, a rehearsal of the time-honored trope of Uncle Tom as shepherd to whites' realization of character.[46] The issue, then, was not *whether* blacks appeared in movies through the 1930s, but *how* they appeared, and toward what ends of prejudice and racist conceit. This degrading state seemed foreordained even when blacks' talents were duly acknowledged: the sound revolution in film in the late 1920s encouraged studios at first to seek out African Americans for voice-over work, because of the industry legend that they recorded better than whites.[47] As time went on, even undisputed first-generation talents like Clarence Muse, Lorraine Beavers, Rex Ingram, and Barnett's own wife Etta Moton found themselves relegated to obsequious type-cast roles or cattle-call positions as primitive extras or silent walk-ons. Several conditions explain the studios' pronounced taste for racial subordination: the anxiety of film moguls over threats of regulation by the southern-dominated Congress; the appeal at the time of the plantation idyll in expressive forms ranging from novel to textbook; the personal prejudice of tastemakers like MGM head Louis Mayer, and the equivalent racism of the majority of white audience members. Whatever the case, Michael Denning's suggestion that "the Southern" was, for film, as definitive an evocation of region as "the Western" would not have seemed off base to African-American performers of the day, given their disheartening circumstances.[48]

According to Thomas Cripps, the institution best positioned to challenge this arrangement was the black press. Well aware that public boycott of film had begun with the NAACP's 1915 campaign against *Birth of a Nation,* studios were more loath to excite black public opinion than their product suggested, as courteous replies to Barnett's entreaties to studios in the run-up to the 1940 exposition indicated. Such conditions anticipated emergence of a generation of uncompromising African-American critics and watchdogs, given growing black urban audiences and expanding journalistic coverage of the arts. Several reviewers, like Dan Burley of the *Amsterdam News,* sought to develop what Cripps would later call a "black cinema aesthetic" through their criticism. Most African Americans engaged with film review in the black press, however, wrote in a manner that paralleled the on-screen obsequiousness of black actors. All credits, however undignified, were extolled as pioneering breakthroughs. Published copy was taken verbatim from studio publicity releases. To be sure, the short-staffed black newspapers at the time necessitated such arrangements—how many publishers or editors, after all, had the resources to base and fund correspondents in Los Angeles, and equip them to cultivate the contacts and sources necessary to do in-depth and independent reporting on the progress of African Americans within the film business? In any case the vast majority of black film writers proved obligated to the industry, to the point where their allegiance rested with it as much as with their readers.[49]

This accurately represented the situation for the ANP, for whom Harry Levette, ex-vaudevillian and former minor actor in the silents, served as the ANP Hollywood correspondent from the 1920s until the late 1950s. Though Levette, thanks largely to tenure of service, has been assessed one of a handful of pioneer independent critics "wrestl[ing] with duality" or the demands of twoness,[50] the record afforded by ANP's own archive offers a less laudatory account. As well, his interchange with Barnett, with whom he sustained a wearying protocol of deference and complaint, reveals much of the working culture of the press, as well as the costs and benefits for the black press of covering Hollywood in the midst of the film industry's greatest period of structural change.

Though Levette supplied the ANP with a steady stream of reviews and scoops from the back lots, all too often he brought more grief than gain to the service. Doubtless Barnett so concluded in 1945, when Fredi Washington, the editor-actress best known for her work in *Imitation of Life,* relayed concerns in the *People's Voice,* the progressive black weekly based in New York City. Reading in a September ANP release that she had engineered Lena Horne's removal from the MGM film *St. Louis Woman* so her sister Isabel Washington (dancer and ex-wife of Adam Clayton Powell Jr.) could secure the role, Washington wrote Barnett demanding explanation and correction. Tracing the erroneous story to Levette's reporting, Barnett in turn wrote his reporter demanding corroboration: Levette's "self-abnegating" explanation back to the Chicago office constituted the extent of restitution Washington enjoyed.[51] Similar questions emerged in 1946, courtesy of Clore Warne, prominent entertainment lawyer representing Hattie McDaniel, over inferences that McDaniel's recent divorce had been precipitated by an affair with a black army lieutenant. This was but one of several times Levette's reporting of McDaniel, still prominent in the public eye following her Oscar, strayed from defensible standards. McDaniel herself objected in 1950 to Levette's gratuitous description of her "young and fair" second husband Larry Williams as a color-struck dig. Here McDaniel took pains to express confidence in Barnett, acknowledging his "tremendous job . . . trying to run herd on hundreds of correspondents," while maintaining that years of questionable stories had convinced her Levette "bore some sort of grudge against her."[52]

Given McDaniel's stature, Levette could only bear her complaints in silence. His posthumous 1951 tribute "I Knew Hattie McDaniel," exacted a minor revenge by claiming that he had provided McDaniel her first industry break in 1931. One can only wonder what his proposal to Barnett in 1953 to write a biography of the pioneering black star might have ultimately contained.[53] Other detractors, however, were engaged more directly. A 1949 proposal from ex-*Ebony* staffer Robert Ellis to generate a syndicated column on what "industry people say and think about Negro actors, Negro problems, Negro life" implicitly pointed out shortcomings in Levette's treatment of these matters, even as it promised to respect ANP's "other arrangements on the Coast."[54] Levette's response to the proposal, which Barnett forwarded with encouragement "to let a chap like this try his wings," was to pillory Ellis in subsequent columns, leading Ellis to plead with Barnett "not to pour any oil with Mr. Levette."[55] A similar proposition in late 1948 by A. S. "Doc" Young, a well-known black sports columnist, to enhance entertainment coverage for the ANP, was more pointed in its critique: though disavowing any desire to succeed Levette, Young nonetheless offered that "it is fact that time has passed him by generally." Levette responded in kind, personally upbraiding Young shortly after hearing news of his offer, and chiding his boss for "editing his stories to the bone . . . reducing my column, meant to be chatty, to a stiff prosaic thing." To Levette, bids to supplement or replace him constituted betrayal at two levels: by competing black journalists that Levette invariably dismissed as "chiselers," and ironically, by Barnett himself, believed to be supplying the chisel to his competitors through a perceived unwillingness to properly value Levette's contributions.[56]

That Young and Ellis's proposals came within weeks of one another signals change in the structure of racial feeling of American film at this moment, in the industry itself and among the specific community of black critics.[57] Cripps cites the 1942 meeting between NACCP representatives and studio executives as cementing the turn toward fair portrayal of blacks in major films, and thus liberalizing conditions of scripting and employment for black performers.[58] While this agreement was the culmination of NAACP campaigns beginning with the start of the feature film era in 1915, the late 1940s scrum of black journalists in Hollywood indicates the enhancing effect of industry realignment, suggesting a more complex timeline for the emergence of racially progressive film. Releases such as *Gentlemen's Agreement, Crossfire,* and *Pinky* in 1949—message films hinging on rejection of racial and ethnic prejudice into their story lines—encouraged Young, Ellis, and others to find more room for race liberalism within a fragmented film industry, reeling from linked crises of theater divestment, the HUAC hearings, and postwar drops in audience size. The demise of vertical integration in film production and distribution—the most important transformation in the cinema of the past half century—here was understood to be attended, in Robert Ellis's cognizant terms, by parting of the "white curtain" southern veto power had imposed on cinematic treatment of African Americans to this time.[59] That the ANP received so many invitations to augment its entertainment coverage evidenced the shifting racial politics of film, and the growing cohort of journalists aware of these changes.

Yet little of this made an impression on Harry Levette. From his vantage point, handouts from studio publicity officials remained the preferred mode of Hollywood reporting, even as studios confessed their confusion about the conditions of public appeal generally, and among increasingly articulate and organized black fans in particular. Forwarding studio stills from Twentieth Century Fox's 1949 *Pinky*—a rehash of its predecessor

Imitation of Life that nonetheless garnered $4 million in receipts and Academy Award nominations for both Jeanne Craig and Ethel Waters—Levette spoke of wanting to get the ANP noticed "in the light of a trade service, just as *Photoplay, Variety, Billboard,* and the many other magazines and metropolitan dailies that are getting part of the millions spent by the motion picture industry."[60] Rather than seeing the opportunity for a new style of coverage and even criticism by black entertainment journalists, Levette addressed race and film consistently along lines of paternalism; how much of studios' largesse could he grab hold of, as opposed to how might he redefine his relationship—and by extension that of his readers—to major film. Ever willing to carry the industry's water, Levette routinely disabused skeptics of any hint of prejudice in the industry, as when he parried claims of an 1950 Academy Awards ceremony whitewash by vouching that Sidney Portier, Sammy Davis Jr., Johnny Mathis were all either performing in Las Vegas or New York.[61] That more established female performers, such as Waters or McDaniel, were not on the program despite being available did not disturb Levette's respect for the industry. The same could not be said of his regard for black performers' individual reputations: in an 1954 episode reminiscent of his painful representations of Hattie McDaniel, Levette corroborated Dorothy Dandridge's rumoured affair with Peter Lawford, a scoop made possible "because I keep on the 'inside' and without guess work."[62]

Acutely aware of the unique appeal of cultural commentary and representation, Barnett's frequent prods of Levette indicated that he remained concerned that the service's film coverage would prove wanting, as film adjusted to the changing conditions of production and society. Yet everyday reliability, as well as capacity to recognize deep historical change, continued to elude Levette as a correspondent. His copy routinely arrived too late for inclusion in the A-list release packet, meaning that much of his work was out of date upon arrival.[63] Mismanagement of funds was a nagging issue, with Levette begging advances and supplements in often bizarre manner. In 1949 Barnett upbraided him for sending a $5.00 telegram (charged to the press) requesting carfare downtown for Los Angeles's Ralph Bunche Day festivities, an event he described, with characteristic grandiosity, as "the most important international event in modern racial or United Nations history."[64] Two years later, Levette would propose a dollar's collection from each of the ANP's nearly eighty member subscribers as due recognition of "years . . . of front page banner lines from my stories."[65] Occasionally, Barnett's patience was pushed too far, as in July 1954 when he trenchantly observed that the service's coverage of Hollywood, "which ought to be a helpful agent in absorbing the high costs of operation, is a bust," fingering Levette's eagerness to serve as "praise agent" for the industry as root cause. Yet Levette, flush in self-assurance if not in talent, resisted all encouragement toward assistance, lecturing Barnett instead on the etiquette of corporate loyalty. The question that then emerges is why Barnett, with so many apparent options, chose to rely on Levette, and part ways with other more able correspondents?

A crucial reason was Levette's ability to play to Barnett's core conservatism. Aware that anticommunism was a trump card for those working in or around postwar Hollywood—the first cold war battleground in the defeat of the American left—Levette seized his opportunities to paint rivals as not only opportunistic, but subversive. Describing Robert Ellis as a "rabid editorial writer of Red stuff," Levette connected him to progressive columnist Leon Hardwick, whom Levette held responsible for the career-ending arrest of Rex Ingram, found with Hardwick and others "partying with young white women."[66] News of threatened libel suits by John Lee, editor at the California *Eagle,* concerning Levette's description of him as a Communist brought nonplused response that "the jealousy is from the other side, who find me in the way of them using ANP for red propaganda, for high pressuring, and for chiseling."[67] For good measure, Levette took pains to note Lee's rumored questioning by the FBI, and invoked the memory of Winston Churchill and the Battle of Britain in seeking "a vote of confidence" for his resilience and constancy, "or at least an encouraging word about my coverage of the Insurance and other conventions this summer."[68] The *Eagle* itself, exemplar by many accounts of the postwar Western progressive press, proved a convenient target as well: by Levette's account, the paper was victim of a leftwing coup by staff fired from the *Sentinel,* a local rival paper.[69]

On occasion Levette, like prominent white contemporaries such as Hedda Hopper and Walter Winchell, sought bigger fish. In July 1955 singer Josephine Baker contacted the press requesting assistance: through a phone conversation and follow-up letter, Barnett learned that she was encountering a city-wide blacklist in Los Angeles due to critical remarks she made on U.S. race relations while on South American tour several years earlier. Asked by Barnett to call on contacts at the Motion Pictures Producers Association for suggestions of a good public relations representative, Levette responded by questioning "her sincerity in the anti-prejudice fight," recirculating charges that she had dodged taxes on receipts from her last Los Angeles visit, and pondering whether efforts on Baker's behalf were worth risking "the good opinion they have of me in Hollywood."[70] Though

Barnett initially expressed sympathy with Baker's plight, Levette's dismissal did its intended work: Barnett wrote one last letter to Levette confirming his opinion of the situation and cautioning him not to get involved "if you find it will hurt you." Barnett was well aware of the intensity of his subordinate's loyalist sentiments—already that year, Levette had personally blocked ANP credentialing of two black reporters on their way to the Bandung Conference on political grounds, despite initial endorsement of their applications.[71]

Levette's relentless portrayal of creeping subversion among African-American journalists, artists, and intellectuals highlights the profound compromises that structured cold-war black thought and opinion making. The paranoid atmosphere of late 1940s Los Angeles, given the rapacity of anti-Communist investigation of film, television, and local social and political circles, made for an especially advanced environment of repression. And this climate of hysteria was, if anything, uniquely pronounced within Los Angeles's African-American community, where local and national law enforcement concerns followed a time-honored tradition of tracing all radical ferment back to breakdowns in racial authority.

It might be argued that Levette's ideological bullying of black writers, performers and workers of the black Hollywood community through the 1940s and into the 1950s offered an unwitting cover for Barnett, a reliable counter to any charge that his interest in circulating news of African-American life might be construed as subversive. If so, it seems clear that the other side of the bargain was the ANP's inability to deepen and sophisticate coverage of black entertainment, at a time when significant inroads were being made by African Americans in film, music, theater, and cultural imagination generally. Coverage of black entertainment achievement and fame constituted an early priority of the ANP, and remained so in Barnett's mind throughout its existence. Ultimately, however, the disabling interrelation of Levette, Barnett, and the press generally meant that other concerns would realize the opportunities a restructuring movie industry offered to African-American critics and performers.

If Levette's incessant red-baiting marked the ANP's approach to entertainment, a subtler language of loyalty characterized his boss's response to gathering demands of ideological conformity, through World War II and into the cold war. Closer examination of ANP's implication in both national and transnational political spheres shows how Barnett's activities outlined an arc of civil fidelity, albeit with finer elaboration than in Levette's case. Recent accounts of the interplay of race and the cold war have focused on insurgent or dissenting figures, in ways that plot risks and costs for those blacks who contested the authority of the state in the United States after 1945. Because he was not an opposition figure, Barnett offers a different yet complementary case study, illuminating the contingencies encountered by those blacks who volunteered for, rather than renounced, induction into the cold war.

Racial lines of loyalty remained uncoordinated through the 1940s, a condition explaining at once widespread black agitation for first class citizenship, the growing trend toward federal concession on matters of race, and the still-punitive approach of Hoover's FBI toward blacks as a potentially subversive force. Barnett, though never radical, recognized the tactical value of complex allegiance, at least during the early years of the cold war. Even as he personally rejected left-of-center affiliations, Barnett nonetheless continued to encourage the interests and careers of progressive associates, in stark contrast to his mentor Washington. Following the resolution of the March on Washington standoff in 1941, Barnett took the lead in advancing Earl Dickerson for a seat on the Fair Employment Practices Commission, encouraging Tuskegee head Fred Patterson, whose opinion was well regarded by President Roosevelt, to nominate Dickerson "in order to prevent the East from dominating all phases of Negro," and adding his own letter to that effect to the White House.[72] Barnett continued to sponsor and advise Dickerson, even after subsequent activities raised suspicions regarding the lawyer's ideological orientation, most notably his 1947 collaboration with W. E. B. Du Bois on the hard-hitting NAACP petition "An Appeal to the World."[73] As well, Barnett's own sentiments at times gravitated toward more dissident positions. A 1942 letter to Kenneth Pangburn, a Talladega College student, recounted a lecture by linguist S. I. Hayakawa advocating cooperatives "and their possibilities for Negro people." Barnett's conjecture about consolidating black economic power through collectivization might have been meant to update the freeholder emphasis of mentor Booker Washington late in life: it was also in line with the dissident radicalism Du Bois championed in the 1940 book *Dusk of Dawn,* a work no doubt familiar to him.[74] Whatever the pressures of threatened censorship of the black press during World War II, Barnett appears to have not allowed it to compromise ANP's editorial mission. Barnett solicited Edward Strong, head of the Southern Negro Youth Congress, for an account "of the plight which faces the disenfranchised Negro and poor whites of the South," and issued nuanced ANP bulletins on Angelo Herndon's expulsion from the Communist Party, for continued opposition to the war.[75] But interest in functioning as a credible broker consistently modified any sympathies he shared with African-American progressives and insurgents.

An early and evocative example of this was Barnett's June 1941 letter to Henry Wallace, which outlined the March on Washington movement, scheduled to culminate in mass protest in the national capital. Barnett offered what can only be described as an informant's narrative, a "back stage view" meant to equip Wallace "if you are in any fashion projected into the picture." Providing a work-up of A. Philip Randolph's rise in leadership circles—updated with a sympathetic account of his resignation as head of the National Negro Congress the year before—Barnett then outlined

his analysis of the bar on black hiring by defense contractors nationally. While acknowledging deficiencies of skill and training in much of the black industrial workforce, Barnett stressed that deliberate exclusion, which he termed "the traditional attitude of industry toward Negroes," constituted the main cause of black underrepresentation in defense industries. This conformed to the opinions of many black leaders and even more of the black public at this moment, yet it was a striking statement for Barnett, given his reputation as a defender of manufacturers against charges of discrimination. Though expressing skepticism for the breadth of support for the march ("for a considerable time it appeared that the march would not excite great interest of participation"), Barnett credited the tactics of Randolph and other leaders, noting their skillful spin of denunciations from the right as well as entreaties from Roosevelt and his emissaries as testament to the value of insurgent pressure in the eyes of the black public.

Having dispensed with the background, Barnett then turned his attention to recommendations for appropriate action. Contrasting rumored Communist vows to disrupt the event with implied concerns that any gathering of African Americans in the capital would be met with white supremacist terrorism, Barnett counseled Wallace that accommodation rather than confrontation represented the best course of state action: "I think that the wisest procedure for the administration is to facilitate the march, to surround it with whatever protection is necessary, to abandon attempts to stop it. That will only strengthen it." Barnett, it can be assumed, was unaware of Roosevelt's impending concession in his executive order 8802 banning war industry discrimination. But had he been privy to the prospect of resolution, his advice to Wallace might well have remained the same. With the exposition experience still coloring his opinion of political leadership, Barnett vouchsafed his appeal to Wallace by noting how "Negro public opinion quite largely looks toward you for calm and fair consideration of the problems which concern the group."[76]

This extraordinary letter fascinates at several levels. While Wallace fulfilled, if not exceeded, Barnett's opinion of him as the decade progressed, no scholarly account has ever documented the conditions of his evolution into a racial progressive. Crediting Barnett wholly for this change would be an exaggeration. Yet Wallace's adult education in progressive race views by Barnett and other tutors nonetheless remains an unresearched area: one that might complicate understanding of this landmark figure, while suggesting, as scholars have recently, that the advent of federal liberalism on matters of race was as much the product of black encouragement and counsel as it was that of white leaders' vision or statecraft.[77] For the purposes of this study, though, the picture presented of Barnett himself is the more compelling issue. Barnett's counsel to Wallace, his most sustained reflection on this defining moment in African-American and national history, demonstrated the publisher's most formidable qualities—flexible intelligence, appreciation of the fundamentally tactical nature of politics, capacity to approach questions from multiple standpoints—alongside his deepest flaw: the desire to insinuate himself into circles of power, functioning as authorized go-between in a still racially separated society.

Barnett's self-definition as racial medium grew more important with the onset of the cold war. Building on the counselor's status he invoked with Wallace, Barnett worked to project his advice and influence beyond the boundaries of the black world. In 1945 he worked to steer the *New York Times* in its search for its first black reporter, who turned out to be George Streator.[78] Writing in 1951 Congressman William Dawson, the ranking black elected representative nationally, Barnett noted the impending reassignment of a black consular official from Liberia to a Southeast Pacific posting, and the need to have a replacement black candidate at the ready, lest other government officials "shift a white man to Liberia on the plea of integration."[79] Barnett's centrist reputation had not placed the ANP above suspicion during the war years, meaning that the wire service found itself the target of FBI inquiries, like so many other race institutions.[80] Yet with tensions concerning the loyalties of African Americans remaining high through the 1940s and into the 1950s, state suspicion was replaced by a growing tendency to invoke Barnett as indeed representative of the centrist line of black opinion. Heads of civil rights commissions based in California and Illinois wrote with requests for advice and support. Edith Sampson, the black Chicago attorney appointed as special advisor to the U.S. ambassador to the United Nations, cited Barnett's opinion along with that of John Johnson in naming mainstream black concerns over State Department plans to tour the musical *Porgy and Bess* through Western Europe in 1952.[81]

Yet if Barnett felt personally validated by the exigencies of the cold war, he could not argue that the ANP had similarly reaped rewards from his collaborations. At various junctures, Barnett had sought to spin off the influence and connections of the service into alternate sectors—beauty products, advertising, even the 1940 exposition. None had provided the structural growth or, as importantly, the residual profits necessary to financially secure the service. Now, shadowed in a most complex manner by the requisites of cold-war loyalty and the incentive to leverage social change, Barnett sought to parlay the service's influence and resources into the most ambitious venture he had engaged in since the founding of the ANP.

In the late spring of 1948, Barnett took time from the pressures of dual loyalty to take in a local picture. The experience left him disturbed, as he related to Ken Blewett, manager of the Regal Theater:

> I visited your theater the other day. My real object was to see a certain scene in the All-America Newsreel. You can imagine my surprise at finding that you did not run the news reel . . . You are conscious, I am sure, of your responsibility to the community you are serving. The theater was full and there were many, many children. These kids see crime, shooting, salacious dialogue, and gangster tactics. Small wonder the kids act as they do. The theater has more influence over them than any other medium . . . Every race is idealized except their own. How can race pride be developed unless they see something worthwhile with Negroes in active roles. I hope you take this into consideration in building programs.[82]

If Blewett, doubtless well acquainted with complaints given his establishment's prominence, was troubled that this one came from Barnett, he might have taken solace that his was not the only theater called out. Barnett sent the same letter to fourteen other picture houses devoted to local audiences, including the Tivoli at 63rd and Cottage Grove, the Virginia and Star Theaters on 43rd Street, the Terrace at 31st and Indiana, and the Metropolitan up the street near 47th and South Parkway.[83] A range of conditions might have motivated Barnett to mount the soapbox. Perhaps his protests were meant to test the waters for more robust protests against local amusements, especially in light of recurrent panics over South Side juvenile delinquency. Possibly Barnett, recalling his 1940 work enabling production of *One Tenth of a Nation,* was seeking to encourage Blewett and other local theater owners to consider the pedagogical possibilities of film for black audiences.

Most probably, though, these letters were meant as a favor to a friend fast becoming one of Barnett's closest collaborators. All-American Newsreel was the brainchild of Emmanuel Glucksman, an energetic entrepreneur and filmmaker of short subjects depicting African Americans—quite possibly the only such operation active in the country at the time. Beginning in June 1942, All-American Newsreel, produced and distributed documentary shorts on black life and news until the late 1950s.[84] Reviews of his product were initially mixed. In 1942 Truman Gibson Jr., by this time established in his army advisor's post, protested the newsreel's exclusive black focus as conducive to white audience backlash: a ironic objection, given the tenacious segregation of the army.[85] Nonetheless Glucksman, based initially in Chicago, established connections with Barnett, hoping to access stories and broader distribution. Barnett, immediately eager to assist, encouraged Glucksman to forward copies of shorts to the Gold Coast, Nigeria, and Liberia, and arranged shipping assistance through the British Overseas Airway Corporation and contacts abroad and in Chicago.[86] Further discussions in 1949 between Glucksman and Barnett on a longer film dealing with black insurance appeared promising, but before they could be acted upon, Glucksman moved to Dallas and fell out of touch with Barnett for two years.[87] When he resurfaced, he brought with him a proposal of still greater interest for Barnett.

Glucksman had sought for years to focus his work in celebration of black achievement, concentrating on distribution possibilities within the emerging medium of network television.[88] By 1951, he had identified a promising partner in tobacco company Liggett and Meyers, which was eager to build on an early toehold in the black consumer market. Agreeing to underwrite one ten minute pilot by Glucksman dealing with race education, Liggett and Myers, through its advertising firm Cunningham and Walsh, proposed to fund three future documentaries, and more if sales for Chesterfield cigarettes sales increased among black consumers. By late 1951, the proposed number of guaranteed short films had risen to six, on the subjects of education, labor and industry, art and literature, science, national affairs, and sports. Plans were already being formulated to identify and obligate interview subjects for the various films, to constitute an advisory board of black leaders, and to generate proposals for future films, provided the series proved a success.

Barnett was deeply involved in the elaborate project from its inception. The series of newsreels, collectively titled *Negro America,* wedded several of his most compelling personal projects—vindicationist portrayal of black achievement, redirection of corporate activity through black consumer leverage, identification of multimedia opportunities for black-related content. The rare prospect of a lucrative payday encouraged him as well: Glucksman contracted Barnett to serve as opening narrator for all of the films, and to provide the obligatory pitch for Chesterfields to viewers.

Barnett was paid $500 per appearance, plus related expenses. Work identifying potential participants, generating storylines, and advising Cunningham and Walsh on promotion and distribution put Barnett in line to garner still more in related fees.[89] But while Barnett was surely inspired by the chance to parlay his stature into the type of personal security that the ANP had never realized for him, the largest attraction of the project remained its prospects as race-related media projected to run in hundreds of theaters nationally, with prospects for television broadcast down the road, and the support of a secure corporate sponsor. Like the exposition over a decade before, it seemed to Barnett the opportunity of a lifetime, given its promise to break new ground in cinematic presentation of black life to date.

Early on, it appeared that these goals—general and social as well as personal—would be met. Feeding a stream of names to Glucksman, his partner Victor Roudin, and Robert Gilham of Cunningham and Walsh, Barnett facilitated agreements with dozens of subjects, including Willard Townsend, Congressman William Dawson, Edith Sampson, Dr. Percy Julian, his close associate Fred Patterson, and wife Etta Moten for a short called "The Negro in Entertainment."[90] Insurance magnate C. C. Spaulding, whose Atlanta Life Insurance Company had vied for years with Supreme Liberty Life for the title of largest black business in the nation, acceded to Barnett's suggestion that he serve on the advisory board for the project, confiding in his reply to Glucksman, "if Mr. Barnett suggested that I serve on your Advisory Board, there is nothing for me to do but accept."[91] He joined Townsend, Barnett, President Rufus Clement of Atlanta University, President Ella Stewart of the National Association of Negro Women, Etta Moten, and Jesse Owens as advisors to the project.[92] Though a healthy portion of the African Americans interviewed, including Dawson, Sampson, Townsend, and Judge Wendell Green, were Chicagoans like Barnett, the *Negro America* series strove to provide a national sample of black life and accomplishment. The pilot feature on black education restricted itself to historically black colleges and universities in the South, while the national affairs program looked to spotlight representative blacks in the federal government. By year's end Glucksman was shuttling across the country to document black culture on film. In Washington D.C. he filmed a parade of the local chapter of the Elks' fraternal group; in Los Angeles renowned architect Paul Williams as well as the new tower offices of the Golden State Mutual Insurance Company.[93] Glucksman's grasp of black life impressed many observers, none more than Barnett, who early on complimented the white filmmaker's understanding of African Americans' "sensitivities and attitudes."[94] Word began to spread of the documentaries' quality and impact,

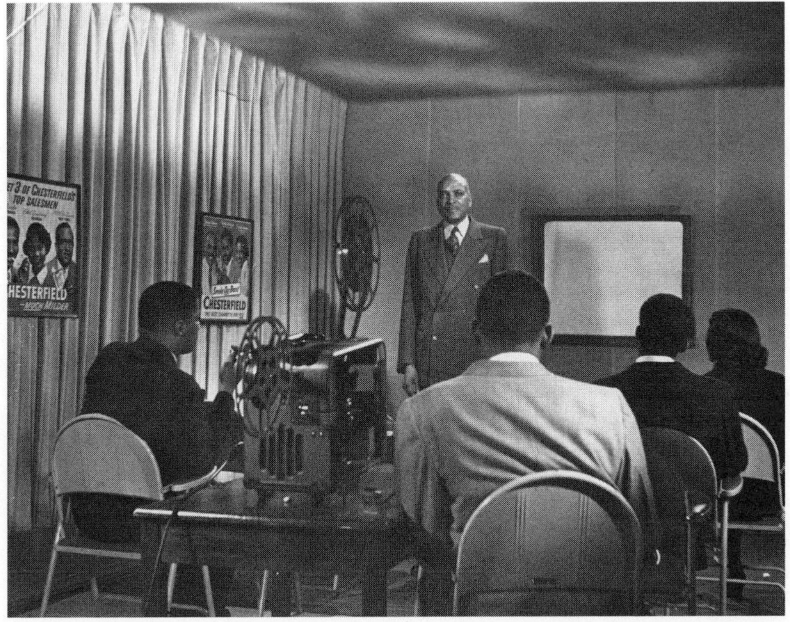

14. Claude Barnett being filmed, either for the *Negro America* series or a Liggett and Myers advertisement. Courtesy of the Claude Barnett Collection/Chicago Historical Society (ICHi-17329).

and inquiries began to emerge from new subjects as well as potential secondary sponsors, including the General Education Board and the Ford Foundation.[95]

A more powerful sponsor seemed within reach late that year. Almost from the beginning of his involvement in *Negro America,* Barnett was struck by the project's value as not only racial but national propaganda. Early in 1952, he detailed to both Glucksman and Roudin the potential usefulness of the films to the State Department, the United States Information Service, the American mission to the United Nations, and various consulates and diplomatic offices desperately seeking to present credible positive portrayals of black life in America.[96] The year was proving a tense one in relation to race and ideology: Pearl Primus, Paul Robeson, W. E. B. and Shirley Graham Du Bois were all forced to surrender passports due to unspecified security concerns, while incidents such as the controversy in New York over the Stork Club's nonservice of Josephine Baker inspired a wave of poor press overseas.[97] The European speaking tour of Edith Sampson the previous fall, meant to divert international attention to critical accounts of U.S. race relations, most notably the Civil Rights Congress's devastating petition *We Charge Genocide,* reinforced to Barnett that "nothing could be more important" in the propaganda arena of the cold war than having the *Negro America* pictures promoted and distributed by diplomatic offices. Renewing his long-standing protest of Communist opportunism in foregrounding domestic racial discrimination, Barnett remained resolute in his faith in the salience of the American creed, even as he acknowledged the question of U.S. race relations as "number one public relations problem in Europe, Asia, and Africa."[98]

Convinced of the film's international value and relevance, Barnett enlisted Glucksman and Roudin in efforts to secure government sponsorship of the films. Attempts to screen the films for Edith Sampson in March of 1952 resulted in her promise to argue the films' value to officials at the UN, USIS, and the State Department, as well as her agreement to sign on as an advisor to the series.[99] State proved unhelpful at first, thanks to the opposition of Turman's special assistant Phileo Nash. Referring to himself (more aptly than intended) as "the bottleneck in the road to producing a film or films to combat Communism abroad," Nash responded negatively to offers to sponsor the films, arguing that backing them would result in southern senators taking revenge on the department's budget.[100] Inquiries to Porter McKeever, the director of information to the United States Mission to the UN, and Wilson Compton, an official in International Information Administration at the State Department, proved more promising. Compton acknowledged Barnett's "frank comments" concerning his department's initial decision and promised a more thorough review of the films. McKeever proposed to screen the films for his staff and discuss distribution to diplomats overseas: unequivocal in his praise of the series, McKeever would also write in support of Barnett's application to the Ford Foundation to facilitate broader distribution for the films through television.[101]

Ultimately, however, these efforts proved insufficient to secure any sustained government funding. Though a broad roster of black arts and entertainment figures—Louis Armstrong, Dizzy Gillespe, even the Harlem Globetrotters—toured Europe, Africa, and Asia from 1951 until 1956 at the behest of the State Department, the *Negro America* films never found international distribution through the U.S. government. This may be explained in part as evidence of the circumscribed ways that the state sought to place African Americans before international audiences. Though kinetic and artistic exhibitions were acceptable, reinforcing time-honored logics of blacks meriting public recognition through their ability to entertain and amuse, a more sober feature of black success in a range of fields—including business and politics—constituted too much of an affront to those still invested in racial hierarchy. Barnett's own ideological adjustments initiated in the late 1940s—summarily dismissing George Padmore as African correspondent, writing touristy accounts of travels in the Caribbean and Africa that evaded hard analysis of material or political conditions—indicated his deferral to such international portrayals of U.S. black life. What represented, then, an attractive and relatively cost-free opportunity for the government to propagandize on behalf of African Americans' full and free access to opportunity in American society went unexercised, mainly due to unwillingness on the part of diplomatic authorities to partner even with obviously loyal African Americans in articulating this message. In this sense, it becomes clearer that even those blacks who volunteered enthusiastically for the cold war found that they could never quite shake official suspicion as to their contributions—or reliability.[102]

Their prospects for sponsorship by the government essentially tabled, Barnett and Glucksman soldiered on, seeking subjects and venues for the *Negro America* films. Subjects addressing fraternal societies, medicine, and African Americans in Los Angeles were planned and shot. A short produced the following year on agriculture would garner praise from the perpetually self-critical Glucksman as "the best picture we have ever made." Inquiries regarding foreign distribution were made with the United African Academy of Culture, Drama, and Sociology in London, as well as Liberian Mission to the United Nations. Yet these initiatives ultimately were something of an overreach, given persistent problems with comprehensive distribution in the United States itself. Barnett wrote several times to Glucksman as well as Robert Gillham and E. H. Ellis, managers of the Liggett and Myers account at Cunningham and Walsh, complaining that theaters in a number of major Midwestern cities, including Chicago itself, were not receiving the films. Prior marketing profiles for the Chesterfield brand saturated exhibitions in areas of the South, but had almost no exposure in the North. Gillham and Ellis's assurances that the imbalance would be corrected apparently lacked follow-through, as Barnett would continue to raise questions about distribution throughout the life of the project.[103]

More difficulties began to emerge in relation to the project thereafter. Barnett's old exposition partner Mary Beattie Brady weighed in with an extensive and frank critique of the series. Venturing that Glucksman's team lacked "the necessary concept" to most effectively feature the various subjects depicted, Brady went on to name that concept as full affirmation of racial integration, "a quality of thinking that is far more important than the spit and polish" she counted as the sum accomplishment of Glucksman's professional abilities. Glucksman responded in kind, calling Brady's objections "a wonderful example of a person writing about motion pictures who doesn't know anything about it." By mid-1952, Glucksman had forced his partner Victor Roudin out of the venture over disagreements concerning responsibilities and profits. The added burden put pressure on Glucksman's company, resulting in missed contracts with Cunningham and Walsh and withheld payments for both Glucksman and Barnett. On occasion, this strained the relationship of the two men. Writing anxiously through 1953 and 1954 regarding back pay often nearing thousands of dollars, Barnett would even hint the possibility of legal action by July 1954. Though he suffered the decreasing revenue stream with Glucksman, he committed so much time and energy to the *Negro America* that it became his most demanding project aside from the ANP itself.[104]

The *Negro America* series continued to run, barely, until 1955—Glucksman would maintain an intermittent relationship with Cunningham and Walsh until they themselves lost the Liggett and Myers account in the summer of 1956. Though problems of overextended production and uneven distribution were key factors in the demise of the series, deeper cultural shifts also played an appreciable role. Barnett and Glucksman found themselves chasing a rapidly receding opportunity: the Supreme Court–ordered break-up of vertical integration of the film industry made it more difficult for them to exploit distribution systems of the shorts. Increasingly, movie houses no longer required short features to fill out extended feature packages. The advent of television also proved unhelpful: the first sign that Cunningham and Walsh were reining in their commitment to the series was news that virtually all of the Chesterfield account was being budgeted for television spots by July 1955. Glucksman had sought access to the television market for the series on his own, almost from the beginning of his partnership with Barnett, pursuing correspondences with southern network stations, and even renaming his company North American Television Productions, Inc., in early 1955. The mushrooming new media, though, posed other problems for Glucksman and Barnett's collaboration: by early 1956, Citizen's Council threats of boycotts resulted in Cunningham and Walsh abandoning all plans of promoting the series to southern stations.[105]

Negro America's end, then, derived from an array of fatal factors: the inability of Barnett and Glucksman to convince sponsors that the series constituted a national and international, rather than regional, marketing vehicle; industry-wide shifts in exhibition policies due to contraction of film generally; and racial vetting of early television programming, due to the cultural specter of massive white resistance. Together, they converged

15. Claude Barnett, 1949. Photograph by Vincent Saunders Jr. Courtesy of the Claude Barnett Collection/Chicago Historical Society (G1980.213.4.7).

to doom what was, for Barnett, his most ambitious and sustained initiative beyond the ANP. As well, the fall of the *Negro America* newsreel series indicated that though the connections and reputation of the service were sufficient to attract erstwhile partners and even sponsors, they were not yet strong enough to provide the means for reliable and independent programming. A fundamentally different type of media institution would be needed before such efforts, and Barnett's strong if equivocal dreams of true institutional autonomy could be realized.

As the *Negro America* project steadily waned, Barnett kept up duties as racial broker, maintaining a national watch through the ANP. Of special interest were growing conditions of racial tension in Mississippi: by 1949, Barnett was writing his favored local contact, Jackson College president

Jacob Reddix, for his views on the conviction and impending execution of Willie McGee. Noting the efforts to raise public awareness by the Civil Rights Council, Barnett expressed opposition to their broad project of insurgency, while acknowledging its effectiveness: "sometimes they get away with statements just because some of the truth around the cases impresses those who read about them." Seeking to enlist Reddix as a counterradical voice on the case ("it would be helpful to have your views"), Barnett would devote increasing attention to events transpiring in that state, singling out black leaders who raised concerns about deteriorating conditions there without moving too far toward the militant camp.[106]

Of course, Barnett would soon discover that the interracial middle ground he was familiar and comfortable with was rapidly disappearing, in Mississippi and across the country. Indeed, he already had access to others providing much different representations of Southern racial conditions from those offered by the patrician Reddix. Writing Barnett in 1945, a young doctor named T. R. M. Howard provided detailed analysis of the adverse effect on planter-managed cotton price ceilings for local sharecroppers, adding for good measure that the arrangement represented a "damnable set-up." Turning to other matters, Howard beseeched Barnett's help in pushing the state's political establishment to follow through on promises to fund the first African-American hospital in the state. Howard noted his recent purchase of the 350 acre Mound Bayou estate of the late Isaiah Montgomery, founder of the historic all-black town—land that had come to Montgomery originally from his father, who in turn had been willed it by his former master, Confederate President Jefferson Davis. Like Reddix—indeed, like Barnett—Montgomery had been a fervent adherent to the custodial style of black leadership, frequently cutting deals with white patrons and sponsors, and generally seeking to stave off any power sharing among fellow African Americans whom he viewed as his obedient constituents.[107]

Howard, though, would prove a different brand of leader. No further record of correspondence between the two men remains. Yet in a decade's time, Howard would stand at the epicenter of pitched struggles between black insurgency and violent white oppression that would grip the state through 1955 and beyond. Indeed, even as Barnett solicited moderate voices to provide their views as to conditions of the moment, Howard would find his relationship to Chicago cemented by a defining moment of tragedy and collective resolve. His ally in solidifying the alliance of Black Metropolis and Delta would turn out to be a Chicago-based media institution like Barnett's ANP, but one that realized the autonomy and material success that eluded Barnett throughout his career, and followed a credo different from the clientage and custodianship defining Barnett and so many before him.

SELLING THE RACE

CHAPTER FOUR

We tell ourselves our individual stories
so as to become aware of our *general* story.
RALPH ELLISON

Johnson Publishing Company occupies a unique place in African-American cultural history. Producer of picture magazines, news and opinion digests, a book publishing operation, and fashion and cosmetics subsidiaries, Johnson Publishing—while not the first example of integrated and sustained culture industry in black life—is indisputably the longest running. Yet many accounts of this Chicago-based company have portrayed it as a decidedly problematic presence in black life, due to its bare-knuckles philosophies of market competition and workplace management, its bourgeois advocacy of a success ethic for African Americans, and the way in which that ethic has been read, most famously by E. Franklin Frazier, as a more suspect call for blacks to remake themselves in the image of American whites.

This chapter proposes a significant rewriting of Johnson Publishing and, more specifically, Ebony*'s place in African-American history. As the most unabashed exemplar of the market turn in black culture during and after World War II, Johnson Publishing demonstrated how race's sale might con-*

Facing page: 16. John Johnson Jr. in Rome, 1950. Photographed by Ben Burns. Courtesy of Harsh Research Collection/Chicago Public Library.

stitute a creative, even transforming experiment in African-American imagination and expression. During the first ten years of Ebony *magazine, an eclectic variety of editorial concerns, and an equivalent diversity of staff talents invoked the broader complexity of African-American life. Through this rich institution of journalistic resource, Chicago's role as pivot of a modern and nationalized African-American community became more apparent. On one hand, race-affirming portrayals of art, accomplishment, work, leisure, and community were disseminated through an unprecedented mass-market medium. At the same time, though, alignment of African Americans with the United States was advocated not along lines of racial abandonment, but instead deep and prophetic engagements with foundational civil and social philosophies.*

In the November 1945 launch issue of *Ebony,* adjacent to the masthead and contents, an editors' column ventured a prediction as to the magazine's future role in black life:

> As you can gather, we're rather jolly folks, we *Ebony* editors. We like to look at the zesty side of life. Sure, you can get all hot and bothered about the race question (and don't think we don't) but not enough is said about all the swell things we Negroes can do and will accomplish. *Ebony* will try to mirror the happier side of Negro life—the positive, everyday achievements from Harlem to Hollywood. But when we talk about race as the No. 1 problem of America, we'll talk turkey.[1]

Such statements read suspiciously cheery in hindsight, given the tensions of race riots, the enforced segregation North as well as South, and the violent, uneven reentry into the labor force marking black life in the aftermath of World War II. Certainly it constituted a break with black journalism's traditional voice of protest. At no time was black print media's identity as a fighting press more evident than during World War II.[2] While members of the old guard like Claude Barnett counseled sanguine ambassadorship, most black journalists loudly decried discrimination, racist violence, and the duplicity of state claims to represent freedom, to a degree nearly precipitating government charges of sedition.[3] *Ebony,* in contrast, encouraged African-American readers "to get away from 'the problem' for a while," or to "reject negativism and advocacy of a cause."[4] Decades later, the rewards of this formula are beyond dispute. Crown jewel of what has become a $400 million annual business, *Ebony* rewrote the rules of imaginative enterprise for African Americans, anchoring the first black cultural conglomerate deserving of the name. But arguments over *Ebony* or Johnson Publishing have never been about material success. Instead, it has been its mission and motive, in particular the recommendation that blacks might turn away from "the problem," that has placed *Ebony* at the center of controversy, to a degree discouraging its full investigation to the present day.

The definitive comment on *Ebony* has remained, for nearly fifty years, that of its harshest reader. Writing in *Black Bourgeoisie,* sociologist E. Franklin Frazier lashed out against *Ebony*'s compensatory "world of make-believe," intended to salve the wounds of a nihilistic black middle class. Cataloging its stories of wealth and luxury, Frazier accused the magazine of elevating status over justice and truth—a variation on the jeremiad against black social distortion that had defined his research from inception. *Ebony*'s aping of mainstream publications—notably *Life*—and its mortgage to advertisers did more than compromise integrity: it raised questions whether the magazine embodied black self-hate. Far from promoting solidarity and group advance, *Ebony* was depicted as encouraging successful blacks to reinvent themselves as "exaggerated Americans" to veil their actual "inferiority and inconsequence in American society."[5]

Over time, the specifics of Frazier's argument have grown hard to recall. Yet a moment's reflection makes clear the long-term influence of his ideas. Critics like LeRoi Jones and Harold Cruse, as well as separatist leaders Elijah Muhammad and Malcolm X, based much of their own work in no small part on depiction of a color-struck, assimilationist black middle class.[6] More recent scholars of the interplay of race and class, while refusing such emphatic dismissal, still retain an underlying assessment of racial elites' incapacity for sustained contribution to group advance. Indeed, the core legacy of Frazier's critique—casting long shadows over Johnson Publishing—is the idea that African-American social mobility has proven solvent rather than wellspring to collective identity.[7] Frazier's representation of the nihilism of the black bourgeoisie proved crucial to benchmarking modern black life as plebeian and proletarian in character, just as his earlier work would engender theories of a racial underclass.[8] The time-honored idiom meant to designate successful yet self-interested blacks—"sell-outs"—is testament to his influence on thinking about race today. Small wonder that *Ebony,* Johnson Publishing, and its founder John Johnson have received little attention, beyond dismissal, in serious accounting of black life.

Yet can we really comprehend modern black community and identity without addressing this singular enterprise? Like the American Negro Exposition, the web of local music business, or Associated Negro Press, *Ebony* and Johnson Publishing retained deep roots in midcentury Black

Chicago. Unlike these predecessors, it departed briskly from its local base to comprehensively rework taste and perception among African Americans across the United States. Initially a shoestring operation staffed by a lapsed white Communist, a late-blooming woman writer from North Dakota, and other improbable characters, *Ebony* and Johnson constituted a multimillion dollar business by the 1950s. Underpinning the company's *deluxe* angle were features on exemplary individuals, as well as rising stars of sport, stage, and the arts, originating ideas of black public presence integral to our own racial lexicon today. Attending to headlines and quotidian minutia alike, Johnson Publishing offered a grammar for postmigration black existence, one matching new realities of urban challenge, societal complexity, and material change. That such transformation derived from the work of entrepreneurs like Johnson hints the need to revisit Frazier's critiques, along with broader presumptions concerning the class roots of modern black racial feeling. Far from selling out African Americans, Johnson Publishing in its early years sold the race new identities, a process that encouraged imagination of a black national community, and made new notions of collective interest—and politics—plausible.

To date, *Ebony*'s legend, along with that of its parent company, has largely gathered around the success story of its founder. John Harold Johnson, like Mahalia Jackson, Al Benson, Claude Barnett, and others fashioning Bronzeville out of the South Side, was product of the serial migrations transforming both the city of Chicago and the nation as a whole. He relocated from Chicago from Arkansas City, Arkansas, in 1933, and turned from houseworker's son to valedictorian; from welfare recipient to multimillionaire businessman. Yet the nature of Johnson's rise ought not obscure his debt to local institutions. As Johnson himself acknowledged, success derived from resources close at hand: vivid testament to Bronzeville's centrality in midcentury black life.

Arriving in Chicago and settling with his mother near South Parkway and 55th Street, Johnson enrolled at Wendell Phillips High School. Phillips had served as beacon for migrants seeking education for their children, much as the Regal Theater, packing companies, and self-help centers like Wabash YMCA or the Urban League inspired other black sojourners. Among Johnson's schoolmates were other luminaries-to-be, whose acquaintance he would in time renew under markedly different circumstances: Dorothy Donegan, Nat Cole, Redd Foxx, and Dempsey Travis, among others. Stimulated by the environment at Phillips and the raucous cityscape surrounding him, Johnson cultivated an outsized ambition.

17. Crowd at Wendell Phillips–DuSable High football game, mid-1940s. Photographed by Wayne F. Miller. Courtesy of Wayne F. Miller.

Maintaining high marks and staffing the school newspaper and yearbook, Johnson was nominated in 1936 to give his class's graduation address. His speech "Building a New World" received report in the *Defender,* the first in a long string of acknowledgments.[9]

Upon graduating, Johnson sought funds for further education. He had won partial scholarship to the University of Chicago, but with his mother working as a domestic, he was compelled to look elsewhere to raise the balance. A benefactor emerged at Johnson's graduation: Harry Pace, serial entrepreneur serving by this time as president of Supreme Liberty Life Insurance. Black insurance companies had constituted the backbone of black economic infrastructure since early in the century, locally and nationally. In Chicago alone, four separate companies were capitalized together at $10 million by 1940, employing 2,000 black workers—a significant share of the local black professional workforce. By this time, Supreme Life had nearly $60 million worth of policies in force, accounting for one-fifth of the black insurance business nationwide. Invited to come on as Pace's personal assistant, Johnson soon abandoned studies at the University of Chicago. Indeed, it is a central irony of Johnson's success that it derived from his background in black insurance, rather than race journalism: circumstances meriting closer examination.[10]

Seeking to convey respect for his first employer, Johnson wrote that "all roads in Black Chicago led to Supreme." So it must have seemed to others as well: on the eve of World War II, the company spearheaded struggles for reform, and provided work and service to a sizable constituency of blacks, in Chicago and beyond. For the hundreds employed at the company, Supreme Life represented one of a handful of businesses offering work commensurate with the advanced education increasing numbers of African Americans received as historically black colleges expanded enrollments and northern white universities modestly expanded access. Supreme Life challenged residential segregation by underwriting black homeownership, quadrupling its stake in the mortgage market from 1936, when Johnson began working with the company, to 1942. The 1940 *Lee v. Hansberry* Supreme Court case, the first successful challenge to restrictive housing covenants, was argued by Earl Dickerson and other company counsel. The legal team represented the Hansberry family (including future playwright Lorraine Hansberry), whose home mortgage was underwritten by the company. Dickerson himself had been the beneficiary of Supreme Life's social involvement previously, finding funds and staff there for a successful city council campaign in 1939. Nor was Supreme Life the only such corporate benefactor active locally: its main competition, Metropolitan Mutual Assurance, was also a bulwark of community life in Chicago. Metropolitan Mutual started a magazine, the *Bronzeman*, in 1930, underwrote the state-of-the-art radio studio used by Jack Cooper that same year, purchased the Chicago American Giants of the Negro League in 1932, and opened the Parkway Ballroom, which rivaled the Regal Theater as a local leisure venue during the 1940s.[11]

The diverse services of companies like Supreme Life and Metropolitan recommend reexamination of long-standing critiques leveled against race commerce generally at this time. Writing in the year of Johnson's arrival at Supreme Life, Abram Harris dismissed the utility of black businesses, citing the low financial ceilings of African-American communities (and markets) along with black entrepreneurs' own exploitative motive for promoting group uplift to argue the impossibility of a viable African-American ownership class. Providing crucial precedent for later studies, Harris used the term "defensive enterprises" to characterize African-American business generally, concluding that given widespread underdevelopment and segregation, black enterprise was consigned to remain a feebly compensatory structure. Like Frazier, Harris sought to demystify the Washingtonian philosophy of racial self-help, emphasizing instead black industrial workers and those institutions, such as the Congress of Industrial Organizations (CIO), seeking to incorporate them into the labor movement, as primary agents of social change. Subsequent arguments of the black middle class's adverse relation to racial advance—notably Harold Cruse's relentless if vitriolic charge of "class incompetence"—drew heavily on Harris's critiques, as they would on Frazier's subsequent theories of racial nihilism.[12]

The history of black insurance from the 1920s through World War II, though, challenges this blanket dismissal. While these companies doubtless maintained focus on their balance sheets, they nonetheless developed and enriched multiple strata of black life politically, economically, and culturally. Such actions were crucial during the Depression, when other sources of risk capital—especially banks—toppled in large numbers within African-American communities. In particular, expansion of mortgage programs by insurance companies encouraged financial stability and therefore material security more broadly in black communities of the time. Lacking reserves with which to make other investments, most blacks earning anything over subsistence found homeownership the only means to secure assets, realize capital gains, and establish some tenuous hold on class stability.[13] Small wonder that with widespread failings elsewhere among comparable businesses, black insurance companies weathered relatively manageable declines during the Depression, retaining their market base of low-cost policies that working-class African Americans somehow found means to purchase.[14]

With this in mind, the effects of commercial business in Black Chicago after the Depression dispute the insolvency—material, political, and ethical—presumed to mark an emergent black middle class. More than defensive or compensatory concerns, black businesses like Supreme Liberty Life abetted vital structures of racial community. Indeed, Supreme Life's example indicates a striking competence on the part of the black bourgeoisie: an ability to foster growth in diverse social spheres, thereby stabilizing multiple class strata within the black community. Most accounts depict black class formation as a fundamentally structural process, with workers shifting from service to industry work after World War II, while the middle class expanded from the 1950s to the 1970s, once again due to broad occupational shifts, especially toward public sector employment.[15] In Black Chicago after 1940, though, this process operated in internal as much as exterior ways. Encouraging homeownership, underwriting church and institutional expansion, and providing services to diverse social strata,

18. Supreme Liberty Life Building, at the corner of 35th Street and South Parkway. Photographed by Wayne F. Miller. Courtesy of Wayne F. Miller.

Supreme Life and related companies helped materially consolidate black working and middle classes simultaneously. Local race businessmen constituted, using the words of E. P. Thompson, a class "present at its own making"—and that of others as well.[16]

The impact of these conditions on Johnson, needless to say, was profound. Though not always well used at Supreme Life—"an underpaid factotum" was how one associate remembered him—Johnson's momentary financial shortfall was counterbalanced by the experience he acquired. Assigned to assist Dickerson's 1939 city-council run, Johnson soon took an integral role, managing publicity for the candidate. Meanwhile, Johnson's regular tasks at Supreme Life consolidated that same year into editing the company newspaper, the *Guardian*, meaning extensive contact with lead staff and even deeper interaction with Pace, by now his closest mentor. This last promotion, it is clear, also planted the seed for Johnson's later journalistic forays. Seeking discreet (he and his family were passing for white in the near-west suburb of Riverside) means to keep up on news concerning black life, Pace had Johnson prepare a monthly digest of relevant items beginning in 1942. Though effective as a source of information for Pace, it proved less successful regarding his other concerns. Pace and his family were racially outed early in 1943—the resulting strain doubtless a factor in his mysterious death later that year. Johnson was left with sober memories (he claims to have warned his boss of plans among disgruntled employees to disclose Pace's identity to neighbors in Riverside), countless lessons, and a promising format for a new publishing venture.[17]

While working at Supreme Life, Johnson began to envision a commercial magazine modeled on Pace's digest. Consulting established black journalists, Johnson encountered uniform pessimism: both ANP editor Frank Marshall Davis and *Crisis* editor Roy Wilkens told Johnson they saw no future for the venture. Nonetheless Johnson persevered, convincing Ben Burns, *Defender* editor and former member of the Communist Party, to join him on a freelance basis. Johnson artfully cobbled together funding for the first issue: a $500 loan paying for subscription letter postage was secured by using his mother's new furniture as collateral. Potential subscribers were identified through policy rolls for Supreme Life, processed thanks to Johnson's facility with the company's Speedaumat mailing system. The end result—5,000 copies of a pocket magazine titled *Negro Digest*—were delivered to subscribers and newsstands in November 1942. Ever attuned to market dynamics, Johnson primed the pump for *Digest* by enlisting friends to purchase multiple copies at newsstands, creating the impression of a hot property meriting further printing and sales.[18]

The magazine itself was unlike any preceding it in black journalism. Close focus on questions of racial justice and its relevance to national affairs was evident in the first issue. Articles by Walter White and Horace Mann Bond advocated full support of war, while round tables related that same war patriotism to imperatives of racial justice, maintaining that "the Negro population's demand for full equality in American life [was] not interfering with or sabotaging the nation's war effort." Other articles highlighted entertainment and culture: a story on Trinidadian musician Hazel Scott as well as Roi Ottley's commissioned feature "Black Jews of Harlem" both ran in the debut issue. An account of the Indian nationalist leader Jawaharlal Nehru was the first of what would prove to be a series of articles that would mirror the shift in the black press toward a more internationalist focus during the 1930s and 1940s. Dr. Julian Lewis, physician at Provident Hospital, excerpted his recent book on the genetic mutability of racial characteristics, meant to prove the fallacy of social Darwinian notions of racial fitness.[19] The first issue's eclecticism hinted its potential as a model for a more national brand of race journalism: only such a bricolage approach could truly articulate the complexity of postmigration African America.

Apparent as well were signs of Johnson Publishing's departure from the fighting press tradition within black life. Though race publications had been historically defined by strong, domineering editors, *Negro Digest* followed a different path: the journal's status as "digest of opinion on the Negro" meant it manifest a more plural personality, not only concerning opinion, but literal editorial control. A combination of circulating stories and eclectically commissioned pieces, *Digest* offered an alternative to the personalized polemics historically characterizing the black press. Indeed, the question of who actually edited the magazine posed a quandary for readers. While Johnson designated himself managing editor on the masthead—in fact the only employee listed for several issues—collaborator Ben Burns claims to have secured most of the pieces during early years, editing and then laying out the magazine while Johnson preoccupied himself with marketing and planning. The complexities of this matter deepen greatly when one considers that Burns was himself white—and an editor of universally recognized brilliance within black journalism. While Burns's talents and meticulous memory support his claims, it seems most appropriate to argue the magazine was, in essence, edited jointly. As Burns himself acknowledged, Johnson articulated *Digest*'s broad focus in conversation, which the veteran journalist sought then to bring into form.[20]

Though the magazine's editorial process defied easy explanation, its appeal proved immediately clear. After first printing 10,000 copies, *Digest* increased circulation to 50,000 by summer 1943, and 200,000 copies monthly by 1945—20 percent of the total for all black magazines combined. Johnson drew together a transregional distribution system, working with postal workers and business owners in Chicago, Philadelphia, Los Angeles, and Atlanta. Though Burns recalled an obsequious tone in *Digest* on questions of racial justice, the articles themselves registered more variegated orientation. Advertisements encouraging the purchase of war bonds coincided with critical discussions of the federal policy of separate blood banks during the war. Sociologist Horace Cayton opined in "What Strategy for the Negro: Patience or Pressure?" that ongoing federal discrimination, together with eruptions of racial violence in Detroit, New York, and Los Angeles in the hot summer of 1943, inspired in blacks "a new critical consideration of [their] position in the social structure of the country and a new attitude toward the theory and practice of democracy." A December 1944 forum titled "Have the Communists Quit Fighting for Negro Rights" drew together authorities across the ideological spectrum—Cayton, conservative George Schuyler, black Communist leader James Ford, ILD (International Labor Defense) attorney William Patterson, and Harlem radical politician Benjamin Davis.[21]

Discussions of popular culture in *Digest* conveyed equal range and nuance. The entertainment focus initiated with the story of Hazel Scott carried through pieces on bandleader and "Father of the Blues" W. C. Handy, photographer Gordon Parks, and even pioneering disc jockey Jack Cooper: premonitions of the cult of black stardom Johnson Publishing would soon perfect. Two articles on writer Dan Burley, digesting his *Original Handbook of Harlem Jive,* described urban black vernacular as a signifying art and strategy of resistance, in a manner predicting recent analyses of black speech. A reprint of a 1943 *New York Times* article offered a genealogy for the zoot suit, emphasizing the interface of dominant and subversive traditions evident in both its emergence and effect. Other articles highlighted various transracial interlocutors, such as linguist, *Defender* columnist, and future California senator S. I. Hayakawa, and Harlem Globetrotters founder Abe Saperstein.[22]

Indeed, these last pieces indicated *Digest*'s unspoken premise that race was itself a construction—the product of disposition and habit rather than biological imperatives. Further evidence of this orientation came with a series of invited columns titled "If I Were a Negro," beginning in December 1942. Including public figures ranging from Orson Welles and Marshall Field to Saul Alinsky, the series sought to personalize liberal interest and empathy for improved race relations by asking prominent whites to imagine an existence stripped of race privilege. The series reached its highpoint in October 1943, when First Lady Eleanor Roosevelt provided the column. The stir surrounding her submission resulted in a doubling of circulation for the magazine from 50,000 to 100,000. Articles on the practice of passing within the black community, and the appropriateness of interracial marriage reinforced the central point that race and racism derived from variable social practice rather than imperatives of biology. Diverse in coverage and editorial interest, the magazine fast became the most acclaimed and popular African-American journal. Johnson began to consult magnates from the white publishing world—including Gardner Cowles of *Look* and Henry Luce of Time-Life—on how to maintain his enviable business position. *Negro Digest* had—at least for the moment—found an answer to the barriers long limiting the growth of black magazines.[23]

Yet clearly Johnson Publishing was not content to rest on initial success. Woven through the *Digest*'s early stories were reflections on one more theme: the burgeoning interest in race marketing. David Sullivan, black founder of an ad agency and market consulting firm based in New York, contributed several articles discussing black consumers and the rules of race-conscious advertising. Articles chronicling black commercial sectors—especially the insurance industry—sought to emphasize the growing material clout of better-paid workers and a growing black white-collar work force. Given the lessons Johnson learned at Supreme Life concerning the social and political significance of this process, it is clear that this focus on the emergence of African Americans as a bona-fide market sector indicated a longer-term agenda. Johnson and his company pursued these goals energetically with their next project, a magazine redrawing sightlines for black journalism still more dramatically than *Digest* had.[24]

Ebony arrived in the late fall of 1945, with a breezy sense of jaunty self-promotion ("a reconversion act out of an ancient hat . . . that would put Houdini to shame") that promised style rather than substance. Yet subsequent claims that it was "a magazine of, by, and for people proud of their color,"[25] indicated that focus on black life's zesty side might yet provide a novel cutting edge to portrayal of group life. Assessment of *Ebony* has rarely moved beyond its purported exploitation of an audience consigned up to that point to poorly capitalized race papers and magazines. Closer examination, however, shows that the magazine redefined what "black community" meant in the wake of two world wars, continued migration, and first hints of the civil authorization to come in the wake of the *Brown* decision.

Like its predecessor *Negro Digest, Ebony* barely made it off of the drawing board. Long discussed by Johnson, Ben Burns, and other *Digest* staffers, actual publication of *Ebony* did not begin until paper rationing strictures were lifted after the surrender of the Japanese in August 1945.[26] With no sense as to demand, the company printed 25,000 copies of *Ebony* in late October, far short of the publication run needed to meet expenses. Burns, continuing to format and edit, remembered the finished product as "less than inspired." Unable to afford the "triple breakthrough" of fast-drying inks, coated paper, and fire dry printing R. R. Donnelley applied to the publishing of *Life* beginning in 1937, *Ebony* instead reproduced the washed grays and imprecise layouts of pre-Depression publications, leaving Johnson and Burns fearing swift critique.[27] To their surprise, reactions proved positive. *Time* and *Newsweek* ran favorable reviews of the magazine, while letters of praise came from Pittsburgh *Courier* editor William Nunn, Los Angeles *Sentinel* publisher Leon Washington, and Langston Hughes, among others.[28] As with *Digest,* demand rapidly grew. Running out of magazines after the first printing, the company published another run of 25,000 copies. By its second issue, *Ebony* had already surpassed the 200,000 circulation figure for *Digest*.[29]

Clues to the magazine's success, along with directions for its growth, were apparent in the first issue. It retained *Digest*'s emphasis on publicly recognized blacks, running features on Hazel Scott, Richard Wright, Eddie "Rochester" Anderson, and Philadelphia banker Major Wright.[30] Survey of economic conditions in Brazil, and an editorial calling for full employment as the war economy contracted indicated concern with the situation of black labor at home and abroad. Joining an article on curators and collectors of African art, the Brazilian overview emphasized transnational and diasporic focus: one advocating cosmopolitan appreciation of non-Western aesthetics, and endorsing unorthodox geopolitics in an emerging decolonized world. Embrace of the vindicationist school of black thought was unmistakable: *Ebony*'s obsession with stories on "the first, the only, the best" in black life of course proved grist for later critiques of the magazine's skewed social perspective. Yet it is worth remembering the novelty of such arguments for racial achievement at this time, when many still questioned the plausibility of these claims.[31]

By the fourth issue, Johnson and Burns were well aware of the project's appeal—and potential. Responding to reader questions regarding the magazine's distinctive title, they offered a telling response:

> A handful of folks . . . have been writing to state their objections [to the magazine's name], i.e., 1. Ebony means black; 2. What does Ebony mean?
>
> On objection No. 1 we enter a dissent based on our contention that there's nothing wrong with blacks as a race; Negroes have much to be proud of. Their achievements stamp black as a color to take pride in. Black is a badge of accomplishment by a people who have stood staunch and steadfast against the worst that is in the white man's soul and yet lifted their heads high through the centuries . . . Black is and should be a color of high esteem.
>
> *Ebony*'s purpose in life is to mirror the deeds of black men, to help blend America's blacks and whites into interracial understanding through mutual admiration of all that is good in both. *Ebony* is a maga-

> zine of, by, and for Negroes who are proud of their color. Therefore the name—*Ebony*.
>
> On objection No. 2, we hope to teach through the medium of *Ebony* what the word means.[32]

The declaration had significance beyond invoking pride and perseverance. By promising to "teach . . . what the word means"—*Ebony* as medium, but also "black" as identity—the editors assumed a role more ambitious than mirroring race achievement of the day. A bid to reshape and extend racial meaning itself was also being offered. Certainly one audience targeted with this intervention were progressive whites, especially in the early months. Receiving a number of letters from interested white readers Johnson would, in late 1946, pursue an ultimately unsuccessful marketing campaign to generate an appreciable white subscriber base.[33] Yet *Ebony* also proposed to rework the thinking of blacks themselves concerning race and racial politics. Extending *Digest*'s strategy of portraying black life and imagination in a nuanced, complex manner, *Ebony* sought to answer Alain Locke's call that African Americans base notions of group upon a shared life, rather than a common problem.[34]

The significance of this becomes more clear when one notes how difficult it remains to historicize ideas of race *within* African-American communities, in this and other periods. Recent analyses of domestic racial formation, ranging from the rationalization of immigration policy, to the modern rise of the racial state, to the emergence of the working class in the nineteenth century, rarely present black identity specifically as a dynamic entity, defying prediction from one moment to the next.[35] In one sense, this omission connotes respect for the stabilizing role of racial identification within African-American thought: black identity in the United States is presumed fully formed, a legacy whose conservation, rather than elaboration, provides the basis of collective feeling.[36] This, as much as anything, has encouraged the emphasis on stories of struggle and constancy in the face of challenge that provide the traditional emphasis on what is termed "race consciousness." Obviously, these accounts deserve places of pride in memory and history, not least because of stubborn aversion toward the basic premise of African Americans' humanity among some scholars and still more of the public even today. Yet just as obvious is the potential for ahistoricity and essentialism resulting when such accounts denote the horizons of group existence. Raising questions as to how African Americans developed a sense of shared being is, at base, a commitment to the idea that racial identity—as well as oppression or resistance—constitutes an entity itself in perpetual formation. With such concerns in mind, the early years of *Ebony* become that much more important, given its potent—and popular—evocation of modern ideas of black community.

Yet one must ask what alternative ideas of African-American community did *Ebony* articulate? How did it transform notions of race within the collective imagination of blacks at this time? Closer examination of core themes established during the magazine's first decade provide answers to these questions.

Among the more striking—and overlooked—characteristics of *Ebony* was its appetite for racially evocative culture and arts, in the United States and beyond. Frazier may have concluded that the magazine "reject[ed] any genuine identification with the black race," but such charges seem difficult, if not impossible, to justify. What Zora Neale Hurston termed "a will to adorn" grounding black aesthetics was evident in a 1946 feature on Rose-Meta Salon in Harlem, whose co-owners Rose Morgan and Olivia Clarke gained credit for their race-proud motto that "no Negro hair is bad."[37] Two years later, similar race-conscious standards marked a spread on African fashion based on Etta Moton's travels there, featuring Yoruban (Nigerian), Faradic and Banga (Congolese), and Sudanese hairstyles and accessories.[38] Early articles extolled the vibrant public life of historic black towns like Eatonville, Florida, and Mound Bayou, Mississippi. Hurston, by now relocated to her Florida hometown, was pictured and listed as "most famous citizen" of Eatonville. A 1948 piece recounted a "rowdy" rendition of Shakespeare's *The Taming of the Shrew* by the Karamu Theater Company in Cleveland—the most venerated little theater to survive the Negro Renaissance years.[39] The magazine often returned to the memory site of slavery, as in a 1954 piece on the descendants of Dred Scott or an earlier one discussing the growing ritual of Juneteenth.[40] Contemporary urban culture offered further occasion for collective validation, through exhaustive accounts of nightclubs and performers in all genres, as well as grass roots intellectuals like Dan Burley.[41] Perhaps no cultural area received more thorough account in the magazine than the kinetic arts. Beginning with a retrospective on Katherine Dunham, *Ebony* documented ritual movement's hold on ethnic, national, and diasporic sensibility, vividly portraying the *rumba*, *mambo*, lindy hop, *beguine*, and *capoeira*, among others.[42] On occasion, more peripheral creative practices were covered, as with a March 1948 article promoting the transsexual stage shows at Joe's DeLuxe Café on the South Side: a noteworthy feature of queer subculture within national media of any kind for this period.[43]

It would be stretching matters to interpret *Ebony*'s survey of expressive

19. Female impersonator Valda Gray backstage at Joe's DeLuxe Café. Photographed by Wayne F. Miller. Courtesy of Wayne F. Miller.

culture as racially exclusive. Even as landmarks of black identity were visited, the magazine held to its promise to promote "interracial understanding through mutual admiration of all that is good in both." Articles on white cultural go-betweens like drummer Louis Belson or singer Johnny Ray lauded their awareness of debt to black predecessors.[44] Other stories advocated interracial fellowship and cross-cultural exchange more broadly. Noteworthy here were a series of pieces discussing Japanese–African-American relations stateside as well as in Japan.[45] Yet throughout emphasis remained on pluralist—what we today would term multiculturalist—embrace of the evocative rather than standards of racial normativity or assimilation. The cultural meaning of blackness in Ebony's estimation was composite, eclectic, often unorthodox—and ever contingent and creative. These qualities suggested a decentered humanism, as much as compensatory self-identification, an approach affirmed in turn by abundant reader response. Virtually all letters sent from white readers, and not a few from blacks, emphasized the suggestive possibilities black expression held for human development at large.

The polymath nature of *Ebony*'s cultural coverage offered powerful argument for addressing black lives in situated context. Place and time were key, the magazine argued, for grasping those lives in appropriate detail. Other lines of coverage proved equally sensitive measures of the epochal shifts in black condition following World War II, the cusp of African Americans' demographic transition from an agrarian to an urban people. Noteworthy among these lines were complex and extensive accounts of black work, and the emerging bifurcation of black occupational life along working and middle-class lines.

Though *Ebony*'s ideal subject was the professional or, better still, the entrepreneur, the predominance of laborers, operatives, and service workers among African Americans demanded that media seeking a black audience make an effective appeal to this majority. Accordingly, the magazine addressed concerns of working class blacks, with empathy if not always solidarity. The lower depths of labor exploitation were consigned to settler nations, garrison territories, and protectorates across the globe like South Africa, Brazil, the Virgin Islands, or the Panama Canal Zone.[46] Worker insurgency was similarly displaced. An August 1947 piece on Federacion de Trabajadores Cubanos's president Lazaro Pena termed him "the Negro who could be Cuba's President," while more muddled survey of the Jamaican political scene extolled the populist credentials of Prime Minister Alexander Bustamante, a long-time trade unionist there.[47] Accounts of U.S. black labor ferment, in comparison, were muted. A 1947 feature on Sam Parks, Willard Townsend, Ferdinand Smith, and other labor activists gave due notice to their efforts on behalf of African Americans engaged in the trades. Yet leadership by left-labor blacks of progressive campaigns in New York, Chicago, Memphis, and Los Angeles gained little mention, besides general allusion in scattered editorials.[48] Given the vanguard role organized labor played in domestic antiracist campaigns during the 1940s, not to mention more general global insurgency at this time, *Ebony*'s cropped coverage of worker initiative recalled the age-old uplift stance of ministering to workers' needs without acknowledging their partnership in struggles for social change.[49]

If the magazine failed to acknowledge the social initiative of African-

American labor, it showed more acuity in detailing the conditions they faced, especially in an economy undergoing runaway restructuring. Expanding occupational sectors detailed in *Ebony*—from postal work to farm equipment manufacture, from Chicago-area steelwork to sandhog digging of tunnels in New York City—gave the magazine the frequent appearance of a job bank. "Employment" even constituted a regular heading in the monthly table of contents until 1950.[50] But less encouraging faces of economic modernization were documented as well. Articles on the closing of the Kaiser Shipyards in San Francisco Bay area and contraction of southern cotton farm work due to mechanization trenchantly noted the upheavals black workers faced after 1945.[51] Prolonged postwar slump inspired concern on several occasions, including one editorial in 1947 where the magazine even warned of the onset of Depression-era levels of joblessness.[52] Clear counsel was rarely forthcoming in these instances—and when it appeared it did not always prove incisive or useful, as with an unfortunate 1948 editorial directed to displaced workers titled "Why Not Go Back to the Farm?"[53] Yet coverage of the changing economy, viewed retrospectively, proved strikingly prescient concerning the coming shift, in the nature and availability of work for blacks as domestic industrial expansion entered its final decades.

More invested coverage was devoted to the professional, commercial, and entrepreneurial sectors. Occasionally, the magazine profiled occupational pioneers among industrial workers, as in a 1948 story on American Airlines mechanic Sarah Patterson.[54] More often, though, stories of occupational entry concerned the more elevated stages of the jobs pyramid. Accounts of barrier busters among faculty at white colleges and universities, marketing agencies, or the sciences joined similarly upbeat coverage of sectors traditionally accessible to African Americans, like black insurance or banking.[55] Even more so than the professions, independent enterprise gained *Ebony*'s interest—and acclaim. Universally recognized successes, like architect Paul Williams or finance magnate C. C. Spaulding, vied with more improbable heroes, like dude ranch owner Lela Murray, mink farmer Robert Alexander Crosby, or leather craftswoman Hazel Washington, who left work as a maid in Los Angeles to found a business "thriving on the trade of the Hollywood's biggest stars and the nation's swankiest shops."[56] Accounts of self-employed blacks, such as Lubbock residents William Lusk (bootmaker), Clarence Lyon (dentist), and Joseph Chapmen (doctor) preached the gospel of commercial utility—the most direct path to "rich incomes and real respect from white clientele." This point was underscored by other stories detailing personal ascensions from sharecropping or even slavery to business success.[57] Publication in mid-1949 of "The Ten Richest

Negroes in America" tilted the magazine decidedly toward the coverage of black wealth, rather than work. Lauding figures like Robert Cole, founder of Metropolitan Mutual Assurance or Birmingham entrepreneur A. C. Gaston as inspiring examples of the $10 billion aggregate income of African Americans, the piece overstated black wealth's causal relation to group improvement.[58] Yet, these stories, though unabashed tributes to a nascent black ownership class, sought a broader audience than narcissistic social climbers. While the modernizing economy held risks for middle-class blacks as well as workers, *Ebony* portrayed the material uncertainty of the times as a universal occasion for opportunity rather than fear. For both classes, future improvement rested on exercise of choice and initiative according to market dictates: a philosophy reflecting the sentiments of *Ebony*'s publisher, but as well the productivity ethic characterizing ameliorative approaches throughout the race since Booker T. Washington.

Excellence or acuity in law proved another important line of coverage. Stories on both men and women lawyers singled that profession out for special recognition and respect: the account of women lawyers, including Judge Jane Bolin, Edith Sampson, and NAACP attorney Constance Baker Motley, proved the first group treatment of working women presented in the magazine.[59] Soon after, the magazine moved from occupational surveys to deeper examination of law and justice. A 1947 article "Does FEPC Work?" detailed the work of New York's State Commission Against Discrimination (SCAD), the only statewide job access program in operation in the United States at the time. Explaining SCAD's impact through reference to the 1946 repeal of FEPC at the federal level, the magazine cataloged its investigative, remedial, and publicity efforts, while acknowledging its effective lack of enforcement powers. Among the article's more novel items was a photo cycle, "Case History of a Discrimination Complaint," documenting step-by-step a black staff member processing a complaint against a New York clothing company. The piece included a plaintiff interview, site visit, examination of records, management testimony, and, ultimately, exoneration of the company. This how-to format would reappear in August 1948, in an article depicting lawyer Gordon Stafford's network of black and white "testers" ascertaining compliance with antibias laws among San Diego area restaurants.[60]

Such accounts of law and policy promoted a basic mission of activation: *Ebony* made this clear in the 1948 piece, quoting Stafford's frustration that more African Americans were not coming forward with actionable complaints. Yet a broader principle was at stake as well, as in the case of coverage of black business initiative. Graphic illustration of the procedures and mechanisms of antidiscrimination not only detailed how law worked—it was also meant to establish, for African-American readers, that law *could work*. Accounts of the turn toward legalism in antiracist organizing after 1940, most notably the NAACP's campaign against school segregation, emphasize the actions of strategists and plaintiffs. The broader black public in these accounts is generally presented as naturally joining the ranks once court victories were secured.[61] Yet legalism was not a self-evident road to justice for African Americans at this time—nor was there much reason it should have been. Even leaving aside the jurisprudence of racial nonstanding running back to the Dred Scott decision in 1857, African Americans had numerous reasons to view law's rule with cynicism: systematic dispossession related to wages, jobs, promotion, and property; grossly unequally rates of arrest, conviction, and sentence; and law's frequent and violent degeneration in tragically large numbers of cases involving African Americans. As Mary Francis Berry, Derrick Bell, and others have shown, these abuses routinely occurred through law's exercise, rather than its absence.[62] The postwar turn toward a rights approach to racial justice, then, required a dramatic shift in black common sense, in addition to altered organizational tactics or strategies. Proof of this can be inferred by the resurgence of cynicism among African Americans regarding the law since the 1960s, marked by emphatic responses to the 1992 LAPD acquittals, or the Simpson trials in 1995 and 1996.[63]

Ebony's illustration of remedial policies, though neither main nor sole precipitant of this turn, vividly anticipated the coming shift of African Americans' resort to law's rule, several years prior to the *Brown* decision. These articles detailing law's work admitted the significance of institutional as well as social racism, and assigned blacks much of the responsibility for challenging and overcoming it. Yet it made clear that they could expect to best do so through law, rather than in spite of it. This commitment proved deeply influential upon *Ebony*'s vision of racial politics, almost from the magazine's inception. In what proved the most significant editorial controversy of *Ebony*'s first decade, the May 1946 issue covered the Columbia (Tennessee) race riot, a prolonged assault on hundreds of the town's blacks resulting in widespread property damage, numerous casualties, and two deaths.[64] Using pictures supplied by *Life* photographer Roger Atkins, the story portrayed white vigilantes, some still in military uniform, hunting down African Americans, with one shot of a bloodied black victim lying on city streets. The obvious parallels to prior cycles of U.S. racial violence were inescapable in the article's rhetorical question: "will 1946 repeat 1919, America's worst year of race violence?" Staff members recalled Johnson banning future portrayals of mob violence, given sponsor and advertiser pressure to steer the magazine clear of such incendiary coverage. Yet a different analysis of this episode might note that the difficulty of the story for *Ebony* lay not so much in its raw representation of racist violence, but rather in its portrayal of legal authority as ineffective or even capricious. It would be nearly a decade before *Ebony* would revisit the topic of racial violence in the United States, despite the regular occurrence of such incidents during these years, nowhere more so than in Chicago. An important reason for this, clearly, was its stake in affirming the remedial and reform capacity of civil law—a position greatly shaping its subsequent approach to the struggles of the civil rights era.

A different—and also significant—area of coverage for the magazine concerned its attention to emotional community, in particular that of the black family. Histories of black migration up to the present day routinely employ the family as a psychic rudder for African Americans coming to midcentury northern cities. Catalysts of black mass movement, ranging from written letters to migration clubs, developed along lines of family as much as those of community or institution. Once arrived, African-American migrants' embrace of new conditions of employment, or novel modes of social and cultural action, often progressed to the extent family provided the necessary financial or emotional margin.[65] Migrants often boarded with relatives, as Richard Wright did with a Chicago aunt in 1927, or sought material support through kin, as John Johnson did in 1945. Of course, Frazier chose to portray urban black families in deep crisis by this time, a tendency evoked more vividly still by Wright's scathing portrayal of black families' incapacity to answer protagonists' needs in his writing, including works relating the story of his own life.[66] Most analysts—particularly those associated with the social history school beginning in the 1970s—choose instead to emphasize black families' resilience, rather than dysfunction, in modern northern cities.

Yet one need not go to Frazier's or Wright's lengths to acknowledge the stress upon African-American families during the 1940s. Formal mobilization of black men, and, to a lesser extent, black women, during World War II coincided with the renewal of racial migration driven by war production to effect the greatest dislocation of African Americans since the antebellum domestic slave market. Military assignments meant breaking parental, sibling, and partner ties, while war production relocation similarly disrupted domestic arrangements. The entry of women into industrial jobs and roles as heads of households rewrote gender relations, even given traditions of women's self-support among African Americans.[67] Rising wages and rates of promotion, a boon for many African Americans during the 1940s, nonetheless brought new personal anxieties around essential and discretionary spending. These challenges had to be met without the reserves or lines of credit enjoyed by whites, creating further strain on black families, not least of which were higher expectations of youth dependents concerning both subsidy and autonomy. Perhaps most dramatically, relocation of over a third of African America since the turn of the century meant extended families—an indispensable social and cultural resource since slavery—were severely dispersed. Though surrogate kin networks of the sort sociologist Carol Stack studied would in time fill these gaps, such improvised relations took time to develop.[68] The emerging ritual of the black family reunion, widespread by this time, offered evidence of the dedication to maintaining family ties in spite of dislocation; at the same time, it registered widespread anxieties over African Americans' capacity to do so.

Ebony's response to these conditions was complex. On occasion the magazine affirmed black families' resilience in uncertain times, emphasizing conventional mores such as patriarchy, fidelity, and juvenile deference. But more often *Ebony* brought a modernizing outlook to bear on the home, as it did with other prior templates of black life like agrarianism or even segregation. Parenting was presented as skill rather than investiture, with psychology and expert counsel emphasized as keys to success. Domestic portraits highlighted nuclear families, celebrating their adaptability and concentration of resources, and questioning, by implication, the utility of extended kin networks. And on occasion, *Ebony* presented nontraditional community as an appropriate alternative to traditional domesticity. The sum result reaffirmed family's importance within modern black experience, but also offered telling record of its revision and redefinition at the same time.

Ben Burns recalled a "no children" rule for *Ebony* covers, because of the staff believed that they proved less attractive to readers than entertainers or models.[69] No such prohibitions existed on couple and family shots, which dominated covers not devoted to individual subjects. Countless articles situated recognizable African Americans in repose at home, ostensibly to level them in the eyes of readers. Though a few such articles proved merely material accounts of lifestyle, others moved past the furniture to portray domestic life more deeply, in terms of familial psyche and emotions. An 1946 article on NAACP President Walter White—the first of several addressing his home situation—emphasized his qualities as "an ideal family man," with testimonials from wife Gladys and account of his warm relations with adult daughter Jane, an aspiring theater actor.[70] The piece's braided story lines—a father's authority, a wife's admiration, a daughter's ambition—anticipated the composite structure of other *Ebony* accounts of black homes, including articles on Jackie and Rachel Robinson during his first year with the Brooklyn Dodgers, Hazel Scott and Adam Clayton

Powell, and insistent cover stories of Joe Louis with wife Marva and children, even as their marriage inexorably dissolved.[71] In such articles, loyalty to family and career were presented as complementary rather than antagonistic commitments, reassurance that the magazine's ethos would not compromise emotional and interpersonal well-being. However, familial devotion did not escape all question. In accounts of children especially, attention to autonomous ambition, such as Jane White's struggles to build an acting career, or even musical prodigy Philippa Schuyler's first date, argued balance between kin obligation and self-definition for blacks as modern individuals.[72]

While black families—especially nuclear families—routinely appeared in *Ebony,* they did not exhaust depiction of emotional community. An article on Roosevelt cooperative house in Cleveland detailed twenty-three black, white, Japanese, and Chinese living together, and featured pictures of Simeon Booker, a black journalist working with the Cleveland *Call and Post.*[73] Another piece detailing the Hollywood travails of struggling actress Avenelle Harris noted not only Harris's close bond with her mother, but reliance on a tight circle of actress friends as well as managers and advisors. Other treatments of transsexual society in Chicago, or prizefighters maternally shepherded by Sarah "Tiny" Paterson, the "lady boxing boss," validated unorthodox emotional communities that answered to more compounded conditions of alienation faced by various subcultures within black life.[74] To be sure, more traditional iterations of psychological sustenance received the greatest emphasis within *Ebony.* A powerful example of this was the implicit role of black public mother assigned to Mary McLeod Bethune within the magazine. Friendships with both Roosevelts as well as her unpretentious philanthropic style provided a pretext for articles that placed Bethune before readers as a universal elder, encouraging a postwar revival of her reputation.[75]

Yet bids to make surrogate parents of public leaders inadvertently underscored the growing impermanence of black families, covered with particular intensity in *Ebony.* The protracted break-up of Joe and Marva Louis was but one of many tales of domestic fracture serialized in the magazine. Walter White's 1949 divorce and remarriage to white South African Poppy Cannon elicited substantial reader mail, coverage of their India honeymoon, and follow-up analyses of the apparent trend toward interracial marriage.[76] Stories of mercurial entertainer romances mirrored the work of publicity departments of the Hollywood studios,[77] but also advised that marriage was neither inevitable nor, it seemed, essential to personal well-being. Divorce rates of 33 percent were cited in a feature on sexual counseling for couples, while another extolled the vitality of black divorcees.[78] This recalled the therapeutic *imprateur* of other pieces, such as an expose of the black female respondent to the Kinsey survey, or Ben Burns's articles on sex education and couples' sexual compatibility, or even the soft Freudianism in the article "Dreams" (an exploration of race's role in the unconscious) all pushing counseling and self-analysis as keys to emotional development and fulfillment.[79] *Ebony*'s tendency toward pop therapy indicated an important gloss on the black home—conventional families could find respect within the magazine, but not necessarily reverence. Depictions of individuated, emotional life were just as prominent, marking the new realities all structures of black social life—including the family—had to adjust to.[80]

It is impossible to limn a clear line—conservative, nontraditional, or compensatory—from *Ebony*'s various accounts of African-American family. Black women were compelled to endorse patriarchal patterns of domestic life, while encouraged to affirm sexual freedom. Children were reminded to defer to parental authority, while being invited to differentiate through consumption, leisure, and even romance. African-American men were instructed in home responsibility, yet also steered toward cooperative and homosocial spheres as alternative emotional communities. What was clear, however, was its prediction of the black family's modification in response to social change ranging from consumerism to modern psychology, star fixation to the scattering of extended kin. Above all, endorsement of black individuation, within and without the family, contrasted starkly with Frazier's warnings that atomization of black life constituted the root source of deeper pathologies. Here, *Ebony*'s take on family did special work, conveying that while blood ties suffered stress or rupture, voluntary links of race community held surrogate capacity to nourish, inspire, agitate—in short to orient and ground.

To say that *Ebony*'s appeal derived largely from features of famous African Americans is to state the obvious. The dream world of successes, romances, and life routines of recognizable black personalities was for readers and staff the signature quality of the magazine. Opinions have varied, naturally, concerning its value: Frazier's was but the first of many to criticize *Ebony*'s society fix as the epitome of delusion and self-hate. On occasion members of the magazine's audience anticipated Frazier's objections, asking why the lives of prominent African Americans dominated its pages so. Many more, though, welcomed the emphasis on black fame. Though black newspapers or wire services like the ANP kept entertainment and society pages whenever budgets allowed, *Ebony*'s resources, contacts, and visual format set a new standard. Indeed, it was *Ebony* that originated the specific concept of black celebrity, a structure central to

African-American culture today, and evocative of deep shifts in racial notions of selfhood since the 1940s.

At first *Ebony*'s feature of famous African Americans was complicated by the historical relation of black status to white control and patronage.[81] The opening profile of Eddie Anderson, better known as Jack Benny's radio manservant Rochester, emphasized a lavish Los Angeles home and well-appointed lifestyle. Yet editors had no choice but to connect Anderson's bounty to his subordinated role on air—troubling reminder of the prevalence of racial servitude's determination of black work and life.[82] Anderson was one of several servant celebrities featured in early editions of *Ebony:* others included Fannie Shipley, head of legendary Baltimore catering service Shipley and Waters, veteran Pullman Porter Ray Duncan, and "movie maid" Lillian Mosley.[83] Recognizing the compromise inherent in deriving black fame from white indulgence, *Ebony* sought less obliged exemplars of prominence. Hazel Scott and Lena Horne were early favorites: Horne's March 1946 cover image, the first color cover for the magazine, caused one rapturous reader to liken her image to "a drink of champagne."[84] Joe Louis, champion of public attentions as well as the ring, garnered eight cover stories between 1946 and 1953, on an array of topics including his profligate lifestyle, business forays, prospective ring comeback, golf game, rumored past lovers—and of course, his tempestuous domestic life.[85] Through its first ten years, the magazine sought tirelessly if not always successfully to predict the rise of future stars, offering the glamour treatment to a range of up-and-coming performers including Francine Everette, June Richmond, Pearl Bailey, and Eartha Kitt.[86]

With the August 1948 cover story "King Cole's Honeymoon Diary," *Ebony*'s celebrity coverage took a pronounced turn. Detailing the Mexico honeymoon of Nat King Cole and singer Marie Ellington, the story followed the format of a photo diary narrated by Cole. Images of bullfights, poolside drinks, boating trips, and beach frolics were provided by staff photographer Griffith Davis, contracted to accompany the Coles on their trip. The story represented the first celebrity profile on foreign location—indicative, among other things, of *Ebony*'s unrivaled budget for features and remote stories. As well, its prearrangement around a moment of personal transition suggested circumstances besides those of work and home could sustain individual coverage. Though Joe Louis, Lena Horne, and others were used to having their daily errata serialized in the magazine, no previous feature had delivered star to public in such terms of celebration and repose. The carefree tone of the piece celebrated not only the Coles' marital bliss, but also travel and recreation more generally. Throughout 1948 the magazine had emphasized black vacationing, with articles on (relatively) race-friendly resorts and national parks, travel to Haiti, and the opening of Bethune Beach, a black-run resort near Daytona, Florida. The honeymoon diary of Nat and Marie Cole differed from these earlier pieces in its portrayal of black tourism unencumbered by concerns of prejudice—or budget. It was, in many ways a landmark, for *Ebony* and the black press historically, in recommending leisure, as opposed to labor, activism, or uplift, as a point of articulation for black existence and identity.[87]

It took time for the leisure ethic to take root in the magazine—initially Cole's first-person voice proved more influential as a format, with 1949 confessional articles by Adam Clayton Powell Jr., and Billie Holiday making clear the public relations utility of *Ebony*.[88] Over time, though, articles on Eddie "Rochester" Anderson's Sierra deer hunt, items on vacation fashions or on "non-Jim Crow" trip packages to Miami demonstrated the magazine's growing recommendation of a leisure ethic to readers.[89] Stories on Frank Yerby's or the Coles' plans to redecorate homes, or on society pages editors at black newspapers "work[ing] hard to chronicle gay doings on the Cadillac set" reinforced growing association of black celebrity with the good life, as much as achievement, productivity, and reputation.[90]

All this signaled a still broader turn away from time-honored values of respectability as the basis for positive reputation among African Americans. Concerning *intra*-racial relations, scholars have established, propriety and duty routinely served as the primary basis of social status among African Americans to this time.[91] Though *Ebony* did not seek to dispense entirely with respectability as a cornerstone of reputation, it is clear that the magazine was willing to play up controversy or even disrepute for public notice. Here true confession features—such as Billie Holiday's "I'm Cured For Good" or even African Methodist Episcopal Church officer Reverdy Ransom's "Confessions of a Bishop"[92]—loomed large, given their implicit argument that questionable behavior ought not impeach the prominent, but instead humanize them and show them as needing compassion (and on occasion intervention) just as with troubled black couples in other stories. Visibility was replacing reputation within the social grammar of black life, reinforcing the liberalization of thought occurring around a broader range of social concerns.

The group most affected by these changes were black women, for whom the politics of reputation had proved a central battleground for generations.[93] All too often, *Ebony*'s portrayal of women took on a prurient quality of exploitation: articles on college co-eds, women lifeguards, or artists' models leavened accounts of accomplishment and skill with a salacious eye, resulting in routine receipt of letters decrying the "risqué" character of the publication.[94] But other features on the personal lives of celebrities like

Lena Horne or Hazel Scott or Marva Louis conveyed as well respect for black women's choice on matters of romance and desire. Before *Ebony,* of course, there had been challenges to the containment of black women's sexuality in black public life—the eroticism of black female performance and corresponding reorganization of popular musical taste during the 1920s, for example, or the growth of the African-American beauty industry.[95] *Ebony*'s complex account of black women's visibility rather than reputation, found its significance in the broad male and female audience it could compel to consider women's sexuality in frank (if at times sensational) terms. In sum, these stories proposed that beauty and sexuality be seen as skills: one of the practices constituting what Stephanie Shaw terms black women's work, a broad sphere of activity ranging well beyond job or vocation.[96]

These commitments proved central to accounts of Dorothy Dandridge who, through her brief life, succeeded Horne, Louis, and others as the magazine's model figure during the 1950s. Though Dandridge was already topic of conversation in entertainment circles for her singing and film work, she had yet to register prominently before the broader public, including many African Americans. Upon Lena Horne's retirement from pictures (to return to live stage work and beat the increasing red-baiting storm), *Ebony* pitched an April 1951 profile of Dandridge as discovery of a new "No. 1 glamour queen." Though the story's occasion—release of B pictures *Tarzan's Peril* and *The Harlem Globetrotters*—revealed *Ebony*'s tendency toward hyperpromotion, it also hinted bigger things in Dandridge's future, in particular rumors of a major picture role to come. Shortly thereafter, the scattered pieces of Dandridge's career fell rapidly into place. Appearances later that year at Los Angeles's Mocambo Supper Club and London's Café de Paris won her coverage in the November 1951 issue of *Life,* and her contract at MGM as Horne's heir apparent. Three years later, Dandridge played the eponymous lead in *Carmen Jones,* for which she received an Oscar nomination, and coronation as queen of Black Hollywood. Having proven its ability to detail black celebrity's lives, *Ebony* had now moved, it seemed, to star-making: placing Dandridge triumphantly before a national public in order to portend her imminent fame.[97]

By this time, *Ebony*'s emphasis on black stardom was thoroughly developed, defining brand identity and reorganizing patterns of public and group life for African Americans. Allure of public recognition, obsession with *de luxe* lifestyles, appetite for the media eye: all of these are by now legitimate, if not determinant, values among African Americans (and most others in the United States), particularly in the post-1960s decades and especially among the young. For some, this turn is one more symptom of nihilism rooted in the antinomies of contemporary society. For others, they represent intriguing (if complex) extension of the tradition of the black folk hero, updated celebration of the rebel or badman whose social challenge now registers by way of luxury display or the platinum fan base. Neither approach, I believe, sufficiently historicizes black celebrity's genesis, nor fully appreciates its redefinition of black subjectivity. Showing how black celebrity succeeded other notions of African-American individuation helps register shifts in racial mores and politics over the past half century precisely, while underscoring, more so than any other issue, *Ebony*'s gateway relation to contemporary black identity.

Though ideas of collectivity—racial, spiritual, diasporic, territorial, global—delineate histories of black life,[98] evolving conceptions of the black individual have played an important, though less acknowledged, role in its development too. From the onset of New World slavery, melding of lingual, ethnic, and cosmological cohorts into a race has been enriched—even hastened—by the virtuosity of blacks as individuals. Eccentricities of faith, outlook, and style, recent scholarship has argued, vitalized the meaning of blackness and its process of formation in the New World, making its unification idiosyncratic and predicated on creative expression.[99] What we refer to today as a vernacular of improvisation among African Americans, in many ways, rests on this impulse toward individuation, as much as it does on folkways of group life.[100] Though much of this activity might be (and has been) understood as native to black folk, motives for personalism among blacks in the New World require some reference to the pressures of white proscription, especially during slavery. Denial of rights, incursion on intimate concerns (particularly related to partners and children), and dehumanization generally meant that validation of the black self through stylized action, as much as unification as a group, proved fundamental to black resistance within New World societies, before and after emancipation.[101]

Toward the end of the nineteenth century—the maturation point for the first free-born generation of African Americans, as well as the linked rise of successor systems of racial supremacy to replace slavery—this tradition of black style coalesced into a body of folklore celebrating what can be called *black characters*. C. L. R. James's definition of character as presentation of the individual "to the point of extreme idiosyncracy" is helpful here, for what distinguished legends like Stagolee and John Henry, or real-life heroes like prizefighters or classic blueswomen, was their outlandishness.[102]The jocular aggression of a Jack Johnson, or the irrepressible wit of a Shine, or the indomitability of a Bessie Smith—all evidenced racial selfhood at a moment when, as during slavery, exercise of personal prerogative by African Americans was aggressively contested at all turns. For Lawrence Levine—the most engaged student of this process—fixation among blacks on characters in culture and myth mirrored larger dynamics of individuation in the United States at the time, driven by urbanization, class differentiation, and deepening material bases of self-worth.[103] Yet ideas of black character, seen in full, challenged norms of American individuality more than they validated them. Black idiosyncrasy and eccentricity disrupted convention and discipline, precisely because individuals manifesting these qualities were black, and thus presumed incapable of self-realization. Herein lay their appeal to African Americans, for in a world where self-expression held potentially fatal consequences, manifest presence of individuated blacks encouraged hope of autonomy and self-determination more broadly.[104]

The most recognized African-American individuals up to the 1940s exemplified this definition of character. Artists like Louis Armstrong, Richard Wright, Zora Neale Hurston, or even representative figures such as Mary McLeod Bethune or Paul Robeson enjoyed standing among African Americans not only for their achievement, but also unique persona. In this sense they recalled James's exemplary account of Charlie Chaplin, particularly his description of Chaplin's tramp as a creature of such anomaly as to belong, paradoxically, anywhere and therefore everywhere. This was, for James, the deepest affirmation possible of humanity in a modern world. One can see such qualities in several black figures spanning the cusp years of World War II, characters like Joe Louis or Billie Holiday—both famous people and folk heroes, and ready sources of coverage in *Ebony* before a grammar of black celebrity had been fully articulated. They are also evident in instant or momentary stars like advertising model Maurice Hunter or farmhand and self-styled "weather prophet" Will Johnson,[105] whose embodiment of local color recalled the tradition of eccentric virtuosity among blacks in the New World. Yet *Ebony* effectively challenged—if not eclipsed—this ethos once it suggested alternate criteria for personal prominence, ones valorizing the familiar rather than the original.

By establishing a philosophy of race celebrity, *Ebony,* more than any institution then or since, shifted black cultural tastes in a modern direction, away from the idiosyncratic and toward the routine. Personal achievement, talent, style, and opinion remained, to be sure, cause for notice and acclaim. Yet as the magazine's stake—figurative and literal—in celebrity deepened, black personality was increasingly portrayed in terms of the recognizable, rather than the distinctive. Chatty revelations concerning home, family, and romantic lives of the black famous encouraged this turn, as did saturation coverage of select personalities, each deepening the presumption of

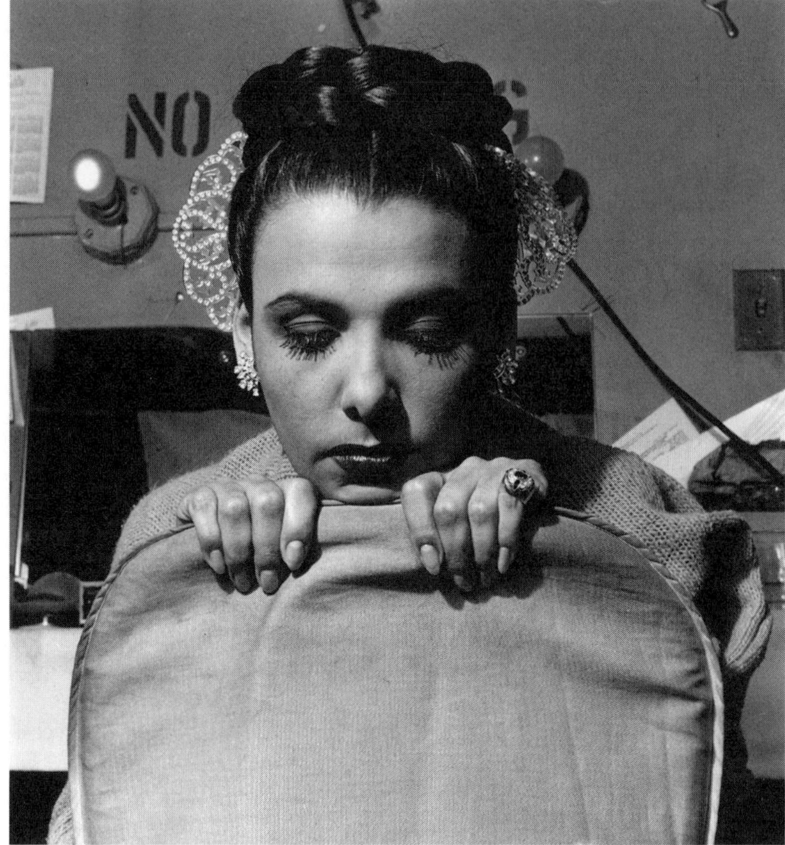

20. Lena Horne, mid-1940s. Photographed by Wayne F. Miller. Courtesy of Wayne F. Miller.

familiarity of reader to subject. Yet rationalization conditioned the expectations of the prominent as well. Given the magazine's utility as an instrument of public relations, the black famous increasingly conformed to limits of behavior and expression suggested by the magazine, even as the expectations of readers and fans were conditioned by desire to identify with those same stars. Here the disparate, even trifling human interest stories on Joe Louis or Hazel Scott, Reverdy Ransom or Dorothy Dandridge took on greater import. Increasingly race entertainers and leaders—the acclaimed as well as the aspiring—crafted selves according to the magazine's evolving template of celebrity, in manner indicating more definitive shift of the cultural attitude of African Americans generally.

In the end, *Ebony*'s emphasis on African-American celebrity advocated an idea of black personality commensurate with the modern age's dominant cultural logic—what Walter Benjamin called an aesthetic of mechanical reproduction.[106] For Benjamin, the emergence of the modern arts signaled an epochal shift in human perception and imagination. Refusing aesthetic theocracies of beauty, genius, or eternal value, Benjamin instead related arts of the mechanical age to repetition, disengagement from history or tradition, and disembodied performance, resulting in modes of aesthetic perception defined not by concentration, but rather distraction. Unlike Adorno or Horkheimer, Benjamin saw this change not as a lamentable crisis of meaning, but rather an overdue opportunity to overhaul radical approaches to art, society, and personality in the modern world. Nonetheless Benjamin warned of the depreciated character of mechanically represented subjects—landscapes, social scenes, even individuals—alienated as they were from their own "substantive duration," from the historical testimony these subjects embodied, and from functioning public communities, at least in any direct sense. For Benjamin, such contradictions were best revealed within the technologies of mechanical reproduction—the snapshot or movie camera—and their products. Yet, as some have since argued, it may be that the most consequential artifact of mechanized imagination is the philosophy and practice of celebrity itself.[107]

These observations are important both to appreciating the significance of *Ebony*'s aesthetic of black stardom and also gaining perspective on its consequences. Black celebrity not only indicated application of the mechanical arts to the black individual, but also announced a new way of seeing—and appreciating—distinct black personality. Given the emergence of the United States as an entertainment society even at this time, *Ebony*'s cult of African-American fame was a vital compensatory institution for still-segregated blacks. The current centrality of black celebrity in countless arenas, from athletics to youth culture, action cinema to charismatic leadership (one less obvious legacy of the last half century's struggles for integration), traces its roots back to the logic of black fame *Ebony* perfected. It is important as well to assess the costs of this transformation—exchange of disparate ideas of activity for a uniform standard of success, suppression of idiosyncrasy in favor of universal appeal, and stories of African-American individuals that often lacked the capacity for what Benjamin termed historical testimony. *Ebony*'s cult of celebrity supplied an emporium of personalities to compel and inspire. Yet these images proved less able to challenge dominant philosophies of self and society, as prior iterations of black selves had done.

While coverage of the black famous in *Ebony* pushed the magazine's view of black individuals toward conformity, the diversity of its own staff counteracted this trend, resulting in a work culture that broke dramatically from the conventions of the black press. From origins in dialogue between Johnson and Ben Burns, the magazine grew into one of the most variegated enterprises in African-American cultural life at the time, as well as one of the more integrated (racially and otherwise) within the United States generally. John Johnson's legendary tendency to micromanage, which would earn him mention in *Fortune* as one of the country's "toughest bosses," caused many observers to characterize *Ebony*'s operation, along with its editorial style, as mere extension of its founder's personality. This constitutes an especially misleading assessment, for *Ebony*'s eclectic staff proved crucial to its institutional growth as well as its expansive impact on thought concerning African Americans in the United States. Though *Ebony* found it increasingly hard to retain emphasis on unorthodox personalities between its covers, it was certainly not due to any surfeit of characters in its offices.[108]

By mid-1950, a glance at *Ebony*'s masthead told the tale of its rise, and promised further growth in the future. Though Arkansan Willie Mae Harmon, the first women hired by Johnson, had by now left the magazine, several others, including writer and associate editor Era Bell Thompson, extended Johnson Publishing's level of gender integration. Allan Morrison, a New York–based journalist with experience as a wartime reporter with *Yank* and *Stars and Stripes*, and Edward Clayton, veteran of the *Louisville Defender*, brought needed experience to the staff, as did Herbert Nipson, a journalism graduate of the University of Iowa. Robert Ellis, Harry Levette's old nemesis, served as Hollywood editor, while A. S. "Doc" Young, another "chisler" decried by Levette, found work at *Ebony* as sports editor a few years later. LeRoy Winbush, whose design skills had been honed since 1940 constructing Regal Theater sets, Loop bank window displays, and countless other projects, brought his expertise to the magazine as arts editor, and soon thereafter Herbert Temple joined him in the arts department. Management of advertising accounts were particularly central operations, and a special source of pride for the company, with *Ebony* having breached, for the first time, print media's color line regarding major corporate sponsorship. Fred Stern and William Grayson managed sponsor accounts at the magazine, which had increased from nothing in early issues to half the copy by mid-1948: among ads at the time were ones from Pepsi, Colgate, Beachnut Gum, Chesterfield Cigarettes, and Seagram. Often they were joined in this work by Johnson himself, whose personal signing of accounts from Zenith, Armour and Swift Meats, Elgin Watches, and Quaker Oats announced his lead advocacy of black consumer market well before the 1960s, when some date his efforts in this sphere. David Jackson was listed as staff photographer, though the most choice assignments still made their way to more experienced freelance cameramen. The notorious 1950s raids by Johnson on black newspapers that netted the company its most distinguished staffers, including Lerone Bennett Jr., Robert Johnson, Cloyte Murdoch, Simeon Booker, and Moneta Sleet Jr., had not yet taken place. But the dynamic, aggressive pattern of growth for the company was already apparent—nine listed editors coordinated the work of nearly one hundred employees, all housed in a recently purchased mansionlike office near the South Loop on 18th and Michigan Avenue.[109]

Overseeing these operations on a day-to-day basis at the magazine was Ben Burns. To have a white Jewish writer serving as executive editor at the most influential black publication of the day was amusingly ironic to some, perverse to others. The incongruities of Burns's presence at Johnson Publishing ran well beneath the skin, however. Burns was a reluctant if active leftist for the better part of his life, and his talent afforded him high reputation as a radical journalist during the 1940s. It had been Burns who, in 1941, penned an acerbic denunciation in *People's World* of Langston Hughes for disavowing "Goodbye Christ" and other proletarian poems written during the Depression. Burns's stature within the Left remained unchanged a year later, when prominent Communist and Scottsboro attorney William Patterson recommended him to the Chicago *Defender* as national editor. While at the *Defender* he oversaw the paper's "Victory Edition" special issue in summer 1942, consulted with Metz Lochard on editorial direction through the years of the "Double 'V,'" and indulged his own bibliophilia through regular book review column. Given Johnson's own emphatic centrism, Burns proved as odd a fit politically as he did racially at *Ebony,* a condition he argued precipitated his abrupt dismissal in 1954. Yet up to that point, Burns proved integral to *Ebony*'s shaping, writing editorials, matching staff to projects, and celebrating the black literary tradition, through accounts of Wright, Hughes, Ann Petry, Chester Himes, and other active writers at the time.[110] Burns's other concerns also influenced *Ebony*'s editorial direction through its first decade: his interest in psychology, his commitment to the interests of labor, and his fascination with race's instabilities and contradictions were clearly important to the magazine's frequent recourse of stories about passing and interracialism.[111]

This last direction constituted, in Burns's case, a classic example of art imitating life. Through the presumed osmosis of years spent in race journalism, Burns often found himself addressed as black, in all seriousness by strangers or clients of the magazine, and with rapine humor by colleagues. To be sure, this was not that unusual according to the phenotypic standards of a society still organized around a one-drop principle. Curly-haired and swarthy, Burns offered more compelling argument for black ancestry than the near-caucasian Walter White, a frequent visitor at Johnson Publishing's offices. More often, though, his misidentification argued identity's derivation from context—the presence of an actual white person in such a thoroughly black-defined environment was fundamentally counterintuitive for most. The contradictions of Burns's identity hinted more general complexities of race politics within the staff. Johnson, for one, was often uncomfortable with actual integrationism in his company, even as he consistently advocated it as a general principle. Others on staff took cues from this ambivalence. Burns recalled reverse stereotyping occasionally taking perverse forms: during editorial meetings, John Johnson would routinely dismiss Burn's opinion as "too black," consequence of his overlong association with race journalism. The joke—humorous to all save Burns—extended beyond the staff, as visitors to the company were occasionally tested to see if they could divine Burns's racial background.[112] His centrality to the company, however, guaranteed job security for years, if not peace of mind. Such was not the case for other whites on staff. Young and talented Kay Cremin lasted but a year in her position as associate editor, because of uproar over her rumored workplace romances, while an unnamed advertising representative was summarily dismissed for excessive attention toward Johnson's wife Eunice during a holiday office party. On occasion the disruptions of whiteness moved beyond the confines of staff. One expose portraying passing at Chicago Loop venues took an unexpected turn when the article's subject was revealed to have passed for black, at the magazine's expense. Though Johnson heartily appreciated the humor of this ruse, the same was not the case with First Lady Roosevelt's request during a visit to company offices to be served fried chicken for lunch, a request Johnson awkwardly declined out of fear of reinforcing stereotype.[113]

Yet there were whites at *Ebony* whose cross-racial adventures proved relatively manageable, notably the freelance photographers fashioning the magazine's initial visual aesthetic. A resonant judgment of *Ebony* at the time and since concerned its derivative format and technique: it was, some argued, a poor imitation of both European journals initiating the photomagazine craze during the 1930s, and its direct American predecessor, *Life*. Certainly *Ebony* did not push photojournalism's boundaries to the degree *Life* did. The arresting war images of Robert Capa, Margaret Bourke-White, and W. Eugene Smith; the industrial abstracts and urban vistas of Bourke-White, Alfred Eisenstaadt, and others; expert lighting of celebrity portraits, high-speed capture of the kinesis of dancers and athletes: all

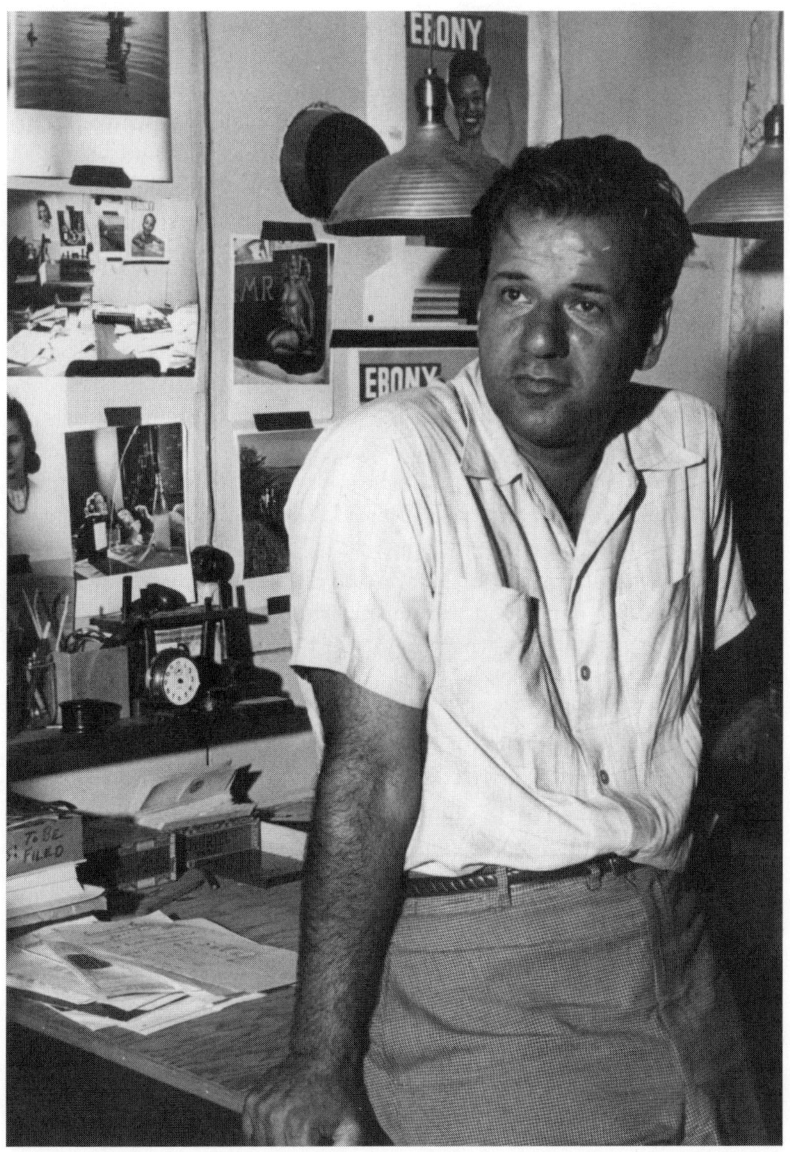

21. Ben Burns in his office at Johnson Publishing Company. Photographed by Wayne F. Miller. Courtesy of the Harsh Research Collection/Chicago Public Library.

demonstrated *Life*'s role in revolutionizing the picture magazine and encouraging similar compositional approach in other visual media like film and, later, television.[114] Yet if *Ebony* was not an equal pioneer in the arts of mass photography, its approach to the unique demands of race-conscious documentation nonetheless heralded a transformed public eye. Some of *Ebony*'s visual innovation, of course, marked the work of talented designers like Winbush and Temple, not to mention Johnson's recognition of the need to literally envision black achievement and success, in ways most mainstream media refused to then and, disturbingly, since. But credit also should go to those generating the images—the raw stuff of Johnson Publishing's visions and dream, as well as the enhanced vistas of black life resonating so powerfully with readers.

Among this group from the start were talented black photographers, to be sure. Gordon Parks, already established through work with *Life* and the Farm Security Administration's group under Roy Stryker, brought nuanced senses of portrait and ensemble style to stories on Hazel Scott and Phil Moore, among others, in the magazine.[115] Earl Leaf Guillumette, prolific if mysterious chronicler of New World blacks, provided breathtaking kinetic studies of dance and movement arts in Brazil, Cuba, and elsewhere.[116] Aside from these two, though, most images from the magazine's first five years were provided by whites. Too cash-strapped initially to cultivate an in-house photography operation, *Ebony*'s limitations inadvertently led to its fuller achievement, as reliance on freelancers resulted in heady cross-fertilization of styles. Gordon Costner, also established among *Life*'s Chicago-based photographers, provided depth-in-focus studies of jazz concert halls and social montages accompanying *Ebony*'s photo-editorials. He also fashioned cityscapes of compelling scope and scale: visual reinforcement of magazine's credo of heroic urbanism.[117] Hungarian immigrant Stephen Deutch, trained as a sculptor and in demand locally as a commercial and fashion photographer, generated portrait as well collage studies for *Ebony* that built on his reputation for three-dimensional and sculptural perspective. Deutch proved crucial to the magazine's early development of visual style, providing nine cover shots between 1947 and 1952 and six from 1947 to 1949. His keen eye for lighting, evident in 1949 pictures of Lena Horne, or of Joe Louis that same year, were well matched by his surrealist sense of experimentation, as with montages accompanying the 1949 story, "What Negroes Dream About."[118] Wayne Miller, Chicago-born and a former member of Edward Steichen's Naval Photography unit, devoted a Guggenheim fellowship to photographing the South Side between 1946 and 1948, thus becoming one of *Ebony*'s most reliable sources. More influenced by documentary principles than

Deutch, Costner, or even Parks, Miller captured numerous eclectic corners of local black life. Photos for "Female Impersonators," "The Truth about Marijuana," and "Society," a feature on the annual ball for the Royal Coterie of the Snakes—all resulted from his Guggenheim-funded work.[119] Other important early photographers—Phil Stern, formerly with *Stars and Stripes,* Werner Wolff, veteran of *Yank* magazine, and Joe Covello, who had served in the U.S. Army Signal Corps—were white freelancers as well.[120] Indeed, besides Parks and Guillumette, Griffith Davis, recommended by Langston Hughes to *Ebony,* and David Jackson were the only black photographers appearing with any regularity prior to the mid-1950s.[121] As with Burns's contributions, the efforts of early freelance photographers make clear *Ebony*'s capture of black experience grew from no easy or obvious racial arithmetic.

It is perhaps no surprise that staffing photography proved *Ebony*'s most heated site of racial tension. While choice (and better compensated) assignments went to these freelancers, David Jackson was initially consigned to managing the darkroom, shooting in-office features for the food and fashion sections or company social functions, and providing filler images for the magazine's back pages. Barely credited by Burns as competent, Jackson returned the sentiment with some of the more pointed baiting Burns endured. Following disciplining by Burns for use of the darkroom as an unofficial social center, Jackson internally circulated a bitter mock-release from the NAACP protesting the campaign "to make the darkroom lily white." Rancor between the two men on occasion took on a more personal aspect. Burns recalled several exchanges between him and Jackson that smacked of anti-Semitism, while Jackson on one instance charged Burns with prejudice during a staff meeting. When Johnson was asked to consider reprimanding or even relieving Jackson, he chose instead to defuse the situation. For Burns, these incidents deepened ongoing doubts regarding the efficacy of his authority at Johnson Publishing. For Jackson, they reinforced an already pronounced essentialism, helping explain the rapid shift by the mid-1950s toward in-house black photographers at *Ebony* once Burns was gone, and Jackson assumed charge of photography operations at the magazine. Their interaction, more so than any other within the staff, demonstrated the limits of interracial trust and reciprocity, even in the relatively ecumenical space of Johnson Publishing.[122]

The tangles of Ben Burns and David Jackson indicated not just racial suspicion, but a decidedly masculine style of office competition. Rife with strong egos, and driven by the top-dog example of Johnson as publisher and owner, the largely male management at the company gave the company the frequent feel of a locker room or lodge hall. This was further reinforced by the many established male writers and photographers providing feature content for *Ebony.* Nonetheless, women remained the majority of regular staff at the magazine, and, as seen above, constituted the subject of much of its visual and written content. Three women were especially instrumental in steering the publication and its day-to day operations toward an alternate institutional culture. Each came from distinct personal and, in two cases, specifically feminized professional backgrounds, these women epitomized *Ebony*'s grasp of even the most sequestered spheres of black life. That their contributions derived not only from gender identity generally, but the specific impact of black women's work on race culture and identity historically, underscores with particular power how the magazine and its parent company ranged well beyond the vision of its founder.

Era Bell Thompson, managing and later international editor at *Ebony,* for decades ranked as the most prominent woman working at Johnson Publishing. Born in North Dakota in 1906, Thompson's first memories of Chicago were painful, as a 1944 fellowship application to the Newberry Library made clear: "Three times I came down from the prairies to live with 'my people' and twice I returned to my plains; hurt, bewildered and a little bit afraid. I couldn't dance, couldn't even snap my fingers or sing the blues. I was 22 before I ever heard of Paul Lawrence Dunbar."[123] Newberry Librarian Stanley Pargellis proved the first of several patrons intrigued by Thompson's renderings of race angst, awarding her a fellowship that yielded in 1945 Thompson's memoir *American Daughter.* Playing on the anomaly of a black childhood in the plains, and offering picaresque rendition of Depression hardships following relocation to Chicago, Thompson's book earned accolades as a congenial take on the race autobiography genre, defined trenchantly that same year with the publication of Richard Wright's *Black Boy.* Invited by Johnson in 1947 to survey the "five most outstanding Negro men" for *Negro Digest,* Thompson detailed her choices and attached a closing comment: "This is fun, Mr. Johnson, now which one can I have?" Hired onto *Ebony* later that year, Thompson took special interest in international coverage, traveling to Hiroshima to report on mission work there, and helping market the magazine in Ghana, Uganda, Kenya, and Nigeria. Thompson extended her globetrotting ways with a 1954 Central and South African tour, leading to a second book, *Africa: Land of My Fathers* and a concurrent *Ebony* feature titled "What Africa Thinks of Us." By this time her role as Johnson Publishing's diasporic conduit was established. Thompson would facilitate St. Clair Drake's appointment as a Ghana-based stringer for *Jet* in 1954, and consult with Madame Diop at *Presence Africaine* on plans to design a four-part volume titled *Africa as Seen by the USA*. Remembered as a model writer and editor (Ben Burns recalled her compensation "for . . . diminutive stature with . . . chip-on-the-shoulder bravado and super sharp wit"), Thompson unsettled decorum more ambitiously on occasion, as when she and other colleagues declared themselves "Chicago branch" of the Mau Mau uprising in Kenya through an interoffice memorandum in 1954.[124]

While not as advanced within corporate hierarchy as Thompson, librarian Doris Saunders proved equally indispensable to *Ebony*'s scope and growth. Before joining Johnson Publishing, Saunders was well known within the community of bibliophiles in Black Chicago.[125] Graduating Englewood High School in the late 1930s along with Timuel Black and Marva Trotter (Louis), and later attending Northwestern University, Saunders opened a South Side bookstore that counted J. A. Rogers among its regular customers—and best-selling authors. In 1942, she took a desk librarian's position at the George Cleveland Hall branch of the Chicago Public Library. Chicago's equivalent of the Schomburg in Harlem, Hall was the key local site of black education and intellectual exchange managed by black women. Though head librarian Vivian Harsh was respected for officiously managing the collection and facility, Saunders, like others, recalls Charlemae Hill Rollins as the guiding force there. Rollins, a Mississippi migrant who left work as a schoolteacher to work at Hall, organized programs and readings that made it a mandatory stop for visiting writers and intellectuals. Vernon Jarrett recalled Langston Hughes's constant presence at the library during his frequent visits and relocations to Chicago. As well, Rollins paid special attention to youth services, maintaining regular children's hours based on Hall's events and collection. Beginning in 1941, she led a campaign to reform textbook and storybook portrayal of African Americans, enlisting librarians and educators across the country—one of the first and most important initiatives of its kind.[126] Glowing recommendations from Rollins resulted in Saunders's promotion as first black reference librarian at the main city branch in the Loop, where she worked until hired away by Johnson in 1948.[127]

Saunders remembers Johnson's job offer with amusement—already making just under $4000 annually, she recalls Johnson offering a mere three-dollar raise to meet that figure, accompanied by promises that "if I make money, you make money." Her work conditions, however, represented clearer improvement over previous circumstances—indeed over virtually any African-American bibliophile. Working to develop the library space at the new office space near the South Loop, Saunders expanded the company's collection from a hundred volumes to several thousand, all paid and approved by the usually parsimonious Johnson without question.

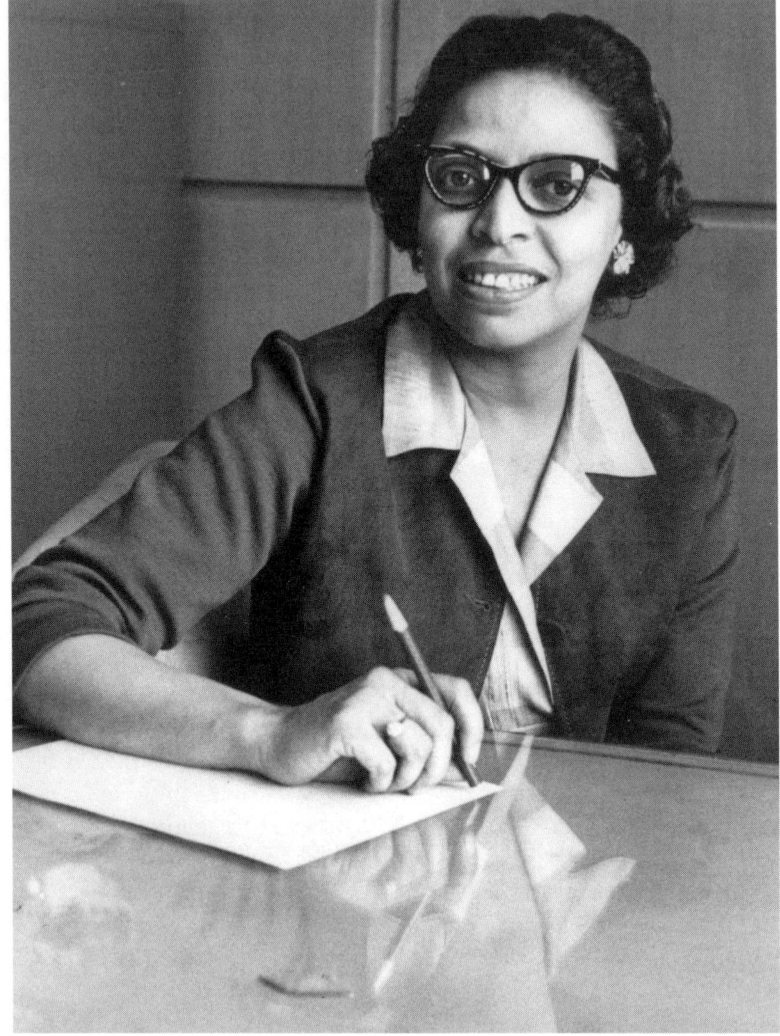

22. Doris Saunders, librarian, Johnson Publishing Company, probably in the early 1960s. Courtesy of the Harsh Research Collection/Chicago Public Library.

Saunders still remembers her prize acquisition—a first edition of Du Bois's *The Philadelphia Negro* secured from an antiquarian bookseller for the then-extravagant sum of $75. Saunders augmented her holdings with full catalogs of federal bulletins and surveys—prior to joining Johnson Publishing, she had been in charge of government publications at the Loop branch. This made the prodigious output of Joseph Houchins and other race-interested researchers accessible to *Ebony* writers and editors; the holdings made up one of the best private libraries on black life anywhere in the country. This enhanced not just editorial, but also marketing operations at Johnson Publishing. Sponsors were enlightened in demographics of racial market segmentation through in-house studies that Saunders played a lead role in generating, which in turn modernized the advertising content reaching *Ebony*'s readers. Together with the emphasis on literary culture in the magazine, Saunders's work shows how black bibliophilia constituted what Raymond Williams called an "active literature," defined by dynamic conditions of generation and reception, rather than canonical strictures of taste and judgment. It also signaled Johnson Publishing's recognition of black intelligence's grassroots in pursuits historically defined as women's work.[128]

As in Saunders's case, food editor Freda DeKnight introduced feminized expertise into the company's institutional culture. Her success in doing so, however, eclipsed not only that of Saunders and Thompson, but all others on staff: no one, not even Johnson himself, supplied a more recognizable face for *Ebony* during its first decade. Like Thompson a plains native (she grew up in South Dakota), DeKnight moved to New York early in the 1930s, starting a catering business, and conducting home economics classes through the Urban League.[129] Johnson recalled meeting her at a Chicago party in honor of Paul Robeson, which she had contracted to cater. Praised by Johnson on her culinary skill, she responded in kind regarding *Ebony*, but noted its lack of a food section.[130] Hired at *Ebony* in summer 1946, she premiered pragmatically with an advice feature titled "How to Glorify the Apple." Running thereafter under the title "Date with a Dish," DeKnight's monthly column followed a format where celebrities identified favorite dishes—tamale pie for Nat King Cole, curry chicken for Lena Horne, fish baked with spring vegetables for bandleader Andy Kirk—which DeKnight designed and executed, to be happily consumed by the stars in accompanying photos. The column found immediate and enthusiastic response from readers: as early as February 1947, calls came for a book of DeKnight's recipes, dutifully published as *Date with A Dish* a year later. In 1949, DeKnight began to tour eastern and midwestern cities with demonstration kitchens sponsored by the Urban League, routinely drawing capacity audiences. Renovation of the company's new offices in 1949 resulted in the installation of a $6,000 test kitchen that DeKnight used for her work, along with a commissary kitchen from which she oversaw the feeding of staff and guests. From 1950 on, DeKnight sponsored multiple product lines through ads in the magazine, including Hunts and Quaker Foods, Carnation Milk, Pillsbury, and Holliwood appliances, along with Lucky Strike Cigarettes, making her the most prominent spokesperson within the magazine, and also an identifiable face for black consumers' long-standing affinity for national brands.[131]

The recipe for DeKnight's success involved, appropriately, an array of ingredients. Though fed by the reflected light of celebrity, "Date with a Dish" was no mere publicity stunt: recipes were based whenever possible on widely available products, and necessary utensils were helpfully described. Columns often appealed to the cost conscious, with advice on appealing use of leftovers, school lunches, and "budget meals for vet wives." As well, they often took on an exotic character: besides Horne's curry chicken, dishes like arroz con pollo or flan encouraged global range for African-American palates. The sense that food constituted a gateway toward expanded social and cultural literacy was underscored by the column's occasional feature of white celebrity "cooks": swing band pioneer Paul Whiteman extolled a hearty interpretation of corned beef and cabbage, while concert baritone Igor Gorin offered his Russian family recipe for peasant potato soup, a "delightful morale builder on cold, icy days of winter." Any tendency to dismiss cooking expertise as gender-specific knowledge was refuted by DeKnight's reference to professional male cooks such as Adolph Roberts of New York's Ship Grill, or Samuel Williams of the Santa Fe rail line, reminding readers that culinary skill was a talent that black men, as well as women, had learned to master out of historical necessity.[132]

Still it was her personal rehabilitation of the kitchen, so long seen as a black women's prison, into a space of proficiency and worldliness that best accounts for DeKnight's unique appeal. If, as Zora Neal Hurston argued in 1937, black women were seen historically as "de mule uh de world"[133] and used in according fashion, it was cooking's correspondence to exploitation that compelled this degradation, as much as any sphere of action. Within *Ebony,* through columns, advertisements, and reverent mail, Freda DeKnight realized a radically different understanding for cooking's place in black lives—especially for black women. DeKnight's columns did not deviate from women's magazines' promotion of new appliances and mask of ongoing obligations of domesticity for women through paeans to "home efficiency"; indeed her legendary concern with implements and reuse of ingredients exemplified the gendered rationalism of home economics. Yet the portrayal of cooking in "Date with a Dish" as a site of voluntary pleasure—leisure more so than self-sacrificing labor—explains, perhaps better than any other section, how *Ebony*'s idealizations of black life conditions found more approval than rejection from its audience. Like quilting, beauty culture, or the curatorial efforts of Saunders and others, DeKnight's countertop intelligence argued the need to credit gendered skills as root source of African-American culture and identity, while showing how redefinition of this work from oppressive to self-interested might transform ideas of both personal and group agency.[134]

In contrast to the varied talents and interests of *Ebony*'s staff, and the corresponding complexity of postwar African-American life in its field of coverage, one uniform area of outlook apparent within the magazine by the mid-1950s was editorial voice. As the cold war's Manichean dynamics grew ever more evident, *Ebony* sailed with prevailing political winds, unambiguously presuming identity on behalf of readers as full and free Americans. Testaments to loyalty, material bounty, and above all opportunity seen to characterize black existence anchored the thinking of *Ebony*'s editors, which on occasion reached the florid patriotism of black cold warriors like Edith Sampson or Max Yergan. Correspondingly, more dissident sectors of black thought were isolated and ultimately dismissed: racial militancy on frequent occasion was critiqued as an alternate pole of race hate, while outspoken champions of the black Left like Paul Robeson were held up for opprobrium. The usual trump card for such arguments—rapid growth of a black middle and even owner class—offered pretext for predictions that race would matter less to future generations of African Americans than occupation, education, achievement, and character. This strikingly postracial thinking came decades before today's neoconservative disavowels of race identification. All this seems strong cause for endorsing criticism of *Ebony* as racially sycophantic and politically accommodating. Yet reconstruction of how this editorial line emerged at the magazine, and examination of its deeper motive, suggests more complex meaning to these views than often acknowledged. Rather than accommodation, political expedience, or simple class interest, *Ebony*'s outlook constituted a political philosophy of both substance and consequence for African Americans, on the eve of profound social and civil change.

Though emphasizing positive dimensions within black life from its inception, *Ebony*'s outlook on occasion departed from optimism. Economic instability in the years after World War II counseled a guarded rather than rosy assessment, especially concerning conditions for black workers. Denunciation of housing discrimination ("the tenth man of America has always been part of the third of the nation ill-housed"), endorsement of labor unity ("the biggest news in . . . race relations is being written these days on picket lines"), and alarm over fatal injustices of health care (the editorial "How Long Can the Negro Live?") announced skepticism concerning the condition of most African Americans, belying the social aversion subsequently attributed to the magazine. As late as October 1949, *Ebony* described societal conditions with a tone of alarm, counseling victims of mass layoffs that year in "How to Beat the Depression." A year later, state inaction in alleviating the crushing housing shortage was also identified as a bar to enhanced black life chances. Existential questions were also pursued, illuminating still more universal consequences of racism: "The Fable of the 'Happy' Negro," run in January 1949, and "Do Negroes Hate Themselves?" written two months later, each detailed the shared psychic costs linked to color prejudice.[135]

The most readily identified adversary in these works proved southern systems and cultures of segregation, and the role of broader institutions—notably the federal government—in abetting them. As with displacement of race insurgency to the periphery of the black world, domestic race oppression was relegated in *Ebony*'s editorials to Dixie states and communities, despite abundant instance of discrimination in northern and western communities as well. Yet focus on the South proved an important rhetorical instrument: racism's regressive and even antimodern character registered most powerfully when regionalized, or even personalized. Constant reference to "Bilbos and Rankins" individuated structural forces of reaction, making answer of its underlying sentiment more plausible. The bossman lore surrounding the figure of "Mr. Charlie" was addressed in like manner: readers were sternly instructed that the means for "remolding the white man's character" lay in southern blacks refusing the small victories of toasts and one-liners signifying on paternalistic authority, which, in *Ebony*'s estimation, did nothing to challenge or reject it. Protest of a revived plantation myth came in January 1947 with "Needed: A Negro Legion of Decency," which slammed Disney's release of *Song of the South*, based on the writings of Joel Chandler Harris and starring James Baskett, veteran of NBC's *Amos 'n Andy* radio show. Though years-long efforts by the NAACP and other institutions to racially monitor Hollywood's content were duly acknowledged, the engine of social change was defined as personal enlightenment and action, be it refusal of gross stereotype by producers like Walt Disney, Southern whites' exchange of progressive present for mythic past in their entertainment tastes, or pressure techniques of boycotts and negative mail for frustrated blacks.[136]

While both well-meaning and antagonistic whites were cited for lapses in affirming values of fair play and brotherhood, ultimately blacks themselves were assigned the majority of the responsibility for hastening equality's arrival. At times this called for renouncing complicity with racial stigma, as in "The Rise and Fall of Uncle Tom," which called on southern blacks to refuse the posture of the "good darky," or "No Biz for Show Biz," which similarly challenged northern entertainers and nightclub denizens to retire minstrel elements within the urban vernacular arts. Most often, African Americans were charged to achieve, develop, and actively pursue opportunity—in work, political affiliations, and social interactions. This incremental philosophy of change received its first and clearest statement in November 1947, in an editorial titled "Time to Count Our Blessings." Citing Chester Himes's second novel *Lonely Crusade* as exemplary of reverse hatred "as virulent as the most rabid race-baiter's," the editorial channeled the magazine's achievement ethic as an explicit philosophy of social reform for the first time. Favorably comparing education, employment, and other indices for African Americans and "90 percent of the world's population," the editorial argued existence worldwide of "countless persons who are fighting and dying to win a measure of the American Negro's standard of living, his civil rights, his everyday enjoyment of life." Meaning to counteract the "cynicism" of frustration and racial bitterness, the editorial "Blessings" argued that blacks' best weapon in confronting prejudice was ultimately their exercise of opportunity:

> No, being a Negro is not so much a handicap as a privilege. For here in the richest, most advanced country in the world, the Negro has made his most significant advancements in history and has a brilliant outlook for the future.
>
> Much remains to be done to give the Negro his just due in the American way of life. But it cannot be done by bitterness, cynicism, and singing the blues.

With homilies to the rise of prior ethnic and immigrant communities through hard work, and appeal to readers to think of themselves as "patriotic Americans," the editorial smacked of collaboration, even in its own time. Indeed, the magazine's editors had to counteract its utility to apologists for the racial status quo almost immediately. Following Alabama senator John Sparkman's compliment of "Blessings" as the work of an "able Negro writer" (it had, of course, been written by Burns), the magazine ran a self-evident rebuttal, "When Bouquets Are Brickbats." Yet its message was not so much one of unquestioning loyalty to the cold-war state as affirmation of core values presumed to animate national society, particularly the equation of individual ambition and development with civil worth. Though expedient in aligning *Ebony* to the currents of consensus society, "Blessings" was more philosophy than opportunistic ideology. The cant of achievement, opportunity, and innovation organizing content within the magazine, now found clear statement within its editorial pages.[137]

From November 1947 forward (a date that Johnson also recalls as the occasion of fiscal and therefore institutional security for his enterprise),

Ebony maintained this editorial line, in protest as well as advocacy. On occasion, endorsement of the United States as a land for black initiative and achievement reached embarrassing levels of hyperbole, as in near-censorious repudiation of Richard Wright's trenchant essay upon revisiting Chicago in 1951, or notorious celebration of Cadillac automobile ownership as a "weapon in the war for racial equality." More often the voice of these editorials was measured, though their arguments were profoundly revealing. Laying reform's burden at the feet of individual whites and blacks,

Ebony increasingly presented race itself as a matter of choice, rather than nature or obligation. Statements assigning responsibility to whites ("Can the Negro Trust His White Friends?" "Etiquette of Race Relations," "Educating Our White Folks"), and blacks ("Do Negroes Really Want Equality?" "Are You Ready For Luck?" "Time to Stop Crying Wolf") presented racial attitude as well as identity in voluntary terms. Primary affinity for ancestral and diasporic black worlds were predictably rejected—more because of foreclosure of individual choice in identification than civilizationist criteria. Direct comment on political questions of election or war refused racially partisan understandings of interest. As one early statement in the magazine put it "Race is not the issue in '48"—or in succeeding years, so much as education, housing, employment, enforcement of law, foreign relations." Contemplation of the future of African-American lives, for *Ebony,* raised questions of personal choice and accomplishment, more so than group responsibility or even social structure.[138]

In their response to Senator Sparkman's unwelcome appropriation of their thinking, *Ebony*'s editors confided the difficulty of locating the road between reaction and radicalism in their work. The dilemma of how to split the difference between postures of "chip-on-shoulder" and "hat-in-hand" was of course not new in black thought and expression. Indeed, it had found potent voice a few years before *Ebony*'s arrival, from sources doubtless familiar to Johnson, Burns, and others on the magazine's staff. Writing in the short-lived digest *Negro Quarterly,* writers Ralph Ellison and Angelo Herndon foresaw emergence of a "third attitude" among African Americans, responding to the dislocations of Depression and war. Refusing both the self-denial of clientage and the grandiosity of more pronounced forms of racial militancy, Ellison and Herndon advocated instead "critical participation" as a mode of action. Based both on a "sharp sense of the Negro people's group personality" as well as need to engage extant structures of power, especially the state, critical participation suggested a racial politics aware both of the strengths and weaknesses of surrounding U.S. society. Was *Ebony*'s emphasis on black ambition and accomplishment an exemplary national idiom, or was its validation of the individual rather than the group symptomatic of this "third attitude"? Though such an association most probably would have given Herndon and Ellison pause at the time, the subsequent path of *Ebony,* and many African Americans (in thinking if not in life conditions), argues that *Ebony* may well have answered this charge first, and to greatest consequence.[139]

If the black bourgeoisie—*Ebony*'s audience and subject of choice—deserved, as Frazier and others believed, to be called "exaggerated Americans," it was because of their embrace of liberalism, far more so than overidentification with whites. Here liberalism means not the hegemonic excesses of neoliberalism, nor even the statist activism of the New Deal, but instead foundational values understood to characterize U.S. society from its beginnings to the present—market criteria of action and value, rule of law, consensual arrangements of social relations, and above all the philosophy of possessive individualism. *Ebony*'s embrace of each of these values was recurrent and strong. Its lead role in modeling African-American identification with them, individually and in concert, was of incalculable consequence. Before the move of racial celebrity to the forefront of cultural spheres of sport, entertainment, and politics; before the advent of the modern black rights movement with its structuring logic of legal remedy and civil equality; before redefinition of market cultures and identities around difference and segmentation rather than homogeneity—before all this, there was first the need to establish for blacks and other minorities that liberal tenets could merit their trust and faith. For better or for worse, *Ebony* did more extensive work to encourage this process in the early postwar years than any other institution—black or white, cultural or otherwise.[140]

To speak of African Americans as liberals of choice, rather than necessity, is to stand black history, and American political history as well, on its head. Blacks, more than any group, confound Louis Hartz's definitive conclusion that Americans, apart from all other national societies, were born rather than made equal, thereby explaining their "natural liberalism," whatever declared ideology or orientation they might claim.[141] Accounts of black politics invariably stress the elite/popular dichotomy as its fault line, the root source for both uplift and mobilization agendas.[142] Yet black liberalism suggests that self-interest was an equally potent fulcrum for black politics over the past half-century, challenging traditional norms of group progress and collective fortune, and showing how reference to the authorized self could (and can) ground diverse notions of black agency, from racial brokerage to charismatic leadership to celebrity cache of the erstwhile renegade in diverse fields of culture and society. Indeed, it may well be that African Americans constitute liberalism's most skilled practitioners over the last half-century of U.S. history, as much as its unwitting victims. For, despite the ways in which liberalism as policy has callously and even brutally betrayed blacks' aspiration for equality in rights and happiness in this country, liberalism's force as ideology and idea remains a potent template for black imagination nationally—allowing community to be seen as the sum of multiple distinct selves. Yet it is important too to remember Hartz's caution that the greatest potential consequence of liberalism was not atomization, but instead unanimity in thought and values.[143] Here *Ebony*'s extraordinary accomplishment in imagining a composite black life along the lines of simultaneity shows a darker side. Was the price of representing modern black life and action in the shape of the dynamic individual paradoxically the flattening of African-American identity more generally? As African Americans continue to struggle today to reckon with their place in an adoptive though often unwelcoming home, the answer to this question remains unclear.

In November 1955, *Ebony* observed its tenth anniversary with a massive special edition—173 pages, the largest in its history. Trumpeting a near $1 million annual payroll and 445 employees, editors framed the issue's overview history, "The Story of *Ebony*," with a double spread image of nearly one hundred staff members gathered in front of the ornate Chicago office. Gone were the worries of early years: the historical backdrop for the magazine—"Ten Years that Rocked the World"—was noted as the occasion of African Americans' "biggest gains since Emancipation Day." Other features related the magazine's decade to the breakthrough achievements of pioneering figures like Ralph Bunche, Jackie Robinson, and Gwendolyn Brooks, articulating social optimism in now routine terms of personal initiative and accomplishment. Anticolonialism, greater economic and political empowerment for blacks in the United States, growing advertising attention to the race market all received due notice. Much of the issue minutely portrayed the magazine's staff, by now its own compelling argument of extended benchmarks within African-American life. Era Bell Thompson, Herbert Nipson, Doris Saunders, Doc Young, Clotye Murdoch, David Jackson, and scores of other staff were cited for their successes as well as their idiosyncratic personalities. Freda DeKnight was shown overseeing the company's test kitchen, now upgraded to a $30,000 facility. Ben Burns, fired the year before, was nowhere to be seen in the issue. Possibly the omission was meant to quell persistent rumors of white ownership of the magazine, which Johnson sought to refute with publisher's statements to the contrary, together with photos of himself, wife Eunice, and mother Gertrude as sole stockholders in the company. Likening its growth to that of a marriage, *Ebony* proclaimed "The First Ten Years Are the Happiest": an inadvertently ambivalent prediction of the future for the enterprise and its African-American constituency, yet surely at the time meant to promise still better things for the future.[144]

Festive though this official commemoration was, an earlier and more poignant observance had already brought *Ebony*'s first decade to poetic close. Before her death, Mary McLeod Bethune had arranged with the magazine to posthumously publish her "last will and testament" to African Americans as a group. Returning to her lifelong dream of "full equality for the Negro in our time," Bethune drew hope from the *Brown* decision the previous year in symbolically bequeathing a series of virtues for blacks as individuals and as a people. Basic resources—"hope," "faith," "education," "racial dignity,"—joined complex and corporate ones—"confidence in one another," "responsibility to our young people." The temptation of what Bethune saw as misguided programs inspired her call for sage and vigilant focus: warning about the potential to "abuse power" in the name of insurgency implied criticism of left radicals like Robeson or W. E. B. Du Bois, whom Bethune had previously worked closely with as an observer at the founding convention of the UN in 1945. Bethune passed on what she considered the essence of her life's work as a legacy of strength and struggle to black people universally, in the hopes "that an old women's philosophy might give them inspiration."[145]

This extraordinary feature, meant to extend the reverence the magazine had carefully cultivated for Bethune during her life as a surrogate racial mother, also suggested the symbolic transition from one age to another for African Americans. A leader of historically black education and inheritor of the black club women tradition, Bethune's dying call for "equality in our time" recalled her own lifelong quest to exchange the world of racially separate life for one of critical participation, in which blacks' limits would derive from their individual development rather than their collective restraint. Her will, it seemed, envisioned a process through which segregation itself could be imagined to die a natural death, free of further sacrifice or rancor.

Such was the hope in August 1955. As it turned out, events took a far different course. Indeed, the degree to which racial change remained marked by atrocity, as so often in the past, found its most profound witness through Johnson Publishing, in ways that reminded African Americans that their interrelation remained rooted in pain as much as newfound power.

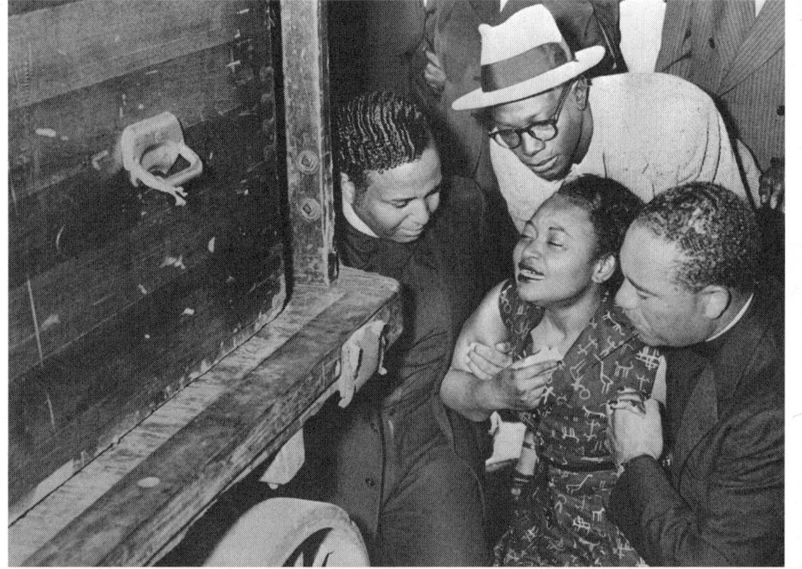

A MOMENT OF SIMULTANEITY

CHAPTER FIVE

> We have seen that physical pain is difficult to express, and that this inexpressibility has political consequences.
>
> ELAINE SCARRY

> I wanted the whole world to see what they had done to my boy.
>
> MAMIE TILL BRADLEY

There have always been innumerable means for African Americans to congregate as groups, as communities, as movements. The inspiration of cultural ritual and affinity, the imposition of forced labor or restricted residence, or the centripetal effect of shared historical consciousness, all compel concentration of black life in collective forms. One other impetus to group orientation for African Americans has been the manifestation of black pain or suffering. Such episodes inspire uncanny recollection of the brutal circumstances under which blacks initially arrived in the New World. They offer evidence of the latent brutality that remains within racism

Facing page: 23. Mamie Till Bradley meeting casket of her son, Emmett Till, as it arrives at Union Station, Chicago, from Mississippi, September 2, 1955. Comforting her are (left to right) Bishop Louis Ford, Gene Mabley, and Bishop Isak Roberts. Photographed by William Lanier. Courtesy of Corbis Photos (or NAACP Papers/ Library of Congress).

today, as an elemental form of dehumanization. They establish the bitter irony of African-American collectivity—that often horrific loss effects the most dramatic forms of racial congregation and affinity.

This chapter presents an iconic episode of black pain and suffering—the brutal murder of Emmett Till in 1955—as the culmination of Black Chicago's conversion into pivot point for modern national imagination among African Americans. Though neither planned nor desired, Till's lynching proved the foundational memory project for blacks nationwide that the American Negro Exposition had projected itself to be fifteen years earlier. Key cultural resources that had emerged in Chicago over the previous decade, from the tradition of social realist literature, to the suggestive power of music, to the truth-effect of black photojournalism, combined with the audacious choice of Till's mother, Mamie Till Bradley, to mourn her son in universal, rather than private, fashion. As with so many other moments of suffering and loss, Till's death became an occasion for African-American congregation. What distinguished this occasion from others before it was the manner in which institutions in Black Chicago transformed congregation into simultaneity, suggesting new conditions of imagination and action, and beckoning toward more activist forms of group life that would transform black and national life over the next decade.

In 1955, with Black Chicago's cultural infrastructure assuming clearer shape, several of its principals took stock, explicitly or through continuing projects. Chess Records, moving from its blues springtime into crossover maturity, released guitarist Chuck Berry's single "Maybelline" that summer, recorded under Willie Dixon's supervision: it topped *Billboard* charts and brought the emerging genre of rock and roll into focus.[1] While *Ebony* celebrated its first decade of publication, the *Chicago Defender* marked its own fifty-year anniversary with an 100-page issue in August, proudly displaying an expanded sponsor base through numerous ads congratulating the paper on a half-century of pioneering journalism.[2] Shortly afterwards, publisher John Sengestacke announced that the *Defender* would move to a daily format early in 1956.[3] Seeking to connect corporate fortunes to broader communal prospects, Sengestacke commissioned studies of local African Americans and their economic conditions. Echoing the boosterism of Johnson Publishing, one survey placed the number of black families with incomes above $5,000 at 40 percent, and used statistics on ongoing migration to predict that Black Chicago would double in size by 1960, and reach one million by 1970.[4]

Yet such halcyon predictions flew in the face of other, more sobering, developments. While black voters constituted the core of the coalition removing incumbent Mayor Martin Kennelly early in 1955, the advent of Richard J. Daley's two decade reign brought neither expansion, nor even preservation of local black political authority. The newly elected mayor moved quickly to box in Congressman Dawson and other established race politicians, diminish and restructure South and West Side Democratic ward organizations, and begin implementing the system of clientage that would come to be known as "plantation politics."[5] Most immediately disturbing was the brutal white resistance to housing desegregation flaring up in Roseland, Englewood, and other area neighborhoods between 1946 and 1955. Characterized by Arnold Hirsch as an "era of hidden violence,"[6] this cycle of civil unrest, reminiscent of the bombings and riots greeting Chicago migrants during and after World War I, proved vexing counterpoint to the optimism Sengestacke, John Johnson, and other African-American cultural entrepreneurs sought to articulate. How meaningful, such events implicitly asked, was social mobility and consumer wealth in general when African-American rights could be so ferociously denied right at home? Speaking at a forum protesting expulsion of black families from the suburb of Cicero in 1951, NAACP head Walter White observed that while African Americans had sought relief from racist violence by migrating to Chicago, events like the unrest in Cicero showed how easy it was for "Mississippi and the South [to follow] them here."[7]

White's own career as a race leader ended in the spring of 1955 with his death. Had he lived a few months more, he would have known how prophetic his words proved to be. In August of that year Emmett Till, a boy vacationing from Chicago, was tortured and murdered near the Mississippi town of Money. The uproar over news of Till's death, his funeral in Chicago, and trial of his accused murderers marked a crucial turn in the generations-old struggle to confront and overturn racial supremacy. African-Americans writers, activists, and public figures routinely recall Till's lynching as an occasion of awakening, one inspiring many to commit themselves to struggles that, over time, constituted the civil rights movement. A critical outcome of the case, of course, was further expansion of the struggle against Jim Crow beyond the borders of Mississippi and the South. While Till's murderers and their advocates spoke unabashedly of the need to reaffirm white supremacy's predominance as a system of social order, blacks in Northern communities—especially Chicago—found the crime occasion for frank calculus regarding collective circumstance and agency. They responded with rallies, letter campaigns, and fund drives for the victim's family that transformed a familiar, if horrific, instance of racist atrocity into the impetus for social change.

Emmett Till's murder was, for blacks, the first modern instance of simultaneity: an occasion in which northern city and southern delta seemed the same place, and the need for collective response among African Americans across the nation seemed urgent as never before. Though the outcry has always been prominent in historical treatments of this crime and surrounding events, its mechanisms and motive have generally remained unexamined. Instead, they have been naturalized and treated as self-evident, as with so many other examples of black mobilization.[8] Central to inspiring the response of African Americans in Chicago, and the massive black outcry around the country, was record of the case generated by local media, in particular Johnson Publishing's pocket magazine *Jet,* begun in 1951. These issues underscore the importance of local media during the 1940s and early 1950s: public outcry and response to the Till case were poignant evidence of the capacity of Black Chicago's cultural infrastructure to offer new ideas of African-American community.

Yet more than institutional capacity is explained by returning to the Till case's roots in Chicago. The murder of Emmett Till represents an incommensurable moment in African-American experience, like the infanticide of Margaret Garner, or the assassination of Malcolm X: an unthinkable episode even given collective familiarity with injury and abuse. The long tradition of pointing to Till's murder and the acquittal of his killers as a moment of black public epiphany hints also at the difficulties in establishing its frames of social meaning. Invocation of its apocalyptic effect has generally substituted in for the complicated work of saying *how* the Till episode revealed the transformed structure of black community, and ultimately the changes possibilities of black politics. I seek to locate these contextual and historical frames, by addressing the Till lynching as a—if not the—modern occasion of black national feeling, confirming Chicago's pivotal role in articulating those notions of racial community. Instead of an atrocity defying context, Till's murder—and the response to it in Chicago and beyond—offered agonized statement of collective racial will, one illuminating an African-American sense of self as comradeship that occupied a shared place and time.

Given the level of development—cultural and otherwise—in Black Chicago during and after World War II, it is noteworthy that few analyses of social mobilization during this period exist. In part, this indicates choices of periodization: scholars interested in Depression-era interaction between local intellectuals and the Communist Party, or those detailing the Southern Christian Leadership Conference's collaboration with local activists beginning in 1965, leave aside the period addressed in this study.[9] Also at work, though, is an interpretive approach recalling that of Allan Spear in addressing the first two decades of Black Chicago's history: as institutions developed and African Americans grew more race-conscious, accommodation and self-ghettoization replaced militant activism.[10] A predecessor of Spear's had already anticipated this approach: James Q. Wilson's negative appraisal of the political submachine managed by William Dawson announced a broader, and more important, argument that Black Chicago lacked a "vigorous civic life" throughout the 1940s and 1950s.[11] Many recent scholars have called for a reassessment of this conclusion. Local affairs through this period saw pitched struggles within groups like the NAACP, pitting traditional leaders against left-wing insurgencies, as well as the emergence of nonviolent protest groups such as the Fellowship of Reconciliation and the Congress of Racial Equality, and mobilizations around a host of equal access issues ranging from schools to parks, Loop restaurants, and lunch counters.[12]

Among these struggles, none was more compelling to Chicago blacks than open housing. Since the turn of the century housing constituted the most volatile point of conflict locally between the races.[13] The decade following World War II was especially noteworthy for its violence. Given the doubling of the African-American population and their ongoing restriction to the South and West Side, the worsening housing shortage citywide (vacancy rates fell from 3.9 percent in 1940 to 0.9 percent in 1942, and 0.8 percent in 1950) created incredible conditions of overcrowding. By the late 1940s, city planning authorities estimated 375,000 African Americans were living in structures intended for no more than 110,000.[14] The extreme crowding resulted in abysmal health and sanitary conditions, and perpetual risk of fire: between 1947 and 1953, 180 African Americans died in local fires, 63 of them children under ten years of age.[15] Many attempted to leave the tenements and kitchenettes of the Black Belt, either by buying homes or by seeking better apartments in border areas. Escaping substandard districts, however, meant braving segregated neighborhoods, and the desire to venture past the color line was more than matched by bitter and violent resistance. Between 1946 and 1953 six episodes of rioting—involving anywhere from 1,000 to 10,000 whites—followed attempts by African Americans to move into communities such as Cicero, Englewood, and Park Manor. Despite the presence of war veterans among many of the black families seeking entry, protestors used guns, arson, vandalism, and mob threats to force removal of the new residents, invoking their own distorted claim of civil rights in doing so.[16]

The most pronounced of these battles—in duration as well as severity—took place at the Trumbull Park Homes on the city's Southeast Side beginning in August 1953. The pitched unrest at Trumbull has increasingly been cited as a watershed in northern race relations, revealing "the shoals upon which the postwar movement for racial equality would founder," in the words of Arnold Hirsch.[17] Indeed, as with other examples of northern resistance to desegregation,[18] Trumbull Park has been examined primarily for the lessons it offers about the politics of working-class whites. Blacks' reaction of grievance and objection, by contrast, when it has been addressed, has been presented as obvious and predictable. Closer discussion of how African Americans engaged the crisis, through their media and other modes of representation, reveals a soberly contemplative reflection on ideas of community and interest.

Details of Trumbull Park's story are sufficiently well known that only abbreviated summary is needed. On July 30, 1953 Donald and Betty Howard, together with their two children, moved into Trumbull Park Homes, a 462-unit, 1,735-occupant development located in South Deering near the city's steel mills. Since the opening of Trumbull Park in 1939, it had been all white.[19] The first of thirty-four black families to arrive between 1953 and 1955, the Howards gained entry through a fluke: despite screening mechanisms to divert black applicants away from Trumbull, Chicago Housing Authority officials failed to note Betty Howard's race during an interview because of her fair complexion. A mandatory home visit was waived due to Donald Howard's status as a Korean War veteran.[20] By the second week after moving in, the Howards found their apartment threatened by mobs of whites from Trumbull and the surrounding South Deering community: crowds on August 9 were between 1,000 and 2,000, causing a tactical alert by police and setting in place elements of the forthcoming siege.[21] At first mobs used bricks and incendiaries to break windows in apartments occupied by blacks; the Howards were eventually forced to replace their windows with plywood. By fall of 1953 they escalated their tactics, as aerial bombs and fireworks, sometimes numbering in the dozens, were discharged at night above apartments occupied by blacks.[22] Conceding the streets to the ever-present white crowds, police addressed the situation by aggressively monitoring blacks, rather than reasserting control of the streets—an especially heinous instance of blaming the victim as a strategy of social order. To go out to work, school, stores, or social visits, Trumbull's blacks had to notify police and wait for officers to "escort" them. Generally this meant riding in the back of a "Black Maria," the same wagon used to ferry arrested persons to jail.[23]

Nonresident African Americans moving through the area—workers at nearby steel and auto plants, or even casual travelers—lacked recourse to even this degrading safeguard, resulting in further violence. On August 10,

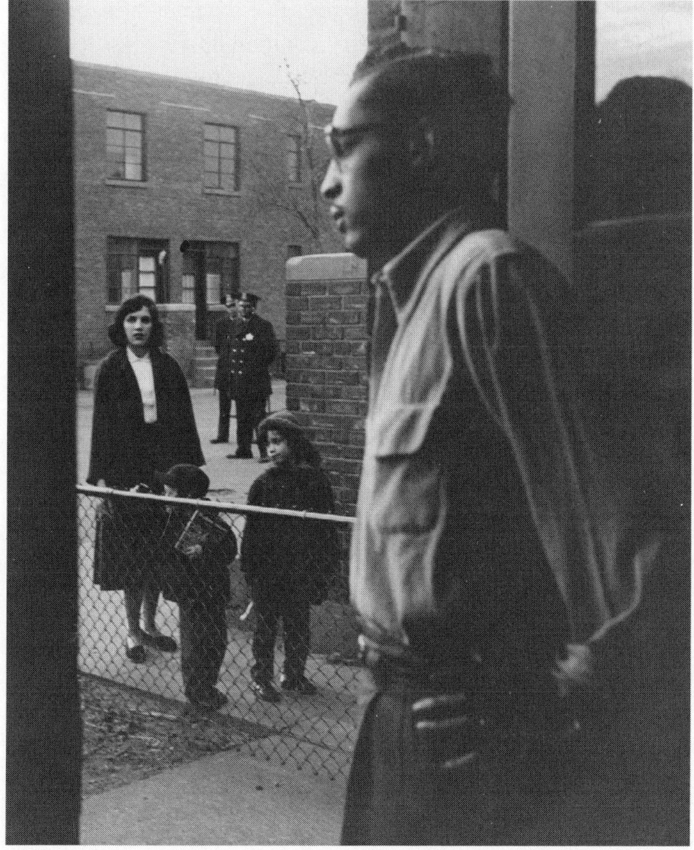

24. Donald Howard watches his wife, Betty, and children approach their apartment in Trumbull Park Homes. Courtesy of the Claude Barnett Collection/Chicago Historical Society (ICHi-15103).

1954, thirty black motorists driving past Trumbull were stoned, while a city bus carrying blacks home from work was attacked and nearly tipped over by crowd of seventy-five whites, in a scene eerily reminiscent of the 1919 Race Riot.[24]

Such contorted arrangements of public safety underscored how officials and most neighboring whites saw blacks as instigators and their tormentors as honorable parties to resistance. While black residents complained of inaction and even abuse on the part of the police "protecting" them, authorities, notably Mayor Kennelly, remained mute,[25] aware of how opposition to integration had mobilized South Deering's whites and heralded the emergence of a new revanchist politics.[26] Reprisals against neighborhood stores serving black customers, as well as attacks against new residents attempting to obtain access to arenas of community life—such as the July 1954 assault of three black worshippers on the steps of St. Kevin's Church by a woman wielding an umbrella—essentially went unpunished.[27] Despite denunciations of the violence from the outside, particularly the national press, conditions remained unchanged through 1954.[28] As more black families moved in, local white commitment to forcing them out of the project grew. Commenting on the ongoing disorder in late October 1954, Federal Housing director Albert Cole termed Trumbull Park a "running sore in our civic life." Chicago politicians and commentators dismissed Cole's statement as partisan meddling in local affairs. Yet several acknowledged that mob defense of "neighborhood rights" was hardly evidence of a healthy body politic. Trumbull's tensions insured that tinderbox questions of housing integration in Chicago would remain unresolved through later years, surfacing again with the arrival of Martin Luther King Jr. and SCLC operatives in 1966.[29]

A crucial—and understudied—element of the Trumbull Park controversy was its unprecedented mobilization of local blacks. Leading the fight was the branch office of the NAACP, reorganized under the leadership of black trade unionist Willoughby Abner, who along with branch president Cora Patton steered the traditional civil rights group toward a more activist agenda.[30] Seeing in Trumbull Park a rare chance to shore up the group's credentials as champion of black common—as opposed to elite—interests, Patton and Abner convened press conferences denouncing the violence, along with its ineffectual handling by courts and police, filed suits against the city, and even organized a July 1954 baseball "play-in" at South Deering's main park.[31] Also supportive of the besieged tenants were the United Packinghouse Workers of America, by now a largely black union with offices relocated to 49th Street and Wabash Avenue in the heart of the South Side.[32] Besides calling for investigation of extremist groups such as the White Circle League, the United Packinghouse Workers of America (UPWA) organized one of the earliest support actions, a picket of CHA offices meant to prevent removal of the Howard family three weeks after their arrival.[33] Response to white massive resistance came as well from less obvious sources. Following the February 1954 near-assault of local businessman S. B. Fuller while he was driving through South Deering, the Chicago Negro Chamber of Commerce called a rally in front of city hall for the following month: 200 black groups signed up to participate. Although the rally failed to meet expectations—fewer than 500 marchers participated, thanks to a well-timed if noncommittal last-minute statement by Mayor Kennelly—it indicated how deep dissatisfaction with the city's handling of the crisis ran within the local black community.[34] Coming several years before massive equal-schools protests energized black Chicago during the early 1960s and over a decade before the Chicago Freedom Movement,[35] activism in support of blacks in Trumbull Park challenges any assessment of local African Americans' as lacking a "vigorous civic life" at the time.[36]

Yet it would be a mistake to conclude that Trumbull Park represented the unambiguous triumph of black mobilization.[37] Nothing makes this clearer than the circumstances of the integrating families, the central players in the drama. Threats and harassment by whites were not just meant to express rejection of the principle of residential integration; they were also aggressive attempts to break the resolve and composure of Trumbull's blacks. On a number of occasions, the effects of this pressure were starkly evident. Jostled by three white teenagers on a project sidewalk in April 1954, Donald Howard responded by drawing a gun and firing several shots, actions for which he would be convicted and fined $100, one of the stiffest penalties resulting from a Trumbull-related arrest.[38] Later that fall the Robinson family moved out of the project: according to the NAACP and black tenants, the cause was Mrs. Robinson, "whose poor health has been aggravated by the circumstances surrounding Trumbull Park."[39] Because of irregularities discovered on their application by the CHA, the Howards were forced to leave Trumbull in May 1954: an ACLU informant reported that local whites took special pleasure in news that one reason for the Howards' departure was the corrosive impact of the crisis on their marriage.[40] Thus, as more black families arrived, those already in Trumbull Park continued to struggle with bricks and bombs, verbal abuse, official indifference, and isolation from the outside world, responding at times in ways that encouraged white resisters to believe that their actions were causing blacks to "[get] the jitters."[41]

Two cultural texts from the period poignantly highlighted Trumbull's cost, rather than its gains, for African Americans. In the June 1954 issue of *Ebony,* an article titled "Riot Victim" told the Howards' story, with a focus on husband and father Donald. Pictured peering from a darkened room at policemen on a project path, Howard's state of mind was established to be one of near paranoia. Another photo reenacted one night's defense of the apartment, with Betty Howard crouched behind her husband, who aimed a "borrowed" gun out another window. With captions like "fear and loneliness haunt Negro family in Chicago's race war" and "Howards live as prisoners for 11 months," the article refused all expressions of optimism about the desegregation struggle. Donald Howard's severe weight loss was mentioned, as was the couple's chain-smoking, evidence of the ordeal's

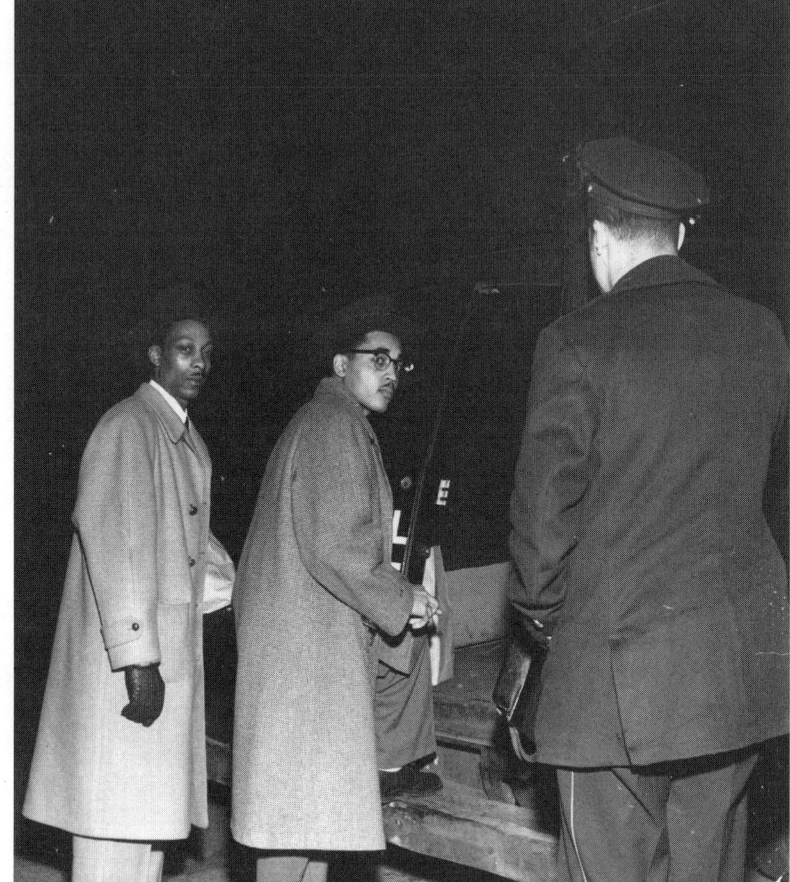

25. Donald Howard and Joseph Sneed board a "Black Maria" police vehicle. Courtesy of Claude Barnett Papers/Chicago Historical Society (ICHi-36837).

"terrific psychological toll." In a photo sequence, the Howard's daughter was shown playing happily with a white friend, and then standing alone rejected, "with an unspeakable look of loneliness on her face," while her playmate moved out front where the mob, as always, was gathered. Asking "why do they stay?"—a question answered by the Howards' departure before the article went to press—*Ebony,* against its well-established precedent, frankly placed the balance of costs in confronting racial animus before black readers across the country.[42]

The second item was the main imaginative work to emerge from the crisis: the novel *Trumbull Park,* written by Frank Brown, an airplane factory worker and member of the tenth African-American family to move into the project. Essentially a fictionalized autobiography, *Trumbull Park* told the story of the Martin family (pseudonym for the Browns), the Davises (Howards), and other black residents as they gained and defended their beachheads within the project. Although events were reordered to enhance the story—while the Browns and Howards overlapped for only a month at the project in reality, their interaction provided the central source of plot tension for the book—*Trumbull Park* nonetheless offered a credible representation of the struggle. The aerial bombings, clashes with police, arrests of Howard and other black residents, even the march in 1954 on city hall were all present in the story. Notable was Martin's recourse to elements of Black Chicago's cultural milieu as a source of psychic grounding during the troubles. References to Muddy Waters, the *Defender,* Club DeLisa, the Regal Theater, Al Benson, and Joe and Marva Louis lent the story an orienting syntax of racial life.[43]

Perhaps the best such example of this was Brown's inclusion of Joe Williams's first and greatest hit, "Everyday I Have the Blues": as much a South Side anthem as any song by Mahalia Jackson or Muddy Waters. Written by Peter Chapman, who as Memphis Slim collaborated with Willie Dixon for decades, the song had anchored Williams's live act at the Club DeLisa since 1951. Observers recalled abandon among the club audience each time he performed the song, asserting common claim to the performance to match Williams's. Melding blues' twin moods of suffering and self-affirmation, "Everyday" resonated with the singer's own history of trials survived: here his oceanic baritone took on a sprightly quality, delivering lines like "speaking of bad luck and trouble, well you know I've had my share" with brio. It was this sense of trenchant faith that Brown sought to impart to his characters at the book's end. Faced once more by an enraged mob, Bugsy Martin and Harry Harvey brave the gauntlet for the first time, reassuring themselves by recalling lines from the song ("nobody loves me, nobody seems to care") and completing their journey, as well as the book, with its closing stanza: "Well there ain't nobody worrying and there ain't nobody crying." Yet such reassurance, ultimately, could not balance the accumulated toll of the assault: when an earlier tenants' meeting was broken up by the sounds of bombs, Martin reflects on the actual distance between Trumbull's blacks and their own community, proximate, yet irrevocably separated:

> the gloom had started to settle—the hopelessness, the loneliness, the fear that the happy people on the corner of 95th and State would not

> be around when the deal went down—fear that the names the *Chicago Defender* might print as the "dead and wounded in the Trumbull Park racial disturbance" would be the only thing that would get through the cool sounds of Ahmad Jamal at the Pershing Lounge down on 63rd Street, through the bluesy tastes that Johnny Griffith laid down at the Basin Street on Cottage Grove. And then it would be too late. Then it would be too goddamned late.[44]

As with the *Ebony* article, the demise most feared in *Trumbull Park* was a more incremental one than that promised by the shouting white mob. Listing assorted pathologies among the black residents of Trumbull—Arthur Davis's alcoholism and paranoia, marital discord, even the high rate of pregnancy among the families—the novel seemed to exemplify Frazier's prior characterization of Chicago as a "city of destruction" for African Americans.[45] Links between Frazier's dim view of postmigration black life, the *Ebony* article, and Brown's novel were strengthened by the concern each text had for prospects for black familial stability, especially patriarchal authority. In the last scene of the book, Martin and another male resident reject dependency on the police—as well as fear of the mob—by walking the streets of the project, rather than riding escorted from work. The ending marks Brown's attempt to recover a measure of male dignity from the tale of Trumbull; yet the accumulated injuries from previous episodes inevitably undermine the intent.

In the end, fictional resolutions could not make up for the realities of Trumbull Park. In 1956 Brown moved out with his family, though as leader of the Tenants' Council he had denounced blacks looking to abandon the fight at Trumbull. Following a July 1957 riot at nearby Calumet Park after black picnickers attempted to enter the area, nine black families left Trumbull Park over the next four months. Nine more left during the next year and a half, leaving only twenty black families by 1959.[46] As with Cicero a few years earlier, the crisis inspired bitter analogy of the supposedly free North with the Jim Crow South: an April 1955 NAACP press release characterized the Trumbull Park Homes as a "little Mississippi."[47] Black Chicagoans were left to wonder, as they had in the summer of 1940, whether their home was in fact a city of refuge—or rather one of destruction.

Not published until the end of the decade, Frank Brown's account of the Trumbull Park crisis confined itself to events prior to 1955. Had he ventured further, Brown might have explored the parallels with an even more disturbing event of racial violence: the death of Emmett Till in Mississippi

26. Police officer watches an unidentified white child throw rocks at Donnie Howard. Courtesy of the Claude Barnett Papers/Chicago Historical Society (ICHi-39059).

in August 1955. Till's murder culminated a year of political tension and violence in Mississippi that paralleled the racial unrest in Chicago. It was brought to the attention of blacks locally and across the country by the same media engendering new notions of community since the war.

In the months leading up to the summer of 1955, African-American readers kept watch on agitation among Mississippi's blacks—as they had other hints of the coming civil rights era—thanks in no small part to Johnson Publishing Company. Instrumental was *Jet* magazine, the pocket weekly first published on November 1, 1951. Meant to allow more timely coverage of current affairs than was possible with *Ebony, Jet* rapidly established itself as an important source of information on struggles to challenge racial inequality. Though officially edited by Edward Clayton, the magazine also showed the influence of the more militant Robert Johnson, a poached recruit along with Lerone Bennett from the Atlanta *Daily World* who would eventually become its executive editor.[48] Its premiere issue noted dismissal of charges against blacks defending themselves during the rioting in Cicero earlier in the year, as well as an NAACP call to revoke the license of New York's Stork Club, following the notorious snubbing of Josephine Baker.[49] Far more so than in the case of *Ebony*, *Jet* sought to emphasize the excesses and absurdities of cold-war anti-Communism. The blackout on news coverage of Paul Robeson did not apply there, as reports of his May 1952 debate with Edith Sampson at AME Zion Church in Brooklyn indicated. Revocation of sociology professor Ira De A. Reid's passport for prior left ties, on the other hand, was criticized, as was the State Department boycott of Walter White's book *A Rising Wind*. Rumors

that Nobel Peace Prize recipient Ralph Bunche was scheduled for questioning by the House Un-American Activities Committee were also scorned. Contrasting stories, such as news that Popular Front icon Angelo Herndon had been arrested in Chicago for housing swindles conducted under an alias, sought to demystify radical tendencies toward deification more than discrediting left politics generally. Herndon's reversal of fortune, an uncanny echo of Ralph Ellison's portrayal of the protean Rhinehart character in his novel *Invisible Man*, illustrated well the local black maxim that all individuals, regardless of reputation or status, inevitably revealed their complicity in some form of hustle.[50]

Given its more uncompromising and hard hitting style, *Jet* was well positioned to address the growing political polarization of the postwar South. An early and somber example of this was the assassination of Florida NAACP head Henry T. Moore on Christmas Night 1951. Detailing ongoing problems in the investigation and the heatedly contradictory recollections of Moore's legacy as tireless advocate of voting rights by local white and black leaders, *Jet*'s article indicated that coverage of gathering tensions in the South would only grow in importance over time. The message was not lost on its sister publication, which returned to the Moore case the following April in a piece provocatively titled "The Bomb Heard around the World": the first coverage of racial violence in *Ebony* since the Columbia Riot of 1946.[51] Articles traced school desegregation cases from the District of Columbia, South Carolina, Virginia, Delaware, and Kansas though the courts to their eventual combination as the *Brown v. Board of Education* lawsuit,[52] noting as well the resolve of Southern governors to resist any future order to desegregate.[53] When the court ruling banning segregated schools was issued in May 1954, *Jet* devoted the next issue to commentary and analysis: writers called the decision "a document that will rank in history with Lincoln's Emancipation Proclamation," and predicted "a Dixie-wide education boom among Negroes."[54] But the company's trademark optimism could not carry in all moments: throughout this time span, *Jet* dutifully chronicled the troubles at Trumbull Park, reporting the Howards' forced exit two weeks before the *Brown* ruling.[55]

Coverage of developments in Mississippi similarly presented two contradictory yet interrelated stories to black readers. To be sure, the groundswell of antiracist activity which had been developing since the end of World War II, received appreciative attention. Concentrating on voter registration and equal schooling, local black efforts had received an important boost with the founding of the Regional Council of Negro Leadership (RCNL) in Mound Bayou in 1951.[56] An early benchmark in the establishment of what Charles Payne calls the organizing tradition in Mississippi and, eventually, the whole of the civil-rights South,[57] the Regional Council combined the activities of previously isolated activists such as Amzie Moore, Medgar Evers, and council president Dr. T. R. M. Howard into a potent statewide movement. By late spring 1955, the council seemed the most significant mobilization of African Americans anywhere in the country. The May 12 issue of *Jet* noted the 13,000 person RCNL voter registration rally during the previous month, an event so impressive that it was covered more extensively in that August's issue of *Ebony*.[58] The coverage of the RCNL rally clearly struck a nerve with readers; it included excerpts from the keynote address by Michigan congressman Charles Diggs, photos showing a massive crowd rushing to a podium to receive registration applications, and lighter asides listing the three tons of barbecue, five hundred cases of soft drinks, and three hundred gallons of ice cream they consumed while doing so. One *Ebony* letter observed that "Negroes . . . staying in the South to fight their own battles are probably making a bigger impression on the country than anything . . . done so far in this area of domestic conflict," while another thanked the magazine for running the piece, observing that "every day Negroes are realizing the full meaning of Civil Rights."[59] Subsequent *Jet* reports on Congressman Diggs's calls for federal enforcement of voting rights in Mississippi, along with RCNL plans to challenge election results in court further underscored the welcome increase in agitation.[60]

Welcome, that is, among African Americans. Indeed, the only news in 1955 more striking than blacks' mobilization in Mississippi was the ferocious white response to it, recounted in detail also for *Jet* and *Ebony* readers. As birthplace not only for the Regional Council of Negro Leadership, but also for the Citizens' Councils, Mississippi served as the first and arguably the most brutal battleground in the clash between antiracist activism and massive resistance during the civil rights era. Beyond losing jobs or suffering boycotts by white customers, having bank credit revoked, and experiencing unending harassment, blacks fighting for citizenship rights in Mississippi routinely found themselves threatened with harm. The same *Ebony* article that lauded the RCNL registration rally also published photos of seven group leaders under the heading "Death List," a reference to threats made by both the Klan and Citizens' Council that continued protests would result in systematic elimination.[61] Speaking at the April RCNL rally, group president T. R. M. Howard noted that while the blacks had weathered the storm of economic reprisals constituting the first wave of backlash activity from the newly formed councils, "the next round will be a wave of violence."[62] Subsequent events proved Howard sadly correct: there were seven politically related murders of blacks in Mississippi during

1955, according to Amzie Moore.[63] Gus Courts, a Belzoni grocer and community organizer who was one of the leaders listed in the *Ebony* article, missed becoming the eighth victim, when he miraculously survived a shotgun attack later that fall.[64] Sharecropper Lamar Smith was not so lucky: after warnings to cease attempts to register to vote, Smith was shot and killed in broad daylight on the steps of the Lincoln County Courthouse.[65]

Beside Emmett Till's, the most brutal of these murders was that of Belzoni minister George Lee. Lee was part of the inner circle of RCNL leadership, co-organizer with Courts of an NAACP branch office, and the first African American in Humphreys County to register to vote. He worked tirelessly for blacks' civil rights locally, and drew numerous threats after the RCNL rally: an anonymous caller informed him soon after that "you're number one on a list of people we don't need around here anymore."[66] A few weeks later while driving home at night from a meeting, Lee's tire was shot out: another car then pulled up alongside the minister and fired a shotgun pointblank at his head. Lee's funeral was attended by over 2,000 agitated mourners, with services interrupted several times by shouts of "he was murdered"—a protest in response to police claims that the tragedy was the result of a traffic accident. Shotgun pellets found in the minister's mouth had been dismissed by local authorities as dental fillings jarred loose upon impact.[67]

In its August article on the RNCL, *Ebony* mentioned Reverend George Lee's murder and presented the restless crowd attending his funeral as further evidence of the significant black mobilization sweeping across Mississippi.[68] Coverage of the shooting and funeral in *Jet*, though, established a more complex view of the tragedy, introducing conventions of narrative that would prove crucial in later reporting of Emmett Till's murder. First, the hypocrisy of the police's refusal to treat the case as a murder was highlighted through charges of an official cover-up. Persons identified by *Jet* as witnesses to the shooting were described as "alter[ing] their story or disappear[ing] altogether." Belzoni blacks told of having all long-distance phone service stopped after the crime, preventing immediate notification of leaders elsewhere and resulting in several driving to Jackson and Mound Bayou in order to relay word of Lee's death.[69] Besides verifying the corruption of local authorities, this material made clear to readers that outside interest and vigilance was requisite to any chance of success in preventing atrocities in Mississippi such as that perpetrated against Reverend Lee.

The second device *Jet* used to relay Lee's death captured its brutal nature far more powerfully than words could. On the first page, set below prose graphically describing the murder, was a photo of Lee's corpse in its casket, with an accompanying image of him alive. Given the severe nature of his injuries, Lee's unremarkable photo at the undertaker's was an anomaly: a contradiction editors highlighted by reminding readers in a caption that the gun blast had torn away the left side of his face.[70] As the *Ebony* article later explained, a local undertaker had labored to conceal the crime's effects, painstakingly sewing Lee's face together for the open-casket service.[71] Coverage of this mortuary work, intended to recover a level of dignity for survivors of George Lee at his funeral, offered a powerful counterpoint to the violence with which this dignity had been wrested from Lee in the first place. Readers were led to see that, at base, the struggle against racism in postwar America was a struggle by blacks to compel recognition of their own humanity. Political controversies—such as the *Brown* legal struggle, race riots from Tennessee to Cicero, and, at least in *Jet*, red-baiting of heroes like Robeson and Du Bois—had been addressed in these magazines previously. Now, though, the rationale for change was being presented in the most immediate terms.

It was within this atmosphere of mobilization and backlash that the Till murder took place, and these were among the concerns that blacks referenced in processing the tragedy. Much of the case's significance appears, on the surface, to derive from stark yet all-too-familiar elements epitomizing racism's savagery in the Jim Crow South: a young boy murdered for an adolescent prank; renowned journalists and politicians greeted with "Good morning, niggers" by the sheriff in Sumner, Mississippi, where the trial of Till's killers took place. Yet at a deeper level, the case, a memory site as much as the American Negro Exposition had been fifteen years earlier, served as opportunity for blacks everywhere to sum up their past, and contemplate their future.

Fourteen-year-old Emmett Till's 1955 visit to uncle Moses Wright in the Delta county of Leflore was not an unusual journey for a black Chicagoan to take. Black migrants in Chicago often made return visits to Mississippi to measure progress since "coming North," maintain ties with distant friends and kin, or just to salve feelings of homesickness.[72] In sending her son South, Mamie Till Bradley, Delta-born herself, doubtless sought some prior sense of place, as others in Chicago had by following the exploits of migrant celebrities like Muddy Waters, Mahalia Jackson, and Al Benson. Till's visit was uneventful until late August, when he entered a country store in Money, Mississippi. It will never be established to the satisfaction of all what occurred during Till and Carolyn Bryant's brief meeting. Did the boy brazenly ask the woman for a date? Did his stutter inadvertently cause him to whistle upon leaving? Either way, subsequent events are clear, thanks to Bryant's husband Roy and brother-in-law J. W. Milam's paid interview in *Look* magazine the following year.[73]

Upon hearing of the encounter from blacks gathered around the store, Bryant and Milam abducted Till late at night from Wright's house. Angered by the boy's insolence while being beaten and threatened, the two men shot him in the head and dumped his body, weighted with a 100-pound gin fan, into the Tallahatchie River. Four days later a fisherman discovered Till's body against a tree near the riverbank. Given advanced decomposition, the identification of the corpse was made through a ring initialed "L. T." found on its hand, a keepsake from Till's father Louis, who died stationed in Italy in 1945. Despite incriminating evidence, testimony by Wright and other witnesses against the men, and the courtroom vigil of Mamie Bradley, Congressman Diggs, and a dozen black journalists throughout the trial, the trial proceeded in farcical fashion. Defendants Bryant and Milam were allowed to roughhouse with their sons and drink Coca-Colas in an atmosphere of casual congregation that mocked the anguish of Bradley and other black onlookers. The all-white jury took but an hour to find Bryant and Milam not guilty of murder; a kidnapping trial held a month later also ended in acquittal.[74]

Despite its objectionable nature and the fever pitch at the time of Mississippi racial politics, Till's murder could not have caused the outcry it did among African Americans were it not for his mother's actions upon the body's return to Chicago. Ignoring a sheriff's order, Bradley, accompanied by local ministers and relatives, opened the casket upon its arrival at the Illinois Central station so that "the world can see what they did to my boy." Journalists from the *Defender* followed her lead, taking photos of the pine box casket (though not the body) and grieving mother at the station.[75] Later, at the Rayner Funeral Home, Bradley insisted that Till's coffin remain open throughout visitation, allowing *Jet* to take the first close-ups of the mangled corpse.[76] It was these images, of course, that conveyed the inhumanity of Till's death to African Americans throughout the country.

The first impression of the *Jet* photos of Till is, of course, their shocking atrocity. Though the September 15 story first detailing the case used other framing visuals—family candids, portraits of witnesses, an image of the gin fan bringing true crime conventions to the story—its centerpiece remains three photos spread over pages 8 and 9. Quarter page images of the body's ravaged frontal view, alongside a photo of Mamie Bradley wanly—yet resolutely—gazing upon her son, were accompanied by a full page close up of Till's face, rotated right to feature its remaining recognizable features (right eye, nose, lips). Dressed in a suit, hair jarringly set and textured, Till's ravaged countenance named the crime more truthfully than much of what would be said in the trial weeks later: in this sense, *Jet*'s caption that the wrenching image constituted "mute evidence" proved not only accurate, but also prescient. As with George Lee, morticians at Rayner faced a daunting task: how to make Till's battered face, beaten beyond recognition, shot at least once from point-blank range, and left to deteriorate in the Tallahatchie River, presentable. Unlike Lee, it proved impossible to achieve lifelike restoration: rough twining rejoining the boy's face stood out across the right temple, and various gestures toward beautification served to emphasize his torture, rather than conceal it . Yet all this ultimately helped establish the documentary power of these images: their *aura,* to return again to Benjamin, their summation of all historically converging in the Till case, was legible in the grotesque and ineffably compelling image of his body.[77]

These pictures, more graphic than those of Lee or any others in Johnson Publishing's history, were of course not the first images of brutality to appear in the black press. Photos of lynchings in weekly newspapers and even journals such as the *Crisis,* had set a stern standard for depictions of racial violence decades before. Even so, the Till photos were unusual. As observers—especially those of Till's age—regularly remarked, it was difficult not to see oneself in the disfigured corpse. Affinity mediated aversion to the macabre image, rendering it one observers were drawn to, as much as repelled by. Nor was this depth of reception mere coincidence. Mamie Bradley's resolve to present her son's body for viewing, and the expert preparation of the corpse worked together to intertwine desecration and adornment, resulting in a poignant public memorial that nonetheless sternly refused any easy compensations of sentimentality. The velvet lining of the coffin, the combed hair crowning the decomposed face, the glimpse of suit and tie veiling the ravaged body complicated the horrifying appearance of the corpse—yes, these images bespoke a heinous crime, but as well a mother's love and a mortician's care, thus anticipating the twinning of indignation and identification that marked its reception among African Americans. Mississippi's brutality, these photos said, was best appreciated juxtaposed to tender reclamation of Till as a boy gone home. Perhaps this explains the absence of protest or objection among African Americans to the photos' publication, despite their disturbance of visual convention, even for those familiar with legacies of racial brutality in the United States.[78]

It is impossible to say whether any of this concerned David Jackson as he set up his equipment at the funeral home, accompanied by Simeon Booker, the *Jet* reporter first introduced to readers as a member of a Cleveland cooperative house in *Ebony* a decade earlier. But if Jackson's thoughts remain a mystery, the significance of the images he generated is by now established. Circulated among hundreds of thousands of subscribers (multiplied in this case by pass-around to probably several million), and corroborated by scores if not hundreds of thousands of black Chicagoans actually viewing Till's body, the photos proved definitive documents of black life and feeling. Few photographs—perhaps the panorama of Martin King addressing the March on Washington in 1963, or iconic portraits of Malcolm X or Angela Davis—can lay claim to equally universal impact upon black observers. And none of these, really, melded feelings of African-American mourning and outrage, of love and loss, as those images of Till did.[79] William Stott speaks of how social documentary balances the two motives of empirical photography—the official need to find fact and the human desire to provoke feeling—by rooting meaning within context and history.[80] It is difficult to think of any other American image exemplifying this union better than these photos of Emmett Till's body, at least for African Americans.

Cursory inventory indicates the universal response to Till's lynching among African Americans during and after 1955. Black memoirs, including those of Anne Moody and Eldridge Cleaver, cited the catalyzing effect of the case on their own politicization. Langston Hughes and Gwendolyn Brooks wrote poems shortly after Milam and Bryant's acquittal, while James Baldwin based his 1964 play *Blues for Mister Charlie* in large part on the case. Till's literary significance remained apparent a generation later in the work of Ishmael Reed, Wanda Coleman, and Audre Lorde. Cleveland Sellers and Robert Terrell spoke for many of the black student activists founding Student Nonviolent Coordinating Committee (SNCC) in 1960 when they recalled for months after not being able "to go into a barber shop or grocery store without hearing someone deploring Emmett Till's lynching." Muhammad Ali, near Till's age and growing up in Louisville at the time, sabotaged a freight train by placing shoe shine stays on the track when he learned of the crime—harbinger of his irrepressibly dissident persona in later years. In virtually all of these cases, it was the photos of Till's corpse that distinguished his story from the countless other atrocities disturbing black memory for generations. If, as Lucious Outlaw maintained, African Americans coming of age in 1955 comprised what he called "the

Emmett Till generation"—one that memorialized his murder not just with poems, memoirs, and plays, but also world-challenging protest—then these images constituted the mechanism of convention for their shared conscience, reminding them that what defined black people was not color, but instead what Du Bois called the "long memory" of pain and outrage.[81]

This response, signifying unity of sentiment and intention among African Americans at the time, raises questions regarding photography's frequent denigration as a demobilizing and deactivating art. "To take a picture is to have an interest in things as they are," Susan Sontag wrote in her classic account of photography as social imagination and action. The correspondence of modern image inventories with increasing public unconcern charged photography as depreciated imagination—"knowledge at bargain prices"—serving to dull rather than strengthen conscience through their ubiquitous presence.[82] Recalling photography's popularity as a strategy for representing violence before, during, and after World War II, Sontag lamented that the "photographic catalogue of misery and injustice" served to "[make] the horrible seem . . . ordinary—making it appear familiar, remote . . . inevitable." Only those rare images constituting "ethical reference points"—for Sontag, images such as those of Nazi death camps—had capacity to redirect individual and collective imagination toward intervention or change. And even here, photography's effect on the balance of social power remained a secondary one of reinforcement or nurture, rather than outright initiation. As Sontag summarily put it: "Without a politics, photographs of the slaughter-bench of history will most likely be experienced as, simply, unreal, or a demoralizing emotional blow."[83]

It is worth revisiting these analyses through the photos of Emmett Till—images that certainly offered ethical reference point to African Americans, then and since; images that not only reinforced, but deepened a critical politics. One must admit the truth of Sontag's analysis at several points. Though the images proved a lodestone for black public consciousness, they had no power to reverse Till's own end: literally, then, they confirmed her definition of photographs as *memento mori*. Explosive though they were, they brought no direct retribution upon his murderers, acquitted weeks later in a notorious show trial. Yet they intervened differently upon the social record—specifically in establishing black injury's authority as a public, if not yet civil, truth. Previous analysts of the Till photos, notably Elizabeth Alexander, stress the photos' power of witness—their record of "murder and defilement" that served to sharpen instincts of survival among African Americans.[84] Yet in their own time the Till photos encouraged not only this general project of resolve, but also a more specific one of verification. Throughout their investigation, Mississippi officials questioned whether the body discovered was Till's, fanning rumors that Bradley had mislead coroners, or that the NAACP had planted the corpse to best exploit the case. These charges, of course, ultimately offered the legal basis for Roy Bryant and J. W. Milam's acquittal. Visual establishment of the *fact* of Till's identity along with his fate, conveyed in *Jet*'s juxtaposition of the boy's portrait standing with his mother with close-ups of his ravaged body, exposed these objections for their inhumanity, as they affirmed the integrity of Till's advocates, in particular his mother. Indeed in 2004, the crime was reopened for investigation by Department of Justice, the first official acknowledgment since 1955 that Till's death, in fact, constituted a crime. Until now, it has remained for African Americans to affirm the crime's truth, and parse its lasting meaning.[85] This they did, through Mamie Bradley's courageous, life-long witness, but also through assembly around imagery of unspeakable malice and harm: an occasion of simultaneity akin to what observers remembered eight years later following news of the Kennedy assassination, or more recently in September 2001 with the attack on and collapse of the World Trade Center.

There was an inherent *truth* to the articulation of black imagination through the photos of Emmett Till's lynching: a truth derived from their testament to history; a truth, indeed, accessible because of their photographic nature, rather than, as Sontag would have it, in spite of it. Elaine Scarry argues that it is pain, more so than any other human condition, that demonstrates language's incapacity to reliably convey social meaning and human feeling. The gulf between the unbearable reality of the sufferer's anguish, and the incomprehension, or indifference, or skepticism of those proximate to abuse, finds illustration in the incredulity of so many whites in Mississippi in 1955, and the ignorance of the case among a vast majority of whites today. It seems even Sontag herself fails to acknowledge these photos in either of her two analyses of modern photography. African Americans, in contrast, claim and have claimed for them a unique fluency in pain's presence and significance, earned through a trying and well-documented history. Yet that the recalled point of encounter for so many with the lynching of Emmett Till was the image rather than the word suggests that pain's confounding of normative language applies for African Americans as well. Pain's inexpressibility, indeed, had political effects for African Americans, compelling them to resort to visual representation to give numbingly familiar atrocity a new meaning, and with it to assert new commitment to action dedicated to change.[86]

Reaction subsequently throughout the country was dramatic. Protest rallies in Detroit, New York, and Baltimore drew scores of thousands as the trial transpired in Sumner, Mississippi. Speakers including A. Philip Randolph, Charles Diggs, Mississippi activists T. R. M. Howard and Medgar Evers, and Mamie Bradley herself—touring the country under NAACP sponsorship—exhorted sympathizers to convey their outrage to authorities both in Mississippi and Washington D.C.[87] Money raised at the events—totaling close to $20,000—was forwarded to the NAACP, authorized by Bradley early in September to "handle the case in their own manner and also to raise funds to finance the prosecution" of the trial.[88] Outrage was apparent even overseas: the International League Against Racialism and Anti-Semitism, headed by Josephine Baker, held a rally of 1,000 in Paris and adopted a resolution to the U.S. Ambassador calling the lynching and subsequent acquittal "a insult to the conscience of the civilized world," while the *Crisis* noted numerous denunciations throughout the French press.[89]

Response to the crime in Chicago was as impassioned as anywhere. Just days before first word of Till's death, a visiting T. R. M. Howard had solicited support for the RCNL in a most upbraiding fashion, blasting migrants in the North for "forget[ting] about conditions back home and about many equally bad conditions in Chicago."[90] In the wake of Till's murder, all of Black Chicago seemed intent on recovering and exercising their collective powers of memory. Relating Till's murder to prior killings and the ongoing campaign of terror in Mississippi, the local NAACP worked closely with Mamie Bradley, sponsoring appearances across the city, notably a September 25 rally at Metropolitan Church drawing 10,000 to hear Bradley, branch president Willoughby Abner, and Simeon Booker speak along with other civic and labor leaders.[91] The branch office also secured counsel for Bradley, assigning attorney William Huff to legally represent the Till family: Huff had experience during the 1940s protecting black fugitives from extradition and thus knew his way around southern courts.[92] One thousand members of the United Packinghouse Workers of America gathered September 15 at their union auditorium to hear Bradley, and they raised $400 in funds.[93] Local disc jockey Daddie-O-Daylie also took up the family's cause, securing contributions from several of his sponsors.[94] The central point of connection to the tragedy, though, took place at the visitation and subsequent funeral. At least 50,000 people came to the Rayner Funeral Home to view the body, horrific in its open casket. Noting the deep wire marks on the barely recognizable face, the *Defender* wrote that "the people saw them and grew angry."[95] The actual service, held at Roberts Temple Church of God, drew an overflow crowd of 12,000: speakers had to be set up in order to broadcast the two-hour service to the far larger crowd blocking off adjacent State Street.[96] The agitated mood of black Chicagoans ran over into other local campaigns: an NAACP rally called to protest the ongoing unrest at Trumbull Park drew 5,000 picketers to city hall in late October 1955, with many in the crowd invoking the Till case as their motivation.[97]

One critical aspect of the Till case was its linkage of Chicago to Mississippi, seen before in Trumbull Park and Cicero, in visits by T. R. M. Howard and other Delta activists, and, of course, the prevalence of the Delta-born among recent migrants. Upon conclusion of the trial, it became clear that the capacity of the Till crisis to embody this connection was based on more than just the victim's Chicago origins. Followers of the tragedy found their attention shifting from anger over Till's death to concern for the welfare of the three Delta residents testifying against the white murderers: sharecroppers Mandy Bradley and Willie Green, and

27. Mourners gather around entrance to Roberts Temple of God Church during funeral services for Emmett Till, September 3, 1955. Courtesy of Corbis Photos.

Till's uncle Moses Wright. Targeted for the same end as Till following their testimony, all made narrow escapes documented by both the *Defender* and *Jet*. Mandy Bradley ran two miles and Willie Green six to avoid potential assailants, eventually catching trains to Chicago where they resettled. Moses Wright, determined to make his cotton harvest before also leaving, thought better of it after sleeping in a church one night and thus avoiding a "visit" from two local whites. He left for Chicago the next day, stating that the only things he would miss from his Delta life were his hunting dogs.[98] Given the abrupt nature of each escape, all three came to Chicago empty-handed: various individuals interested in the case, notably Simeon Booker, made appeals for funds, jobs, and homes for the former fugitives.[99] For these individuals, the journey from Delta to Bronzeville was more hopeful than the somber return of Till's corpse. Concern about sustaining those still living grew out of mourning for the deceased. Interviewed extensively following their escapes, Wright, Bradley, and Green proved eloquent spokespersons for the significance of the recent events: eighteen-year-old Green echoed T. R. M. Howard's earlier thoughts when he challenged listeners at the September 25 NAACP rally to "quit shouting and begin to help their people in the South,"[100] a challenge that many in Chicago responded to in assisting Green and others begin new lives.

Other fugitives resurfacing in the city cemented the connection of modern locale and predecessor region. Following the murder, Till's cousins Curtis Jones and Wheeler Parker were "spirited out of town" back to Chicago, accompanied by their aunt Elizabeth Wright, who vowed she would "never come back" to Mississippi.[101] Sharecropper Leroy "Too Tight" Collins's appearance on the South Side early in October created a minor sensation: a hand on Milam's farm rumored to have washed blood from the truck carrying Till's body, Collins was brought north for safekeeping and to convince him to testify in the upcoming kidnapping trial of his former employer.[102] Even more startling was announcement that T. R. M. Howard was planning to move to Chicago. Observing that he could accomplish more for southern blacks "alive outside than . . . underneath six feet of soil in Mississippi," Howard, after selling $200,000 worth of property and initially shuttling his family to California for safety, resettled in Chicago. In 1958 he would unsuccessfully challenge Congressman Dawson as a Republican, claiming that "our people have grown tired of leaders who are lions among Negroes, but lambs among others."[103] Together with the tales of Wright, Reed, and Mandy Bradley, these stories did more than reignite and expand interest in the tragedy: they designated Chicago as a city of refuge, rather than one of destruction. Recalling the most effective template of antebellum black politics—the flight from slavery and its narration—the Till refugees provided a modern interpretation of the black fugitive as well as invocation of the enduring challenge to the slave system, the erstwhile parent of the Jim Crow social code that compelled Till's own gruesome fate.[104] Something approaching hope could be drawn from the tragic end of Emmett Till, an ironic circumstance that goes some way to explaining how African Americans, then and since, could feel inspiration, along with revulsion, in responding to the tragedy. Yet in order to better grasp this inspiration—and also to comprehend how the response to the crime not only challenged racial supremacy but also momentarily reversed the post-migration predictions of E. Franklin Frazier and others—we must consider the case of the survivor closest to Till.

As Ruth Feldstein has pointed out, analysis of the Till tragedy is notable for its focus on the interplay of black men (and boys), white women, and white men in the Jim Crow South. Black women, by contrast, have not been seen as important figures within the story: a surprising and compromising omission given Mamie Bradley's central role. Although the NAACP and media led by the *Defender* and *Jet* coordinated protest and facilitated near-universal identification with the murdered Till, it is clear that Mamie Bradley was the catalyst for much of this activity, a point developed convincingly by Feldstein.[105] Tracing the tortuous path Bradley negotiated—from caricature in the southern white press as an irresponsible mother for sending Till south in the first place, to contradictory expectations of stoicism and maternal grief from black newspapers, and later to sniping from national NAACP leadership in response to Bradley's requests for renumeration for speaking in some thirty states through the fall—Feldstein maps the meaning of black motherhood in the mid-1950s, indicating how it was reworked into an object "to be positioned, defined, and contained . . . across the political landscape."[106] While noting that Bradley in the end was let go as a spokesperson by the NAACP, leaving her with a previous job as an air force clerk and, of course, haunting memories of her son's awful end, Feldstein shows how Bradley's example demonstrates the racial discrepancy in the public respect accorded motherhood, as well as the ingenious ways that Bradley directed attention to this discrepancy, to great political effect.

Certainly this juxtaposition offered inspiration to poet Gwendolyn Brooks, who in her 1960 collection *The Bean Eaters* offered her own appraisal of the two motherhoods. In the extended poem "A Bronzeville Mother Loiters in Mississippi. Meanwhile, A Mississippi Mother Burns Bacon," Brooks revisited the crime as remembered by its white "victim," Carolyn Bryant. Warmed at first but eventually troubled by the chivalric

28. Gwendolyn Brooks reading to audience at Hall Branch, Chicago Public Library 1949 or 1950. Courtesy of Harsh Research Collection/Chicago Public Library.

pretense in her husband's revenge upon Till, Carolyn Bryant confides that, far from vindicated, recent events had left her vulnerable: "The one thing she did know and knew / With terrifying clarity was that her composition / Had disintegrated. That although the pattern prevailed / The breaks were everywhere. That she could think / Of no thread capable of the necessary / Sew-work."[107] Observing her husband striking their son's face or roughly gripping her from behind, Bryant is haunted by spectral images reminiscent of the murder: "a red that had no end" on her child's cheek, a bloody ooze "spreading darkly, thickly, slowly" over her own shoulders.[108] Recognizing by poem's end that she, like Mamie Bradley, would relive the tragedy in her mind without end, Bryant realizes the price she alone must pay for defense of her white womanhood:

Then a sickness heaved within her. The courtroom Coca-Cola,
The courtroom beer and hate and sweat and drone,

Pushed like a wall against her. She wanted to bear it.
But his mouth would not go away, and neither would the
Decapitated exclamation points in that Other Woman's Eyes.[109]

In contrast, Brooks's rendition of Mamie Till Bradley emphasized her dignity and integrity in mourning, completing reversal of the uneven valuation of motherhood according to race:

Emmett's mother is a pretty-faced thing;
the tint of pulled taffy.
She sits in a red room,
drinking black coffee.
She kisses her killed boy.
And she is sorry.
Chaos in windy grays
through a red prairie.[110]

Like Feldstein, Brooks seeks here to highlight the cruelly contradictory manner in which "good" and "bad" motherhood were coded according to race, and establish a counter narrative that allows for a more sensitive stance in relation to the Till tragedy.

Yet moving though these characterizations were, they might have gone further in relating black motherhood to concerns at that time over the black family. As Feldstein notes, public response to Mamie Bradley's performance as grieving mother drew on a critical vocabulary formulated by Frazier in his research: even as Bradley was asked to embody the race's grief, she was also scrutinized as a single black mother, understood to hold debilitating capacity to disempower adult men and stunt the growth of offspring. While never a dominant point of discussion among black media or racial organizations in Chicago, the spectacle of a single black mother operating in such activist fashion provoked its own challenge to Frazier's ideas. Certainly the concern—in the end unsatisfied—of recovering some sense of male social and political agency during the concurrent Trumbull Park crisis occurring only amplifies this interpretive dimension of the Till protests. Reviewing other events that marked Bradley's personal priorities—her hiring of her own father and cousin as traveling companions during her short-lived yet spectacular career as a national spokesperson, or her reunion with elder Delta relatives in Chicago—one sees an improvised, hopeful model of black family resulting from the tragedy: one that, if atypical and even irreparably tainted by its origins in loss, nonetheless functioned in social and political terms. Mamie Bradley's loss of her son was irreplaceable, and an awful reminder to other African Americans of the price of living under racial supremacy. Yet the senses of familial and racial community that sustained her transfiguring actions after the crime, and in turn were redefined through her intervention, offered a hopeful example allowing others to take something of value from Emmett Till's death.

As much as anything, it was this hope that provided a memory alternative to the racial future warned of by Frazier at the American Negro Exposition back in 1940. Reappraising the social value of the single black mother, redefining the gender of African-American activism, the various elements of the Till tragedy—lynching and protest, fugitive escape, a mother's grief and anger transfigured into universal and simultaneous demand for change—suggested that urban blacks could present themselves, and by extension their community, as deepened politically as well as culturally: a far cry from Frazier's forecast of self-destruction. It is impossible to know if these thoughts persisted for Mamie Bradley: abruptly cut off from NAACP support before 1955 had ended, she was left to the harsh work of reconstructing her life, even as she continued to agitate around the killing of her son. For African Americans generally the case argued, against precedent and propriety alike, that they might see themselves in a more self-determining light.

Yet subsequent stories of mobilization nationally and in Chicago caution against crediting the Till episode with lasting shift of African-American politics. Nationally, the case offered an insurgent counternarrative for the origins for the civil rights movement, contrasting the reformist tone of *Brown* the year before. Its sense of epiphany only deepened in subsequent decades, as Mississippi came to signify the movement's deepest battleground. Challenges emerging in the Delta state—the violent desegregation of Ole Miss, Freedom Summer, the controversies of the Mississippi Freedom Democratic Party (MFDP), and of course the many martyrs who followed Lee, Till, and the others after 1955—reinforced the movement's multiple organizing legacies, giving the sense of an irreversible teleology of struggle. Yet these all revealed the movement's devastating contradictions, as well as its heroic successes—which traced back to Till as well. The question of interracial trust and fellowship that plagued organizing and staffing decisions traced back, ultimately to the differential calculus of human worth that the case exemplified. Though Mamie Bradley's example mirrored those of other women activist leaders including Ella Baker, Daisy Bates, Ruby Hurley, Fannie Lou Hamer, and Unita Blackwell, her marginalization at the hands of the NAACP anticipated the problems of misogyny constraining capacity and vision in groups like SCLC and SNCC.[111] Even the litmus question of nonviolence gestured back to the case: how often in strategy and bull sessions among young organizers in Mississippi might Till's example have been invoked to prove that direct action without self-defense would ultimately end in brutalization?[112] Thus, even as the catalyzing effect of the case was clear, the extent to which its enduring lessons were similarly remembered remained in question.

Political conditions in Chicago proved still more ambiguous in the wake of Till. Mass agitation did carry through the decade and into the 1960s, indicating continued civil energy and concern among local blacks. Ongoing residential segregation, and the linked issue of educational inequity proved especially catalyzing. In 1962, black parents documented underfunding and overcrowding, despite obstruction from the city school board, and staged a series of sit-ins in area elementary schools: the following year, the campaign grew into a 250,000-student boycott of city high schools.[113] Linkage of educational inequality and ongoing housing-related violence to overarching issues of neighborhood segregation led to demands for eradication of slum conditions in the city, calls which would be joined by Martin Luther King and SCLC in the Chicago Freedom Movement of early 1966. Yet ultimately, these challenges proved too great for the unprecedented coalition. Often thought of as King and SCLC's most crippling defeat, the CFM was outmaneuvered by Mayor Daley and his numerous allies among municipal leadership, and viciously harassed by white mobs in Gage Park, Cicero, and other white bungalow communities. King channeled Walter White's 1951 words following the Gage Park march that he had "never seen anything so hostile and so hateful as I've seen today." Lacking enforceable agreements, and suffering countless recriminations from black constituents, King and SCLC left without realizing any of their announced goals. A bitter sense of betrayal carried through to the end of the decade, corresponding to worsening school and neighborhood conditions, joblessness, and anger over police repression, exemplified by the brutal assassination of local Black Panther Party leader Fred Hampton in 1969. That event, involving a charismatic community leader only a few years older than Till himself, showed how the pain associated with the case could prove as important a legacy locally as its agitating promise.[114]

The Till case's most direct consequence, we must remember, was its *convention* of African Americans, more so than its *mobilization* of them. A great accomplishment in recent research, not to mention evolving perspective among black folk generally over two generations, has been healthy skepticism regarding the efficacy of unanimity as a pretext for a racial politics.[115] At the same time, it is also important to note those moments when interests among African Americans could be said to converge, inspiring diverse responses to a shared crisis or affront. This precipitation of community should not be read as choice or preference, much as some might wish to. Certainly editorial policy of Johnson Publishing had by this time diverged from circulating sensational images of violence and injury; and obviously neither Till nor his mother sought out such a gruesome end. Out of unanticipated conditions, though, emerged an instance of virtual racial assembly, a moment of simultaneity that concentrated senses of past, present, and future for blacks, and marked Chicago as a different sort of pivot for black imagination than it had constituted for generations of migrants previously.

No self-conscious racial nation emerged from this occasion of convergence—black lives and aspirations, ever varied and eclectic, proved too dynamic to conform to a single agenda or identity. Ironically, the force of the episode may well have been to orient African Americans more firmly to the United States as a civil structure: despite the travesty of justice that the case's *denouement* represented, blacks still found ways to hold faith in rule of law, in possessive individualism and the opportunity of the market, in the redemptive possibilities of participatory democracy. The extent to which these commitments have been betrayed, as Mamie Bradley and others were betrayed in 1955 when they journeyed to Sumner, Mississippi, in search of justice is well documented, if not yet well known. Nonetheless, these must be categorized as consequences of blacks' convention in 1955 around the ritual of protest and remembrance that the Till case constituted. The sort of "horizontal comradeship" that Benedict Anderson posits as representative of nationalist sensibility at its most elemental finds apt expression in the premise of an "Emmett Till generation" among African Americans of the time. If their simultaneity did not yield the enduring structural conditions of autonomy and self-determination that we equate with "real" nationalism, it did nonetheless signify capacity for its feelings of collective expanse: an indelibly modern structure of imagination—politically as well as culturally.[116] Yet the means by which this sense of expansive community was articulated advances its own questions concerning how durable this sense could have been expected to be.

Anderson terms print capitalism—market production and distribution of cross-hatching modes of cultural representation like the novel or daily newspaper—as the modern mechanism of national feeling. What does it mean, then, that the image, rather than the word, provided the call for African Americans to convene around Till's murder and remembrance? In one sense, this means of transmission marked its simultaneity as all the more modern. Open as photographic images are to innumerable strategies of context and association, the Till images proved specific artifacts related to particular events, and also elastic vessels able to carry endless personal and historical narratives. In this sense, they gave modern gloss to a deep structure of black thought and feeling: terror, after all, has routinely accessed black experience throughout American history. What Douglass famously termed "the blood stained gate" (for him, the whipping of an aunt, but for other blacks, a fear and pain that went by innumerable names) was, as many have by now pointed out, its own empty and malleable time. Sadiya Hartman eloquently cautions regarding the consequences of sensationalizing African-American experience as pain and terror: among whites, these events far too often have proven site of voyeuristic fascination instead of corrective action. For her, black pain constitutes the quintessential scene of subjection—the point where modern humanism inevitably returned to its latent motives of domination. Yet this is a critique directed at the presumptions of interracial sympathy. Ought the empathy of black people for one another to be similarly interrogated?[117]

In its own moment, the Till episode indicated a robust sense of black community, able to effect correspondence not only around interest, but also feeling. Yet the simultaneity of this moment, like all instances of great social and political convergence, proved fragile, and impermanent. If the level of ignorance of this case among whites presently constitutes an affront, the degree to which its indictment of human domination in specific forms—as sexualized aggression, as imposed subordination, even as infanticide—has not registered as powerfully with African Americans at present as has its exemplification of the depths of American racism. We return to the case to tell us how heinous life could be at the time, but fail to return to it as a warning of the human capacity for degeneration generally. That lesson, too, is legible in the horrific images of Emmett Till that, for a moment, convened a black national community. The frequent failure, since that time, to affirm a common humanity—to say nothing of a common polity—reminds us that in history, as in all things, that which is gained is easily lost.

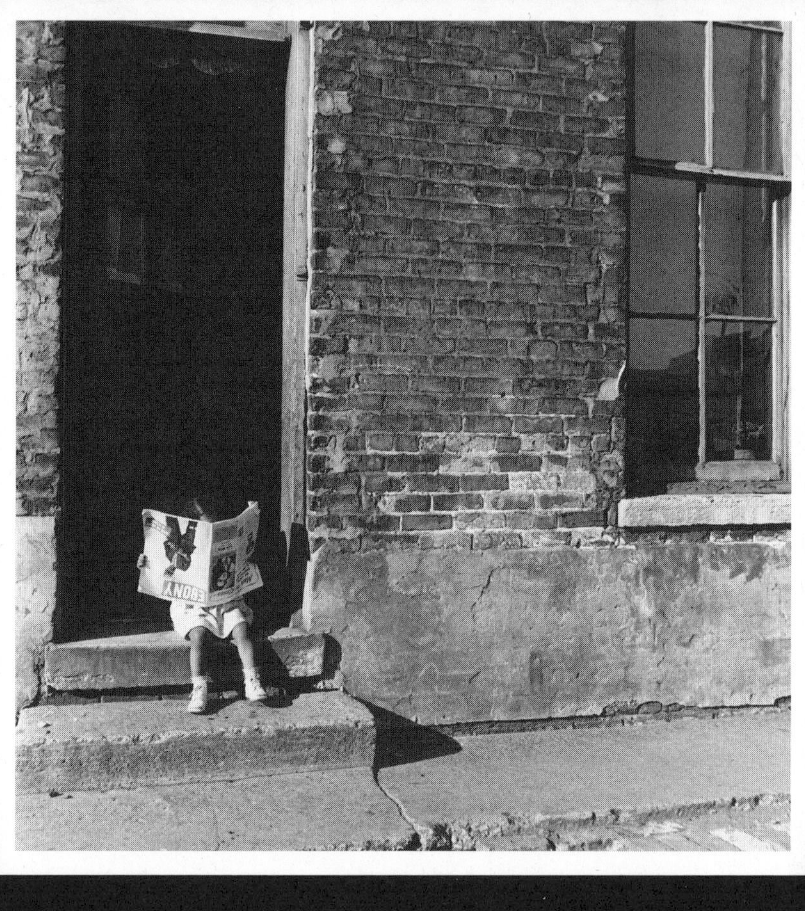
EBONY

AN AFRICAN-AMERICAN DILEMMA

CONCLUSION

It registers at first as an innocuous yet endearing image. Outlines of broader meaning emerge the more one looks at it, suggesting something of a historical cusp—a portal between the hopeful legend of blacks' arrival in Chicago and the urban trials presumed to overwhelm them thereafter. A young girl, no more than four or five, intently scans the August 1949 *Ebony,* with the cover story "Negro FBI Agents in Action": among the more improbable portrayals of black workplace fortune offered by the magazine in its first decade. Her winning preciosity—she reads the issue, after all, upside down—seems the stuff of a cherished family photo. Yet other elements complicate the picture's meaning—the entry door ajar, suggesting latchkey childhoods decried in later years as a structuring condition of black underclass life; worn exteriors belying the South Side's dilapidated appearance; even the diminutive human presence against oversized background, echoing the style of FSA photographers like Russell Lee and Edwin Rosskam who shot Black Chicagoans dwarfed by their surroundings, much as Richard Wright represented them as overwhelmed by urban challenges. Seen against this backdrop, her inverted attention disturbs as much it endears. The black life she finds there, one might surmise, is one seen through the looking glass, a dangerous distortion of both social reality and group responsibility. Intimate, documen-

Facing page: 29. Girl "reading" *Ebony.* Photographed by Wayne F. Miller. Courtesy of Wayne F. Miller.

tary, and prescient at once, the photo gathers together disturbing elements of local history to come: miseducation, fragmented families, children living (and dying) by their wits.

It would be impossible, in closing this book, not to acknowledge the sobering future that Black Chicago would face after 1955, the hyperreality of arrested campaigns for justice, jobless ghettos, and lost youth that by now seems as much the stuff of local legend as the optimism of migrant masses first arriving here. Black Chicago *was* a land of trial and even tra-

gedy, as much as it was a land of hope. Surely, its instructive value as apocryphal tale—warning of how societies can degenerate once jobs, education, services and resources are systematically divested—must be retained. How else are we to reckon with the full cost of the cynicism informing the urban social contract today? How else can we acknowledge the persistence of racial division through the ages of Myrdal and Kerner, to our own time when inner cities like the South Side are written off as liabilities, or fire-sold as assets for developers or latter-day homesteaders looking to enter a booming residential market on the cheap? The misuse of generations of African Americans, in Chicago and other communities, as U.S. society entered and exited its urban era, remains a fundamental gauge of how our society has changed—for worse as much as for better—over time.

And yet, what do we miss when we view Black Chicago's history through such a rueful and fatalistic lens? What of changes in local music culture—the rise of the disk jockey, conversion from the large-label to small-label principles of recording, validation of the realist vocal style—that reworked not only black entertainment but American popular culture generally? Or struggles with the philosophy of clientage evident in the American Negro Exposition or *Negro America* newsreels, posing—though never answering—all-important questions of cultural self-determination well before the consciousness-raising years of late 1960s? Where might we place discussion of Johnson Publishing Company, whose prominence derives not only from the success of its business model or the opportunism of its founder, but also its novel articulation of the core political precepts of intertwined national societies? How do we approach the challenges of relating a black present to experiences of the past—from slavery to Southern terror—crucial grounding for imagining a future in meaningful historical and existential context?

And what of addressing, finally, black identity—collectively and individually—as open narrative, subject to innovation and revision, rather than as constant preserved and recited, unchanged, over time? Our contemporary model for African-American history remains the saga of recognition: either affirmation of black people's truth claims to humanity from beyond the circle of race, or revelation of affinities and obligations within it. Yet the more searching work on black folk has always asked us to suspend presumption of settled meaning: the story remains to be told, the dilemmas persist, out of reach of any easy resolution. Black Chicago's history from 1940 to 1955, as viewed through its cultural producers, speaks to this tendency: it is the thick irony of black existence, rather than its clarified meaning, which emerges through its telling. That by 1955 blacks in Chicago belonged in equal parts to black race and American nation seems compelling cause to resort to African-American history not so much for better answers, but rather better questions.

Another Chicago story poised to emerge in the decades after 1955 was that of race's growing sale. Michael Jordan, R. Kelley, Oprah Winfrey—even personal leadership brands like Jesse Jackson or Louis Farrakhan signify market logics of being that have reorganized contemporary understandings of blackness, much as the privations of the underclass have. Indeed, a walk anywhere on the streets of the South Side today show these two conditions coexisting, signalling modernity's deep contradictions well into the postindustrial age. Much has been said (and remains still to be said) about African Americans' implication within the market ethic of the United States, as buyers, sellers, and product alike. Yet underneath such discussions is the nagging question, tethering epochs of black life much as the little girl standing *Ebony* on its head ties present and future: can blackness ever be sold without recalling its original conditions of sale in the New World through slavery? All those examined in the previous pages wrestled with this conundrum—some openly, others in sublimated or aversive fashion. None, it seems, ever resolved it. Can members of a group profitably sell when they themselves once were sold? Can one belong—socially, culturally, civilly—to a country where one was once a possession? These should be questions always animating politics insofar as it concerns black folks' relation to the United States: but one should not expect easy answers. All we might ask for, in the end, is a more accurate sense of how African Americans themselves reckoned with these vexing issues, often well in advance of the general interest.

One last way to illustrate this observation is to recover Black Chicago's generative links to the greatest story, individually speaking, to emerge from later African-American life. Martin Luther King's biography, of course, already includes a prominent Chicago chapter: one firmly rooted in the adverse conditions of black existence that preoccupied Richard Wright, Horace Cayton, St. Clair Drake, and others. Drawn to the slums of the West

Side, recently occupied by hundreds of thousands of Delta refugees reversing Emmett Till's last journey, King joined local and national organizers in a 1966 omnibus campaign to "end slums" through mass challenge to segregated real estate markets structuring the vast majority of the city. It was to be the opening of SCLC's northern phase—following victories in Birmingham and Selma (not to mention realigning legal gains in the statehouses of Washington), King and his allies predicted a sweep through the Windy City, outflanking the local Democratic machine and allied munici-

pal power structure, and proving the efficacy of nonviolent direct action in the nation's second largest city. Instead, they endured what most observers, then and since, understood to be the death knell of the modern civil rights movement. Outmaneuvered by Mayor Daley, discredited by establishment blacks and militants alike, and confronted by white hostility King famously termed in excess of anything seen in the South, the nonviolent civil rights movement and its leader left burdened with their greatest defeat—further evidence of the enervating state of public life and spirit in Black Chicago.

Preceding this well-known history by roughly a decade was a more hopeful link of King to Chicago. In July 1956, as the Montgomery Bus Boycott entered its final months, *Ebony* magazine published "The King Plan for Freedom," an extensive piece chronicling the organizational development of the campaign, and elevating its young leader to the front ranks of national black life. The first of many feature articles by Lerone Bennett Jr., who had attended Morehouse College at the same time as King, the piece stresses cornerstones of what it termed his personal vision of black freedom and racial justice: nonviolent resistance as a "weapon of love," pursuit and exercise of citizenship rights, reliance on an activated black clergy, closing the gap "between the classes and the masses." *Ebony* and Bennett played up for the first time King's gathering air of destiny ("the leader Negroes have been seeking for a quarter of a century") and emphasized the prophetic symbolism of a racial justice campaign so intertwined with the institutional resources of African-American Christianity. Years before the mainstream press would do the same, King was being presented to black readers as the personification of the civil rights movement: an individual whose deeds, character, and personal life served as harbinger of the coming fortunes of African Americans generally. Over the next two years, *Ebony*'s fascination with King would deepen. Comprehensive coverage of the 1957 Prayer Pilgrimage in Washington, involving six different photographers working on site under David Jackson's supervision, would designate King "the number one Negro leader of men," while by September that year, King was running the occasional column "Advice for Living" in the magazine, addressing readers' queries on military discrimination, interracial marriage, anger management—even the propriety of minister-congregant flirtation.[1]

A generation of revisionist work on the civil rights period has by now taught us the truth of Ella Baker's comment that "Martin did not make the movement; the movement made Martin." Attempts to personify its struggles in King's name are often challenged as attempts to limit its scope, and therefore, its aims. Yet what Johnson Publishing's pioneering interest in King indicates is that the cult of personality that has emerged around him did not begin with neoconservative attempts to appropriate his legacy, nor even with the eruption of white liberal attention in the wake of the 1963 Birmingham struggles. Rather, King had been promoted as an exemplary black individual by *Ebony, Jet,* and subsequently other race media years before. That this agreed with the fundamentally liberal perspective of the magazine is clear: a way to think about the veneration of King since his tragic death is to think about how his life has authorized the ethic of black individual agency and responsibility, an intervention that has quickened activist energies and curtailed radical aspirations at once. When we view his contradictory legacy as a product of black life, as much as an imposition upon it, we are forced to think in different ways about the deeper consequence of *Ebony*'s effort, as well as those of cultural producers in Black Chicago and elsewhere.

All we might say in the end then is that the imaginative life, and thus social experience, of African Americans over the past half century has been far richer than most have understood—indeed, it has time and again proven root source for many of the conventions by which we live today. To begin to get at the good questions that might help lead to better answers, we have to credit and consult that imaginative life. With this in mind, perhaps the best way to read the picture of the little girl on the stoop is not to ground her in her structural and material constraints, but instead to follow her thoughts and dreams through the pages of her magazine, seeing the strange and wide horizons she undoubtedly sees.

NOTES

IN SEARCH OF AFRICAN-AMERICAN MODERNITY: AN INTRODUCTION

1 Richard Wright, introduction to St. Clair Drake and Horace Cayton's *Black Metropolis: A Study of Negro Life in a Northern City* (New York: Harcourt, Brace and Jovanovich, 1945), xviii.

2 Leon Forrest, "Character Behind the Walls of Residential Segregation," *The Furious Voice of Freedom: Essays on Life* (Wakefield, RI: Asphodel Press, 1994), 53; Clifford Geertz, "Notes on the Balinese Cockfight," *The Interpretation of Culture: Selected Essays* (New York: Basic Books, 1973).

3 For discussion of a distinctively black or African diasporic sense of modernity and modernism, see Houston A. Baker Jr., *Modernism and the Harlem Renaissance* (Chicago: University of Chicago Press, 1987); Paul Gilroy, *The Black Atlantic: Modernity and Double Consciousness* (Cambridge, MA: Harvard University Press, 1994); Saidiya V. Hartman, *Scenes of Subjection: Terror, Slavery, and Self Making in Nineteenth Century America* (New York: Oxford University Press, 1997); and Brent Edwards, *The Practice of Diaspora: Literature, Translation, and the Rise of Black Internationalism* (Cambridge, MA: Harvard University Press, 2003). Especially illuminating is the work of Michael Hanchard—in many ways the most ambitious scholar of what he terms "Afro-modernity." See Hanchard, "Afro-Modernity: Temporality, Politics, and the African Diaspora," *Public Culture* 11 (Winter 1999).

4 For introduction to modernity as a field of inquiry and analysis, see Arjun Appadurai, *Modernity at Large: Cultural Dimensions of Globalization* (Minneapolis: University of Minnesota Press, 1996); Walter Benjamin, *Illuminations: Essays and Reflections* (New York: Harcourt, Brace, Jovanovich, 1968); Marshall Berman, *All That Is Solid Melts into Air: The Experience of Modernity* (New York: Simon and Schuster, 1982); Michael Denning, *Culture in the Age of Three Worlds* (London: Verso, 2004); Ann Douglas, *Terrible Honesty: Mongrel Manhattan in the 1920s* (New York: Farrar, Straus, and Giroux,

1995); Jürgen Habermas, "Modernity: An Incomplete Project," in *The Anti-Aesthetic,* ed. Hal Foster (Port Townsend, Washington: 1983): 3–15; Michael Hardt and Antonio Negri, *Empire* (Cambridge, MA: Harvard University Press, 2000); David Harvey, *The Condition of Postmodernity: An Enquiry into the Origins of Cultural Change* (London: Blackwell, 1989); Max Horkheimer and Theodor W. Adorno, *Dialectic of Enlightenment* (1944; reprint New York: Continuum Press, 1991); Karl Polanyi, *The Great Transformation: The Political and Economic Origins of Our Times* (Boston: Beacon Press, 1944); Mary Louise Pratt, *Imperial Eyes: Travel Writing and Transculturation* (London: Routledge, 1992); James C. Scott, *Seeing Like a State: How Certain Schemes to Improve the Human Condition Have Failed* (New Haven: Yale University Press, 1998); Raymond Williams, *The Politics of Modernism: Against the New Conformists* (London: Verso, 1989), as well as the works of Baker, Gilroy, Hanchard, Hartman, and Edwards listed above.

5 My thoughts on the symbiotic relation of urbanism and modernism draw most substantively on Berman, *All That is Solid Melts into Air;* Harvey, *The Condition of Postmodernity;* and Williams, "Metropolitan Perceptions and Emergence of Modernism," in *The Politics of Modernism:* 37–48.

6 Robert Bone, "Richard Wright and the Chicago Renaissance," *Callaloo* 9/3 (1986): 446–68; Margaret Walker, *Richard Wright: Daemonic Genius* (New York: Warner Books, 1988); Bill V. Mullen, *Popular Fronts: Chicago and African-American Cultural Politics, 1935–1946* (Urbana: University of Illinois Press, 1999).

7 Richard Wright, *Twelve Million Black Voices* (New York: Viking Press, 1941): 93–136; Wright, introduction to St. Clair Drake and Horace Cayton's *Black Metropolis: A Study of Negro Life in a Northern City* (New York: Harcourt, Brace, Jovanovich: 1945), xvii. On contemporary pejorative representations of black urban life, see Nicholas Lemann, *The Promised Land: The Great Black Migration and How it Changed America* (New York: Vintage Books, 1991); William Julius Wilson, *The Truly Disadvantaged: The Inner City, The Underclass, and Public Policy* (Chicago, University of Chicago Press, 1987); and Christopher Jencks, *Rethinking Social Policy: Race, Poverty, and the Underclass* (Cambridge, MA: Harvard University Press, 1992).

8 James R. Grossman, *Land of Hope: Chicago, Black Southerners, and the Great Migration* (Chicago: University of Chicago Press, 1989); Arna Bontemps, "The Slave Narrative: An American Genre," in *Great American Slave Narratives,* ed. Bontemps (Boston: Beacon Press, 1969), x; Williams, "Metropolitan Perceptions and the Emergence of Modernism," 38.

9 For an introduction to the voluminous literature on black nationalism, see John H. Bracy Jr., August Meier, and Elliot Rudwick, eds., *Black Nationalism in America* (Indianapolis: Bobbs Merrill, 1970); Robert Carr, *Black Nationalism in the New World: Reading the African-American and West Indian Experience* (Durham: Duke University Press, 2002); Michael A. Gomez, *Exchanging Our Country Marks: The Transformation of African Identities in the Colonial and Antebellum South* (Chapel Hill, University of North Carolina Press, 1998); Wilson Jeremiah Moses, *The Golden Age of Black Nationalism*

(New York: Oxford University Press, 1988); Edwin S. Redkey, *Black Exodus* (New Haven: Yale University Press, 1969); Sterling Stuckey, *Slave Culture: Nationalist Theory and the Foundations of Black America* (New York: Oxford University Press, 1987); William Van De Burg, ed., *Modern Black Nationalism: Marcus Garvey to Louis Farrakhan* (New York: New York University Press, 1997); Komozi Woodard, *A Nation within a Nation: Amiri Baraka (LeRoi Jones and Black Power Politics)* (Chapel Hill, University of North Carolina Press, 1999).

10 My thinking here is of course deeply influenced by the work of Benedict Anderson and its concentration on the ideational habits and basis of modern nationalism. See Anderson, *Imagined Communities: Reflections on the Origins and Spread of Nationalism* (London: Verso, 1983).

11 Horace Cayton and St. Clair Drake, *Black Metropolis: A Study of Negro Life in a Northern City* (New York, Harcourt, Brace and Company, 1945), 379.

12 Louis Wirth, *Local Community Fact Book of Chicago* (1949), 38; William Julius Wilson, *The Declining Significance of Race: Blacks and Changing American Institutions* (Chicago, University of Chicago Press, 1978), 90; Herbert R. Northrup, *Negro Employment in Basic Industry: A Study of Racial Policies in Six Industries* (Philadelphia, 1970), 55–67; Robert Puth, "Supreme Life: The History of a Negro Insurance Company," Ph.D. diss., Northwestern University, 1967; Bureau of the Census, *U.S. Census of the Population: Census of the Population: 1940,* vol. 3, part 1, p. 88; *U.S. Census of the Population: 1950* (Washington, 1953), vol. 2, part 1, 276, 298, vol. 2, part 13, table 87; *U.S. Census of the Population: 1960* (Washington, 1964), vol. 1, part 1, 217, 225, and vol. 1, part 15, table 124.

13 Kevin Gaines, *Uplifting the Race: Black Leadership, Politics, and Culture in the Twentieth Century* (Chapel Hill: University of North Carolina Press, 1996); Joy James, *Transcending the Talented Tenth: Black Leaders and American Intellectuals* (London: Routledge, 1997); Mary L. Dudziak, *Cold War Civil Rights: Race and the Image of American Democracy* (Princeton: Princeton University Press, 2000); Penny Von Eschen, *Race Against Empire: Black Americans and Anticolonialism, 1937–1957* (Ithaca: Cornell University Press, 1997); Robin D. G. Kelley, "How the West Was One: The African Diaspora and the Remapping of American History," in Thomas Bender, ed., *Rethinking American History in a Global Age* (Berkeley: University of California Press, 2002); Wilson Jeremiah Moses, *Afrotopia: Roots of African American Popular Culture* (Cambridge: Cambridge University Press, 1998); Ula Taylor, *The Veiled Garvey: The Life and Times of Amy Jacques Garvey* (Chapel Hill: University of North Carolina Press, 2002).

14 Though many scholars could be listed as important contributors to this field of work, I will restrict myself to a few exemplary practitioners. See Robin Kelley, *Race Rebels: Culture, Politics and the Black Working Class* (New York: Free Press, 1994); Tera Hunter, *To 'joy My Freedom: Southern Black Women's Lives and Labors After the Civil War* (Cambridge, MA: Harvard University Press, 1997); Barbara Ransby, *Ella Baker and the Black Freedom Movement: A Radical Democratic Vision* (Chapel Hill: University of North Carolina Press,

2003); Charles Payne, *I've Got the Light of Freedom: The Organizing Tradition and the Mississippi Freedom Struggle* (Berkeley: University of California Press, 1995); and Steven Hahn, *A Nation Under Our Feet: Black Political Struggles in the Rural South From Slavery to the Great Migration* (Cambridge, MA: Harvard University Press, 2003).

CHAPTER 1: IMAGINING THE FUTURE

1 Letter from Claude Barnett to James W. Washington, president and general manager of the Afra-American Emancipation Exposition, December 27, 1939, Claude A. Barnett Papers, box 366, folder 3, Chicago Historical Society (hereafter Barnett Papers). On reorganization of the Exposition Authority, see the *Chicago Defender,* February 10, 1940, p. 15. For early history of the planning of the exposition, see American Negro Exposition Committee, *American Negro Exposition: 75 Years of Negro Achievement* (Chicago, 1940), 6–7. For other analyses of this event, see Bill Mullen, *Popular Fronts: Chicago and African-American Cultural Politics, 1935–1946* (Urbana: University of Illinois Press, 1999); and Robert Rydell, *World of Fairs: The Century of Progress Expositions* (Chicago: University of Chicago Press, 1993).

2 *Chicago Defender,* June 29, 1940, supplement.

3 Interview with Truman Gibson Jr., May 5, 2000, Chicago.

4 *American Negro Exposition,* 1.

5 Interview with Dr. Margaret Taylor Goss Burroughs, May 5, 2000; *American Negro Exposition,* 10, 11.

6 *Exposition,* 2.

7 Ibid., 1.

8 On the Rosenwald Fund's work on black public schools, see James D. Anderson, *The Education of Blacks in the South, 1860–1935* (Chapel Hill: University of North Carolina Press, 1988), 155. On the fund's sponsorship of arts and scholarship, especially in Chicago, see Robert Bone, "Richard Wright and the Chicago Renaissance," *Callaloo* 9, no. 3 (Summer, 1986), 446–69. Gibson to Barnett, March 1, 1940, box 366, folder 3, Barnett Papers; *American Negro Exposition,* 15.

9 *American Negro Exposition,* 4, 9–10; Barnett to "Tom," February 29, 1940, box 366, folder 3, Barnett Papers. On perpetuation of segregation by both liberals and conservatives within the New Deal, see Desmond King, *Separate and Unequal: Black Americans and the U.S. Federal Government* (New York: Oxford University Press, 1995), esp. chapters 1, 2, and 6; Raymond Wolters, *Negroes and The Great Depression: The Problem of Economic Recovery* (Westport, CT: Greenwood Press, 1970), esp. 42–43. Harvard Sitkoff's *A New Deal for Blacks. The Emergence of Civil Rights as a National Issue: The Depression Decade* (New York: Oxford University Press, 1978), while much more complimentary of the racial politics of the Roosevelt administration, particularly after 1936, also offers abundant documentation of segregationist effects of the New Deal.

10 Barnett to Mary McLeod Bethune, March 13, 1940; Barnett to Robert Weaver, March 13, 1940, box 366, folder 3; Barnett to Emmer Lancaster, June 19, 1940, box 367, folder 4; W. J. Trent to Barnett, July 12, 1940, box 368, folder 1, Barnett Papers.

11 Jackson Davis to Barnett, March 2, 1940; Donald Slesinger to Barnett, March 7, 1940; Barnett to Davis, March 14, 1940, box 366, folder 3, Barnett Papers; John H. Stansfield, *Philanthropy and Jim Crow in American Social Science* (Westport, CT: Greenwood Press, 1985), 152–58.

12 Barnett to Grove Edwards, March 14, 1940, box 366, folder 3; Barnett to Willa Brown, April 22, 1940 box 366, folder 4; Emmer Lancaster to Willa Brown, June 11, 1940, box 367, folder 4; Enoch Wolters, "Peacetime Flyers," undated clipping, box 261, folder 1, Barnett Papers. At this point, Chicago was arguably the center for black aviation nationally, with eight of thirty-one black commercial pilots, five of twelve amateur pilots, and seventeen of eighty-two student pilots located there. See "Negro Aviators" bulletin 3 (January 1939), Office of the Acting Specialist, Negro Statistics, Bureau of the Census, Department of Commerce, box 261, folder 1, Barnett Papers. For more general discussion of black interest in aviation, an important precedent to the Tuskegee Airmen, see Ann Douglas, *Terrible Honesty: Mongrel Manhattan in the 1920s* (New York: Farrar, Straus and Giroux, 1995), 434–61; Robert J. Jakeman, *The Divided Skies: Establishing Segregated Flight Training at Tuskegee, Alabama, 1934–1942* (Tuscaloosa, University of Alabama Press, 1996); Bernard Nalty, *Strength for the Fight: A History of Black Americans in the Military* (New York: Free Press, 1986), 143–61; and Richard Wright, *Native Son* (New York: Harper and Row, 1940).

13 Barnett to Elmer Simms Campell, box 366, folder 4; Eleanor Fournier to Barnett, May 3, 1940, box 366, folder 6, Barnett Papers.

14 *American Negro Exposition,* 2; Dorothy Porter to Barnett, March 26, 1940, box 366, folder 4, Barnett Papers.

15 Richard L. Beard and Cyril E. Zoerner II, "Associated Negro Press: Its Founding, Ascendency, and Demise," *Journalism Quarterly* (Spring 1969): 51.

16 Woodbridge E. Morris, M.D. to Barnett, March 13, 1940; Barnett to Woodbridge E. Morris, M.D., March 19, 1940, box 366, folder 3, Barnett Papers.

17 Letter from "Assistant to the Governor" to Congressman Arthur Mitchell, March 4, 1940; Congressman Mitchell to Barnett, March 8, 1940; Barnett to Congressman Mitchell, March 19, 1940, box 366, folder 3; Congressional Record, Senate (1940): 9285, box 367, folder 1, Barnett Papers.

18 Barnett to Lawrence Cremer, governor of the Virgin Islands, and Gabriel Dennis, secretary of the treasury, Republic of Liberia, March 26, 1940, Barnett to Hon. M. Stenie Vincent, president of the Republic of Haiti, April 1, 1940, box 366, folder 4; Barnett to Rev A. A. Louw, Missionary Conference, Great Zimbabwe, Southern Rhodesia; Rev. A. J. Cross, General Missionary Conference, Nkana, Northern Rhodesia; Rev. J. M. du Toit, Christian Council of South Africa, Pretoria, Transvall; M. le Pasteur P. Patton, Evangelical Missionary Association, Nissao Suica, Recatla, CP 21; Rev. L. J. Bakewell, Consulatative

Board of Federated Missions, CMS Training School, Bukoba, Tanganyika Territory; Rev. John T. Rucker, Alianca Evangelica de Angola Dondi, Chiguar, Angola; Mr. J. G. T. Obaka-Torte, Accra, Ivory Coast; Rev. W. M. Marke, United Christian Council, Sengea, Sierra Leone; Rev. J. Bardsley, Achimota College, Accra, Gold Coast; Mr. L. B. Greaves, Missionary Council, Nairobi, Kenya; Rev. H. Wakelin Coxill, Conseil Protestant du Congo, Leopoldville-Ouest, Congo Belge, April 23, 24, 26, 1940, box 366, folder 5, Barnett Papers.

19 Barnett to Nickerson, May 28, 1940, box 367, folder 2; Nickerson to Barnett, June 7, 1940, box 367, folder 3, Barnett Papers.

20 Barnett to Mayor LaGuardia, March 14, 1940, box 366, folder 1, Barnett Papers.

21 Barnett to Gibson, May 6, 1940, box 366, folder 6, Barnett Papers.

22 David Levering Lewis, *When Harlem Was in Vogue* (New York: Knopf, 1979).

23 Lewis, *When Harlem Was In Vogue,* 262–63.

24 Barnett to Mary Beattie Brady, March 15, 1940, box 366, folder 3; Beattie Brady to Barnett, March 25, 1940, box 366, folder 4, Barnett Papers.

25 Frank Marshall Davis to Robert S. Pious, April 22, 1940, box 366, folder 5, Barnett Papers.

26 Charles Johnson to Barnett, May 29, 1940, box 367, folder 2, Barnett Papers.

27 Barnett to Alain Locke, March 5, 1940, box 366, folder 3; Locke to Barnett, May 26, 1940, box 367, folder 2, Barnett Papers.

28 Barnett to L. D. Reddick, March 19, 1940, box 366, folder 3; Reddick to Barnett, June 17, 1940, box 367, folder 4, Barnett Papers.

29 Julius Adams to Frank Marshall Davis, May 29, 1940, box 367, folder 2, Barnett Papers.

30 Barnett to John Thompson, June 28, 1940, box 367, folder 5, Barnett Papers.

31 Telegram from Brady to Barnett, June 19, 1940, box 367, folder 4, Barnett Papers.

32 Andy Razaf to Barnett, May 2, 1940, box 366, folder 6; William Smith to Barnett, June 8, 1940, box 367, folder 3, Barnett Papers.

33 Laurence Jones to Barnett, May 28, 1940, box 367, folder 2; Barnett to Laurence Jones, June 13, 1940, box 367, folder 3, Barnett Papers.

34 Letter from Mabel K. Staupers to Barnett, June 3, 1940, box 367, folder 2, Barnett Papers.

35 Barnett to Emory Ross, March 26, 1940, box 366, folder 4, letter from Clara Bentley (Africa Bureau) to Barnett, April 24, 1940, box 366, folder 4; "Enlargements sent to Mr. Barnett" (African Bureau inventory), July 2, 1940, box 367, folder 6, Barnett Papers.

36 Margaret Walker, "Epic for the Jubilee Year of Negro Freedom," copy in possession of Barnett, box 367, folder 3, Barnett Papers.

37 Frank Marshall Davis to Truman Gibson Jr., June 24, 1940, box 367, folder 5, Barnett Papers.

38 Telegram from John Sengestacke to Barnett, June 17, 1940, box 367, folder 4, Barnett Papers. See also open letter from George W. Lawrence, chairman, Cit-

izens' Committee, Afra-American Emancipation Exposition, Inc., June 12, 1940, box 367, folder 3, Barnett Papers.

39 Proposed itinerary for Mr. James W. Washington, box 366, folder 6, Barnett Papers.

40 Letters from J. Arnett Murphy, advertising manager, Baltimore *Afro-American,* to Barnett, May 14, 16, and 21, 1940, box 367, folder 1, Barnett Papers.

41 Barnett to D. Kenneth Rose, July 13, 1940, box 368, folder 1, Barnett Papers. All indications are that this dispute had its origins in the weeks before July 4, and only reached its resolution after the opening of the event.

42 Letter from Barnett to Senator James Slattery, June 15, 1940, box 367, folder 4, Barnett Papers.

43 Letter from Bethune to Barnett, June 28, 1940, box 367, folder 5, Barnett Papers.

44 Letter from Roy Wilkens to Barnett, June 26, 1940, box 367, folder 5, Barnett Papers.

45 Letter from Barnett to Stephan Early, June 7, 1940, box 367, folder 3; Early to Barnett, June 25, 1940, box 367, folder 5, Barnett Papers.

46 Telegram from Stephen Early to Barnett, July 2, 1940; program for the Fourth of July opening exercises, box 367, folder 6, Barnett Papers.

47 Undated memo from Major R. R. Jackson, Barnett Papers, box 369, folder 1.

48 Letter from Barnett to George Luker, August 5, 1940, box 368, folder 3, Barnett Papers.

49 George Washington Williams, *History of the Negro Race In America,* vol. 2 (New York, 1883); W. E. B. Du Bois, *Black Reconstruction in America, 1860–1880* (New York: Antheneum, 1935), 81–87. For current analyses of the Emancipator mystique of Lincoln, among both blacks and whites, see Lerone Bennett Jr., *Forced Into Glory: Abraham Lincoln's White Dream* (Chicago: Johnson Publishing Company, 2000), and Scott A. Sandage, "A Marble House Divided: The Lincoln Memorial, the Civil Rights Movement, and the Politics of Memory, 1939–1963," *Journal of American History* 80 (June 1993): 135–67."

50 *American Negro Exposition,* 16, 20–22; third assistant postmaster general to Barnett, June 24, 1940, box 367, folder 5, Barnett Papers; Chicago *Defender,* April 13, 1940, 9.

51 *American Negro Exposition,* 19, 24–25; Writers' Program of the Works Projects Administration (Illinois), *Cavalcade of the American Negro,* 95. Other Chicago-area black institutions featured at the exposition were Eighth Infantry Regiment, the acclaimed army volunteer unit from World War I, the Wabash YMCA, and the local Urban League. For introduction to historic race institutions in Chicago, the best source remains Allan Spear, *Black Chicago: The Making of a Negro Ghetto, 1890–1930* (Chicago: University of Chicago Press, 1967).

52 *American Negro Exposition,* 22; Arnold Hirsch, *Making the Second Ghetto:*

Race and Housing in Chicago, 1940–1960 (Cambridge: Cambridge University Press, 1983), 10–11.

53 Memo from Barnett to Gibson, May 6, 1940, box 366, folder 6, Barnett Papers; for White's mural, now in display at the *Defender* office in Chicago, see *American Negro Exposition,* 12.

54 *American Negro Exposition,* 15–16.

55 Memo from Barnett to Gabriel Dennis, April 27, 1940, box 366, folder 6; Walter Walker to Barnett, June 8, 1940, box 367, folder 3, Barnett Papers; *American Negro Exposition,* 25.

56 Letter from Barnett to Alvin White, June 21, 1940, box 367, folder 4, Barnett Papers.

57 *American Negro Exposition,* 23. On Wright at the exposition, see Michel Fabre, *The Unfinished Quest of Richard Wright* (Urbana: University of Illinois Press, 1993), 206, 563–64.

58 *American Negro Exposition,* 19.

59 D. Kenneth Rose to Barnett, July 23, 1940, box 368, folder 2; Margaret Sanger to Wendell Green, July 23, 1940, box 368, folder 2, Barnett Papers; "Cancels Exhibit on Birth Control," *New York Times,* July 8, 1940, 18.

60 Irene Wilson to Barnett, April 18, 1939, box 285, folder 5, Barnett Papers.

61 *Defender,* June 25, 1940, supplement; Ethel Waters to Claude Barnett, June 24, 1940, box 367, folder 5, Barnett Papers. For information on Katherine Dunham's early career in Chicago, see Joyce Aschenbrenner,"Katherine Dunham" in Darlene Clark Hine, et al., eds., *Black Women in America: An Historical Encyclopedia* (Brooklyn, NY: Carlson Publishers, 1993), 363–67; and Ve Ve Clark, "Performing the Memory of Difference in Afro-Carribean Dance: Katherine Dunham's Choreography, 1938–1987," in Geneviève Fabre and Robert O'Meally, eds., *History and Memory in African-American Culture* (New York: Oxford University Press, 1994), 188–204.

62 Locke, "The American Negro Exposition's Showing of the Works of Negro Artists," introduction to American Negro Exposition, *Exhibition of the Art of the American Negro, 1851–1940* (Chicago, 1940), box 286, folder 16, Barnett Papers.

63 American Negro Exposition, *Exhibition of the Art of the American Negro,* box 286, folder 16, Barnett Papers; letter from Albion Holsey to Barnett, July 22, 1940, box 368, folder 2, Barnett Papers.

64 *Exhibition of the Art of the American Negro,* box 286, folder 16, Barnett Papers; interview with Leroy Winbush, February 8, 2000.

65 Letter from Holger Cahill to Barnett, July 11, 1940, box 368, folder 1, Barnett Papers.

66 Locke, "The American Negro Exposition's Showing of the Works of Negro Artists."

67 James V. Herring to Barnett, March 28, 1940, box 366, folder 4, Barnett Papers.

68 *American Negro Exposition,* 17.

69 *American Negro Exposition,* 24.

70 See comments on Frazier's exhibit in "Exposition," 24.

71 E. Franklin Frazier, *The Negro Family in the United States* (Chicago: University of Chicago Press, 1939). The exposition diorama titles corresponded exactly to the section headings of this landmark book, making clear his interest in using the exposition to disseminate his ideas among a broad black audience.

72 American Negro Exposition, *American Negro Exposition,* 15.

73 "Dustin' Off the News," *Defender,* July 6, 1940, 2.

74 Unsigned and undated letter, box 368, folder 4, Barnett Papers. Hammurabi, unknown outside black Chicago, was a central presence locally from the 1920s until his death in 1977. As Frederick Robb, he helped anchor New Negro society in Chicago through the 1920s, organizing lyceums and debates, and compiling two vivid almanacs of local black life known as the Wonder Books, in 1927 and 1931. Increasingly disenchanted with bourgeois routine, Hammurabi changed both name and career, opening the House of Knowledge, a bookstore and learning center emphasizing links of U.S. blacks to African civilizationist traditions. House of Knowledge proved a key inspiration to the array of Africentered artists, activists, and educators flourishing in Chicago from the Depression to the present. For discussion of Hammurabi's early career, see Adam Green, "The Rising Tide of Youth: Chicago's Wonder Books and the 'New' Black Middle Class," in *Middling Sorts: Explorations in the History of the American Middle Class,* ed. Burton J. Bledstein and Robert D. Johnston (New York: Routledge, 2001).

75 Robert W. Rydell, All the World's a Fair: Visions of Empire at America's International Expositions, 1876–1916 (Chicago: University of Chicago Press, 1984), chapter 2.

76 Frank Marshall Davis to John Hammond, March 14, 1940, box 366, folder 3, Barnett Papers. On Hammond, see Arnold Shaw, *Honkers and Shouters: The Golden Years of Rhythm and Blues* (New York: MacMillen Publishing Company, 1978), 25; Robert Palmer, *Deep Blues: A Musical and Cultural History of the Mississippi Delta* (New York, Viking Penguin, 1981): 130–31; Michael Denning, *The Cultural Front: The Laboring of American Culture in the Twentieth Century* (London: Verso, 1996), 90–91.

77 Barnett to Gibson, June 22, 1940, box 367, folder 5, Barnett Papers.

78 Gibson to Duke Ellington, undated, box 367, folder 6, Barnett Papers.

79 Letter from Howard Dietz to Barnett, March 8, 1940, box 366, folder 3; Barnett to Howard Dietz, March 26, 1940, and John LeRoy Johnston to Barnett, April 17, 1940, box 366, folder 4; letters from Barnett to Monroe Greenthal, George Borthwick, and Will Hays, May 11, 1940; and George Borthwick to Barnett, May 14, 1940, box 367, folder 1, Barnett Papers.

80 *Defender,* January 26, 1940; February 3, 1940; March 2, 1940.

81 Thomas Cripps, *Slow Fade to Black: The Negro in American Film, 1900–1942* (New York: Oxford University Press, 1977), chapter 13.

82 Barnett to David and Donald Selznick, June 18, 1940, box 367, folder 4, Barnett Papers.

83 Letter from Selznick to Barnett, June 24, 1940, box 367, folder 5, Barnett Papers.

84 Letter from Daniel O'Shea to Barnett, July 11, 1940, box 368, folder 1, Barnett Papers.

85 Telegram from O'Shea to Barnett, July 18, 1940, box 368, folder 1, Barnett Papers.

86 Barnett to L. D. Reddick, March 19, 1940, box 366, folder 3, Barnett Papers.

87 Barnett to Hale Woodruff, July 20, 1940, box 368, folder 2, Barnett Papers.

88 *Defender,* July 13, 1940, 1; Barnett to Elizabeth Simon, July 23, 1940; Arthur McLendon to Barnett, July 19, 1940, box 368, folder 2, Barnett Papers.

89 Barnett to Dorothy Porter, July 13, 1940, box 368, folder 1, Barnett to Hale Woodruff, July 20, 1940, Barnett to Dorothy Porter, July 20, 1940, box 368, folder 2, Barnett Papers.

90 Memo from Barnett to Gibson, April 21, 1940, box 366, folder 5, Barnett Papers.

91 For materials related to Barnett's work against the organizing drive of the Brotherhood of Sleeping Car Porters, see box 278, folders 4 and 5; box 279, folders 1–4, Barnett Papers. See chapter 3, note 16 for further discussion of Barnett and the sleeping-car porters.

92 Philip S. Foner and Ronald L. Lewis, eds., *Black Workers : A Documentary History from Colonial Times to the Present* (Philadelphia: Temple University Press, 1989), 447.

93 *American Negro Exposition,* 33. The strike, pitting black drivers against white fleet owners, exemplifies racialized labor politics locally after the Depression. Increases in rentals and gas costs compelled 400 drivers to unionize and walk out in June, winning settlement a month later after the owners suffered $35,000 in business losses. The conflict proved a compelling point of interest during the exposition's first weeks. *Defender* stories predicted the action would "paralyze the South Side," noted efforts of the Illinois Housewives League, Urban League, and the National Negro Congress to broker a settlement, and described battles between picketers and replacement drivers in front of large crowds. One sympathetic columnist warned residents that they could expect injury if caught in strikebreaking cabs, since "the boys have a strike on and anything goes." Building on prior insurgencies such as the Don't Buy Where You Can't Work boycotts of 1932, the taxi strike underlines the correspondence of race and class issues for Chicago blacks, most of whom were far more sympathetic to unions than Barnett. For information on the strike, see *Defender,* June 8, 1940, 1; June 15, 1940, 1; June 29, 1940, 1; July 6, 1940, 1. For column commentary, see "Everybody Goes When the Wagon Comes," by "Ole Nosey," June 15, 1940.

94 Edward Lawson to Gibson, May 31, 1940, box 367, folder 2; Gibson to Barnett, June 10, 1940, box 367, folder 3, Barnett Papers.

95 Pittsburgh *Courier,* August 24, 1940, 1. The piece covered Kelly's arrest on racketeering charges, substantiating rumors that Kelly reported to Frank Nitti and Dan Stanton, Al Capone's successors as Chicago mob heads. Local labor leaders, including Willard Townsend, were quick to condemn the Kelly-

controlled syndicate as a "strong arm" organization that pocketed most of the workers' dues.

96 Barnett to Dorothy Porter, July 13, 1940, box 368, folder 1; Barnett to Mary Beattie Brady, July 31, 1940; Barnett to Fred D. Patterson, July 31, 1940, box 368, folder 2; Barnett to Wendell Dabney, August 1, 1940, box 368, folder 3, Barnett Papers.

97 Telegram from Robert McKeague to Barnett, July 30, 1940; attachment to letter from Barnett to Frederick D. Patterson, July 31, 1940, box 368, folder 2, Barnett Papers.

98 Letter from Langston Hughes and Arna Bontemps to Barnett, July 22, 1940, box 368, folder 2, Barnett Papers.

99 Letter from Langston Hughes and Arna Bontemps to Barnett, July 22, 1940, box 368, folder 2, Barnett Papers.

100 Frederick Patterson to Barnett, August 3, 1940, box 368, folder 3, Barnett Papers.

101 Robert Bishop to Barnett, August 5, 1940, box 368, folder 3, Barnett Papers.

102 Barnett to Robert Bishop, August 10, 1940, box 368, folder 3, Barnett Papers.

103 Memo from Frank Marshall Davis to Barnett, July 16, 1940, box 368, folder 1, Barnett Papers.

104 Jules Herbuveaux to Barnett, July 18, 1940; letters from Barnett to Ulmer Turner (WAAF) and Don Kelly (WLS), July 31, 1940, box 368, folder 2, Barnett Papers.

105 Barnett to the American News Company, July 31, 1940, box 368, folder 2, Barnett Papers.

106 *Defender,* August 10, 1940, 1; Roster of Gate Winners, August 13, 1940, box 368, folder 3; exposition handbill, box 369, folder 5, Barnett Papers.

107 Form letter from Barnett to "The Merchants of Chicago," August 15, 1940, box 368, folder 4, Barnett Papers.

108 Memo from Early Taylor to A. W. Williams (undated), box 368, folder 3, Barnett Papers.

109 *Defender,* August 10, 1940, 1; Barnett to Elder Solomon Lightfoot Micheaux, September 12, 1940, box 368, folder 5, Exposition Handbill, box 369, folder 5, Barnett Papers.

110 *American Negro Exposition,* 38.

111 Letter from Robert Bishop to Truman Gibson Jr., July 23, 1940, box 368, folder 2, Barnett Papers.

112 Barnett to Homer Smith, August 14, 1940; Samuel Ross (NBC Artist Services) to Barnett, August 19, 1940, box 368, folder 4, Barnett Papers.

113 William Trent to Barnett, August 22, 1940, box 368, folder 5, Barnett Papers.

114 Memo from James Gentry to Frank Marshall Davis, August 10, 1940, box 368, folder 3, Barnett Papers; *American Negro Exposition,* 35.

115 Frank Marshall Davis to Carl Murphy, July 29, 1940. Davis's rebuttal is attached to the original letter. Box 368, folder 2, Barnett Papers.

116 Frank Marshall Davis to Roy Wilkens, January 7, 1941, box 368, folder 6, Barnett Papers.

117 Carl Loneia to Barnett, September 7, 1940, Cayton to Barnett, September 13, 1940; Barnett to Cayton, September 16, 1940; Cayton to Barnett, October 16, 1940, box 368, folder 5, Barnett Papers.

118 Emory Ross to Barnett, September 23, 1940; memo from Barnett to A. W. Williams, October 1, 1940 box 368, folder 5, Barnett Papers.

119 Thomas Clark to Barnett, October 16, 1940, box 368, folder 5, Barnett Papers.

120 Irvin C. Mollison to Barnett, June 11, 1941, box 368, folder 6, Barnett Papers.

121 Mary Beattie Brady to Wendell Green, April 22, 1941; Barnett to Brady, May 26, 1941; Brady to Barnett, December 7, 1942; Barnett to Brady December 14, 1942, box 368, folder 6, Barnett Papers.

122 Edwin Embree to Truman Gibson Jr., March 17, 1941; Gibson to Embree, March 19, 1941, box 368, folder 4, Barnett Papers.

123 Barnett to Thomas Young, December 20, 1941, box 368, folder 6, Barnett Papers.

124 Barnett to Brady, May 26, 1941; Barnett to Young, December 20, 1941, box 368, folder 6, Barnett Papers.

125 Barnett to Brady, June 10, 1944, box 368, folder 6, Barnett Papers.

126 Barnett to Brady, June 10, 1944; Charles Dawson to Barnett, September 3, 1945; Albion Hosley to Barnett, June 19, 1946; Barnett to Hosley, June 21, 1946, box 368, folder 6, Barnett Papers.

127 Barnett to Carter G. Woodson, March 25, 1940, box 366, folder 4, Barnett Papers.

128 Barnett to Woodson, March 25, 1940, box 366, folder 4, Barnett Papers.

129 Barnett to Charles E. Edison, May 15, 1940, box 367, folder 1, Barnett Papers.

130 *American Negro Exposition,* 34.

131 The best analysis of the Arts Center is Bill Mullen's work, which discusses it, along with other projects including the exposition itself, as demonstrative of the orthodox radical spirit of local cultural work. This argument extends prior interpretations to black cultural vitality in Chicago during and after the Depression: it is one that I seek to complicate and question with this study. See Mullen, *Popular Fronts: Chicago and African American Cultural Politics, 1935–1946* (Urbana: University of Illinois Press, 1999), 75–105. For prior accounts of the role of ideological radicalism in Black Chicago after 1930, see both Robert Bone, "Richard Wright and the Chicago Renaissance," *Calalloo* 9, no. 3 (1986): 446–68; and Richard Wright, *American Hunger* (New York: Harper and Row, 1977). Extensive primary records concerning the center are available through their own institutional files, and also at the Harsh Collection at the Woodson Branch of the Chicago Public Library, in the William McBride Papers.

132 Benedict Anderson, *Imagined Communities: Reflections on the Origins and Spread of Nationalism* (London: Verso, 1983); Etienne Balibar and Immanuel Wallerstein, *Race, Nation, Class: Ambiguous Identitities* (London: Verso, 1991); Homi K. Bhabba, ed., *Nation and Narration* (New York: Routledge, 1990).

133 Walter Johnson, "Possible Pasts: Some Speculation on Time, Temporality, and

the History of Atlantic Slavery," *Amerikastudien/American Studies* 45, no. 4 (2000): 485–99.

134 W. E. B. Du Bois, *Black Reconstruction in America, 1860–1880* (New York: Harcourt Brace, 1935): see especially foreword, chapters 1, 4, and 17; introduction to Charles T. Davis and Henry Louis Gates Jr., eds., *The Slave's Narrative* (New York: Oxford University Press, 1985); Jerrold Hirsch's introduction to B. A. Botkin, ed., *Lay My Burden Down: A Folk History of Slavery* (1945; reprint, Athens, GA: University of Georgia Press, 1989). For early (and still most effective) utilizations of the slave testimonies beginning in the 1970s, see George Rawick, ed., *The American Slave: A Composite Biography.* vols. 1–19 (Westport, CT: Greenwood Publishing, 1972); and John Blassingame, *The Slave Community* (New York: Oxford University Press, 1972).

135 The literature on the FWP slave narratives is extensive, as they informed much of the benchmark scholarship on U.S. slavery during the middle of the nineteenth century and up to emancipation. For introduction to the story of their generation, as well as valuable interpretation, see Jerrold Hirsch's foreword to B. A. Botkin, ed., *Lay My Burden Down;* introduction to George P. Rawick, *From Sundown to Sunup: The Making of the Black Community* (Westport, CT: Greenwood Publishing, 1972); and introduction to Ira Berlin, et al., eds., *Remembering Slavery: African Americans Talk About Their Experiences of Slavery and Emancipation* (New York: New Press, 1998).

136 Arna Bontemps, "The Slave Narrative: An American Genre," in Bontemps, ed., *Great American Slave Narratives* (Boston: Beacon Press, 1969), vii.

137 Rawick, *From Sundown to Sunup,* xvii.

CHAPTER 2: MAKING THE MUSIC

1 William Broonzy and Yannick Bruynoghe, *Big Bill Blues: William Broonzy's Story* (London: Cassell, 1955), 3; LeRoi Jones, *Blues People: The Negro Experience in White America and the Music That Developed From It* (New York: Morrow Quill Paper, 1963), 131; Jones, *Black Music* (New York: William Morrow, 1967), 187.

2 Stuart Hall, "What Is This 'Black' in Black Popular Culture," in *Black Popular Culture: A Project by Michelle Wallace,* ed. Gina Dent (Seattle: Bay Press, 1992), 21–33; Jones, *Black Music,* 187. It is useful to note periodization schemes shared by various discussions of music's place in African-American history. Lawrence Levine traces black oral culture from the antebellum period to 1940s, arguing that "major patterns of change wrought by freedom" had crystallized by World War II. Sterling Stuckey, in a similarly polyvalent history, ends his analysis in the 1940s as well, with Paul Robeson. Other treatments—those of Jones, Albert Murray, and William Barlow, for example—emphasize the period prior to World War II as determinate for black music as a whole. What I am suggesting here is we extend our focus from, as Barlow puts it, the "*emergence* of blues culture" to its *elaboration* in the postmigration and

urban context. See Levine, *Black Culture and Consciousness: Afro-American Folk Thought From Slavery to the Present* (New York: Oxford University Press, 1977), xix; Stuckey, *Slave Culture: Nationalist Thought and the Foundations of Black America* (New York: Oxford University Press, 1987); Jones, *Blues People;* Albert Murray, *Stomping the Blues* (New York: McGraw-Hill, 1976); and William Barlow, *Looking Up at Down: The Emergence of Blues Culture* (Philadelphia: Temple University Press, 1989).

3 Philip H. Ennis, *The Seventh Stream: The Emergence of Rock'n'Roll in American Popular Music* (Hanover, NH: Wesleyan University Press, 1992); Kerry Segrave, *Payola in the Music Industry: A History, 1880–1991* (London: McFarlans, 1994); Robert D. Leiter, *The Musicians and Petrillo* (New York: Bookman and Associates, 1953). In a 1944 letter to the AFM, the NAACP pointed out that of 673 AFM chapters nationwide, 32 were independent "colored" locals, and 8 were all-black branches subordinate to white locals, with minimal access to royalties or work. None of the chapters were integrated. The NAACP's protest, citing President Roosevelt's executive order 8802 banning discrimination in war industries, forced promotion of the 8 branches to full chapter status. It would be another decade before any locals formally desegregated. See Leiter, *The Musicians and Petrillo,* 92.

4 Barlow, *Looking Up at Down,* 130–31; Ennis, *The Seventh Stream,* 42–62; J. Fred MacDonald, *Don't Touch That Dial: Radio Programming in American Life from 1920 to 1960* (Chicago: Nelson-Hall, 1979); and Arnold Passman, *The Deejays* (New York: MacMillen, 1971). The 1932 compact called for a sliding percentage on gross revenues from the networks—3 percent in the first year, 4 percent in the second, and 5 percent in the third—to go to the ASCAP. Clearly a deal that favored the songwriters, it was renewed once in 1936.

5 For exemplary arguments on this point, see Nathan Huggins, *Harlem Renaissance* (New York: Oxford University Press, 1971); Kathy Ogren, *Twenties America and the Meaning of Jazz* (New York: Oxford University Press, 1989) and Ann Douglas, *Terrible Honesty: Mongrel Manhattan in the 1920s* (New York: Farrar, Straus and Giroux, 1994).

6 TOBA, as the agency was known, was reviled for imposing conditions of near-indenture upon black artists. Over time, the acronym came to stand for "Tough on Black Asses."

7 Lawrence Levine has provided the most compelling version of this argument. See Levine, *Black Culture, Black Consciousness,* 224–33, esp. 228.

8 Race records sold on average for between $0.75 and $1.00 during the 1920s. On remuneration for Smith specifically and for black artists generally, see Barlow, *Looking Up at Down,* 130–33.

9 "Ink" Williams, for example, had an uneven reputation among black artists. Bill Broonzy recalled being enticed into signing away his royalties while drunk at a 1927 Paramount recording session that Williams supervised. Bessie Smith had similar memories of her manager, black songwriter Clarence Williams. Upon discovering that Williams had withheld half her initial royalties, Smith fired him, subsequently negotiating directly with Columbia's management.

See Broonzy with Bruynoghe, *Big Bill Blues,* 20–21; and Chris Albertson, *Bessie* (New York: Stein and Day, 1974), 39, 44–46.

10 Mike Rowe, *Chicago Blues: The City and the Music* (New York: Da Capo Press, 1975), 14; Barlow, *Looking Up at Down,* 133; Arnold Shaw, *Honkers and Shouters: The Golden Years of Rhythm and Blues* (New York: MacMillan Company, 1978), 12. The collapse of the race record market raises an important question: did the market collapse because of decreased purchasing by blacks, or constricting supply from the companies? Studies such as Samuel Adams's work on sharecroppers in Mississippi suggest that purchase of record players among blacks *increased* during the 1930s, indicating that the market's implosion had little to with demand. See Adams, "The Acculturation of the Delta Negro," *Social Forces* 26 (December 1947): 202–12. Here again we are reminded how little control blacks—as producers, artists and consumers—had over the music industry at this point.

11 The story of black music in Depression-era Kansas City is a significant one, both with regards to the development of blues and jazz, as well as the relation of black music to political and underworld systems. See Murray, *Stomping the Blues;* Ronald L. Morris, *Wait Until Dark: Jazz and the Underworld, 1880–1940* (Bowling Green, OH: Bowling Green University Popular Press, 1980), 184–89; and Nathan W. Pearson Jr., *Goin' to Kansas City* (Urbana: University of Illinois Press, 1987).

12 As mentioned in chapter 1, similar explanations have been given for the demise of the Harlem Renaissance as a coherent literary movement. See David Levering Lewis, *When Harlem Was In Vogue* (New York: Knopf, 1981).

13 Charlie Gillet, *The Sound of the City: The Rise of Rock and Roll* (New York: Pantheon Books, 1970), 5; Segrave, *Payola in the Music Industry,* 50.

14 By 1940, 28.5 million—over 80 percent—of American families owned radio sets. Mark Newman, *Entrepreneurs of Profit and Pride: From Black Appeal to Radio Soul* (Westport, CT: Greenwood Press, 1988), 41. For discussion of radio's centrality during the Depression, see Warren Sussman, *Culture as History: The Transformation of American Society in the Twentieth Century* (New York: Pantheon Books, 1984), chapters 8, 9, and 13; and Lizabeth Cohen, *Making a New Deal: Industrial Workers in Chicago, 1919–1939* (Cambridge: Cambridge University Press, 1990).

15 Segrave, *Payola in the Music Industry,* 51.

16 Ennis, *The Seventh Stream,* 101–2. Of more than passing interest here is the local presence of the juke box industry: the three companies—Wurlitzer, Rock-Ola, and Seeburg—that monopolized the trade into the 1960s were all Chicago-based. See Robert Pruter, *Chicago Soul* (Urbana: University of Illinois Press, 1991), 2–3.

17 Leiter, *The Musicians and Petrillo,* 135.

18 Max Horkheimer and Theodor W. Adorno, *Dialectic of Enlightenment,* trans. John Cumming (New York: Continuum Publishing Co., 1991), 120.

19 Richard Middleton, *Studying Popular Music* (London: Open University Press, 1990), 61.

20 *An Antonio Gramsci Reader: Selected Writings, 1916–1935,* ed. David Forgacs (New York: Schoken Books, 1988), 200–206, 217–19. I am indebted here to Stuart Hall's reading of Gramsci's discussion of hegemony. See Hall, "Gramsci's Relevance for the Study of Race and Ethnicity," *Journal of Communications Inquiry* 10 (Spring 1990): 14–17.

21 Several now-classic studies have challenged this position. Notable among these are Tricia Rose's work on hip-hop music and Janice Radway's discussion of romance novel audiences. See Rose, *Black Noise: Rap Music and Black Culture in Contemporary America* (Hanover, NH: Wesleyan University Press, 1993); and Radway, *Reading the Romance: Women, Patriarchy and Popular Literature* (Chapel Hill: University of North Carolina Press, 1984).

22 William Howland Kenney, *Chicago Jazz: A Cultural History, 1904–1930* (New York, Oxford University Press, 1993), 162. For more on the early years of the Regal and Savoy, consult Milt Hinton, interview (n.d.), tape 7, at the Institute for Jazz Studies (IJS), Rutgers University, Newark, NJ.

23 Dempsey Travis, *An Autobiography of Black Jazz* (Chicago: Urban Research Institute, 1983), 83–84.

24 Travis, *An Autobiography of Black Jazz,* 157–61.

25 Bandleader Johnny Otis referred to five venues—the Regal, Harlem's Apollo, the Paradise in Detroit, Howard in Washington D.C., and Royal in Baltimore, as "around the world theaters," flagship venues seen by performers as a cut above the "chitlin' circuit" of neighborhood clubs in post-Depression black communities. See Shaw, *Honkers and Shouters,* 167.

26 Ronald Morris gives a thorough, if partisan, account of underworld involvement with black music. See Morris, *Wait Until Dark,* esp. chapter 7.

27 Nat Shapiro and Nat Hentoff, *Hear Me Talkin' to Ya: The Story of Jazz as Told By the Men Who Made It* (New York: Dover Publications, Inc., 1966), 130; Morris, *Wait Until Dark,* 141; Lionel Hampton with James Haskins, *Hamp: An Autobiography* (New York: Amistad Books, 1993), 16, 24. Hampton went so far as to call Capone "the savior of the black musician" during the Depression because of his stake in South Side entertainment.

28 Travis, *An Autobiography of Black Jazz,* 113, 124–25.

29 Ibid., 45–46. Ronald Morris argues that Chicago gangsters curtailed the careers of at least two jazz legends—Jelly Roll Morton and Joe "King" Oliver. After Morton and Oliver asserted greater autonomy (and, in Morton's case, a stake in the bootlegging and gambling trade), a blacklist was issued, which ended their performance and recording careers. See Morris, *Wait Until Dark,* 153–54, 156.

30 Travis, *An Autobiography of Black Jazz,* 113–14, 166, 270–71. To be sure, some black-managed clubs fared better than others. A 1940 *Defender* article reporting a police crackdown on liquor curfew violators mentioned only three establishments securing "exemptions" from enforcement: Joe's DeLuxe, Club DeLisa, and Square's Boulevard Lounge, another black-owned venue at 51st and Michigan. *Chicago Defender,* June 22, 1940, 11.

31 Travis, *An Autobiography of Black Jazz,* 128, 470.

32 Gray renegotiated contracts for Red Saunders in 1937, Earl Hines in 1941, and Erskine Tate despite threats of harm from white club owners. No doubt much of this newfound power derived from Gray's close relations with union national president James Petrillo. See Travis, *An Autobiography of Black Jazz,* 46–48, 128, 130. Ironically, Gray was ultimately bested by Red Saunders in 1963, when the Regal bandleader successfully organized a drive for integration of the two AFM locals. Gray, whose effectiveness and authority over the years derived from the imperatives of segregation, opposed the campaign to the end.

33 The most compelling version of this argument addresses "acculturation" projects conducted by black elite institutions—race newspapers, community associations, fraternal groups, and prominent churches—who feared that unsupervised activity by Southern migrants would erode their own social capital. See Grossman, *Land of Hope;* Kenneth Kusmer, *A Ghetto Takes Shape: Black Cleveland, 1870–1930* (Urbana: University of Illinois Press, 1976); and Earl Lewis, *In Their Own Interests: Race, Class and Power in Twentieth-Century Norfolk, Virginia* (Berkeley: University of California Press, 1991). For more pointed discussion of the ambivalence of postmigration black leaders towards the mass of black people, see Robin D. G. Kelly, *Hammer and Hoe: Alabama Communists in the Great Depression* (Chapel Hill: University of North Carolina Press, 1990).

34 *Chicago Defender,* January 8, 1949, 26; Travis, *An Autobiography of Black Jazz,* 189, 271, 301.

35 *Chicago Defender,* January 11, 1941; February 15, 1941.

36 Travis, *An Autobiography of Black Jazz,* 468.

37 Willie Dixon with Don Snowden, *I am the Blues: The Willie Dixon Story* (New York: Da Capo Press, 1989), 45.

38 Travis, *An Autobiography of Black Jazz,* 93–109, 134. See *Chicago Defender,* January 1, 1949, 21, for a preview of a Moore show at Club DeLisa on New Year's Eve.

39 *Chicago Defender,* January 1, 1949, 21 and 29; January, 1949, 27. Reaction to these shows echoes recent arguments that transsexual and gay subcultures were far from closeted within postmigration black urban communities: "Joe Hughes' night spot, majoring in the presentation of female impersonators, is packed over the weekend and not without reason. To begin with there is hardly a show boasting more speed, song and dance than the one offered by Valda Gray at Hughes' hot spot. Among the stars are Petite Swanson, Dixie Lee, "Caldonia," Nina Mae McKinney, and Pretty Vicki, all song and dance stars of the first rank. Added to this list of course is emcee Clarence Weems to take care of dramatic numbers included in the list" (*Chicago Defender,* January 29, 1949, 27). For discussion of urban black gay and transsexual nightlife, see Hazel V. Carby, "It Jus Be's Dat Way Sometime: The Sexual Politics of Women's Blues," *Radical America* (1986): 9–22; Eric Garber, "A Spectacle in Color: The Lesbian and Gay Subculture of Jazz Age Harlem," in *Hidden from History: Reclaiming the Gay and Lesbian Past,* ed. Martin Duberman, Martha

Vicinus, and George Chauncey Jr. (New York: Meriden, 1989); George Chauncey, *Gay New York: Gender, Urban Culture and the Making of the Gay Male World, 1890–1940* (New York: Basic Books, 1994), 244–67; and Kevin J. Mumford, *Interzones: Black/White Sex Districts in Chicago and New York in the Early Twentieth Century* (New York: Columbia University Press, 1997).

40 Travis, *An Autobiography of Black Jazz,* 169, 469; Shaw, *Honkers and Shouters,* 144–45.

41 Michael W. Harris, *The Rise of Gospel Blues: The Music of Thomas Andrew Dorsey in the Urban Church* (New York: Oxford University Press, 1992).

42 Apart from Harris's study, the best work on black gospel remains Anthony Heilbut, *The Gospel Sound: Good News and Bad Times* (New York: Proscenium Publishers, 1971).

43 Currently, there is no scholarly study of Mahalia Jackson, one of the more important black cultural figures of the twentieth century. A good source of information on Jackson's life is the chatty but rich companion memoir by Laurraine Goreau, *Just Mahalia, Baby* (Gretna, LA: Pelican Publishing, 1975).

44 Heilbut, *The Gospel Sound,* 64–65; Goreau, *Just Mahalia,* 116.

45 Goreau, *Just Mahalia,* 130–144.

46 "The Mahalia Jackson Show," Promotional booklet for CBS Radio (ca. 1954), Mahalia Jackson Clippings File, Institute for Jazz Studies (IJS), Rutgers University, Newark, NJ.

47 Goreau, 84–88, 99–100, 116, 128.

48 *Ibid.,* 122–23, 195.

49 C. Eric Lincoln and Lawrence Mamiya, *The Black Church in the African American Experience* (Durham: Duke University Press, 1990), 7–10.

50 Heilbut, *The Gospel Sound,* 58. Among those who solicited Jackson's services were Earl Hines, Louis Armstrong, and Duke Ellington. Only Ellington's request was granted: the bandleader backed Jackson at the 1958 Newport Jazz Festival and at a later Columbia recording session.

51 Harris, *The Rise of Gospel Blues,* 270.

52 Charles Wolfe, liner notes for *Mahalia Jackson: The Apollo Sessions,* Compact Disc PCD-2–1332 (Pair Records, 1994).

53 Shaw, *Honkers and Shouters,* 135. Notably, a key catalyst for do-wop—one of the primary rhythm and blues streams that fed into both rock and roll and soul in the 1950s—was the AFM music strike from 1942–44. During the strike, the recording ban applied to instrumental musicians only, and vocalists continued to record, with several early black groups replicating jazz and blues instrumentation in *a capella* form.

54 Heilbut, *The Gospel Sound,* 4, 10, 75–93; Peter Guralnick, *Sweet Soul Music: Rhythm and Blues and the Southern Dream of Freedom* (New York: Harper and Row, 1986), 28–37.

55 I use this term here with Houston Baker's discussion of the blues tradition in mind. See Baker, *Blues, Ideology, and Afro-American Literature* (Chicago: University of Chicago Press, 1984), esp. 3–14.

56 Jerry Watts, *Heroism and the Black Intellectual* (Chapel Hill: University of North Carolina Press, 1994), esp. chapter 2.

57 Heilbut, *The Gospel Sound,* 62.

58 Levine, *Black Culture, Black Consciousness,* 185

59 It is ironic that Jackson never acknowledged this synthesis that so many others noted. Often, while denying characterization of herself as a blues singer, Jackson would pronounce that "blues are the songs of despair, but gospel songs are the songs of hope." Guitarist Bill Broonzy recalled how "he would never play a blues song in front of Mahalia Jackson," out of respect for her devotion to sacred songs. See Levine, *Black Culture, Black Consciousness,* 174; Shaw, *Honkers and Shouters,* 32.

60 Jordan is revered not only by students of black music, but also early rhythm and blues and soul artists. Chuck Berry stated he identified with Jordan "more than any other artist." B. B. King cited Jordan's music as "the origins of rap." When asked whether Jordan had influenced him, James Brown, who routinely covered Jordan compositions early in his career, stated; "He was everything!" See Shaw, *Honkers and Shouters,* 61–85; Nelson George, *The Death of Rhythm and Blues* (New York: Pantheon Books, 1988), 19–20; Jacques Lubin and Danny Garcon, *Louis Jordan Discographie* (Paris: Lavallois-Perret, 1987); and John Chilton, *Let the Good Times Roll: The Story of Louis Jordan and His Music* (Ann Arbor: University of Michigan Press, 1994).

61 In 1947, Adams cofounded Mercury Records, a Chicago-based company highly involved in rhythm and blues and soul music, and sufficiently successful to be classified a "major" national label by the mid-1950s. Among its artists was Dinah Washington, the label's top star into the mid-1960s. See Shaw, *Honkers and Shouters,* 76–85, and Bernard Asbell, "Music in Chicago," *Downbeat,* June 29, 1955, 19–26.

62 Shaw, *Honkers and Shouters,* 67.

63 Chilton, *Let the Good Times Roll,* 95, 97–98, 130, 131. At Billy Berg's, Jordan and the Tympany Five were signed to play at $3,500 a week, near the top of the club's fee scale. For information on Jordan at the Regal, see *Downbeat,* September 23, 1946, 8.

64 Ben Sidran, *Black Talk* (New York: Da Capo Press, 1971), 78–79.

65 Eric Lott, "Double V, Double Time: Bebop's Politics of Style," in *Callaloo* (Fall 1988): 597–605.

66 George Lipsitz, *Class and Culture in Cold War America: A Rainbow at Midnight* (New York: Praeger, 1982), 195–200; George, *The Death of Rhythm and Blues,* 19–20.

67 Keil, *Urban Blues,* 64. Jordan was a master not only at involving audiences during performance, but also simulating such interplay on record. One example of this is "Beware" (1947), in which Jordan, egged on by the band, cautioned male "audience members" to defer all romantic propositions for the sake of their "rights" as men. Consult "Beware" on Jordan, *The Best of Louis Jordan,* Compact Disc MCAD-4079 (MCA Records, 1975).

68 Here I am thinking of discussions of World War II social politics tied to what Robin Kelley called "the riddle of the zoot." First proposed by Ralph Ellison in a 1943 *Negro Digest* essay, the figure points out how racial politics were rooted in "hidden territories" of fashion, dance, and street talk along with more obvious sites such as polling booths or union halls. This culturalist method—reminiscent of Gramsci and, more recently, James Scott—informs many contemporary works on post-Depression black activism, most notably those by Kelley himself. See Kelley, *Race Rebels: Culture, Politics, and the Black Working Class* (New York: Basic Books 1996), especially chapters 2, 4, 5, and 7. For similar discussions by British scholars, see Dick Hebdige, *Subculture: The Meaning of Style* (London: Methuen and Co., 1979; reprint, London: Routledge, 1987); and Stuart Cosgrove, "The Zoot Suit and Style Warfare," in *Zoot Suits and Second-Hand Dresses: An Anthology of Fashion and Music,* ed. Angela McRobbie (Boston: Unwin Hyman, 1988), 3–22.

69 Travis, *An Autobiography of Black Jazz,* 419–21.

70 The connection between Jordan and Caribbean culture is a fascinating aspect of Tympany Five history. In addition to attracting Pan-American "advisors" such as Thomas and Merrick, a robust island audience for Jordan's music evolved through stateside broadcasts of jump music from U.S. coastal cities. Jordan's hemispheric popularity was made clear in 1951, when the band made a tour through Jamaica, Trinidad, Guyana, and Haiti, playing without fail to overflow audiences. See Chilton, *Let the Good Times Roll,* 161.

71 Chilton, *Let the Good Times Roll,* 80–81. Burley, a Chicago-based jazz pianist during the 1920s and author of *Original Handbook of Harlem Jive* (1941), worked as a featured columnist with the *Amsterdam News* during his years of association with Jordan.

72 Jordan's story behind "Is You Is or Is You Ain't (Ma Baby)?" gives some indication of his eclectic system of lyrical procurement: "I was playing Lakota's Lounge on Wisconsin Avenue in Milwaukee. He (the songwriter) was a little hunchback fellow about the size of Chick Webb. He'd come in every night and talk to this girl. They'd have dinner and stay for lunch. He just loved me, and he'd hang around so long as I was there. She'd be talking to someone else and he'd say to her, "Is you is or is you ain't ma baby?" And he was strictly Caucasian—no black blood in him at all. Soon I started sayin' it. And he said, "let's write a song." You can't say because of color or race that a person would not say a thing or would not do a thing" (Shaw, *Honkers and Shouters,* 70–71). For more on Jordan and white collaborators, see Chilton, *Let the Good Times Roll,* 94.

73 Chilton, *Let the Good Times Roll,* 89–90.

74 Their interests were characterized by, more than anything else, their implication within a market-driven process of music creation and dissemination. In this sense, the fact that Jordan's claim that he sought to "play for the people" was intended to separate himself from what he saw as the artistic arrogance of most bebop musicians (with the intriguing exception of Dizzy Gillespie) is

telling. See Charles Keil, *Urban Blues* (Chicago: University of Chicago Press, 1968), 64.

75 Baker, *Blues, Ideology and Afro-American Literature;* Henry Louis Gates Jr., *The Signifying Monkey: A Theory of African-American Literary Criticism* (New York: Oxford University Press, 1988). The quote is from Baker, 3.

76 Here it is important to note Louis Jordan's link to the jukebox market. Although his popularity derived from diverse venues—live performance, radio, armed forces concerts, even movie shorts—it was as a jukebox artist that Jordan was best known. Recording over 160 songs between 1941 and 1950, Jordan and Berle Adams followed a strategy under which songs were "market-tested" live, with audience favorites then recorded and the best of those shipped to jukebox distributors. Often this meant a large portion of Jordan's sales went to automatic players (estimates of jukebox sales for Jordan's "Buzz Me" (1945) were 400,000), further defining Jordan as a "public" artist. See Chilton, *Let the Good Times Roll,* 109. For recording data on Jordan, see Lubin and Garcon, *Louis Jordan Discographie,* 22–51. For more on Jordan's prominence as a jukebox artist, see "Jackpot for the Jukes" in *Negro Digest* (September 1948): 8–11.

77 Georgia Tom was the stage name for Thomas Dorsey, prior to his switch to gospel composing in 1932. For more on Dorsey's blues career, see Harris, *The Rise of Gospel Blues,* 47–90, 117–50.

78 For more on Melrose's role in the early development of Chicago blues, see Rowe, *Chicago Blues,* 17–24; Dixon with Snowden, *I am the Blues,* 42–44; Barlow, *Looking Up at Down,* 306–24.

79 For lyrics and discussion of the two songs, see Paul and Beth Geron, *Woman with Guitar: Memphis Minnie's Blues* (New York: Da Capo Press, 1992), 222–26; and Barlow, *Looking Up at Down,* 322–23.

80 Although her reputation has not carried to the present, there are more than a few testimonies to Green's importance. Robert Harris, lead for the Soul Stirrers gospel quintet, recalled encountering Green's singing while she was an inmate at a Texas prison camp during the Depression, and using it as an important model for his own technique. Researching jukeboxes in Clarksdale, Mississippi, 1941, Tony Russell discovered that Green was one of a handful of artists (Louis Jordan, Fats Waller, Count Basie) featured on every juke in town. See Heilbut, *The Gospel Sound,* 81; Rowe, *Chicago Blues,* 213. For a sample of Green's music consult Foremothers Series, vol. 5, *Lil Green: Chicago, 1940–1947,* Disc RR1310 (Rosetta Records, 1985).

81 While Broonzy and Memphis Minnie were key popularizers of guitar amplification, they were not the first to employ the new technology: black Texans Eddie Durham and Charlie Christian both used amplification prior to 1940. See Shaw, *Honkers and Shouters,* 115–16.

82 Rowe, *Chicago Blues,* 17–25. For discussion of the larger implications of long-term contracting for black musicians, see Shaw, *Honkers and Shouters,* 56.

83 Think, for example, of how various popular conceptions of "soul" music were rooted in the divergent processes and personalities—not to mention racial pol-

itics—of the Motown, Stax, and Atlantic studios. For more on this, see Guralnick, *Sweet Soul Music.*

84 Dixon with Snowden, *I am the Blues,* 60–62.

85 Rowe, *Chicago Blues,* 40–45.

86 On Rhumboogie and Hy-Tone, see Rowe, *Chicago Blues,* 61. On the Leaner brothers and United Records, see Rowe, *Chicago Blues,* 20; Pruter, *Chicago Soul,* 4–5, 8; and Norman Spaulding, "History of Black-Oriented Radio in Chicago, 1929–1963," Ph.D. diss. (University of Illinois, 1981), 59–62.

87 Albert Murray, *The Omni-Americans: Black Experience and American Culture* (New York: Da Capo Press, 1970), 54–66.

88 Levine, *Black Culture and Black Consciousness,* 221–24. Ben Sidran also makes this argument in connection to turn-of-the-century jazz in New Orleans. According to Sidran, the turn toward a more autonomous idea of musicianship could be seen in the emphasis on instrumental craft in Storyville artists like trumpeter Buddy Bolden. See Sidran, *Black Talk,* 30–45. Notably, both Sidran and Levine link the emergence of blues and jazz—as individualized and therefore "modern" black arts—to the self-help philosophy of Booker T. Washington and other black "accomodationists."

89 National membership of the AFM, after decreasing from 146,421 in 1928 to 101,111 in 1934, grew to 134,372 in 1940, 232,370 in 1948, and 242,167 in 1952. See Leiter, *The Musicians and Petrillo,* 80.

90 Figures between the years 1940 and 1955 indicate the fluctuating membership of the local:

1940: 428	1948: 550
1941: 456	1949: 480
1942: 555	1950: 476
1943: 302	1951: 450
1944: 315	1952: 267
1945: 348	1953: 266
1946: 375	1954: 230
1947: 500	1955: 223

The numbers are taken from American Federation of Musicians, Local 208, "Dues Invoices," 1940–55, archives, Chicago Federation of Musicians, Chicago.

91 Rowe, *Chicago Blues,* 49.

92 *Time,* May 7, 1956; Segrave, *Payola in the Music Industry,* 97.

93 Dixon with Snowden, *I am the Blues,* 112–13.

94 For information on the early history of Chess Records, see Rowe, *Chicago Blues,* 63; Dixon with Snowden, *I am the Blues,* 78–82; Mary Katherine Alden, liner notes, *Chess Blues* Compact Discs CHD/C 4–9340 (MCA Records, 1992). The business records of Chess Records, unfortunately, were irreparably scattered during the business's hasty buyout by GRT in 1969.

95 Palmer, *Deep Blues,* chapters 3 and 4; Rowe, *Chicago Blues,* 63–70.

96 Palmer, *Deep Blues,* 159–60; Rowe, *Chicago Blues,* 70–72, 79–81.

97 Palmer, *Deep Blues,* 160.

98 Dixon was involved in numerous Waters sessions for Chess as writer and musician, during the 1950s and 1960s. In addition Dixon encouraged Waters to treat club gigs as "tryouts" for studio material, much like Louis Jordan was doing at the time. Waters's signature song, "Hootchie Cootchie Man" (1954), evolved in this way: Dixon gave him the song prior to a performance, working out the arrangement just before the band took the stage. After the debut, the band recorded the song at Chess. The release was a national hit, remaining on *Billboard* store list for one month and the jukebox list for over three. See Dixon with Snowden, *I am the Blues,* 83–86, 253; for the song's sales see *Billboard,* March 24–June 5, 1954.

99 The Brown signing indicates the hustling, seat-of-the-pants nature of independent recording during the postwar years. Toward the end of 1955 Brown and the Fabulous Flames cut a demo copy of "Please, Please, Please" from a Macon, Georgia studio, and had their agent mail copies to the major independent labels, including Chess and King Records. Leonard Chess ultimately made the best offer, and was scheduled to come to Atlanta to finalize the contract in early 1956, but a snowstorm held up his plane. This complication allowed Ralph Bass, a King agent traveling through the South, the opportunity he needed to turn the tables, inducing Brown to break his commitment to Chess by providing a $200 advance. See Guralnick, *Sweet Soul Music,* 225–26. For information on Chess Records, see Rowe, *Chicago Blues,* esp. chapters 4, 5, 7, and 9.

100 The best source on Dixon is his autobiography, published three years before his death in 1992. See Dixon with Snowden, *I am the Blues.*

101 Rowe, *Chicago Blues,* 171–73.

102 Dixon with Snowden, *I am the Blues,* chapters 4, 6, and 7.

103 In this sense, current discussion over rap music's role in amplifying popular misogyny can be seen as a continuation of a long-standing tradition of linking music and declarative black masculinity. There are of course many parties to this discussion, but it is helpful to begin with Keil—in many ways the first methodical student of black popular music and gender. See Keil, *Urban Blues,* introduction.

104 Though influenced by Keil, the nuanced connection of "songs of love and loss" to histories of racial terror is Gilroy's own reading; one marking a rich path for future analysis of African diasporic music. See Paul Gilroy, *The Black Atlantic: Modernity and Double Consciousness* (Cambridge, MA: Harvard University Press, 1993), 83–85, 201–4.

105 Paul Gilroy, *There Ain't No Black in the Union Jack: The Cultural Politics of Race and Nation* (Chicago: University of Chicago Press, 1991), chapter 5, especially 199–203. For further discussion of the idea of "anti-productivism" in African-American history, see Kelley, *Race Rebels,* especially chapters 1 and 2.

106 Dixon with Snowden, *I am the Blues,* 114–15.

107 George, *The Death of Rhythm and Blues,* 26–28.

108 The Chicago-based Impressions indicate local soul music's impact on ideas of black community, both nationally and internationally. Prominent in all discus-

sions of 1960s soul music because of Black Pride anthems like "Keep on Pushin'" and "People Get Ready," the Impressions have recently been defined as a crucial influence on Black British popular music as well. See Gilroy, *There Ain't No Black in the Union Jack,* 174; and *The Black Atlantic,* 94–95.

109 For information of Vee-Jay Records and the local soul scene, see Pruter, *Chicago Soul,* especially chapters 1 and 2. Michael Haralambros, *Soul Music: The Birth of a Sound in Black America* (New York: Drake Publishing, 1974), while not as rich in local detail as Pruter's work, also has some relevant information.

110 Travis, *An Autobiography of Black Jazz,* 190–201.

111 Hampton with Haskins, *Hamp,* 100.

112 The unnamed company had accounts with 60,000 local black customers, and used that customer base to generate the survey group of 200. See Newman, *Entrepreneurs of Profit and Pride,* 74.

113 Newman, *Entrepreneurs of Profit and Pride,* chapter 3. See also Newman, "On the Air with Jack L. Cooper: The Beginnings of Black Appeal Radio," *Chicago History* 12 (Summer 1983): 51–58.

114 "Program Guide" (ca. 1955), Jack L. Cooper Papers, Manuscript Collection, Chicago Historical Society.

115 For discussion of Cooper's public service programming, see Newman, *Entrepreneurs of Profit and Pride,* esp. 67–69.

116 Jones, *Blues People,* 96.

117 Alain Locke, ed., *The New Negro: An Interpretation* (New York: Arno Press, 1968), especially the introduction.

118 The best discussion of this symbiosis between black print media and the Great Migration remains Grossman, *Land of Hope,* 74–89.

119 In 1930, the percentage of local black households owning radios was 42.6 percent. By 1940, the figure was close to 90 percent, as indicated by surveys of black neighborhoods. See Newman, *Entrepreneurs of Profit and Pride,* 44, and Wirth, *Local Community Fact Book, 1940,* especially entries for Douglas, Grand Boulevard, and Washington Park.

120 Roland Marchand, *Advertising the American Dream: Making Way for Modernity, 1920–1940* (Berkeley: University of California Press, 1985), 64.

121 Marchand, *Advertising the American Dream;* Cohen, *Making a New Deal;* Sussman, *Culture as History.*

122 Drake and Cayton, *Black Metropolis,* 84–85, 733, 743; Mark Naison, *Communists in Harlem During the Great Depression* (Urbana: University of Illinois Press, 1983); Cheryl Greenberg, *"Or Does It Explode?": Black Harlem in the Great Depression* (New York: Oxford University Press, 1991), chapter 5.

123 Cohen, *Making a New Deal,* chapter 8, conclusion; Lewis, *In Their Own Interests,* chapters 2 and 6; Kelley, *Hammer and Hoe,* chapters 6–8.

124 Mark Tushnet, *The NAACP's Legal Strategy Against Segregated Education, 1925–1950* (Chapel Hill: University of North Carolina Press, 1992); Adam Fairclough, *Race and Democracy, The Civil Rights Struggle in Louisiana, 1915–1972* (Athens: University of Georgia Press, 1995).

125 Brenda Gayle Plummer, *Rising Wind: Afro-Americans and U.S. Foreign Affairs, 1935–1960* (Chapel Hill: University of North Carolina Press, 1996), Nikhil Singh, *Black Is a Country: Race and the Unfinished Struggle for Democracy* (Cambridge, MA: Harvard University Press, 2004).

126 Newman, *Entrepreneurs of Profit and Pride,* 69–70.

127 Robert Weems, *Black Business in the Black Metropolis: The Chicago Metropolitan Mutual Assurance Company, 1925–1984* (Bloomington: University of Indiana Press, 1996), 57–58. To be sure, Cooper never gained the number of black sponsors and advertisers he hoped to: his wife and partner Gertrude estimated that only one in five programming sponsors were black businesses or institutions. See Newman, *Entrepreneurs of Profit and Pride,* 70.

128 Newman, *Entrepreneurs of Profit and Pride,* 73.

129 In this light the view of Newman, Keil, Nelson George, and Michael Haralambros that black radio was the progenitor of the "soul consciousness" undergirding cultural and political notions of African-American singularity during the 1960s has particular significance: indeed, Newman calls the early black disk jockeys in Chicago "the first soul men." See Newman, *Entrepreneurs of Profit and Pride,* chapter 7; Keil, *Urban Blues,* chapter 7; George, *The Death of Rhythm and Blues;* and Haralambros, *Soul Music,* chapters 3 and 4.

130 "Disc Jockeys," *Ebony* (December 1947): 44–49.

131 Newman, *Entrepreneurs of Profit and Pride,* 82; Spaulding, "History of Black-Oriented Radio in Chicago," 78, 79. Benson's ties with Dawson survived the latter's switch in party loyalties and subsequent ascension; although Benson never publicly endorsed Dawson, they enjoyed what Norman Spaulding called an "amiable" relationship, one that no doubt provided unique benefits for both men. See Spaulding, "History of Black-Oriented Radio in Chicago," 81.

132 For discussion of Benson, see Newman, *Entrepreneurs of Profit and Pride,* 82–85 and Spaulding, "History of Black-Oriented Radio in Chicago," 78–82.

133 While providing rich detail on Benson, both Spaulding and Newman juxtapose the two broadcasters according to class identity defined in this manner.

134 Spaulding speaks of Benson increasing Regal Theater attendance figures during the early 1950s to 125,000 a week, by gathering cutting-edge blues and rhythm and blues talent and getting them to play several shows a night, building on local appeal already generated by Benson's regular airplay of their music. See Spaulding, "History of Black-Oriented Radio in Chicago," 80.

135 See *Chicago Defender,* December 4, 1948. While deeper examination is needed, it is clear that Benson's "election" was not well received by either traditional leaders or the newspaper itself. Listings of previous candidates show a common profile of traditional institutional leadership: I find no evidence of a figure with ties to popular culture or this sort of mass constituency before Benson. Of course, this reiterates a key theme in the argument here: before to the war, black cultural infrastructure was not sufficiently developed to offer a legitimate institutional presence locally that was capable of consistently providing models of leadership and community-building. For more on the history of

the "Mayor of Bronzeville" campaigns, see Susan Herbst, *Politics at the Margin: Studies of Public Expression Outside the Mainstream* (Cambridge: Cambridge University Press, 1994), chapter 4.

136 Spaulding, "History of Black-Oriented Radio in Chicago," 55, 78–82.

137 For more on payola and radio, see Segrave, *Payola in the Music Industry.*

138 Segrave, *Payola in the Music Industry,* 122.

139 These conditions might explain Benson's lack of success within the recording business. In 1949, Benson started a label using his on-air nickname, "Old Swingmaster," that lasted only for a year. He would return in 1953 with the Parrot label, renamed Blue Lake a year later. Although this label released a few songs of local interest, it never matured, and Benson was eventually blacklisted, in an ironic twist, by the AFM for using nonunion musicians. No doubt he also realized at this point that his fortunes rested with the trade in, not recording of, black popular music. See Rowe, *Chicago Blues,* 61, 113, 123–25.

140 Newman, *Entrepreneurs of Profit and Pride,* 84.

141 Spaulding, "History of Black-Oriented Radio in Chicago," 81.

142 "Black Radio," program produced by Public Radio International, broadcast on WBEZ (Chicago), February 2, 1996.

143 "Black Radio," WBEZ (Chicago), February 2, 1996.

144 Pruter, *Chicago Soul,* 24.

145 To be sure, others had more ambivalent feelings about Benson and his impact on the local music scene. Willie Mabon, a Chess vocalist, found all $5,000 in royalties from his first hit song "I Don't Know" (1952) going to Benson, who had brokered Mabon's signing. Dizzy Gillespie recalled a somewhat more humorous dispute with Benson in 1961. Appearing with Dinah Washington at the Regal, Gillespie and his band played for twice as long as the theater contract stipulated. Benson responded by sending angry telegrams to Gillespie after each performance, inspiring the artist to comment on what he saw as the "Old Swingmaster's" limited appreciation for jazz. Yet while anecdotes like these counter reminiscences of Benson as altruistic and generous, one need only compare his reputation to that of "Ink" Williams a generation earlier to see how within the more dynamic music commerce of the 1940s and 1950s, entrepreneurs such as Benson were more subject to charges of intraracial partisanship than parasitism. On Benson and Mabon, see Dixon with Snowden, *I am the Blues,* 86. On Benson and Gillespie, see Travis, *An Autobiography of Black Jazz,* 176.

146 Spaulding, "History of Black-Oriented Radio in Chicago," 90–91; Rowe, *Chicago Blues,* 80. According to Evans's widow, he started out playing jazz, but switched over to blues when he decided to "stop playing the music that he liked and start playing the music that his people liked." Among his contributions, it seems, is the origination of the term "soul food": several of Evans's listeners recall his regular on-air accounts of "going to the basement and eating some soul food on a chicken crate" as an unpretentious but resonant statement of racial pride that helped inspire later equations of authentic black identity with "soul." See Spaulding, "History of Black-Oriented Radio in Chicago," 123–24.

147 Spaulding, "History of Black-Oriented Radio in Chicago," 83, 84.

148 Travis, *An Autobiography of Black Jazz,* 214. For advertisements of Fitzhugh's programming, see *Chicago Defender,* January 30, 1954, 14.

149 Travis, *An Autobiography of Black Jazz,* 262–73; Spaulding, "History of Black-Oriented Radio in Chicago," 95, 96.

150 Spaulding, "History of Black-Oriented Radio in Chicago," 87–88. The programming of Brown and Durham has been recently examined by Barbara Savage. See Savage, *Broadcasting Freedom: Radio, War and the Politics of Race, 1938–1948* (Chapel Hill: University of North Carolina Press, 1999).

151 Spaulding, "History of Black-Oriented Radio in Chicago," 47.

152 Ibid., 50.

153 George, *The Death of Rhythm and Blues,* 40, 41. Although still in need of development, one can see more and more attention to early black-appeal radio: one of the fundamental modernizing developments in African-American cultural history. In addition to George, Spaulding, and Newman, see Palmer, *Deep Blues,* Haralambros, *Soul Music,* and Louis Cantor, *Wheelin' on Beale Street: How WDIA-Memphis Became the Nation's First All-Black Radio Station and Created the Sound that Changed America* (New York: Pharos Books, 1992).

154 Haralambros, *Soul Music,* 14; Spaulding, "History of Black-Oriented Radio in Chicago," 107–8.

155 Jones, *Blues People,* 140.

CHAPTER 3: THE ENDS OF CLIENTAGE

1 David Levering Lewis, *W. E. B. Du Bois: The Fight for Equality and the American Century, 1919–1963* (New York: Henry Holt, 2000), 243.

2 Claude Barnett to Harry Pace, December 20, 1932, box 266, folder 6, Barnett Papers.

3 Lawrence D. Hogan, *A Black National News Service: The Associated Negro Press and Claude Barnett, 1919–1945* (Rutherford: Fairleigh Dickinson University Press, 1984). That Hogan's meticulous work, the sole extensive account of Barnett's work at the ANP, stops in 1945, indicates the need to revisit Barnett and ANP in contextual relation to the issues animating this study.

4 Adolph Reed Jr., *Stirrings in the Jug: Black Politics in the Post-Segregation Era* (Minneapolis: University of Minnesota Press, 1999): 18, 28.

5 Reed, *Stirrings in the Jug,* 23. On the effects of clientage on local black life through out the twentieth century, see Drake and Cayton, *Black Metropolis;* Harold F. Gosnell, *Negro Politicians: The Rise of Negro Politics in Chicago* (Chicago: University of Chicago Press, 1935); Grossman, *Land of Hope;* and especially Allan H. Spear, *Black Chicago: The Making of a Negro Ghetto, 1890–1919* (Chicago: University of Chicago Press, 1967).

6 W. E. B. Du Bois, *The Souls of Black Folk* (Boston: Bedford Books, 1997), 67.

7 Hogan, *A Black National News Service,* 41.

8 Ibid., 44–45.

9 Roi Ottley, *The Lonely Warrior: The Life and Times of Robert S. Abbott* (Chicago: Henry Regnery Co., 1955), 136.

10 Frank Marshall Davis, *Livin' the Blues: Memoirs of a Black Journalist and Poet,* ed. John Edgar Tidwell (Madison: University of Wisconsin Press, 1992), 226–28; Barnett to Emmanuel Glucksman, October 5, 1952, box 292, folder 2, Barnett Papers; Louis Jordan to "Theatrical Editor" (ANP), 1949 n.d., box 286, folder 1, Barnett Papers.

11 Brenda Gayle Plummer, *Rising Wind: Black Americans and U.S. Foreign Affairs, 1935–1960* (Chapel Hill: University of North Carolina Press, 1996), 25–27.

12 Davis, *Livin' The Blues,* 227.

13 Linda J. Evans, "Claude Barnett and the Associated Negro Press," *Chicago History* (Spring 1983): 49.

14 L. C. Bates to Barnett, July 27, 1946; Barnett to L. C. Bates, July 31, 1946; Barnett to L. C. Bates, November 30, 1946, box 358, folder 1, Barnett Papers.

15 Hogan, *A Black National News Service,* 146.

16 Scores of letters between Barnett and Pullman Company officials attest to the greater degree of Barnett's identifications both with management, and with white corporate authority through the Brotherhood Drive. See box 278, folders 4 and 5, and box 279, folders 1–4, Barnett Papers for detailed records of Barnett's anti-Brotherhood efforts. For a comprehensive account of the Brotherhood's historical development and impact, see Beth T. Bates, *Pullman Porters and the Rise of Protest Politics in Black America, 1925–1945* (Chapel Hill: University of North Carolina Press, 2001).

17 Barnett to J. Carlisle McDonald, July 26, 1936; Barnett to W. Sykes, July 25, 1936; Barnett to John A. Stephens, August 1, 1936; memo for Mr. John A. Stephens, August 1, 1936; Barnett to McDonald, October 31, 1936, box 280, folder 1, Barnett Papers. Many similar letters are also in this file for the second half of 1936 and throughout 1937.

18 Barnett to Noel Sargent, secretary, National Association of Manufacturers, July 19, 1941; Sargent to Barnett, July 21, 1941; Barnett to Sargent, July 23, 1941; Barnett to Sargent, July 24, 1941; Sargent to Barnett. August 4, 1941. Barnett had made similar overtures to Sargent and the NAM during 1937 and 1940. See box 259, folder 1, Barnett Papers.

19 Barnett to Mr. Test, April 20, 1942; Barnett to Maj. Wm. Dorough, July 7, 1942; Barnett to Maj. Wm. Dorough, August 29, 1942, box 278, folder 5, Barnett Papers. For an example of these stories, see "Negroes Fill Vital Posts in Turning Out Wings for Army," Chicago Sun Times, October 1, 1942.

20 Barnett to J. Carlisle MacDonald, January 6, 1942; E. C. Logelin to Frank Marshall Davis, July 29, 1942, box 280, folder 1, Barnett Papers.

21 "Arms Program Fails to Benefit Negro Reliefers: They Make up 41% of CRA Rolls," clipping from the *Chicago Tribune,* May 18, 1941, box 282, folder 2, Barnett Papers.

22 "Some War Gains for Negro but Still Big Reservoir of Manpower is Not Used," clipping from St. Louis *Dispatch,* October 11, 1942, box 282, folder 4, Barnett Papers.

23 Frank Marshall Davis to Truman Gibson Jr., April 4, 1942, box 278, folder 5; "Negro Workers, Irked By Discrimination, Close Big War Plant," ANP release by Davis, July 12, 1943, box 280, folder 2, Barnett Papers.

24 Undated form letter from Frank Marshall Davis and undated reply from Barnett, box 342, folder 8, Barnett Papers.

25 Barnett to Paul Robeson, July 13, 1938; Barnett to Essie Robeson, March 15, 1942, Essie Robeson to Barnett, March 1942, box 294, folder 3, Barnett Papers. The precise nature of Buck's remarks, issued in China, is unclear and contradict the author's progressive reputation at the time. See Buck, *American Unity and Asia* (New York: John Day, 1942), as discussed in both John W. Dower, *War Without Mercy: Race and Power in the Pacific War* (New York: Pantheon Books, 1986), 5, 26; and Mary L. Dudziak, *Cold War, Civil Rights: Race and the Image of American Democracy* (Princeton: Princeton University Press, 2000), 8–9.

26 "6000 Jam Church, Crowd Street to Hear Robeson Speak, Sing in Chicago," ANP release, September 26, 1949, box 294, folder 4, Barnett Papers.

27 Thyra Edwards to Barnett, July 13, 1939, box 267, folder 5, Barnett Papers.

28 Luther Peck to Barnett, May 3, 1943; Barnett to Peck, May 7, 1943, box 346, folder 4, Barnett Papers.

29 Barnett to Albion Holsley, October 1, 1940, box 346, folder 4, Barnett Papers.

30 Wright to Barnett, February 5, 1941; Barnett to Wright, February 8, 1941; Wright to Barnett, February 10, 1941; Barnett to Wright, February 12, 1941, all in box 289, folder 26, Barnett Papers.

31 Hazel Rowley briefly outlines the State Department response to Wright's passport application in 1941. See Rowley, *Richard Wright: The Life and Times* (New York: Henry Holt, 2001), 251.

32 Wright to Barnett, February 5, 1941; Barnett to Wright, February 8, 1941; Wright to Barnett February 10, 1941; Barnett to Wright, February 12, 1941; Barnett to Cordell Hull, April 10, 1941; Wright to Barnett, May 19, 1941; Barnett to Wright, May 21, 1941; Barnett to Wright, October 5, 1948; Barnett to Wright, January 5, 1949, box 289, folder 26, Barnett Papers. On previous international reporting by black journalists, see Brenda Gayle Plummer, *Rising Wind: Black Americans and U.S. Foreign Affairs, 1935–1960* (Chapel Hill: University of North Carolina Press, 1996), 25–27, 52, 71. On Wright's pronounced interest in global politics as experienced in colonized and quasi-colonial locations, see Wright, *Black Power: A Record of Reactions in the Land of Pathos* (New York: Harper, 1954); *The Color Curtain: A Report on the Bandung Conference* (New York: World Publishing Company, 1956); and *White Man, Listen* (New York: Doubleday, 1957); see also Michel Fabre, *The Unfinished Quest of Richard Wright* (Urbana: University of Illinois Press, 1993): chapters 16, 17, and 19; and Hazel Rowley, *Richard Wright: The Life and Times* (New York: Henry Holt, 2001), 235–36; chapters 23–25.

33 Hurston to Barnett, February 1943; Hurston to Douglas Gilbert, February 4, 1943; "When Negro Succeeds, South Is Proud, Zora Hurston Says," *New York World-Telegram* clipping, February 1943; Barnett to Hurston, February 15,

1943, box 289, folder 4, Barnett Papers. For discussion of this episode within the biographical literature on Hurston, see Robert Hemenway, *Zora Neale Hurston: A Literary Biography* (Urbana: University of Illinois Press, 1980), 289; and Carla Kaplan, ed., *Zora Neale Hurston: A Life in Letters* (New York: Doubleday, 2002).

34 Barnett to Bill Robinson, June 29, 1939, Bill Robinson to Barnett, July 5, 1939, box 291, folder 3, Barnett Papers; "Declares 'Mammy' Type of Negro Mother Gave Us Sojourner Truth and Other Great Women," ANP release n.d., box 287, folder "Hattie McDaniel," Barnett Papers.

35 Bayard Rustin to Barnett, May 2, 1952, box 358, folder 3, Barnett Papers. Following his Africa trip, Rustin helped effect a shift in proposed emphasis among American pacifist groups toward alignment and cooperation with nonviolent anticolonialists in Ivory Coast, Nigeria, and elsewhere on the continent. What might have proven among the more novel transcontinental activist initiatives of the 1950s was essentially neutralized by Rustin's controversial arrest on sex charges in Pasadena in 1953. See John D'Emilio, *Lost Prophet: The Life and Times of Bayard Rustin* (New York: Free Press, 2003), 184–205.

36 Herbert Garfinkel, *When Negroes March: The March on Washington Movement and the Organizational Politics of the FEPC* (Glencoe, Ill: Free Press, 1959); Barbara Dianne Savage, *Broadcasting Freedom: Radio, War, and the Politics of Race* (Chapel Hill: University of North Carolina Press, 1999); Harvard Sitkoff, *A New Deal for Blacks: The Emergence of Civil Rights as a National Issue,* vol. 1, *The Depression Decade* (New York: Oxford University Press, 1978).

37 Desmond King, *Separate and Unequal: Black Americans and the U.S. Federal Government* (New York: Oxford University Press, 1995), esp. chapter 3.

38 King cites FEPC files from 1943 listing seventeen African-American professional-grade employees at the Commerce Department out of a black work force of 1,392, and a general work force of 11,218. Houchins's contacts are recorded in the member list of the Federal Council of Negro Affairs, available in the records of the ANP. See "Table and Summary of Employment of Negroes in Federal Government, December 1943," table 3, Office Files of Joy Davis, box 405, folder "Employment of Negroes in Federal Gov't"; President's FEPC, in King, *Separate and Unequal,* table A3.3, 230; "Members of the Federal Council on Negro Affairs and Other Negro Officials in Federal Government Agencies," box 281, folder 6, Barnett Papers.

39 "Racial Composition of the Population, for the United States, By States: 1940," series P-10, no. 1, February 2, 1942; "Urban Places With 2,500 Negro Inhabitants or More: 1940," series NP, no. 10, August 11, 1942; "Significant Facts Concerning the Negro Population," series P-1943, no. 4; all U.S. Department of Commerce, Bureau of the Census; box 283, folder 3, Barnett Papers. Also noteworthy is the presence of Philip M. Hauser as assistant director of the census during the early 1940s. Hauser would relocate to University of Chicago, and coedit the *Chicago Fact Book,* for 1950–70, a preeminent empirical sources for Chicago-related studies in years to come.

40 Joseph R. Houchins to Barnett, January 16, 1946, box 283, folder 1; Barnett to E. M. Glucksman, August 29, 1953, box 292, folder 4; Barnett to Sinclair Webb, January 16, 1954, box 283, folder 1, Barnett Papers.
41 Theodore Porter, *The Rise of Statistical Thinking, 1820–1900* (Princeton: Princeton University Press, 1986), 5–6, 17, 20.
42 Anderson, *Imagined Communities,* 165–66.
43 For an especially acute analysis of the census as an instrument of social control in this fashion, see Vincente Rafael, "White Love: Surveillance and Nationalist Resistance in the U.S. Colonization of the Phillippines," in *Cultures of U.S. Imperialism,* ed. Amy Kaplan and Donald Pease (Durham: Duke University Press, 1993), 185–218.

44 George Fredrickson *The Black Image in the White Mind: The Debate on Afro-American Character and Destiny, 1817–1914* (Middletown, CT: Wesleyan University Press, 1972), esp. chapter 8; Eugene Genovese, *Roll, Jordan Roll: The World the Slaves Made* (New York: Vintage Books, 1974); Walter Johnson, *Soul by Soul: Life Inside the Antebellum Slave Market* (Cambridge, MA: Harvard University Press, 1999); Mark M. Smith, *Mastered by the Clock: Time, Slavery and Freedom in the American South* (Chapel Hill: University of North Carolina Press, 1997).
45 Michel Foucault, "Governmentality," in *Essential Works of Foucault, 1954–1984.*—vol. 3, *Power,* ed. James D. Faubion (New York: New Press, 1994), 201–22.
46 Thomas Cripps, *Slow Fade to Black,* chapter 11.
47 Cripps, *Slow Fade to Black,* 269.
48 Denning, *The Cultural Front,* 35
49 Cripps, *Slow Fade to Black,* 179–80, 340–41.
50 Ibid., 6.
51 Fredi Washington to Barnett, September 21, 1946; Washington to Barnett, October 6, 1946, both in box 285, folder 6; Barnett to Washington, October 12, 1946, box 288, folder 2, Barnett Papers.
52 Hattie McDaniel to Barnett, November 22, 1950, Barnett to Hattie McDaniel, November 29, 1950, box 286, folder 1, Barnett Papers.
53 "I Knew Hattie McDaniel," ANP feature release by Harry Levette, November 5, 1952, box 287, Hattie McDaniel Folder; Levette to Barnett, August 2, 1953, box 288, folder 2, Barnett Papers.
54 Robert Ellis to Barnett, February 30 [*sic*], 1949, box 287, folder 9, Barnett Papers.
55 Robert Ellis to Barnett, February 30 [*sic*], 1949; Barnett to Ellis, March 9, 1949; Ellis to Barnett, April 23, 1949, all box 287, folder 19, Barnett Papers; Barnett to Levette, March 8, 1949, box 288, folder 2, Barnett Papers. Negotiations with Ellis, which progressed to a test run of three columns running intermittently among member papers, and both Barnett and Levette's response to them, are vividly evocative of the dynamics of entertainment coverage within the black press at this time. An extensive run of letter among the three men can be found in box 287, folder 19 and box 288, folder 2 of the Barnett Papers.

56 A. S. "Doc" Young to Barnett, December 24, 1948 and March 7, 1949; Barnett to Young, January 18, 1949, Levette to Barnett, March 14, 1949, box 288, folder 2, Barnett Papers.

57 The concept of "structures of feeling" originates of course with Raymond Williams. His intention to close the separation in Marxist theory of social from personal might be seen here as approaching the problem of reflexive black political agency, introduced under the preceding heading in this chapter, from the other side as it were. Just as depersonalized character of the modern state power ought to be appreciated with similarly complex ideas of social agency, so too should structural change, in this case within the culture and industry of postwar American film, be articulated through grammars of feeling as well as more the concrete terms of materialism. See Raymond Williams, *Marxism and Literature* (Oxford: Oxford University Press, 1977), 128–36.

58 Cripps, *Slow Fade to Black*, 6, 375–76.

59 Ellis, "Hollywood at Dawn," undated and unpublished column, box 287, folder 19, Barnett Papers. For accounts of the deep structural changes in the film industry in the late 1940s, see Tino Balio, ed., *The American Film Industry* (Madison: University of Wisconsin Press, 1976), esp. part 4; and Thomas Schatz, *Boom and Bust: American Cinema in the 1940s* (Berkeley: University of California Press, 1997), part 3.

60 Levette to Barnett, May 15, 1949, box 288, folder 2, Barnett Papers. For background on Fox's *Pinky*, see Schatz, *Boom and Bust*, 384, 385–86.

61 Levette to ANP office, April 9, 1950, box 288, folder 2, Barnett Papers.

62 Levette to Barnett, October 20, 1954, box 288, folder 2, Barnett Papers.

63 Levette to Barnett, November 14, 1948, box 288, folder 2, Barnett Papers.

64 Telegram from Levette to Barnett, July 15, 1949; Barnett to Levette, July 18, 1949, box 288, folder 2, Barnett Papers. Levette had made an emergency request for $8.00 previously in 1949, to attend the Academy Awards. Barnett fulfilled the request—without comment. See telegram from Levette to Barnett, March 23, 1949, box 288, folder 2, Barnett Papers.

65 Levette to Barnett, May 26, 1951, box 288, folder 2, Barnett Papers. Levette would write Irene Rowland, the office manager of the main ANP office in Chicago, eighteen separate times between 1949 and 1956, asking that space rate payments be hastened to him. See various letters from Levette to Irene Rowland, box 288, folder 2, Barnett Papers.

66 Levette to Barnett, March 14, 1949; Levette to Barnett, May 26, 1950, box 288, folder 2, Barnett Papers.

67 Edward Carter Maddox to Barnett, September 14, 1950; Levette to Barnett, September 18, 1950; Barnett to Levette September 21, 1950; Levette to Barnett September 23, 1950, all in box 288, folder 2, Barnett Papers.

68 Levette to Barnett, September 23, 1950, box 288, folder 2, Barnett Papers.

69 Levette to Barnett, May 26, 1950, box 288, folder 2, Barnett Papers. This allegation is less surprising for its content and more for its source—according to Levette, the characterization of a black left *coup* at the Eagle came from its publisher, Charlotta Bass. Bass, who has been described as a crucial black pro-

gressive leader in postwar Los Angeles and ran as the Progressive Party vice presidential nominee in 1952—the first black women to run for national office—comes across here and elsewhere in the Barnett Papers as less radical than generally presumed. At least, such accounts indicate the fineness of distinction made among Africans Americans on the left—if less so on the right—regarding ideology and solidarity during heated years of the early cold war. For more on Bass, see Gerald Horne, *Fire This Time: The Watts Uprising and the 1960s* (Charlottesville: University of Virginia Press, 1990).

70 Josephine Baker to Barnett, July 9, 1955; Barnett to Levette, July 13, 1955; Levette to Barnett, July 22, 1955; Barnett to Levette, July 23, 1955, box 288, folder 2, Barnett Papers. The Baker controversy, like the similar incident surrounding remarks made by Paul Robeson at the Paris Peace Conference in 1949, proved a landmark event in the policing of African Americans' discussion of the United States overseas. Mary L. Dudziak, "Josephine Baker, Racial Protest, and the Cold War," *Journal of American History* 81, no. 2 (September 1994): 543–70.

71 Levette to Barnett, April 8, 1955. The two reporters seeking ANP credentials to cover Bandung were James Jones and M. Goodlett.

72 Barnett to Fred D. Patterson, July 8, 1941, box 267, folder 4; Barnett to Roosevelt, July 7, 1941, Patterson to Roosevelt, July 11, 1941, box 346, folder 4, Barnett Papers.

73 Memo from Barnett to Earl Dickerson, December 23, 1954; memo from Barnett to Dickerson, October 15, 1955; box 266, folder 6, Barnett Papers. Barnett also played an important role in 1952 efforts to maintain Dickerson's slot on the NAACP Board of Directors, at a time when the association was clearly trying to move well to the right of Dickerson concerning political orientation. Joining Barnett in this effort was a complex cross section of national black leadership, including Hubert Delany, Ralph Bunche, Channing Tobias, and Ella Baker. See Circular Letter from Committee for the Reelection of Earl B. Dickerson to the National Board of the NAACP, November 24, 1952; and Dickerson to Barnett, December 18, 1952, box 267, folder 5, Barnett Papers.

74 Barnett to Kenneth Pangburn, March 16, 1942, box 358, folder 1, Barnett Papers.

75 Barnett to Edward Strong, December 5, 1941, box 358, folder 1; "Angelo Herndon Ousted by Reds," undated ANP release, box 343, folder 2, Barnett Papers.

76 Barnett to Wallace, June 20, 1941, box 279, folder 5, Barnett Papers.

77 This remains a vexed topic in the social and political history of the United States over the past half-century or so. Scott Sandage's instructive analysis, which is focused on the Lincoln Memorial as a racialized memory site, emphasizes how official representations of emancipation defined it as a gift from beneficent whites to blacks, as opposed to the historical outcome of social struggle. This approach to a specific episode of the recent past helps isolate the present tendency to consider civil rights change as the product of an enlightened national political establishment, rather than itself the product of struggle, opposition, and even threat. Such questions are central to the period

of 1940s generally, a period whose racial liberal icons—from Roosevelt's executive order to Truman's own order desegregating the military to Gunnar Myrdal's publication of *An American Dilemma* to Wallace's own quixotically heroic 1948 campaign—have led some observers to implicitly argue for emancipator effect in considering the lead-up years to the civil rights movement beginning in the mid-1950s. For a deeply significant alternative approach, one that offers a most convincing genealogy of national racial liberalism's roots in 1940s black protest, see Martha Biondi, *To Stand and Fight: The Struggle For Civil Rights in Postwar New York City* (Cambridge, MA: Harvard University Press, 2003)

78 Barnett to Turner Catledge, May 22, 1945; Catledge to Barnett, July 10, 1945; Catledge to Barnett, November 23, 1945; all box 358, folder 4, Barnett Papers.

79 Barnett to William Dawson, November 10, 1951, box 346, folder 6, Barnett Papers.

80 Patrick S. Washburn, *A Question of Sedition: The Federal Government's Investigation into the Black Press during World War II* (New York: Oxford University Press, 1986); Robert Hill, ed. *The FBI's RACON: Racial Conditions in the United States during World War II* (Boston: Northeastern University Press, 1995); Barnett to J. Edgar Hoover, May 22, 1943; Hoover to Barnett, June 3, 1943; box 281 folder 6, Barnett Papers.

81 Edith Sampson to Howland Sargent, July 24, 1952, box 286, folder 1, Barnett Papers.

82 Barnett to Ken Blewett, June 9, 1948, box 291, folder 7, Barnett Papers.

83 For letters to managers of the other thirteen theater managers, see box 291, folder 7, Barnett Papers.

84 Press release for North American Television Productions, Inc., April 19, 1955, box 292, folder 6, Barnett Papers.

85 Truman Gibson Jr. to Barnett, December 14, 1942, box 291, folder 7, Barnett Papers. For a more positive early notice, see "Negro Newsreel Makes Its Debut," clipping from the Buffalo *Star,* box 291, folder 7, Barnett Papers.

86 E. M. Glucksman to Barnett, June 10, 1948; Barnett to British Overseas Airway Corporation, July 10, 1948; Barnett to Glucksman, July 14, 1948; box 291, folder 7, Barnett Papers. Barnett's own contacts included Gabriel Dennis, the secretary of state in Liberia, and a Captain J. Stocker of the Nigerian Public Relations Department. No further record exists as to whether the films were received in any of the African countries, and what use might have been made of them.

87 Barnett to Glucksman, December 4, 1948; Barnett to Glucksman, June 9, 1949, box 291, folder 7, Barnett Papers.

88 Glucksman to Barnett, April 5, 1949, box 291, folder 7, Barnett Papers.

89 Barnett to Fred Patterson, August 4, 1951; Barnett to Glucksman, August 9, 1951; Glucksman to Barnett, August 21, 1951; Barnett to Louis Wright, October 24, 1951; invoice from Barnett to American Newsreel Corp., Inc., December 22, 1951; all in box 291, folder 7, Barnett Papers.

90 Barnett to Wright, October 24, 1951; telegram from Glucksman to Barnett No-

vember 2, 1951; box 291, folder 7, Barnett Papers; Victor Roudin to Barnett, January 7, 1952, box 292, folder 1, Barnett Papers.

91 C. C. Spaulding to Glucksman, January 8, 1952, box 292, folder 1, Barnett Papers.

92 Glucksman to Barnett, May 2, 1952, box 292, folder 1, Barnett Papers.

93 Barnett to Glucksman, October 7, 1952; Glucksman to Barnett, December 2, 1952; Barnett to Glucksman, December 31, 1952, box 292, folder 2, Barnett Papers.

94 Barnett to Glucksman, March 24, 1952, box 292, folder 1, Barnett Papers.

95 Barnett to Glucksman, March 15, 1952; Barnett to Roudin, March 19, 1952, box 292, folder 1, Barnett Papers.

96 Barnett to Roudin and Glucksman, February 9, 1952, box 292, folder 1, Barnett Papers.

97 "Pearl Primus Surrenders Passport to State Department," ANP release, May 26, 1952, box 391, folder 1, Barnett Papers. For accounts of the Stock Club controversy, see Biondi, *To Stand and Fight,* 186–90.

98 Barnett made this statement in a year-end grant application to the Ford Foundation from the American Committee for Films on Minorities: "A Project to Implement Current Efforts of the United States Government to Defeat Soviet Propaganda About American Minorities" (undated and unsigned), box 292, folder 2, Barnett Papers.

99 Barnett to Glucksman, March 15, 1952; Barnett to Glucksman, March 16, 1952; Barnett to Roudin, April 25, 1952, box 292, folder 1, Barnett Papers.

100 Roudin to Barnett, March 24, 1952, box 292, folder 1, Barnett Papers.

101 Porter McKeever to Barnett, March 5, 1952; McKeever to Barnett, April 4, 1952; Wilson Compton to Barnett, April 7, 1952; Barnett to Edwin Arnold, April 28, 1952; box 292, folder 1, Barnett Papers.

102 On State Department Goodwill tours of black artists and entertainers between 1951 and 1956, see Von Eschen, *Race Against Empire: Black Americans and Anti-Colonialism, 1937–1957* (Ithaca: Cornell University Press, 1997): 167, 177, and Mary L. Dudziak, *Cold War, Civil Rights: Race and the Image of American Democracy* (Princeton: Princeton University Press, 2000): chapter 2, On Barnett's "enlistment" in the cold war during the late 1940s, and the larger impossibility of establishing beyond question African American loyalty during the cold war, see Von Eschen, 159, 163–64, and Biondi, esp. 181–86.

103 Barnett to Glucksman, August 30, 1952; Glucksman to Dr. Obiesia Macjajah, September 2, 1952; Barnett to B. F. Few, October 1, 1952; Barnett to Glucksman, October 7, 1952; Memo from Barnett to Glucksman, undated; Glucksman to Barnett, December 12, 1952; Barnett to Glucksman, December 31, 1952; box 292, folder 2, Barnett Papers. Barnett to Robert Gillham, June 12, 1953; Barnett to E. H. Ellis, May 13, 1953; Ellis to Barnett, June 15, 1953, box 292, folder 3, Barnett Papers. Memo from Glucksman to Barnett, September 5, 1953; Barnett to Hon. Richard S. Bright, November 11, 1953, box 292, folder 4, Barnett Papers.

104 Glucksman to Barnett, June 9, 1952, box 292, folder 1, Barnett Papers. Beatty

Brady to Barnett, October 10, 1952; Glucksman to Barnett, October 17, 1952; box 292, folder 2, Barnett Paper. Glucksman to Barnett, February 16, 1953, box 292, folder 3, Barnett Papers. Barnett to Glucksman, July 30, 1954, box 292, folder 5, Barnett Papers.

105 Glucksman to Barnett, July 5, 1952, box 292, folder 1, Barnett Papers. Offering Circular, North American Television Productions, Inc., n.d.; Glucksman to Barnett May 13, 1955; Glucksman to Barnett, July 7, 1955; box 292, folder 6, Barnett Papers. On the decreasing recourse to short films and newsreels in theaters by the early 1950s, see Tino Balio, ed., *The American Film Industry* (Madison: University of Wisconsin Press, 1985), 400–47.

106 Barnett to Jacob Reddix, October 12, 1949, box 342, folder 8, Barnett Papers; Jacob Reddix to Barnett, October 21, 1949, box 358, folder 2, Barnett Papers; Barnett to Dr. A. H. McCoy, May 25, 1955, box 358, folder 3, Barnett Papers.

107 T. R. M. Howard to Barnett, November 10, 1945, box 346, folder 4, Barnett Papers. For discussion of Isaiah Montgomery's fidelity to racial clientage, see Neil McMillen, *Dark Journey: Black Mississippians in the Age of Jim Crow* (Urbana: University of Illinois Press, 1989), 50, 51, 116, 186; and Reed, *Stirrings in the Jug*, 21–24.

CHAPTER 4: SELLING THE RACE

1 "Backstage," *Ebony* (November 1945): 2.

2 Gunnar Myrdal, *An American Dilemma: The Negro Problem and Modern Democracy*, 908. For account of the black press in wartime, see Drake and Cayton, *Black Metropolis*, chapter 15; Bill Mullen, *Popular Fronts*, chapter 2; Robert Hill, ed., introduction to *The FBI's RACON: Racial Conditions in the United States During World War II* (Boston: Northeastern University Press, 1995); Percival L. Prattis, "The Role of the Negro Press in Race Relations," *Phylon* 7, no. 3 (1946); Penny Von Eschen, *Race Against Empire*, chapter 2; and Patrick Washburn, *A Question of Sedition: The Federal Government's Investigation of the Black Press During World War II* (New York: Oxford University Press, 1986).

3 Washburn, *A Question of Sedition*.

4 John Johnson with Lerone Bennett Jr., *Succeeding Against the Odds* (New York: Warner Books, 1989), 157; Ben Burns, *Nitty Gritty: A White Editor in Black Journalism* (Jackson: University of Mississippi Press, 1996), 88.

5 The phrase "exaggerated Americans," was first applied to African Americans by Gunnar Myrdal; albeit with less pejorative intent than in Frazier's case. See Gunnar Myrdal, *An American Dilemma*, 952. E. Franklin Frazier, *Black Bourgeoisie: The Rise of a New Middle Class* (New York: Free Press, 1957; reprint, New York: Collier Books, 1962), chapter 8.

6 Jones, *Blues People*, chapter 9; Cruse, *The Crisis of the Negro Intellectual* (New York: Morrow, 1967), 83–85; Elijah Muhammad, *Message to the Blackman in America* (Chicago: United Brothers and Sisters, 1965), 129–31; Mal-

colm X, "Message to the Grass Roots," in Breitman, ed., *Malcolm X Speaks: Selected Speeches and Statements* (New York: Grove Weidenfeld, 1990).

7 William Julius Wilson, *The Declining Significance of Race: Blacks and Changing American Institutions* (Chicago: University of Chicago Press, 1978). See also Alphonso Pinkney, *The Myth of Black Progress* (Cambridge: Cambridge University Press, 1984), and Kevin Gaines, *Uplifiting the Race: Black Leadership: Politics and Culture in the Twentieth Century* (Chapel Hill: University of North Carolina Press, 1996). For other work meant to reorient discussions of the black middle class, see Michael Dawson, *Behind the Mule: Race and Class in African-American Politics* (Princeton, NJ: Princeton University Press, 1994); Jennifer Hochschild, *Facing Up to the American Dream: Race, Class and the Soul of the Nation* (Princeton, NJ: Princeton University Press, 1995); and Mary Patillo McCoy, *Black Picket Fences: Privilege and Peril Among the Black Middle Class* (Chicago: University of Chicago Press, 1999).

8 The term paraphrases Cox's elaborate thinking on how capital operated through social and structural effects to "proletarianize a whole people." See Cox, *Caste, Class, and Race: A Study in Social Dynamics* (New York: Doubleday and Co., 1948; reprint, New York: Monthly Review Press, 1970), 344.

9 Grossman, *Land of Hope,* chapter 9; Johnson with Bennett, *Succeeding Against the Odds,* chapters 6 and 10. For parallel recollections of Phillips at the time, see Dempsey Travis, *An Autobiography of Black Jazz.*

10 Johnson with Bennett, *Succeeding Against the Odds,* 85, 88. Cayton and Drake, *Black Metropolis* 462–64. The only extensive study of Supreme remains Robert Puth, "Supreme Life: The History of a Negro Insurance Company," Ph.D. diss. (Northwestern University, 1967).

11 Drake and Cayton, 182–90, 465–66; Johnson with Bennett, *Succeeding Against the Odds,* 97–103; Plummer, *Rising Wind,* 33; Puth, 50, 116, 134; Robert E. Weems Jr., *Desegregating the Dollar: African American Consumerism in the Twentieth Century* (New York: NYU Press, 1998), 23–24, 72 and chapter 4. Restrictive covenants were contractual agreements, legal and binding up to the 1940 ruling, that white home owners could not rent or sell to blacks within a designated area. Widespread by the mid 1920s, it was estimated that three-fourths of all Chicago residential property was subject to such restrictions by 1930. Prior to the *Hansberry* case, no effective challenge had been mounted against the practice, which had implicit support of municipal authorities up to the mayor.

12 Abram Harris, introduction to *The Negro as Capitalist: A Study in Banking and Business among American Negroes* (Philadelphia: American Academy of Political and Social Science, 1936; reprint, Chicago: Urban Research Press Institute, 1992), 66, 211; Cruse, *The Crisis of the Negro Intellectual,* 70, 80, 329.

13 Clarence Taylor, *The Black Churches of Brooklyn* (New York: Columbia University Press, 1994) chapter 3; St. Clair Drake, "Churches and Voluntary Associations among the Negroes of Chicago" (Chicago, 1940); Drake and Cayton, *Black Metropolis,* 688–710. Figures on homeownership in seven black Chicago neighborhoods—Near West Side, Douglas, Oakwood, Kenwood,

Grand Boulevard, Washington Park, and Woodlawn—increased almost 240 percent from 1940 to 1950, while populations there grew by only 50 percent. Wage increases and occupational mobility explain some but not all of this increase, evident in other urban areas at this time. Hauser and Kitagawa, eds., *Local Community Fact Book of Chicago: 1950*, 119, 147, 151, 159, 163, 167, 175.

14 The African American insurance industry carried a total of $235 million in policies in 1978 ($86 million in ordinary insurance and $149 million in industrial) to $177 million in 1935 ($39 million ordinary and $136 million industrial). Between 1928 and 1938, the number of black insurance companies nationwide actually *expanded* from fifteen to twenty-nine. By 1940, the figure for the industry was $294 million. Robert Weems suggests that some firms, like Metropolitan Funeral Systems Association, specialized in serving a black working class market, while others like Supreme, catered to middle-class blacks. However, industrial insurance totals indicate all companies moving toward a black worker customer base at this time. Supreme itself had over 80 percent of its business—some $47 million dollars worth of policies—devoted to industrial insurance by 1940. Weems, *Desegregating the Dollar,* xiii, chapters 1 and 2; Puth, appendix C.

15 On black working class formation, see Ira Katznelson, *Black Men, White Cities: Race Politics and Migration in the United States, 1900–1930, and Britain, 1948–1968* (London: Oxford University Press, 1973); Carole Marks, *Farewell, We're Good and Gone: The Great Migration* (Bloomington: Indiana University Press, 1989); and Joe William Trotter, *Black Milwaukee: The Making of an Industrial Proletariat* (Urbana: University of Illinois Press, 1984). On consolidation of the black middle class, see Wilson, *The Declining Significance of Race;* Bart Landry, *The New Black Middle Class* (Berkeley: University of California Press, 1987); and Charles T. Banner-Haley, *The Fruits of Integration: Black Middle Class Ideology and Culture, 1960–1990* (Jackson: University Press of Mississippi, 1994). Significantly, literature on race and class in the nineteenth century approach them, by contrast, as social rather than structural processes, thereby assigning more agency to African Americans themselves. See Rawick, *From Sundown to Sunup;* Levine, *Black Culture and Black Consciousness;* and Willard Gatewood, *Aristocrats of Color: The Black Elite, 1880–1920* (Bloomington: Indiana University Press, 1990).

16 E. P. Thompson, *The Making of the English Working Class* (New York: Vintage, 1963), 9. See also Gareth Stedman Jones, *Languages of Class: Studies in English Working Class History, 1832–1982* (Cambridge: Cambridge University Press, 1983); and Herbert Gutman, *Work, Culture, and Society in Industrializing America: Essays in American Working-Class and Social History* (New York: Alfred A. Knopf, 1976).

17 Ben Burns, *Nitty Gritty,* 27; Davis, *Living the Blues,* 274–75; Johnson with Bennett, *Succeeding Against the Odds,* 93, 97–101; "Secret of Pace's Death a Mystery," *New York Age* (July 31, 1943).

18 Johnson with Bennett, *Succeeding Against the Odds,* 114–17, 124–26; Davis with Tidwell, *Livin' the Blues,* 274–75; Burns, *Nitty Gritty,* 27–32.

19 Walter White, "This Is the Army—As Negroes See It"; Horace Mann Bond, "Should Negroes Care Who Wins The War?" and "Round Table: Should Negroes Demand Equality Now?" *Negro Digest* (November 1942): 3–4, 21–23, 47–53, respectively. "Round Table: Is the Negro Demand for Full Equality Sabotaging the Nation's War Effort," *Negro Digest* (November 1942): 47–48; and Burns, *Nitty Gritty,* 32–33; *Time,* "She Made Jive Respectable"; Roi Ottley, "Black Jews of Harlem": all in *Negro Digest* (November 1942): 7–8, 25–27; Krishnalai Shridharani, "Nehru of India: A Man To Watch," *Negro Digest* (November 1942): 35–36; Julian Lewis, "Biology of the Negro," *Negro Digest* (November 1942): 45. Roi Ottley's piece later found its way into his definitive collection of essays on wartime Harlem, *'New World A-Coming': Inside Black America* (Cambridge, MA: Riverside Press, 1943), one of many occasions when *Negro Digest* serialized landmark works of race literature or analysis. Among the later authors who presented work in the magazine in this fashion were Richard Wright, Gunnar Myrdal, Zora Neale Hurston, Paul Robeson, and Lillian Smith.

20 Burns, *Nitty Gritty,* 26–28, 30–38.

21 Johnson with Bennett, *Succeeding Against the Odds,* 126–28; Burns, *Nitty Gritty,* 34–35; *Negro Digest,* October 1943: back cover; Dorothy Thompson, "Blood Does Not Tell," *Negro Digest* (January 1944): 31–33; Horace Cayton, "What Strategy for the Negro: Patience or Pressure?" *Negro Digest* (August 1943): 49–52; "Round Table: Have the Communists Stopped Fighting for Negro Rights?" *Negro Digest* (December 1944): 57–70. For more information on the wartime and postwar black Left, see Biondi, *To Stand and Fight;* and Gerald Horne, *Black and Red: W. E. B. Du Bois and the Afro-American Response to the Cold War, 1944–1963* (Albany, NY: State University of New York Press, 1986); *Communist Front? The Civil Rights Congress, 1946–1956* (East Rutherford, NJ: Associated Universities Press, 1988).

22 "Maker of the Blues," *Negro Digest,* January 1943: 37–38; "Photo by Parks," *Negro Digest* (January 1944): 41–2; "The Voice with A Smile," *Negro Digest* (February 1945): 11–12; "Mellow Like a Cello," *Negro Digest* (August 1943): 7–9; "The Jive Is On!" *Negro Digest* (July 1944): 11–15; "Origins of the Zoot Suit," *New York Times,* reprinted in *Negro Digest* (August 1943): 69–70; S. I. Hayakawa, "Happy Birthday," *Negro Digest* (November 1943); "He Ballyhooed a Race," *Negro Digest* (December 1942): 45–47. According to the *Times* piece, a black busboy in Gainesville, Georgia, Clyde Duncan, ordered a suit made to written specifications at a local clothier, Frierson-McEver, in 1940. The tailor, puzzled by the measurements (thirty-seven-inch coat length, twenty-six-inch knees, fourteen-inch pants bottoms), sent the design to Globe Tailoring Company in Chicago and "washed his hands" of the matter. The suit, known first as the "Killer Diller," was connected to an even more interesting inspiration within the article. Apparently "Gone with the Wind" had opened in Gainesville months before Duncan presented his request: several of the ensembles worn by Clark Gable in the film suggested the later zoot suit style. The ironies of this provisional genealogy—from apology for the planta-

tion myth and Confederacy to signifier of racial alterity and oppositional style—are striking, to say the least, and highlight *Digest*'s role of suggesting to its audience the complexities of racial identity.

23 Johnson with Bennett, *Succeeding Against the Odds,* 130–32; Eleanor Roosevelt, "If I Were a Negro," *Negro Digest* (October 1943): 8–9; Otto Kleinberg, "Passing: A National Hoax," *Negro Digest* (May 1944): 94–98.

24 David J. Sullivan, "The Negro Market," *Negro Digest* (February 1943): 60–62; Sullivan, "A Catalogue of Don'ts," *Negro Digest* (June 1943): 49–51; Sullivan, "'Export' Market at Home," *Negro Digest* (September 1944): 45–48; Archibald Rutledge, "'Double C' Insurance," *Negro Digest* (May 1943): 47–51; A. T. Spaulding, "Half a Billion in Insurance," *Negro Digest* (March 1944): 79–82. For more information on Sullivan and other African American marketing pioneers, see Weems, *Desegregating the Dollar,* esp. chapter 2.

25 "Backstage," *Ebony* (November 1945): 2; "Backstage," *Ebony* (February 1946): 2.

26 Johnson with Bennett, *Succeeding Against the Odds,* chapter 20; Burns, *Nitty Gritty,* 85–86. This was not the first time Johnson Publishing locked horns with the War Production Board. In April 1945, the company was cited by the Board for violating paper ration limits in printing *Digest*. Only an elaborate appeal by Johnson in front of the board's Appeals Department averted the potential demise of the company. See Johnson with Bennett, *Succeeding Against the Odds,* chapter 19.

27 William Stott, *Documentary Expression and Thirties America* (Chicago: University of Chicago Press, 1973, 1986): 129–30. Donnelley's printing techniques, Stott argues, were as critical to sustaining *Life*'s claims to have revolutionized photojournalism and magazine publishing generally, as were its unprecedented photographic or editorial scope.

28 Burns, *Nitty Gritty,* 86; *Ebony* (December 1945): 51.

29 Johnson with Bennett, *Succeeding Against the Odds,* 162; "Backstage," *Ebony* (December 1945): 2.

30 "Rochester," *Ebony* (November 1945): 13–18, "Black Boy in Brooklyn," *Ebony* (November 1945): 26–27; "Bye-Bye to Boogie," *Ebony* (November 1945): 31–35; and "Slave to Banker," *Ebony* (November 1945): 43–47.

31 Clarence E. Walker, *Deromanticizing Black History: Critical Essays and Reappraisals* (Knoxville: University of Tennessee Press, 1991).

32 "Backstage," *Ebony* (February 1946): 2.

33 Johnson with Bennett, *Succeeding Against the Odds,* 183–84; "Backstage," *Ebony* (December 1946): 4. The campaign consisted of purchasing space in Sunday editions of the *New York Times* and *Chicago Tribune,* as well as in *Newsweek* during that month. While no definitive figures are available, Johnson pronounced the campaign "a mistake": and the subscription base for the magazine would remain close to entirely African American. No further efforts were made thereafter to directly appeal to white subscribers.

34 Locke, ed., *The New Negro,* 7.

35 Mae M. Ngai, *Impossible Subjects: Illegal Aliens and the Making of Modern America* (Princeton: Princeton University Press, 2004); Michael Omi and Howard Winant, *Racial Formation in the United States: From the 1960s to the 1980s* (New York: Routledge, 1986); David Roediger, *The Wages of Whiteness: Race and the Making of the American Working Class* (London: Verso, 1991); Eric Lott, *Love and Theft: Blackface Minstrelsy and the American Working Class* (New York: Oxford University Press, 1994). It is important here to distinguish between how such accounts take blacks seriously as helping effect the racialization of key social sites (the state, the working class, mass vernacular cultural) and yet fail see blacks themselves as racially formed, thus making their collective experience—and political and cultural profile—historically contingent. This persistent lacuna constitutes a special obstacle to Paul Gilroy's recommendation of a "reintroduction of history" to the study of black people. For how is such revision possible without acknowledging the unpredictability of black existence as its most salient and resonant point: that of collective identity? Gilroy, *The Black Atlantic,* 26–27; see also Stuart Hall, "Gramsci's Relevance for the Study of Race and Ethnicity," *Journal of Communications Inquiry,* 10, no. 2 (Spring 1990): 5–27.

36 Adequate summary of this idea's impact on scholarship is impossible: in essence it structures most if not all of the field. A selection of classic works cited so far—Levine's *Black Culture, Black Consciousness,* Stuckey's *Slave Culture,* Jones's *Blues People*—illustrate the breadth of commitment to this approach in the study of African-American history. One genealogy of its inception might begin with the 1940 statement by W. E. B. Du Bois locating the unity of African diasporic interest and sensibility around neither ties of blood nor ancestral culture, but instead "the social heritage of slavery, the discrimination and the insult." W. E. B. Du Bois, *Dusk of Dawn: An Essay Toward an Autobiography of a Race Concept* (New York: Harcourt, Brace, and World, 1940; reprint: New Brunswick, N.J.: Transaction Publishers, 1984), 117. Lest readers take him solely as witness to structured black identity, though, Du Bois offered the subtitle for this work, as reminder that collective racial experience was unpredictable, "open" narrative, as well as ledger of social injury.

37 Zora Neale Hurston, "Characteristics of Negro Expression," in *Negroes: An Anthology,* ed. Nancy Cunard (New York: 1934); "House of Beauty," *Ebony* (May 1946): 25–27.

38 "African Influences on Fashion," *Ebony* (June 1948): 48–52.

39 "Brown Town," *Ebony* (February 1946): 37–43; "Mound Bayou," *Ebony* (September 1946): 19–24; "The Bard at Karamu," *Ebony* (October 1948): 36–40.

40 "Juneteenth," *Ebony* (June 1951): 27–31; "Dred Scott's Children," *Ebony* (April 1954): 83–86.

41 "Jive Papa," *Ebony* (August 1946): 19–24. By the 1950s, Burley was the magazine's most prolific freelance writer, contributing frequently with stories ranging in topic from true crime to profiles of prominent entertainers.

42 "The Schoolmarm Who Glorified Leg Art," *Ebony* (January 1947): 14–18;

"The Rumba," *Ebony* (April 1947): 23–27; "How the Beguine Began," *Ebony* (May 1948): 62–65; "African Jiu-Jitsu," *Ebony* (January 1948): 37–39; "New Home for Happy Feet," *Ebony* (June 1956): 88–90; cites for lindy hop. The feature on *capoeira* focused on Salvadoran-based teacher Manoel dos Reis Machado, better know as Mestre Bimba, founder of the first school of *capoeira* instruction. For more on Bimba and *capoeira,* see J. Lowell Lewis, *Ring of Liberation: Deceptive Discourse in Brazilian Capoeira* (Chicago: University of Chicago Press, 1992). Both the *rumba* and *capoeira* pieces featured images from photographer Earl Leaf Guillumette who, judging from *Ebony* bylines, was among the more prolific sources of images on New World motion art in the 1940s. Further information on Guillumette is unavailable as I write this chapter.

43 "Female Impersonators," *Ebony* (March 1948): 61–65. For historical context of transsexual performance at this time, see Joanne Meyerowitz, *When Sex Changed: A History of Transsexuality in the United States* (Cambridge, MA: Harvard University Press, 2002); for specific account of black transsexual performance in Harlem, see Eric Garber, "A Spectacle of Color: The Lesbian and Gay Subculture of Jazz Age Harlem," in *Hidden From History: Reclaiming the Gay and Lesbian Past,* ed. Duberman, Vincus, and Chauncey (New York: New American Library, 1989), 318–33. *Ebony* and Johnson Publishing were, at best, marginally tolerant environments. Burns recalls Johnson holding to a strict "don't ask, don't tell" policy regarding employment of gay staff, and clearly the magazine did not significantly disrupt normative media valorization of straight relationships and desire. Yet articles on the Joe's DeLuxe revue were not the only instances where sex norms were complicated in the magazine. An article recounting the contributions of a black female informant to the Kinsey survey recounted lesbian sexual encounters without opinion, while a 1952 story detailed with appreciable sensitivity impending sex-change surgery for a year-old hermaphrodite in St. Louis. Clearly, though, editorial preference tilted discernibly toward transparency rather than ambiguity in matters of sexual identity. In an August 1952 article "I am a Woman Again" the magazine lauded legendary transvestite performer Gladys Bentley for having "found happiness in love after medical treatment to correct her strange affliction (93–98). See "What I Told Kinsey about My Sex Life," *Ebony* (December 1948): 45–50; "Half-Boy, Half-Girl" *Ebony* (February 1952): 83–84.

44 "Negroes Taught Me to Sing," *Ebony* (March 1953): 48–58; "This Time It's Love," *Ebony* (May 1953): 123–29. For similar white testimonials to black influence, see "Whites Who Sing Like Negroes," *Ebony* (February 1951): 49–55; "The World's Greatest Musician," by Tallulah Bankhead, *Ebony* (December 1952): 102–13; "How Negroes Influenced My Career," by Sophie Tucker, *Ebony* (December 1953): 80–92; and "Harlem Taught Me To Sing," by Martha Raye, *Ebony* (November 1954): 50–58.

45 "The Race War That Flopped," *Ebony* (July 1946): 3–9; "The Truth about

Japanese War Brides," *Ebony* (March 1952): 17–25; "The Loneliest Brides in America," *Ebony* (January 1953): 17–25; "Every GI a King in Japan," *Ebony* (April 1953): 36–42. Though concerned with Korean rather than Japanese war brides, Ji-Yeon Yuh's recent book is an important model for analysis of the articles listed here that deal with military marriages. See Yuh, *Beyond the Shadow of Camptown: Korean Military Brides in America* (New York: NYU Press, 2002).

46 "Weep for the Virgins," *Ebony* (December 1945): 13–16; "His Majesty Jim Crow," *Ebony* (April 1946): 13–15; "Photo-Editorial: Black and Yellow Gold," *Ebony* (May 1947): 36–37; "The World's Worst Slums," *Ebony* (November 1947): 39–42.

47 "The Man Who Could Be Cuba's President," *Ebony* (August 1947): 32–35; "The World's Most Colorful Politician," *Ebony* (April 1951): 96–100.

48 Biondi, *To Stand and Fight;* Rick Halpern, *Down on the Killing Floor: Black and White Workers in Chicago's Packinghouses, 1904–1954* (Urbana: University of Illinois Press, 1997), esp. chapters 6 and 7; Michael Keith Honey, *Black Workers Remember: An Oral History of Segregation, Unionism and the Freedom Struggle* (Berkeley: University of California Press, 1999); Horne, *The Fire This Time.* See also, "Labor's Love Gained," *Ebony* (March 1946): 44–45; "One Year after V-Day," *Ebony* (September 1946): 40–41; "Can Negro Labor End Housing Woe?" *Ebony* (December 1947): 32–33.

49 Frederick Cooper, *Decolonization and African Society: The Labor Question in French and British Africa* (Cambridge: Cambridge University Press, 1996).

50 "Mail Order Job Boom," *Ebony* (November 1947): 31–35; "Men of Steel," *Ebony* (December 1947): 25–28; "The World's Most Dangerous Job," *Ebony,* (March 1949): 13–17.

51 "Wanted: Jobs for a Million Vets," *Ebony* (September 1946): 5–9; "What Happened to the War Workers?" *Ebony* (December 1946): 5–10; "Where are the War Heroes?" *Ebony* (January 1947): 5–11; "Revolution in Cottonland," *Ebony* (March 1947): 27–30. See also "Dixie Comes to California," *Ebony* (April 1950): 15–21, for discussion of the plight of migrant cotton pickers there, in particular the impending effects of mechanization.

52 "What's Ahead for the Negro In '47?" *Ebony* (January 1947): 40–41.

53 "Why Not Go Back to the Farm?" *Ebony* (September 1948): 44–45.

54 "Lady Plane Mechanic," *Ebony* (January 1948): 28–31.

55 "Negro Profs at White Colleges," *Ebony* (October 1947): 14–18; "The Brown Hucksters," *Ebony* (May 1948): 13–18; "Scientists," *Ebony* (September 1950): 15–20; "Insurance," *Ebony* (October 1947): 31–35; "Biggest Bank," *Ebony* (July 1947): 32–33; "Negro Jobs in White Banks," *Ebony* (December 1951): 15–23.

56 "Designer for Living" *Ebony* (February 1946): 24–29; "Mink Ranch," *Ebony* (January 1947): 19–23; "California Dude Ranch," *Ebony* (February 1947): 5–11; "Leather Craft," *Ebony* (September 1947): 29–33.

57 "Texas Negroes Strike It Rich," *Ebony* (October 1948): 46–52; "Lumber Con-

tractor," *Ebony* (July 1951): 63–67; "Slave to Banker," *Ebony* (November 1945): 43–47.

58 "The Ten Richest Negroes in the United States," *Ebony* (April 1949): 13–18. This article provided Frazier's most vivid evidence in his critique of the magazine. See Frazier, *Black Bourgeoisie,* 152–53. For examples of the coverage turn this article precipitated , see "Death Comes to World's Richest Negro," *Ebony* (October 1950): 66–70; "America's Richest Negro Minister," *Ebony* (January 1952): 17–23; "Negro Millionaires of Texas," *Ebony* (August 1952): 15–25; "Park Avenue Doctor," *Ebony* (March 1953): 16–24; "Death is Big Business," *Ebony* (May 1953): 16–31; "Who Are the Newly Rich?" *Ebony* (March 1954): 26–32; and "How I Made a Million," *Ebony* (September 1954): 43–56, a profile of Robert Cole.

59 "Lawyers," *Ebony* (April 1947): 15–18; "Lady Lawyers," *Ebony* (August 1947): 18–21.

60 "Does FEPC Work?" *Ebony* (September 1947): 9–11; "Crusade against Jim Crow," *Ebony* (August 1948): 13–18. The California article linked Stafford's initiative to contemporaneous sit-ins organized by CORE in Chicago restaurants beginning in the 1940s. For more information on these precursors of civil rights–era direct action, see August Meier and Elliot Rudwick, *CORE: A Study in the Civil Rights Movement, 1942–1968* (New York: Oxford University Press, 1973).

61 Waldo Martin, ed., *Brown v. Board of Education: A Brief History with Documents* (Boston: Bedford/St Martin's, 1998); Richard Kluger, *Simple Justice: The History of Brown v. Board of Education and Black America's Struggle for Equality* (New York: Knopf, 1975); Genna Rae McNeil, *Groundwork: Charles Hamilton Houston and the Struggle for Civil Rights* (Philadelphia: University of Pennsylvania Press, 1983); Mark Tushnett, *The NAACP's Legal Strategy Against Segregated Education, 1925–1950* (Chapel Hill: University of North Carolina Press, 1987). For a detailed account in *Ebony* of the extensive NAACP legal office headed by Marshall, see "The World's Biggest Law Firm," *Ebony* (September 1953): 17–24.

62 Mary Francis Berry, *Black Resistance–White Law: A History of Constitutional Racism in the United States* (New York: Penguin, 1971); Derrick Bell, *Race, Racism, and American Law,* 3rd edition (Boston: Little Brown, 1992). See also A. Leon Higgenbotham, *In the Matter of Color: Race and the American Legal Process: The Colonial Period* (New York: Oxford University Press, 1978); and Herbert Hill, *Black Labor and the American Legal System: Race, Work, and the Law* (Madison: University of Wisconsin Press, 1985).

63 Robert Gooding-Williams, ed., *Reading Rodney King, Reading Urban Uprising* (London: Routledge, 1993); Toni Morrison and Claudia Brodsky Lacour, eds., *Birth of a Nation'hood: Gaze, Script, and Spectacle in the O. J. Simpson Case* (New York: Pantheon Books, 1994); Angela Davis, *Are Prisons Obsolete?* (New York: Seven Stories Press, 2003).

64 "Race Riot," *Ebony* (May 1946): 5–9; for further account of the riot in Columbia, Tennesseee, see Herbert Shapiro, *White Violence and Black Response:*

From Reconstruction to Montgomery (Amherst: University of Massachusetts Press, 1988), 362–65.

65 Grossman, *Land of Hope,* 105–7; Herbert G. Gutman, *The Black Family in Slavery and Freedom, 1750–1925* (New York: Random House, 1976); Earl Lewis, *In Their Own Interests: Race Class and Power in Twentieth Century Norfolk, Virginia* (Berkeley: University of California Press, 1990); Gretchen Lemke-Santangelo, *Abiding Courage: African American Migrant Women and the East Bay Community* (Chapel Hill: University of North Carolina Press, 1996); Joe William Trotter Jr., *Black Milwaukee: The Making of an Industrial Proletariat, 1915–1945* (Urbana: University of Illinois Press, 1985)

66 Frazier, *The Negro Family in the United States,* especially part 4. Frazier's conclusion that migrants tended toward pure individuation—"the final stage of demoralization"—provided the touchstone for numerous critiques of inner city mores over the past twenty years. On Wright, who expanded Frazier's ideas into definitive renditions of modern personality, see Richard Wright's *Native Son* (New York: Harper and Brothers, 1940); *Twelve Million Black Voices* (New York: Viking Press, 1941); *Black Boy: A Record of Childhood and Youth* (New York: Harper and Brothers, 1945); and *American Hunger* (New York: Harper and Row, 1977).

67 Darlene Clark Hine, "Black Migration to the Urban Midwest: The Gender Dimension, 1915–1945," in *The Great Migration in Historical Perspective* ed. Joe W. Trotter Jr. (Bloomington: Indiana University Press, 1991): 127–46; Jacqueline Jones, *Labor of Love, Labor of Sorrow: Black Women, Work and Family from Slavery to the Present* (New York: Basic Books, 1985); Lemke-Santangelo, *Abiding Courage;* Carol B. Stack, *All Our Kin: Strategies for Survival in a Black Community* (New York: Harper and Row, 1974).

68 Stack, *All Our Kin,* esp. chapter 4.

69 Burns, *Nitty Gritty,* 86. Despite several child covers following the first issue's image of elementary schoolers at the Henry Street Settlement, Johnson eventually vetoed photos of children in favor of publically recognizable adults. See also Burns's unpublished memoir, written in 1953–54, detailing this policy. Burns, "Manuscript," 37, Ben Burns Papers (H/W-CPL).

70 "The White House," *Ebony* (April 1946): 3–7.

71 "A Day at Marian Anderson's Country Hideaway" *Ebony* (April 1947): 9–14; "Family Man Jackie Robinson," *Ebony* (September 1947): 15–17; "My Life with Hazel Scott," *Ebony* (January 1949): 42–50; "Can Joe Louis Make Good in Business?" *Ebony* (June 1949): 20–24.

72 "The White House," *Ebony* (April 1946): 3–7; "Super Girl," *Ebony* (April, 1946): 21–25.

73 "Co-Op House," *Ebony* (March 1946): 8–9.

74 "I Tried to Crash the Movies," *Ebony* (August 1946): 5–10; "Lady Boxing Boss," *Ebony* (May 1947): 31–35; "Female Impersonators," *Ebony* (March 1948): 61–65.

75 "My Secret Talks with FDR," *Ebony* (April 1949): 42–51; "Some of My Best Friends Are Negro," by Eleanor Roosevelt (February 1953): 16–27.

76 "Famous Negroes Who Married White," *Ebony* (December 1949): 20–30. The White-Cannon marriage proved an attractive topic for the magazine—see "How We Made Our Mixed Marriage Work" *Ebony* (June 1952): 24–40; and "How We Erased Two Color Lines" *Ebony* (July 1952): 46–58, both written by Poppy Cannon; as well as "Ex-Wives of Celebrities," *Ebony* (November 1952): 103–12, which discussed Gladys White's life since the remarriage of her former husband.

77 Molly Haskel, *From Reverence to Rape: The Treatment of Women in the Movies* (New York: Penguin Books, 1973); Maria La Place, "Producing and Consuming the Woman's Film: Discursive Struggle in *Now Voyager,*" in *Home is Where the Heart Is: Studies in Melodrama and the Woman's Film,* ed. Christine Gledhill (London: British Film Institute, 1987), 138–66; Thomas Schatz, *Boom and Bust: American Cinema in the 1940s* (Berkeley: University of California Press, 1997), esp. chapter 6. For examination of how these dynamics affected exemplary black entertainers, see Donald Bogle, *Dorothy Dandridge: A Biography* (New York: Amistad, 1997).

78 "What Married Couples Should Know about Sex," *Ebony* (May 1950): 50–58. "Gay Divorcees," *Ebony* (February 1950): 72–77. An earlier 1947 article was noteworthy in its presentation of the barriers to black marriage as mainly a problem for black women ("800,000 Negro girls will never get to the altar, experts predict" reads the subtitle). "Marriage," *Ebony* (June 1947): 21–24.

79 "What to Teach Youngsters About Sex," *Ebony* (April 1948): 38–44; "What I Told Kinsey About My Sex Life," *Ebony* (December 1948): 44–50; "Dreams," *Ebony* (May 1949): 52–59; "What Married Couples Should Know About Sex," *Ebony* (May 1950): 50–58. Response to *Ebony*'s informed and nonjudgmental coverage of sex was generally positive, although the magazine nonetheless seemed anxious about possible protests. In December 1950 Maudelle Bousfield, recently retired as principal of Chicago's Wendell Phillips School, wrote an article decrying the "looseness" of her former students—clearly an attempt within the magazine to counter charges that it was too libertine in its views. "Sex in High School," *Ebony* (December 1950): 24–32.

80 Along these lines, the annual features on black bachelors and bachelorettes, which became a much sought-after mark of social prominence by the 1970s and 1980s, underscores the magazine's interest in validating individuated black adults, even as it exerted subtle pressure that they seek to couple. See "Single Men," *Ebony* (May 1948): 54–59; "Eligible Men," *Ebony* (November 1949): 76–80; "Wealthy Bachelors," *Ebony* (October 1952): 31–38.

81 Prior to the 1920s, black social status was a fundamentally derivative asset: reference to white ancestors, or the prominence of the white patron or (far usually) employer one claimed, generally established the bona fides of elite African Americans. See Willard Gatewood, *Aristocrats of Color: The Black Elite, 1880–1920* (Bloomington: University of Indiana Press, 1990).

82 "This is House That Jack Built" *Ebony* (November 1945): 14–20.

83 "Food for Bluebloods," *Ebony* (September 1947): 34–35; "Memoirs of a Pull-

man Porter," *Ebony* (February 1948): 51–58; "Secrets of a Movie Maid," *Ebony* (November 1949): 52–62.

84 Johnson and Bennett, *Succeeding Against the Odds,* 126. For further coverage of Horne in the magazine, see "Meet the Real Lena Horne," *Ebony* (November 1947): 9–14.

85 "How Joe Louis Lost Two Million Dollars," *Ebony* (May 1946): 10–13; "Will Joe Louis Be Golf Champ Next?" *Ebony* (December 1948): 13–18; "Can Joe Louis Make Good in Business," *Ebony* (June 1949): 20–24; "Why I Quit Joe," *Ebony* (December 1949): 61–71; "Why I'm Fighting Again," *Ebony* (October 1950): 15–20; "The Love Life of Joe Louis," *Ebony* (July 1951): 22–34; "Why I Won't Marry Again," *Ebony* (November 1952): 34–48; "The Ten Biggest Lies About Joe Louis," *Ebony* (August 1953): 52–61; "How I Discovered Joe Louis," *Ebony* (October 1954): 64–78.

86 "Is Jazz Going Highbrow?" *Ebony* (July 1946): 15–17; "Negro Movies Hit Paydirt," *Ebony* (September 1946): 42–44; "The Schoolmarm Who Glorified Leg Art," *Ebony* (January 1947): 14–18; "Hollywood Debut for Pearl Bailey," *Ebony* (April 1947): 38–39; "Sammy Davis, Jr.," *Ebony* (December 1950): 45–49.

87 "King Cole's Honeymoon Diary," *Ebony* (August 1948): 24–28. On earlier accounts of black travel and recreation, see "Where to Go for a Vacation," *Ebony* (July 1947): 14–17; "Florida's First Negro Resort," *Ebony* (February 1948): 24–26; "Vacation in Haiti," *Ebony* (July 1948): 52–55; and "Jamaica," *Ebony* (November 1948): 44–50.

88 "My Life with Hazel Scott," *Ebony* (January 1949): 42–50; "I'm Cured for Good Now," *Ebony* (July 1949): 26–33.

89 "High Sierra Deer Hunt," *Ebony* (February 1949): 19–23; "Florida Package Vacation," *Ebony* (April 1950): 61–63; "Where to Vacation in the West Indies," *Ebony* (March 1951): 34–38; "Fashion Fair: Summer Tropicals," *Ebony* (August 1950): 40–43. The byline of the last story was the first time that "fashion fair" appeared in relation to Johnson Publishing. It would designate the multimillion-dollar line of cosmetics launched by the company in 1974. Beginning in 1958, *Ebony* held annual fashion tours in various U.S. cities. Through the 1960s and 1970s the *Ebony* Fashion Tour, managed by Eunice Johnson, would reach hundreds of cities, raising $25 million charity dollars by the early 1990s. It also constituted what Johnson called the introduction to *couture* for a large portion of African Americans—one further indication of *Ebony*'s synergy of celebrity coverage, leisure ethic, and luxury culture marking the magazine's imprint on black culture and society. Johnson with Bennett, *Succeeding Against the Odds,* 250–52, 342–50.

90 "King Cole Decorates His New Home" *Ebony* (April 1949): 26–30; "Frank Yerby Remodels His Long Island Home," *Ebony* (June 1949): 53–55; "Nellie Lutcher's New Home," *Ebony* (December 1949): 41–43; "Society Editors," *Ebony* (March 1950): 52–57.

91 Drake and Cayton's *Black Metropolis* is worth consulting here: see especially

chapters 18, 19, 22, 23. For further discussions of respectability's impact on black thought and behavior, see Kevin K. Gaines, *Uplifting the Race,* and Stephanie Shaw, *What a Woman Ought to Be and to Do: Black Professional Women Workers during the Jim Crow Era* (Chicago: University of Chicago Press, 1996).

92 "I'm Cured for Good," *Ebony* (July 1949): 26–33; "Confessions of a Bishop," *Ebony* (March 1950): 71–80.

93 Although connection of respectability and black femininity reached its highpoint around the turn of the century, such concerns had defined the horizons of plausible social activity for black middle- and upper-class women through the first half of the twentieth century as well. See Paula Giddings, *When and Where I Enter: The Impact of Black Women on Race and Sex in America* (New York: Bantam Books, 1984); Carby, *Reconstructing Womanhood;* and Miriam DeCosta-Willis, ed., *The Memphis Diary of Ida B. Wells* (Boston: Beacon Press, 1996). For discussions of the continued salience of respectability among black women into the twentieth century, see Shaw, *What a Woman Ought to Be and to Do;* and Darlene Clark Hine, "Rape and the Inner Lives of African-American Women in the Middle West: Preliminary Thoughts on the Culture of Dissemblance," *Signs* 14 (Summer 1989): 912–20.

94 "Glamour Is Global," *Ebony* (July 1946): 18–23; "Artists' Model," *Ebony* (February 1948): 63–66; "Lady Lifeguard,"*Ebony* (July 1948): 19–22; "What Men Notice about Women," *Ebony* (January 1950): 34–36. For varied reader response to provocative photographs of women in the magazine—in particular cover shots—see letters from December 1946, April 1947, May 1947, August 1947, May 1949, and August 1950 issues.

95 On the eroticization of black women's performance in popular music, see Hazel Carby, "'It Jes Be's Dat Way Sometime': The Sexual Politics of Women's Blues," *Radical America* 20 (June–July 1986): 9–22. For introduction to the African-American beauty industry, see Kathy Peiss's entry "Beauty Culture," in *Black Women in America: An Historical Encyclopedia,* ed. Darlene Clark Hine, Elsa Barkeley Brown, and Rosalyn Terborg-Penn (Bloomington: Indiana University Press, 1994), 100–104.

96 Shaw, *What a Woman Ought to Be and to Do,* esp. 166. Shaw's own characterization of black professional women's "work" as activity and responsibilities extending well beyond their "jobs" has little to say about sexual expression or desire. Nonetheless, I find her framework sufficiently flexible to accommodate my usage here, given the evidence within the text of *Ebony,* and the clear interest of the magazine's readers in this coverage. As well, Shaw's refusal to more fully discuss ideas of sexuality among middle and upper class black women can be taken to indicate the degree of shift in postwar common sense that *Ebony*'s discussion gender and sexuality represented—if not inspired.

97 "Hollywood's New Glamour Queen," *Ebony* (April 1951): 48–52. For further coverage of Dandridge in the magazine, see "Don't be Afraid of Sex Appeal," *Ebony* (May 1952): 24–31; "See How They Run," *Ebony* (April 1953): 43–48; "Dorothy Dandridge," *Ebony* (December 1953): 99–101; "Screen Test," *Ebony*

(September 1954): 37–42, which covers her successful audition for the film *Carmen Jones;* and "Dorothy Dandridge's Greatest Triumph," *Ebony* (July 1955): 37–41, an account of her subsequent Academy Award nomination.

98 John Blassingame, *The Slave Community: Plantation Life in the Antebellum South* (New York: Oxford University Press, 1972); Michael Gomez, *Exchanging Our Country Marks: The Transformation of African Identities in the Colonial and Antebellum South* (Chapel Hill: University of North Carolina Press, 1998); Lawrence Levine, *Black Culture, Black Consciousnesst;* Sidney W. Mintz and Richard Price, *An Anthropological Approach to the Afro-American Past: A Caribbean Perspective* (Philadelphia: Institute for the Study of Human Issues, 1976); Albert J. Raboteau, *Slave Religion: The "Invisible Institution" in the American South* (New York: Oxford University Press, 1978); Sterling Stuckey, *Slave Culture: Nationalist Theory and the Foundations of Black America* (New York: Oxford University Press, 1987). John Thornton, *Africa and Africans in the Making of the Atlantic World, 1400–1680* (Cambridge: Cambridge University Press, 1992).

99 Ira Berlin, "From Creole to African: Atlantic Creoles and the Origins of African-American Society in the Mainland North America," *William and Mary Quarterly* 53, no. 2 (April 1996): 251–88; Shane White and Graham White, *Stylin': African American Expressive Culture from Its Beginnings to the Zoot Suit* (Ithaca: Cornell University Press, 1998): especially chapters 1–4.

100 On the interplay of vernacular and improvisation in African American culture, see Henry Louis Gates, *The Signifying Monkey;* and Houston Baker Jr., *Blues, Ideology, and African American Literature: A Vernacular Theory* (Chicago: University of Chicago Press, 1984).

101 Here I am thinking not only about the more innocuous varieties of dress, music, courtship and social etiquettes so imaginatively cataloged by Shane and Graham White, but also individuated rejection of slavery's authority through sabotaging tools, verbally defying masters and overseers, running away, or producing slave narratives. These actions, taken often to constitute a more or less universal template of black resistance, suggest that the most common—and perhaps most effective—mode of slave resistance was individual rather than collective. For examples from this voluminous literature, see Eugene D. Genovese, *Roll, Jordan, Roll: The World the Slaves Made* (New York: Random House, 1972); Gerald Mullin, *Flight and Rebellion: Slave Resistance in Eighteenth-Century Virginia* (New York: Oxford University Press, 1975); and Brenda E. Stevenson, *Life in Black and White: Family and Community in the Slave South* (New York: Oxford University Press, 1996).

102 C. L. R. James, *American Civilization* (London: Blackwell, 1993): 133. It is important here, I think, to distinguish this definition of modern personality from the idea of the "performed self" that Erving Goffman and others pushed as a theory of individuation within the consensus society of the cold war. See Goffman, *The Presentation of Self in Everyday Life* (New York: Doubleday, 1959).

103 Lawrence Levine, *Black Culture and Black Consciousness,* 223. Levine richly

inventories the varieties of character circulated among turn of the century African Americans in his final chapter to the book, "A Pantheon of Heroes."

104 This underscores the specific quality of irrepressibility related to these cultural heroes. The antics of Bessie Smith at the plush parties of Carl Van Vechten and other Negrophiles, Jack Johnson's defiant consort with white women, Shine's cool swim to survival and waiting beer in the legend of the Titanic's sinking: all realized that while African-Americans difference in a segregated world might be recognized, feared, mimicked or even appealed to by whites, it would never be fully subsumed or assimilated.

105 "The Man in the Ads," *Ebony* (January 1947): 35–39; "Weather Prophet," *Ebony* (September 1947): 24–26.

106 Walter Benjamin, "The Work of Art in the Age of Mechanical Reproduction," in *Illuminations: Essays and Reflections* (New York: Harcourt, Brace, Jovanovich, 1968), 217–52. Others have built on Benjamin's cautionary though appreciative approach to the mass arts—especially their core qualities of repetition, as well as irreverence toward the more theological conceits of high art—to black culture with power and insight. Tricia Rose, *Black Noise: Rap Music and Black Culture in Contemporary America* (Hanover, NH: Wesleyan University Press, 1993); and James Sneed, "On Repetition in Black Culture," *Black American Literature Forum*, 15, no. 4 (1981): 146–54. Here, though, I am less concerned with the established oppositional aspect of mechanical commodities like hip-hop beats or lyrics and more with the general implications of mechanical reproduction for black personality, both individually and in the aggregate form of public community and political will.

107 James's work, while not attentive to the implications of celebrity to black culture specifically, clearly had Benjamin's work in mind while formulating his own sympathetic readings of the political implications of mass media tastes in the United States. See James, *American Civilization,* esp. chapter 5. Aside from James's work, the closest thing we have to a Benjaminian reading of celebrity as a social phenomenon remains Richard Dyer, *Stars* (London: British Film Institute, 1979). Conversations with Timuel Black greatly enhanced my understanding of black celebrity's relation to local life in Black Chicago. Interview with Timuel Black, May 3–4, 2000.

108 Burns, *Nitty Gritty,* 98.

109 Masthead, *Ebony* (May–December 1950); Johnson with Bennett, *Succeeding Against the Odds,* chapters 22, 23, and 26; author's interview with LeRoy Winbush, February 2000; author's interview with Herbert Nipson, May 2000; author's interview with Doris Saunders, June 2000; for discussion of Johnson's leadership advocacy of black-appeal marketing in the 1960s, see Weems, *Desegregating the Dollar,* chapter 2.

110 "Black Boy in Brooklyn," *Ebony* (November 1945): 26–27; "First Novel," *Ebony* (April 1946): 35–41; "Angry Author from Brooklyn," *Ebony* (July 1946): 48–49; and Arna Bontemps, "Langston Hughes," *Ebony* (October 1946): 19–27.

111 Burns, *Nitty Gritty,* chapter 1; for account of Burns's scathing denunciation of Hughes, which he deeply regretted throughout his life, see page 15; see

also Arnold Rampersand, *The Life of Langston Hughes, Volume 1: 1902–1941* (New York: Oxford University Press, 1986), 394–95.

112 Burns, *Nitty Gritty,* chapters 7–9.

113 Burns, *Nitty Gritty,* 97, 113, 116–17, 129–43; Burns, "A White Man in Black Journalism" Ben Burns Papers, Harsh Collection (CGWB-CPL): 11–21, 76–78, 141–43; "Passing," *Ebony* (May, 1949): 27–30.

114 There are several expert analyses of *Life*'s suggestive relation to the development of modern photography. See Carl Fleischauer and Beverly W. Brannen, eds., *Documenting America, 1935–1943* (Berkeley: University of California Press, 1988); Maren Stange, *Symbols of Ideal Life: Social Documentary Photography in America, 1890–1950* (Cambridge: Cambridge University Press, 1992); William Stott, *Documentary Expression and Thirties America* (Chicago: University of Chicago Press, 1973), 129–30, and Warren I. Sussman, *Culture as History: The Transformation of American Society in the Twentieth Century* (New York: Pantheon Books, 1984), 159. For a sample of images from *Life* up to the early 1940s, see *Life: The First Decade, 1936–1945* (New York: Time, Inc., 1979).

115 "Bye-Bye Boogie," *Ebony* (September 1945): 31–35; "Meet Mr. Moore," *Ebony* (December 1945): 41–45; "Zanzibusiness," *Ebony* (April 1946): 23–30; "Reporter with a Camera," *Ebony* (July 1946): 24–29.

116 "The Rumba," *Ebony* (April 1947): 23–27; "African Jiu-Jitsu," *Ebony* (January 1948): 37–39. Further information on Guillumette is unavailable as I write this chapter.

117 "Jazz Concerts" *Ebony* (September 1946): 29–34, esp. 29–30; "Skin Wizard of the World," *Ebony* (February 1946): 7–13; "Sixty Million Jobs or Else . . . This Again?" *Ebony* (September 1945): 50–51; "The House We Live In," *Ebony* (January 1946): 20–21. Here I am recalling the popularity of deep focus as a technique of cinematography at the time, exemplified by Gregg Toland's contributions to *Citizen Kane* in 1941. Meant as an aesthetic representing pronounced and even irresolvable narrative tension, Costner's own application of deep focus seems motivated by its peculiar capacity to convey urban complexity and instability in grand scale. Its incorporation in *Ebony* suggests once more the sophistication of the visual grammar presented to its readers. Robert L. Carringer, *The Making of Citizen Kane* (Berkeley: University of California Press, 1985), especially chapter 4; and David Bordwell, "Deep Focus Cinematography," in Janet Staiger, ed., *The Studio System* (New Brunswick: Rutgers, University Press, 1995), 93–124. Costner's work is also archived in his collected papers. See Gordon Costner Papers (Chicago Historical Society).

118 Kenneth C. Burkhart and Larry A. Viskochil, eds., *Stephen Deutch, Photographer: From Paris to Chicago, 1932–1989* (Chicago: Tri-Quarterly Books, 1989). Deutch, who maintained a Loop studio with wife and colleague Helen Deutch, pursued his extraordinary career over four decades, moving from jobs for fashion magazines *Coronet* and *Mademoiselle* to extensive work for Marshall Field's, U.S. Gypsum, and advertising firms Leo Burnett and Young and Rubicam. Subsequent photographic series, such as "Doors and Windows" "Bench

Sitters," and "Twilight World" (nominated for a Pulitzer Prize), extended his reputation. For overview of Deutch's work, see Abigal Foerster, "Sculptor of Light," in *Stephen Deutch: Photographer,* ed. Burkhart and Viskochil. For further survey of Deutch's work, see the Stephen Deutch Papers (Chicago Historical Society)

119 Wayne F. Miller, *Chicago's South Side: 1946–1948* (Berkeley: University of California Press, 2000): esp. 46, 51, 53, 54. These are only a few examples of Miller's work for *Ebony:* between 1946 and 1948, he was the magazine's most prolific photographer. For stories accompanying this work, see "Female Impersonators" *Ebony* (March 1948): 61–65; "The Real Truth about Marijuana," *Ebony* (September 1948): 46–51.

120 For information on Stern, see *Ebony* (March 1946): title page; for Wolff, *Ebony* (May 1947): title page; for Covello, *Ebony* (August 1947): title page.

121 On Davis, see "Backstage," *Ebony* (October1948). Jackson's first listed credits at the magazine appeared in July and August, 1949, two months after Gordon Parks's last listed credits for *Ebony* "Global Honeymoon," *Ebony* (September 1952): 95–101, recounted Davis's three-continent honeymoon with Muriel Corin, through photos he took while traveling.

122 Burns, *Nitty Gritty,* 147–51.

123 Thompson to Stanley Pargellis, May 24, 1944, Era Bell Thompson Papers, box 1, folder 2, Harsh Collection (Woodson-Chicago Public Library).

124 John Johnson to Thompson, November 8, 1946, box 1, folder 4; Floyd Schwartz to Thompson, undated 1950, box 1, folder 7; intraoffice memo from Thompson, box 1, folder 12; Zeline Dickerson to Thompson, March 11, 1954, David Wasawo to Thompson, January 15, 1954, and Symons Onynago to Thompson, March 25, 1954; St. Clair Drake to Thompson, undated, box 2, folder 1; and Thompson to Madame A. Diop, December 1, 1954, box 2, folder 1, Era Bell Thompson Papers, Harsh Collection (Woodson-Chicago Public Library). See also Era Bell Thompson, *American Daughter* (Chicago: University of Chicago Press, 1946) and *Africa: Land of My Fathers* (Garden City, NY: Doubleday and Co., 1954) as well as Thompson's preview of her African memoir in "What Africans Think about Us," *Ebony* (February 1954): 36–41.

125 "The 1950 Census," *Ebony* (April 1950): 31–38.

126 Charlemae Hill Rollins, a Mississippi migrant who left a teaching post to work at Hall, organized programs and readings at Hall Library, including regular children's hours. Beginning around 1941, she launched a campaign to improve textbook and storybook depictions of African Americans, enlisting librarians and educators across the country, and representing one of the first and most important initiatives of its kind. For more information on Rollins, see Shaw, *What a Woman Ought to Be and to Do,* 204–6.

127 Interview with Doris Saunders, June 6, 2000. For invaluable information on area high schools during the 1930s and 1940s, I am indebted to Timuel Black. Interview with Timuel Black, May 3–4, 2000.

128 Saunders, June 6, 2000. Doris Saunders remains active in publishing today. Un-

til recently she was manager of the company's book catalog, including works of *Ebony* editor and historian Lerone Bennett Jr. She is finishing up her own biography of Congressman William L. Dawson. For *Ebony*'s use of government statistics following Saunders's arrival, see "The 1950 Census," *Ebony* (April 1950): 31–38, which discussed Joseph Houchins prominently. For account of Saunders's importance to marketing operations at the company, see "Ebony Pioneers in Negro Advertising," *Ebony* (November 1955): 130–32. On the idea of "active literature," see Williams, *Marxism and Literature* (New York: Oxford University Press, 1977), 2. For profound account of this tendency in black intellectual and cultural life over time, see Elizabeth McHenry, *Forgotten Readers: Recovering the Lost History of African American Literary Societies* (Durham: Duke University Press, 2002).

129 "Backstage," *Ebony* (August 1946).

130 Johnson with Bennett, *Succeeding Against the Odds,* 196.

131 "How to Glorify the Apple," *Ebony* (October 1946): 28; "Tamale Pie For New Year's Eve," *Ebony* (January 1947): 42–43; "Lena Horne's Valentine Party, *Ebony* (February 1947): 17–18; "Baked Fish," *Ebony* (April 1948): 33; Letters to the Editor, *Ebony* (February 1947): 9; Advertisement for DeKnight's "A Date with a Dish," *Ebony* (June 1948): 27; "Backstage," *Ebony* (March 1949): 10; for examples of De Knight ads, see December 1948, and November and December 1950 editions of *Ebony.*

132 "Budget Meals for Vet Wives," *Ebony* (September 1947): 27–28; "School Lunches," *Ebony* (September 1948): 62; "Pepper and Spices from the Islands," *Ebony* (June 1947): 25; "Fruit Pies," *Ebony* (March 1948): 45; "Corned Beef and Cabbage," *Ebony* (August 1948): 62; "Peasant Potato Soup," *Ebony* (February 1949): 50; "Leg of Lamb," *Ebony* (March 1949): 33.

133 Zora Neale Hurston, *Their Eyes Were Watching God* (Urbana: University of Illinois Press, 1991), 16. Elizabeth Clark-Lewis, *Living In, Living Out: African American Domestics in Washington D.C., 1910–1940* (Washington: Smithsonian Institution Press, 1994); Tera W. Hunter, *To 'Joy My Freedom': Southern Black Women's Lives and Labors After the Civil War* (Cambridge, MA: Harvard University Press, 1997); Stevenson, *Life in Black and White,* 192; Angela V. Davis, *Women, Race, and Class* (New York: Vintage Books, 1981); Deborah Gray White, *Ar'n't I a Woman? Female Slaves in the Plantation South* (New York: W. W. Norton, 1989), chapter 4.

134 On 1940s the emphasis on home economics in women's magazines, see Nancy A. Walker, ed., *Women's Magazines: 1940–1960* (Boston: Bedford Books, 1998).

135 "The House We Live In," *Ebony* (November 1945): 20; "Labor Love's Gained," *Ebony* (March 1946): 44; "How Long Can the Negro Live?" *Ebony* (April 1946): 40; "The Fable of the 'Happy' Negro," *Ebony* (January 1949): 60–61; "Do Negroes Hate Themselves?" *Ebony* (March 1949): 53–53; "How to Beat the Depression," *Ebony* (October 1949): 42–43; "The Plot to Kill Public Housing," *Ebony* (June 1950): 92–93.

136 "The Right Not to Discriminate," *Ebony* (August 1948): 60–61; "Don't Blame

Only the South," *Ebony* (December 1948): 66–67; "Challenge to Mister Charley," *Ebony* (April 1948): 20–21; "Needed: A Negro Legion of Decency," *Ebony* (January 1947): 36–37.

137 On the limits of white support, see "Can the Negro Trust His White Friends," *Ebony* (August 1946): 40–41; "Was Lincoln Anti-Negro?" *Ebony* (February 1948): 48–49; and "Do Do-Gooders Do Good?" *Ebony* (March 1948): 46–47. On black reinforcement of race stereotype, see "The Rise and Fall of Uncle Tom," *Ebony* (December 1946): 34–35; and "No Biz for Show Biz," *Ebony* (October 1947): 42–43. "Time to Count Our Blessings," *Ebony* (November 1947): 44–45; "When Bouquets Are Brickbats," *Ebony* (June 1948): 46–47.

138 "Return of the Native Son," *Ebony* (December 1951): 100–101; "Why Negroes Buy Cadillacs," *Ebony* (September 1949): 34–35; "Can the Negro Trust His White Friends?" *Ebony* (August 1946): 40–41; "Etiquette of Race Relations," *Ebony* (December 1949): 78–79; "Educating Our White Folks," *Ebony* (March 1952): 98–99; "The Carrot or the Club," *Ebony* (August 1947): 46–47; "Do the Negroes Really Want Equality?" *Ebony* (June 1949): 56–57; "Yesterday's World of Tomorrow," *Ebony* (July 1949): 54–55; "Are You Ready for Luck?" *Ebony* (September 1950): 78–79; "Time to Stop Crying Wolf," *Ebony* (June 1952): 116–17; "A Future in America, Not Africa," *Ebony* (July 1947): 40–41; "Race Is Not the Issue in '48," *Ebony* (July 1948): 56–57; "The Negro Choice for President," *Ebony* (November, 1948): 36–37; "Is It a War of Color?" *Ebony* (October 1950): 94–95.

139 "When Bouquets are Brickbats," *Ebony* (June 1948): 46–47; "The Fable of the 'Happy' Negro," *Ebony* (January 1949): 60; "Editorial Comment," *Negro Quarterly* 1, no. 4 (Winter–Spring 1943), reprinted in *African Americans in the Industrial Age: A Documentary History, 1919–1945*, ed. Joe W. Trotter Jr., and Earl Lewis (Boston: Northeastern University Press, 1996), 297–302.

140 Frazier, *Black Bourgeoisie,* 193; John Dunn, "Measuring Locke's Shadow," in John Locke, *Two Treatises of Government and a Letter Concerning Toleration,* ed. Ian Shapiro (New Haven: Yale University Press, 2003), 265–66.

141 Louis Hartz, *The Liberal Tradition in America* (New York: Harcourt Brace, 1955), esp. 5–14.

142 Reed, "The Jug and Its Contents," in *Stirrings in the Jug,* esp. 16–28, 29, 50–51.See also Michael C. Dawson, *Black Visions: The Roots of Contemporary African-American Political Ideologies* (Chicago: University of Chicago Press, 2001): esp. chapter 6; Gaines, preface to *Uplifting the Race;* Saidiya V. Hartman, introduction to *Scenes of Subjection: Terror, Slavery and Self-Making in Nineteenth-Century America* (New York: Oxford University Press, 1997).

143 Hartz, *The Liberal Tradition in America,* 11.

144 *Ebony* (November 1955). On *Ebony* staff, see "The Story of *Ebony,*" 122–28; "*Ebony* Pioneers in Negro Advertising," 130–32; and "Around the World with *Ebony* Staffers," 140–41. On national and global events, see "Ten Years That Rocked the World," 134–38; and "The Jackie Robinson Era," 152–55. On editorial and publisher comment, see "Backstage," 14; "A Message from the Publisher," 121; and "The First Ten Years Are the Happiest," 98–99.

145 Mary McLeod Bethune, "My Last Will and Testament," *Ebony* (August 1955): 105–10.

CHAPTER 5: A MOMENT OF SIMULTANEITY

1 Rowe, *Chicago Blues,* 165–66; Dixon with Snowdon, *I am the Blues,* 88–92.

2 *Chicago Defender* (August 6, 1955).

3 Speech by John H. Sengestacke, location unknown, December 9, 1955, in *Defender* Pamphlet File, Manuscript Collection (Chicago Historical Society).

4 "The Chicago Daily *Defender:* 'The Newspaper that Looks Ahead,'" promotional brochure (ca. 1956); *Chicago Defender, First Annual Consumer Market Survey* (Chicago: Abbott Publishing Co., 1953); and *Chicago Defender, Second Annual Consumer Market Survey* (Chicago: Abbott Publishing Co., 1955); all in the *Defender* Pamphlet File, Manuscript Collection (Chicago Historical Society).

5 William J. Grimshaw, *Bitter Fruit: Black Politics and the Chicago Machine, 1931–1991* (Chicago: University of Chicago Press, 1992).

6 Arnold Hirsch, *Making the Second Ghetto: Race and Housing in Chicago, 1940–1960* (Cambridge: Cambridge University Press, 1983), chapter 2.

7 "Words of the Week," *Jet* (November 1, 1951): 26.

8 Taylor Branch, *Parting the Waters: America in the King Years, 1954–1963* (New York: Simon and Schuster, 1988), 181; Charles M. Payne, *I've Got the Light of Freedom: The Organizing Tradition and the Mississippi Freedom Struggle* (Berkeley: University of California Press, 1995), 39–40, 53–54; Aldon Morris, *The Origins of the Civil Rights Movement: Black Communities Organizing for Change* (New York: Free Press, 1984), 29–30; Williams, *Eyes on the Prize: America's Civil Rights Year, 1954–1965* (New York: 1987), chapter 2; Stephen J. Whitfield, *A Death in the Delta: The Story of Emmett Till* (New York: Free Press, 1988).

9 Robert Bone, "Richard Wright and the Chicago Renaissance"; Margaret Walker, *Daemonic Genius;* William V. Mullen, *Popular Fronts: Chicago and African-American Cultural Politics, 1935–1946* (Urbana: University of Illinois Press, 1999); Alan B. Anderson and George W. Pickering, *Confronting the Color Line: The Broken Promise of the Civil Rights Movement in Chicago* (Athens, GA: University of Georgia Press, 1986); James R. Ralph Jr., *Northern Protest: Martin Luther King, Jr., Chicago, and the Civil Rights Movement* (Cambridge, MA: Harvard University Press, 1993).

10 This is Spear's well-known argument that the establishment by Blacks of an "institutional ghetto" exacerbated the effects of the white-imposed "physical ghetto," making Chicago a singularly stubborn case of racist community in the North. See Spear, *Black Chicago*.

11 James Q. Wilson, *Negro Politicians: The Search for Leadership* (New York: Free Press 1960), 7.

12 Christopher Reed, *The Chicago NAACP and the Rise of Black Professional Leadership, 1910–1966* (Bloomington: Indiana University Press, 1997); August

Meier and Elliot Rudwick, *CORE: A Study in the Civil Right Movement, 1942–1968* (New York: Oxford University Press, 1973), chapters 1 and 2; Anderson and Pickering, *Confronting the Color Line,* chapters 2 and 3.

13 Spear, *Black Chicago,* especially chapters 1 and 11; Chicago Commission on Race Relations, *The Negro in Chicago,* 3, 152–230; Thomas Lee Philpott, *The Slum and the Ghetto: Neighborhood Deterioration and Middle Class Reform* (New York: Oxford University Press, 1978); Drake and Cayton, *Black Metropolis,* chapters 3, 4, and 8.

14 Hirsch, *Making the Second Ghetto,* 19–20, 23.

15 Ibid., 25–27.

16 Ibid., chapter 2.

17 Hirsch, "Massive Resistance in the Urban North: Trumbull Park, Chicago 1953–1966," *Journal of American History* 82 (September 1995): 522–50; quote is from p. 523. Similar to Thomas Sugrue's work on race and labor in postwar Detroit, Hirsch's essay counters the conclusions of Thomas and Mary Edsall, Jim Sleeper, and others that the New Deal coalition of white labor, blacks, and liberal intellectuals collapsed during the late 1960s and 1970s, due to divisive calls for African-American autonomy and independent leverage through movements such as local school control and civilian police review, or the diffuse groundswell of "Black Power." Given Hirsch and Sugrue's findings, it is clear that working class white resistance to racial liberalism predated these developments during the sixties; indeed they preceded the very emergence of black civil rights as an issue of national-popular concern, raising questions as to whether a "New-Deal coalition" as such ever existed. See Sugrue, "Crabgrass-Roots Politics: Race, Rights, and the Reaction against Liberalism in the Urban North, 1940–1970," *Journal of American History* 82 (September 1995): 551–78.

18 J. Anthony Lukas, *Common Ground: A Turbulent Decade in the Lives of Three American Families* (New York: Alfred A. Knopf, 1985); Jonathan Reider, *Canarsie: The Jews and Italians of Brooklyn Against Liberalism* (Cambridge, MA: Harvard University Press, 1985).

19 Chicago Commission on Human Relations (CCHR), *The Trumbull Park Homes Disturbances: A Chronological Report, August 4, 1953 to June 30, 1955* (Chicago: Chicago Commission on Human Relations, n.d.), 7, 10. This unpublished document, digesting items that the commission gathered over two years, offers a helpful case study in urban race relations for the period.

20 Hirsch, "Massive Resistance in the Urban North," 522–23.

21 CCHR, *The Trumbull Park Homes Disturbances,* 11–12.

22 Hirsch, "Massive Resistance in the Urban North," 527; the use of aerial bombs, meant to deprive the Howards and other black tenants of any semblance of comfort and security at night, was most extensive during the winter and spring of 1954. While detonations reduced as the summer approached, they continued sporadically into the next year. See CCHR, *Trumbull Park Homes Disturbances,* esp. 11–56.

23 Hirsch, "Massive Resistance in the Urban North," 527, 533.

24 CCHR, *Trumbull Park Homes Disturbances,* 12; "Hate Mob Storms Project, Nab 41," *Chicago Defender* (August 13, 1953): 1, 2. For information on parallel 1919 attacks on public streetcars, see Chicago Commission on Race Relations, *The Negro in Chicago,* 6, 10–11.

25 Evidence of official reluctance to challenge the actions of white protestors can be found in arrest statistics. Out of 202 Trumbull arrests between August 1953 and May 1955 for offenses such as aggravated assault, resisting an officer, disorderly conduct and riot, only one case resulted in a jail sentence (of ten days). The weak standards of enforcement did not escape the attention of black Alderman Archibald Carey, who pointed out that during the first seven months of the crisis, only 167 arrests had been made even though estimates were that fifty to sixty thousand whites took part in the often disorderly protests, and expenditures to muster police details often numbering in the hundreds had reached $2 million. On arrests, see CCHR, *Trumbull Park Homes Disturbances,* appendix; on Carey, see Reed, *The Chicago NAACP,* 169.

26 Although links between street violence and local organizations, such as the South Deering Improvement Association (SDIA), have never been clearly established, there is no doubt that local whites—from Alderman Emil Pucini to Joseph Beauharnais of the supremacist White Circle League—saw themselves as soldiers to a common cause. By October 1954, SDIA leader Louis Dinnocenzo warned that the group would screen candidates "from U.S. Senator on down" on housing integration issues for the upcoming election: their sense of entitlement doubtless derived from an August 21 outdoor benefit attended by ten and fifteen thousand local whites, with most expressing what the Commission on Human Relations termed "sympathy for South Deering's cause." See Hirsch, "Massive Resistance in the Urban North" and CCHR, *Trumbull Park Homes Disturbances,* esp. 51 and 53.

27 CCHR, *Trumbull Park Homes Disturbances,* 17, 27, 31, 49.

28 *Time* magazine ran two pieces on Trumbull Park in 1954; while the *Nation* published an article by Robert Gruenberg, a local reporter who had followed the crisis since its beginnings. Eric Sevareid devoted his national television program, *American Week,* to Trumbull Park on the Fourth of July 1954. Alan Paton, South African author of *Cry the Beloved Country* was commissioned by *Collier's Magazine* to write an article on the crisis: Chicago Housing Authority officials reported Paton "collecting material" in the area in late April 1954. See "Seven Months' War," *Time* (March 1, 1954): 19, and "We Suffered," *Time* (May 22, 1954): 33; Robert Gruenberg, "Chicago Fiddles While Trumbull Park Burns," *Nation* (May 22, 1954): 441–43; Hirsch, "Massive Resistance in the Urban North," 542; and CCHR, *Trumbull Park Homes Disturbances,* 41, 43, 48.

29 Nor was desegregation of Chicago's neighborhoods achieved by the Chicago Freedom Movement of local activists together with King and SCLC from 1965 and 1967. While an agreement negotiated with Mayor Daley and realtors in August 1966, following the infamous Gage Park and Cicero marches, was supposed to initiate residential integration, weak enforcement left supporters dis-

illusioned—and Chicago's residents ever more divided by race. As late as the 1980s, Chicago was known as "the nation's most segregated central city." On the Chicago Freedom Movement, see Anderson and Pickering, *Confronting the Color Line,* and Ralph, *Northern Protest,* esp. chapters 3, 4, and 6. On recent measures of housing segregation in Chicago, see Massey and Denton, *American Apartheid: Segregation and the Making of the Underclass* (Cambridge, MA: Harvard University Press, 1993), chapter 3.

30 After years of inactivity and internal strife, nearly resulting in the chapter's demise, Abner, who headed the branch's Nominating Committee, helped engineer the election of Cora Patton (the first woman president in branch history) in 1953, and then succeeded her in 1956. Although Abner's consolidation of power was not the first time labor had bid for control of the group—Sam Parks of the United Packinghouse Workers of America and Abner briefly gained control of the branch in 1948 after enlisting scores of black unionists to "swing" the election—it marked the first and only occasion when the group enjoyed sufficient coherence and stability to translate such insurgency into a distinct political approach. See Reed, *The Chicago NAACP,* chapters 7–9; on the 1948 "coup," see Halpern, *Down on the Killing Floor,* 241.

31 CCHR, *Trumbull Park Homes Disturbances,* 15, 31, 33–34, 47–48, 50; Reed, *The Chicago NAACP,* 168.

32 Halpern, *Down on the Killing Floor,* 241, 244–45.

33 CCHR, *Trumbull Park Homes Disturbances,* 15, 44.

34 CCHR, *Trumbull Park Homes Disturbances,* 35–37; Reed, *The Chicago NAACP,* 170. Fuller's close escape, as well as the telling actions of nearby police—who drove away as Fuller sought protection from the mob—are detailed in the indignant editorial "A Matter for Our Alderman," *Chicago Defender* (February 27, 1954): 10.

35 See Anderson and Pickering, *Confronting the Color Line;* Ralph, *Northern Protest.*

36 Wilson, *Negro Politics,* 7.

37 Halpern, *Down on the Killing Floor,* 241; Reed, *The Chicago NAACP,* 172–73.

38 CCHR, *Trumbull Park Homes Disturbances,* 38–39.

39 Ibid., 52.

40 Hirsch, "Massive Resistance in the Urban North," 530.

41 Ibid.

42 "Riot Victim," *Ebony* (June 1954): 17–24.

43 Brown, *Trumbull Park,* frontispiece, 132, 152, 226–27, 374, and chapter 41.

44 Brown, *Trumbull Park,* 254. On Williams's live performances of "Everyday," see Dempsey Travis, *An Autobiography of Black Jazz,* 138–40. For two recorded versions of the song listen to *Count Basie Swings: Joe Williams Sings,* Disc MGC678 (Clef, 1955; reissue CD 314 519 852–2: Verve, n.d.), and *Joe Williams Sings Everyday, Everyday, Everyday . . .* Regent MG 6002 (Savoy 1955; reissue CD SV-0199, Denon, 1992), which includes the earliest recorded version of the song, regrettably marred by studio reverb. For account of

Williams's life and career at this time, see "Everyday He Has the Blues," *Ebony* (January 1956): 61–65.

45 Although Frazier's *Negro Family* had no index entries for "housing," this aspect of black urban life has of course come to symbolize the declension that Frazier warned of. As such, it has proven one of the most crucial contextual landmarks for modern African-American writing: along with Brown's *Trumbull Park,* objectionable housing conditions play a central role in works by Richard Wright Ralph Ellison, Gloria Naylor, and Gwendolyn Brooks, among others. Probably the work that most fully offered precedent to Brown's in this sense is Ann Petry's *The Street* (Boston: Beacon Press, 1946), the pioneering account of single mother Lutie Johnson's battle to retain her humanity within the squalor of postwar tenement life. Links between Frazier's predictions for black urban living and central works of modern black fiction raise questions about defining its thematic impulse as "ghetto pastoral," as Michael Denning recently has. See Denning, *The Cultural Front,* chapter 6.

46 Hirsch, "Massive Resistance in the Urban North," 546–48.

47 Reed, *The Chicago NAACP,* 172.

48 Author's interview with Lerone Bennett Jr., May 2000.

49 "Four Cicero Indictments Quashed," *Jet* (November 1, 1951): 3–4; "Jo Baker Snubbed at Stork Club," *Jet* (November 1, 1951): 4. For details and context of this episode, see Martha Biondi, *To Stand and Fight,* 186–89.

50 "Sampson and Robeson Meet Face to Face," *Jet* (May 29, 1952): 3–4; "Bunche to Be Investigated by Red Probes, Powell Says," *Jet* (June 18, 1953): 4–5; "Walter White Book Banned by State Department," and "State Department Lifts Dr. Ira De A. Reid's Passport," *Jet* (July 2, 1953): 4–5; "Swindle Suspect Identified as Ex-Red Angelo Herndon," *Jet* (April 29, 1954): 6–7. Herndon's earlier heroic work as a Georgia-based organizer for the Communist Party is well documented in his own autobiography. See Herndon, *Let Me Live* (1935; reprint, New York: Arno Press, 1969). Ellison's study of Rhinehart comes toward the end of his novel: see Ralph Ellison, *Invisible Man.* My thoughts on the Herndon story's exemplary illustration of Black Chicago stem from Leon Forrest's brilliant "Character behind the Walls of Residential Segregation," where he maintained that the first of four attributes shaping this character in Chicago was the community's identity as a "hustling town." See Forrest, "Character behind the Walls of Residential Segregation," in *The Furious Voice for Freedom: Essays on Life* (Wakefield, RI: Asphodel Press, 1994), 49–65. I must also acknowledge debt to the late Charles Walton, who made this same point, with equal eloquence, in conversation. Author's interview with Charles Walton, December 1999.

51 "FBI Probes Slaying of NAACP Head," *Jet* (January 10, 1952): 3–5; "The Bomb Heard Around the World," *Ebony* (April 1952): 15–22.

52 "U.S. Court Upholds Unequal Schools," *Jet*(March 20, 1952): 3–4; "U.S. High Court Weighs School Case," *Jet* (December 25, 1952): 3–5; "U.S. to Argue Against Jim Crow Schools," *Jet* (November 26, 1953): 3–4; "High Court Tackles School Bias, Hottest Racial Case in 96 Years," *Jet* (December 3, 1953):

8–9. For definitive analysis of the *Brown* case—nonetheless lacking any mention of the role played by *Jet* and other black media in generating public awareness and support for the NAACP litigation campaign—see Kluger, *Simple Justice.*

53 "South Vows to Defy Supreme Court if Jim Crow Schools Go," *Jet* (December 18, 1952): 4–5. Herman Talmadge of Georgia and James Bryne of South Carolina were among the governors interviewed in the article.

54 "U.S. High Court Outlaws School Segregation," and "What U.S. Supreme Court Decision Means for South," *Jet* (May 27, 1954): 3–7.

55 "300 Policemen Quell Chicago Housing Riot," *Jet* (August 27, 1953): 5; "Cops Break Barricade of Women to Quell Chicago Housing Riot," *Jet* (October 29, 1953): 6–7; "Negro Family Ordered Out of Housing Project," *Jet* (November 12, 1953): 4; "Quelling Chicago Housing Riot Cost Chicago $1.5 Million," *Jet* (January 21, 1954): 8; "Justice Dept. Studies Chicago Housing Row," *Jet* (March 18, 1954): 2–3; "Chicago Riot Victim Jailed For Firing At Whites," *Jet* (April 22, 1954): 4; "'Too Much Sacrifice' Forces Family from Chicago Riot Site," *Jet* (May 13, 1954): 4–5.

56 John Dittmer, *Local People: The Struggle for Civil Rights in Mississippi* (Urbana: University of Illinois Press, 1995), 32; Payne, *I've Got the Light of Freedom.*

57 Payne, *I've Got the Light of Freedom,* 3–4. By speaking of an "organizing tradition," Payne (following SNCC leader Bob Moses) makes the distinction within civil rights activism between the work of mobilization—marches, press conferences, and other public activities Payne terms "the movement of popular memory . . . the only part of the movement that has attracted scholarly attention"—and the work of organizing—those more intimate and innocuous everyday actions without which the marches, rallies and (most crucially) collective confidence of Mississippi blacks to "change the conditions of their own lives" could not have existed. The most revisionist—even revolutionary—aspect of Payne's approach here is his presentation of black radicalization as an inherently historical phenomenon—not ever-present and eternal, but instead operative depending both on the times, and complex actions of ordinary people as opposed to motivational leaders. This position is one that I find especially suggestive for my own argument that African Americans could not understand themselves as a "national"—or even a "racial"—community without establishing an everyday level of comfort with "imagining" themselves in such a way, a process that accelerated during the postmigration period, and was catalyzed by the emergence of a vital public cultural infrastructure, whose center during this period was in Chicago.

58 "13,000 Hear Diggs Hit Bias in Miss. Speech," *Jet* (May 12, 1955): 3–5; "The New Fighting South," *Ebony* (August 1955): 69–74.

59 "Letters to the Editor," *Ebony* (October 1955): 6.

60 "Congressman Demands Probe of Miss. Voting," *Jet* (August 18, 1955): 3–4.

61 "The New Militant Fighting South," *Ebony* (August 1955): 71.

62 Ibid., 69.
63 Payne, *I've Got the Light of Freedom,* 35.
64 Ibid., 39.
65 "2nd Negro Leader Slain In Miss. Vote Drive," *Jet* (August 25, 1955): 3–4.
66 Payne, *I've Got the Light of Freedom,* 37.
67 Ibid.
68 "The New Fighting South," *Ebony* (August 1955): 70.
69 "Mississippi Gunmen Take Life of Militant Negro Minister," *Jet* (May 26, 1955): 8–11.
70 Ibid., 8.

71 "The New Fighting South," *Ebony* (August 1955): 70.
72 Grossman, *Land of Hope,* 93–94.
73 William Bradford Huie, "What Happened to the Emmett Till Killers?" *Look* (January 24, 1956): 46–49.
74 Besides coverage in publications like the *Defender* and *Jet,* the best summary of the events surrounding Till's murder is Stephen Whitfield's *A Death in the Delta,* see esp. chapter 2.
75 Photos from the station can be found in "Grieving Mother Meeting Body of Martyr Son," a special two-page photo insert depicting Till's return and funeral in the *Chicago Defender* (September 10, 1955).
76 "Nation Horrified by Murder of Kidnapped Chicago Youth," *Jet* (September 15, 1955): 8–9. Despite repeated requests, representatives of Johnson Publishing Company regrettably declined to release these images for publication in this book.
77 "Nation Horrified by Murder of Kidnapped Chicago Youth," *Jet* (September 15, 1955): 7–11; photos of the body are on pages 8 and 9. Benjamin's idea of *aura*—that which he characterized as the irrevocable loss of cultural artifacts in the Mechanical Age, is outlined in his essay, "The Work of Art in the Age of Mechanical Reproduction," in *Illuminations,* 221–23.
78 On circulation of images of atrocity among blacks historically, see Herbert Shapiro, *White Violence and Black Response;* and Roi Ottley, *The Lonely Warrior: The Life and Times of Robert S. Abbott* (Chicago: Henry Regnery Company, 1955). My remark on African Americans' credit of these photos as valid if abhorrent addressed in part the frequent disorientation and even disengagement of others encountering visual reminders of racial torture. Think of W. E. B. Du Bois's "turn aside" from his work upon seeing lynching victim Sam Hose's knuckles displayed in an Atlanta butcher shop in 1900; or Elizabeth Alexander's rhetorical query of the 1991 videotaped beating of Rodney King: "Can You Be BLACK and Look at This?" Think, finally, of Hilton Als's recent essay protesting the volume of lynching photos it accompanied, as well as the complex reactions (including leave-taking) of black visitors to exhibitions of these same photos. See David Levering Lewis, *W. E. B. Du Bois: Biography of a Race, 1868–1919* (New York: Henry Holt, 1993), 226; Elizabeth Alexander, "'Can You Be BLACK and Look at This? Reading the Rodney King Video(s)," in

The Black Interior, ed. Alexander (St. Paul: Greywolf Press, 2004), 175–205; Hilton Als, introduction to James Allen, *Without Sanctuary: Lynching Photography in America* (Santa Fe: Twin Palms, 2002).

79 I credit Jackson for these images based on the recollection of Simeon Booker. See "Best Civil Rights Cameraman in Business Dies," *Jet* (April 21, 1966): 28–29. Generally these images have been tied to Ernest C. Withers, the legendary civil rights photographer. Withers, it is clear, took his own photos of Till's body at Rayner Funeral Home, along with other iconic images related to the subsequent trial in Sumner, Mississippi. These pictures, however, were not the ones used in the *Jet* story, according to Booker. To see Withers's own Till images, see his self-published pamphlet, *Complete Photo Story of Till Murder Case* (1955). For a more extensive review of his work, from the Till case to his stunning chronicle of the Memphis sanitation workers' strike in 1968, see Michelle Furst, Ronald C. Bailey, and Ernest C. Withers, *Scenes Let Us March On: Selected Civil Rights Photography of Ernest C. Withers, 1955–1968* (Boston: Massachusetts College of Art, 1992).

80 William Stott, *Documentary Expression and Thirties America* (Chicago: University of Chicago Press, 1973), 6, 7, 18.

81 I am grateful for Christopher Metress's and Elizabeth Alexander's work in digesting numerous comments on the Till lynching. Alexander, "'Can You Be BLACK and Look at This?' Reading the Rodney King Video(s)"; Christopher Metress, ed., *The Lynching of Emmett Till: A Documentary Narrative* (Charlottesville: University of Virginia Press, 2002).

82 Susan Sontag, *On Photography* (New York: Anchor Books, 1977), 11.

83 Ibid., 6, 11, 18–19, 20–21, 24.

84 Alexander, "'Can You Be BLACK and Look at This?'" 194.

85 This recalls photography's role as a technology of evidence, used by police as well as state institutions from the nineteenth century to the present. See Sontag, *On Photography*, 21. By the 1930s and 1940s, criminal investigation no longer constituted the primary rationale for official resort to the camera. Yet projects of verification—of poverty, of citizens' equality, of the depth of affirmative national feeling—remained central to state initiatives drawing on the camera, most famously the Farm Security Administration Photography unit headed by Roy Stryker. See Stott, *Documentary Expression;* Carl Fleischauer and Beverly W. Brannen, eds., *Documenting America, 1935–1943* (Berkeley: University of California Press, 1988); and Maren Stange, *Symbols of Ideal Life.*

86 Elaine Scarry, *The Body in Pain: The Making and Unmaking of the World* (New York: Oxford University Press, 1985), 3–23. On Sontag, see her *Regarding the Pain of Others* (New York: Farrar, Strauss, Giroux, 2003). My observation here is not intended to single her, nor any contemporary observer out. Instead, based on direct and observed testimonies on the part of whites to have never heard of the case before, it seems to me profound evidence of how segregation continues to separate blacks from whites not only in social life and relations, but also more ephemeral realms of memory and imagination.

87 "50,000 New Yorkers Urge 'Dixie March,' *Jet* (October 6, 1955): 3–4; "100,000 Across Nation Protest Till Lynching," *Chicago Defender* (October 1, 1955): 3. Attendance at the rallies, each held in a prominent black church, were listed in the *Defender* as 50,000 in Detroit, 15,000 in New York, and 2,500 in Baltimore.

88 "NAACP Heads Till Campaign," *Chicago Defender* (September 10, 1955): 4; "100,000 Across Nation Protest Till Lynching," *Chicago Defender* (October 1, 1955): 3.

89 "Paris, Jo Baker Hold Till Rally," *Chicago Defender* (October 1, 1955): 1; "L'Affaire Till in the French Press," *Crisis* 62 (December 1955): 596–97.

90 "Howard Raps Apathy of Urban Negro," *Chicago Defender* (September 3, 1955): 1.

91 "10,000 Jam Till Mass Meet Here," *Chicago Defender* (October 1, 1955): 1–2.

92 Reed, *The Chicago NAACP,* 180.

93 "Packinghouse Workers Give to Till's Mom," *Chicago Defender* (September 17, 1955): 36.

94 "How the Till Case Changed 5 Lives," *Jet* (November 24, 1955): 13.

95 "Thousands at Rites for Till," *Chicago Defender* (September 10, 1955): 3. Discrepancy exists within the paper as to whether the number of people viewing Till's corpse during the four-day visitation was 50,000 or 250,000. See "250,000 View Slain Youth's Body," in the same issue of the *Defender,* p. 1.

96 "Thousands at Rites for Till," *Chicago Defender* (September 10, 1953): 3.

97 Hirsch, "Massive Resistance in the Urban North," 541; "NAACP Pickets Circle City Hall," *Chicago Defender* (October 29, 1955): 1–2.

98 "How I Escaped from Mississippi," *Jet* (October 13, 1955): 5–11; "Emmett's Kin Hang on in Miss. to Harvest Crop," *Chicago Defender* (September 17, 1955): 36; "Two Who Fled Mississippi Tell Stories," *Chicago Defender* (October 1, 1955): 1–2.

99 "Ticker Tape U.S.A.," *Jet* (October 13, 1955): 53; "Two Who Fled Mississippi Tell Stories," *Chicago Defender* (October 1, 1955): 2.

100 "50,000 New Yorkers Urge 'Dixie March,'" *Jet* (October 6, 1955): 4.

101 "Mother Waits in Vain for Her 'Bo,' *Chicago Defender* (September 3, 1955): 1–2, "Warned: Flee Dixie or Else," *Chicago Defender* (September 10, 1955): 1–2; "Nation Horrified by Murder of Kidnapped Chicago Youth," *Jet* (September 15, 1955): 7–8; "How I Escaped from Mississippi," *Jet* (October 13, 1955): 6–11.

102 "U.S. to Probe 'Hiding' of Till Witness," *Jet* (October 15, 1955): 3–4.

103 "Two Top Negro Leaders Plan to Leave Mississippi," *Jet* (December 22, 1955): 3; Alan Ehrenhalt, *The Lost City: Discovering the Forgotten Virtues of Community in the Chicago of the 1950s* (New York: Basic Books, 1995), 164.

104 Charles T. Davis and Henry Louis Gates Jr., *The Slave's Narrative* (New York: Oxford University Press, 1985); Arna Bontemps, ed., *Great American Slave Narratives* (Boston: Beacon Press, 1969).

105 Ruth Feldstein, "'I Wanted the Whole World to See': Race, Gender, and the Constructions of Motherhood in the Death of Emmett Till," in *Not June*

Cleaver: Women and Gender in Postwar America, 1945–1960, ed. Joanne Meyerowitz (Philadelphia: Temple University Press, 1994), 263–303.

106 Feldstein, "'I Wanted the Whole World to See'," 266–67. Also helpful in defining the distinct—and often derogatory—ways in which black motherhood was represented in mainstream public discussion at this time is Regina G. Kunzel, "White Neurosis, Black Pathology: Constructing Out-of-Wedlock Pregnancy in the Wartime and Postwar United States," also in Meyerowitz, ed., *Not June Cleaver,* 304–31.

107 Gwendolyn Brooks, "A Bronzeville Mother Loiters in Mississippi. Meanwhile, a Mississippi Mother Burns Bacon" (1960). Brooks's poems are available in her definitive self-edited collection *Blacks* (Chicago: David Company, 1987). Quote is from p. 335.

108 Brooks, "A Bronzeville Mother," 338.

109 Ibid., 339.

110 Brooks, "The Last Quatrain of the Ballad of Emmett Till," in Brooks, ed. *Blacks,* 340.

111 Daisy Bates, *The Long Shadow of Little Rock* (Fayetteville, AK: University of Arkansas Press, 1988); Cynthia Griggs Fleming, "Black Women Activists and the Student Nonviolent Coordinating Committee: The Case of Ruby Doris Smith Robinson," in *We Specialize in the Wholly Impossible,* ed. Darlene Clark Hine, Wilma King, and Linda Reed (Brooklyn, N.Y.: Carlson Publishing, 1995), 561–77; Barbara Ransby, *Ella Baker and the Black Freedom Movement: A Radical Democratic Vision* (Chapel Hill: University of North Carolina Press, 2003); Joanne Gibson Robinson, *The Montgomery Bus Boycott and the Women Who Started It* (Knoxville, TN: University of Tennessee Press, 1987).

112 Clayborne Carson, *In Struggle: SNCC and the Black Awakening in the 1960s* (Cambridge, MA: Harvard University Press, 1981); Morris, *Origins of the Civil Rights Movement;* Payne, *I've Got the Light of Freedom.*

113 Anderson and Pickering, *Confronting the Color Line,* chapters 3 and 4.

114 Ralph, *Northern Protest,* esp. chapter 6 and epilogue; David Garrow, *Bearing the Cross: Martin Luther King and the Southern Christian Leadership Conference* (New York: William Morrow and Company, 1986), 500; Ward Churchill and Jim Vander Wall, *Agents of Repression: The FBI's Secret War Against the Black Panther Party and the American Indian Movement* (Boston, South End Press, 1988), 63–71.

115 Cathy J. Cohen, *The Boundaries of Blackness: AIDS and the Breakdown of Black Politics* (Chicago: University of Chicago Press, 1999); Dawson, *Black Visions;* Philip Brian Harper, *Are We Not Men? Masculine Identity and the Problem of African-American Identity* (New York: Oxford University Press, 1996).

116 Anderson, *Imagined Communities,* 7. The degree to which the crushing conditions of black life in Mississippi remain in many ways unchanged since the struggles of the 1950s and 1960s are well illustrated in the work of Clyde Woods. See Woods, *Development Arrested: The Blues and Plantation Power in the Mississippi Delta* (London: Verso, 1998).

117 Gilroy, *The Black Atlantic,* 53–58, 117–20; Hartman, introduction to *Scenes of Subjection;* W. E. B. Du Bois, *Dusk of Dawn,* 130–33. Characterization of modern time—and modern black time—as empty, of course, recalls Walter Benjamin's description of modern temporality as "empty, homogenous time," even as it recovers some greater political substance in that condition than he was prepared to acknowledge. See Benjamin, "Theses on the Philosophy of History," in *Illuminations* (New York: Schoken, 1969), 261. For a groundbraking examination of the question of modern black temporality, see Michael Hanchard, "Afro-Modernity: Temporality, Politics, and the African Diaspora," cited above.

CONCLUSION: AN AFRICAN-AMERICAN DILEMMA

1 Lerone Bennett, "The King Plan for Freedom," *Ebony* (July 1956): 65–68; "Prayer Pilgrimage to Washington," *Ebony* (August 1957): 16–22; Reverend Martin Luther King, "Advice for Living," *Ebony* (September 1957): 74.

INDEX

Page numbers in italics refer to photographs